Culturally Responsive
School-Based Practices

Culturally Responsive School-Based Practices

Supporting Mental Health and Learning of Diverse Students

ANISA N. GOFORTH

AND

ANDY V. PHAM

OXFORD
UNIVERSITY PRESS

OXFORD
UNIVERSITY PRESS

Oxford University Press is a department of the University of Oxford. It furthers
the University's objective of excellence in research, scholarship, and education
by publishing worldwide. Oxford is a registered trade mark of Oxford University
Press in the UK and certain other countries.

Published in the United States of America by Oxford University Press
198 Madison Avenue, New York, NY 10016, United States of America.

CIP data is on file at the Library of Congress
ISBN 978-0-19-751692-8

DOI: 10.1093/med-psych/9780197516928.001.0001

9 8 7 6 5 4 3 2 1

Printed by Marquis, Canada

I dedicate this book to my parents, Bruce and Cathy Goforth, who opened my eyes to the beauty in difference and the excitement in culture. To my love and partner in life, James, who continually and patiently encouraged and supported me. Finally, to my daughter Kora, who I raise to be brave, strong, and generous in order to make change in our world.
—Anisa

I dedicate this book to my family and to the students in the school psychology program at Florida International University. I have learned so much from them, which enabled me to become a better person.
—Andy

CONTENTS

LIST OF ILLUSTRATIONS

FIGURES

TABLES

BOXES

ACKNOWLEDGMENTS

We are incredibly grateful to the colleagues, friends, and graduate students who supported and contributed to this book. These are individuals who we deeply respect for their passion in supporting culturally and linguistically diverse students and their families. Specifically, we thank our colleagues and friends Stacy Bender, PhD, Amy Burton, EdS, Ryan Farmer, PhD, D'Andrea Jacobs, PhD, Philip Lazarus, PhD, Sara Lewandowski, PhD, Danielle Palmer, PhD, and Cameo Stanick, PhD. Your perspectives, insights, and critiques in the development and writing of this book were greatly appreciated! We also thank our graduate students at the University of Montana: Diana Diaków, Emily Hattouni, and Jennifer Rotzal. And at Florida International University we thank Sarah Abulkheir, Cristina Criado Barrios, Renee Bastian, Quennie Dong, Denisse Gonzalez, and Matthew Netina. The future is bright with these talented, passionate leaders.

Introduction

Culturally Responsive Practice for Mental Health and Learning

In her book, *The Spirit Catches You and You Fall Down: A Hmong Child, Her American Doctors, and the Collision of Two Cultures*, Anne Fadiman writes,

> I have always felt that the action most worth watching is not at the center of things but where edges meet. I like shorelines, weather fronts, international borders. There are interesting frictions and incongruities in these places, and often, if you stand at the point of tangency, you can see both sides better than if you were in the middle of either one. (p. viii)

As practitioners in schools, we are often standing on the shorelines and weather fronts where we witness the frictions and connections between and among students, caregivers, educators, administrators, and community members. Our roles are often to stand in the middle so we can see both sides in order to support students' learning and mental health. This ability to see both sides can sometimes elicit feelings of discomfort and distress, particularly when it can disrupt relationships. Yet, this ability to navigate the shorelines is what brings strength to our roles—as school counselors, school psychologists, school social workers, and other professionals.

An additional challenge we may experience as practitioners is understanding how to support students whose culture, values, and traditions may differ from our own. Although we may have good intentions in providing culturally responsive practice, sometimes we fall into a state of paralysis. We fear making a mistake to such a degree that we are unable to move forward. Further, when students' culture, values, and norms do not necessarily align with those of schools, we often discuss how the student is "different" from our expectations, rather than the other way around. This is particularly the case when students from culturally, ethnically, and linguistically minoritized groups experience oppression and marginalization, caused by the systems and environment that have often shaped our expectations and practices. Thus, we often are not prepared or do not know how best to ensure their success.

During these past few years, schools have also faced a great deal of turmoil that has divided our country. The challenges of remote learning, the tolls of illness, and the disruptions of routines as a result of the COVID-19 pandemic have left students academically and emotionally exhausted, particularly students of color and those from low-income families. The U.S. Surgeon General's Advisory (Department of Health and Human Services, 2021) highlighted the increased concerns about the mental health of children and adolescents, especially those from culturally and linguistically diverse (CLD) backgrounds. The pandemic has also put additional pressure on teachers, leading to concerns about teacher's mental health stress, self-efficacy, and compassion fatigue (Baker et al., 2021; Yang, 2021). Many feel unprecedented levels of stress in their work. On the other hand, we have also learned through these experiences that our students are incredibly resilient. From developing responsive and compassionate relationships to learning coping strategies that buffer from harm, students can adapt positively to such adversities. Although the well-being of students and teachers are paramount, the current climate exacerbates these issues, requiring mental health practitioners to re-examine their roles in schools.

There has also been heightened attention on the current sociopolitical context and racial injustices. The killings of George Floyd, Breonna Taylor, and many other Black people by police and the resulting protests have underscored the historical and contemporary racial injustice and inequitable distribution of power that have occurred in the country (Roberts & Rizzo, 2020). Unless systems change, more injustices will likely occur, and by the time of this reading, this list may tragically be longer. Further, there has been an especially visible backlash by certain groups about race, power, and privilege that has taken center stage in many school districts in the United States. For example, school board elections, bans on books on certain topics due to fears of "indoctrination," and legislative efforts to block curriculum related to social-emotional learning, diversity, and critical race theory have evoked emotionally charged conversations about the role of race and power in the educational system.

Many efforts to address disparities and disproportionalities have been rooted in deficit orientations that reflect the perception of White superiority and the validity of White middle-class practices, expectations, and experiences. Classroom approaches that denounce deficit orientations have evolved to reflect strength-based approaches, where we view student differences as potential assets, contesting the ways differences are too often reduced to deficiencies. Some of the most widely cited approaches include culturally responsive teaching (Gay, 2018), culturally responsive pedagogy (Ladson-Billings & Tate, 1995), and Funds of Knowledge (González et al., 2006), among others.

Clearly, our educational systems are not perfect, and there is a great deal of work we must do to change those systems to enhance equity for all students. We want to promote schools as positive and supportive environments, and to reframe our work with students in a similar way. Our roles as practitioners (for us, as school psychologists) historically have taken a medical model based on a deficit-based approach, which have led to inequities in how we teach, assess, intervene, and make educational decisions about students. Research in mental health has attempted to move away from this model toward a focus on resilience and well-being (Lazarus et al., 2021; Masten et al., 2021). Even the "problem-solving model" often implies deficit thinking (e.g., "The student can't read on grade level") rather than examining how the schools are structured and how Eurocentric practices persist to prevent some students from succeeding. It does not mean we ignore the causes of traumas or the gaps in learning that students' experience. The issue is *how we talk and think about* our students because of these causes. Too often, we hear of these conversations in teacher's lounges, where we attribute a student's difficulties to "turmoil at home." Instead, we need to shift our thinking and language to consider what supports we are failing to provide in schools. For example, we can reframe these thoughts as the student "may benefit from more consistent classroom supports, clearer positive feedback, and carefully structured routines." Focusing on how we can change our environments and schools can help us improve as people and as professionals. Reframing, but not ignoring, can be one way to understand, support, and advocate for students.

Advocacy is needed to ensure voices are heard when injustices persist, but even these efforts still require planning and building alliances. Our actions and decision-making practices have a direct impact on our students and their future. Despite heroic efforts from our teachers, staff, and school leaders to ensure that students' needs are met, we also need to invest our resources to restore trust and rebuild relationships. We should be mindful that our actions or inactions can have long-lasting impressions on students. Like most relationships, there will be ups and downs, conflicts and successes, and improvement efforts that are never ending. Our work to promote and sustain mental health and academic support are needed now more than ever. Students should grow to be empathetic and thoughtful contributors to our society.

As practitioners, it is our responsibility to figure out how best to support them, yet there are few resources that help practitioners understand how to meet the needs of culturally, racially, and linguistically diverse students. We wrote this book because we recognize that practitioners need specific strategies for their practice in schools. These strategies need to be practical, not just theoretical. Thus, this book is designed to provide specific strategies for culturally responsive practice across a number of domains of practice. The first section of the book focuses on the foundations of culturally responsive practice, the second section on culturally responsive assessment, and finally, the last section on promoting resilience through counseling, interventions, and evaluation of programs. Not all of these sections are directly relevant to the roles and responsibilities of all practitioners who provide learning and mental health support to students in schools. Indeed, this book is written for a broad range of practitioners in schools and can be useful for general educators, special educators, and administrators who are interested in understanding how to provide culturally responsive services to CLD students.

ENGAGING IN CRITICAL REFLEXIVITY
WITHIN OURSELVES

The foundation of this book is culturally responsive practice and engaging in cultural humility. During the writing of this book, we practiced what we preached: we engaged in critical reflexivity about our professional work and our identities. Critical reflexivity refers to self-questioning and self-examination of our assumptions, beliefs, and past experiences that affect our current practice and ways of thinking. What is slightly different about this process compared with "self-reflection" is determining how we are directly or indirectly contributing to systemic inequities or the status quo. These could be based on our actions or inactions. Our weekly meetings were not only about the organization or flow of a chapter. It was also discussing important questions: *How do the current sociopolitical context and the pandemic differentially affect students from minoritized groups? Do our personal and professional identities shape our perceptions of culturally responsive practice? Why are you using that particular term/word/acronym?* We share our reflexivity here as a way to introduce ourselves to you, our reader, as well as to emphasize that providing culturally responsive practice to students and their families requires vulnerability, discomfort, and openness.

Andy Pham: A Vietnamese American's Never-Ending Navigation

As a Vietnamese American, growing up in a small urban city north of Boston made it difficult for me to understand my own cultural identity and determine why I looked different from others. It was not until I moved to the affluent suburb of Lexington, Massachusetts, that I realized there were no other Vietnamese students or those of Southeast Asian descent. Because of this realization, I felt different from many of my Asian American peers who mainly were of Korean or Chinese heritage. After graduating from college, I finally traveled to Vietnam for the first time with my family and realized that many of the local residents quickly knew I was an outsider just from the way I looked, spoke, or dressed. This experience led to a question I often ask: "How do I fit in this community, or am I OK with being so different that I stand out like a sore thumb from my heritage culture?" It was like being a tug of war between both American and Vietnamese cultures. In either case, I have always felt like a minority, but wanting to explore more of these thoughts, rather than suppress them.

As I tried to determine my own cultural identity during my schooling, most of my Vietnamese heritage was lost. My parents seemed to understand this (as they also were adapting to living in the Boston suburbs), yet they wanted my brother and me to learn, speak, and understand as much as we could from both cultures. Nevertheless, most of the stress I experienced during schooling was trying to fulfill expectations given to me by family, teachers, and society, so that I was not able to devote time to explore my cultural identity. Although my teachers and school counselor were approachable, I have never communicated any of my personal struggles with them or to my peers. I never acted out, I had good grades, and I was not seen as a "problem" student. At the same time, my heritage culture viewed "mental health" as a stigma and that being gay is a "disease." Therefore, I did not ask questions or share my internal struggles with anyone at school.

These types of issues can be easily overlooked by many school professionals. Mental health is not equated simply as the absence of disability but involves subjective well-being, autonomy, competence, and realization of one's own strengths and potential, and their role in society. It is one of the reasons why I became a school psychologist—not only to support children to thrive in schools, but also to ensure that we understand more about them beyond what we teach in the classroom. I have had the opportunities to work in schools in Michigan, Massachusetts, Virginia Beach, New York City, Costa Rica, and now Florida. The collaboration with Miami-Dade County Public Schools, the fourth largest school district in the United States, with over 90% CLD students, allowed me to refocus my research and efforts so that we learn from our communities and understand their needs. The shortage of school psychologists and special educators locally and nationally has made it difficult for school professionals to address the learning and mental health needs of every student adequately. One of my professional goals is not only to work with our school communities, but also to provide mentorship: to check in with students, to ensure they feel safe and supported, and to listen their stories. This mindset allows me to become more mindful and reflective of my work, and to appreciate students' efforts and contributions to the school. I have come to understand and appreciate the complexities of my cultural identity.

I have to remind myself that schools and their classroom environments have changed over time since I was a student. From our increasing student diversity to advances in technology, we must learn to adapt to these changes. On the other hand, critical shortages of teachers and school professionals, the rise in stress and burnout, and the disparities in school resources have led to wider gaps in educational opportunity across high-poverty schools and low-poverty schools (Cancio et al. 2018). As faculty, I have power (even though at times I believe I don't), but often I am still learning how to use it to advocate for others. Our initial efforts to support individual students and families can perhaps put a band-aid on problems temporarily, but if these issues are not resolved collectively and at a deeper systems level or policy level, these challenges are likely to worsen, affecting our most vulnerable students. However, systemic changes do not occur unless the individual person changes. I hope our book achieves the goal in serving as a catalyst for change in people, no matter how small the change may be.

Anisa Goforth: Where Am I from? Everywhere

On my home office wall, there's a picture of the deep red mountains of Yemen where I was born. I don't remember this small Arab town where my American father and Australian mother met and eventually had me, as we left to live in Latin America, Southeast Asia, and South Asia. That picture, however, represents the beginning of my learning and connection to traditions, values, and social norms of cultures around the world. I attended international schools where my peers were British, Japanese, Pakistani, Brazilian, who followed Buddhist, Muslim, and Catholic faiths. As a White, cisgender girl who was an Australian and American national (but never lived in either place), I encountered different cultural traditions and spoke multiple languages.

These experiences shaped my understanding of cross-cultural interactions in educational systems. I saw the strengths of these interactions, seeing my friends play during recess, speaking multiple languages on the playground. I also saw the disadvantages, whereby colorism and racism revealed itself on that playground as well. When I lived in Lahore, Pakistan, for example, my Pakistani friends with darker skin were teased relentlessly, and my female friends would lather their skin with Whitening lotions in an attempt to become "fairer." I also experienced the privilege associated with being White, although in different ways than perhaps in the United States with its history of racial injustice. Colonialism, on the other hand, was embedded within many of the nations I lived in, from the British Victorian buildings in Pakistan to the Spanish influences in Nicaragua.

As I entered college in the United States and experienced significant culture shock (I didn't understand my friends' pop culture references nor how to use an ATM), I became more interested in understanding the psychological outcomes associated with cross-cultural interactions and acculturation. This interest evolved after teaching in an international school in Cambodia and eventually beginning my graduate program at Michigan State University. My dissertation focused on the acculturation process and stress experienced by Arab American adolescents—an immigrant group that was neglected in research yet had so many strengths in their community. It was also after the events of September 11, where many members of that community (including my friends) encountered staggering racism and anti-Muslim discrimination. My friends' experiences with federal agents coming to their home as well as frequently being stopped in airports drove me to address racism and xenophobia in my research as well as in my personal life.

These research and life experiences drive me to advocate for culturally and linguistically diverse children. The idea for this book evolved out of teaching clinical practicums and courses on assessment and intervention, where I realized that the specific strategies and helpful tools weren't really accessible to school-based professionals. I wanted to make sure that professionals were able to have one book that covered a number of different areas of practice. I also believe that cross-cultural interactions are needed to enhance professionals' lives. Experiencing other cultures can shift people's perspectives, fostering empathy and understanding. I look at the picture of Jibla, Yemen, on my office wall and connect my real-life experiences with my passion for culturally responsive services in schools and hope this book prompts similar discussions about supporting all children's well-being.

LANGUAGE MATTERS

As practitioners and scholars, we also engaged in critical reflexivity in the development of the book proposal all the way through the final stages of editing. Language matters, so we want to highlight our rationale for some of the terms and words we have chosen to use in this book. We had lengthy and difficult discussions about which terms we will be using to describe students. For example, when we proposed the book, the term *Black, Indigenous, and people of color* (BIPOC) was being used often in discussion about race, racism, and oppression. We considered using the term, as we wanted to center the discussions on people who have been historically and contemporarily oppressed and marginalized. Yet, we also heard from colleagues and leaders in our profession about the challenges of this term—that it combines a diverse group of people under one acronym.

Ultimately, we have chosen to use "culturally and linguistically diverse" because the focus is on students who have varying values, norms, traditions, beliefs, race, and ethnicity. Also, we are specific when we describe students who have been systematically marginalized, where we are intentional about noting their race (e.g., Black students), sovereign identities (e.g., Indigenous students' Tribal Nations), or their experience of acculturation (e.g., forcibly displaced students). Further, we recognize that historically, the field has use deficit-based terms when describing students (e.g., "at-risk students"), and terms have been used that rarely recognize the way that systems have marginalized and oppressed certain groups of students. Thus, we often use the adjective "minoritized," when describing students who are from groups who have been systematically oppressed. Importantly, we also wanted to recognize intersecting identities (Crenshaw, 1989) and have made sure to include cases that include intersecting identities by race, ethnicity, language, gender, and sex.

In addition, we are using gender inclusive language to the extent possible. We use the singular "they," even when referring to a single practitioner or student. This aligns with the American Psychological Association's endorsement of the singular "they." Not only does this facilitate better reading, but it is also more inclusive of the broader gender identities. Similarly, we have chosen the use the term "Latinx" to be gender inclusive, although we recognize that some individuals may not prefer this term.

Language does matter, *and* we recognize we are certainly not perfect. We engaged in a great deal of critical reflexivity prior to and throughout the writing of this book. It is likely that we may review this book in a few years and change our minds about certain words. Most importantly, we will continue to engage in critical reflexivity as we learn, practice, and train.

AN INVITATION TO JOIN US IN LIFELONG LEARNING

Culturally responsive practices require us to engage in lifelong learning. Every student in the classroom is unique, and we need to adapt our ways of thinking and interaction to each student's strengths and needs. Culture is a fluid and dynamic construct. Thus, we may never get to the point of "cultural competence" when it comes to our personal and professional growth. Our understanding of culture may conflict with what we have come to learn about standardized assessment or evidence-based practice. Should we be implementing practices the same way for every student, or is there room to adapt these practices and tailor them to the individual's culture? Because culture and specific sociocultural variables influence whether classroom instruction or delivery of school-based services are effective, these issues must always be in the forefront of our work with students and families. We must learn about their intersecting identities, their histories, and their experiences, and the sociopolitical-economic contexts from which they reside. We must also learn more about ourselves and how our different forms of privilege and oppression exist simultaneously in shaping our biases, beliefs, and actions. Thus, we invite you to stand at the point of tangency in order for you to see both sides better than if you were in the middle of either one.

Foundations of Culturally Responsive Practice

Culturally responsive school-based services are critical to supporting the mental health and learning of culturally and linguistically diverse students. In this section, we highlight the foundations of culturally responsive practice, which include reflexivity, relationships, responsiveness, and relational empowerment as foundational elements. We then describe how culturally responsive practices integrates social justice principles, by leveraging student strengths and addressing issues of privilege, power, and oppression in society. Finally, we provide ways to foster authentic school-family-community partnerships, emphasizing ways to engage with families to promote students' mental health and learning.

The 4Rs of Culturally Responsive Practice

Catherine is a White American, cisgender female and school social worker. She was raised in the Midwest, where it was expected that she would uphold her family values by being a hard worker and avoid "rocking the boat," or causing a stir, among the tight-knit community. Catherine's parents are Catholic, and she attended Mass throughout her childhood. Her family's traditions include celebrating Christian holidays, such as Easter and Christmas. Since adulthood, Catherine no longer identifies as Catholic and now identifies as an atheist, but she still enjoys the holidays with her family. When entering the field of social work, Catherine realized that her career choice may have been influenced by her religious upbringing and religious norms, through which she believed women tend to follow more caring and emotionally intensive careers than men.

A few months ago, a Pakistani American student, Nadia, enrolled in the high school where Catherine works. She and her family moved from a large metropolitan city to a small suburb to find a home more conducive for their lifestyle. Now living in a community where there is little racial or cultural diversity, Nadia has struggled to find a social group, which has increased her social anxiety. As a result, she has begun to skip school, reporting stomachaches or headaches, and her grades have begun to slip below failing. Nadia's teachers reached out to Catherine for guidance, noting that even when Nadia was in class, she rarely made eye contact or spoke with peers or teachers. When speaking to Nadia's parents, they expressed great concern about her current grades, as she excelled academically in her previous school.

- *What should Catherine consider about her values, culture, and social norms that may influence her ability to provide culturally responsive practices to Nadia?*
- *What sociocultural factors might Catherine want to consider in order to provide effective services?*

Reflexivity, relationships, responsiveness, and relational empowerment are the foundational elements in providing culturally responsive school-based services to the support mental health and learning of culturally and linguistically diverse students. As practitioners, we may worry that when we work with culturally and linguistically diverse (CLD) students, including students who are Black, Indigenous, and people of color (BIPOC), that we may make a mistake, offend someone, or worse, unintentionally cause harm. These worries sometimes paralyze us, to the point that we are so cautious and so concerned that we may not put in the effort and time that is necessary to really ensure that we're providing effective mental health services. Further, the paralysis can also occur because we may not know where to start looking for information, or perhaps that information is not the right information for the specific student. However, fundamentally, culturally responsive practice is simple: It is about being reflexive in our work as practitioners, it is about the relationships we have with students and their families, it is about being responsive to the needs and strengths of students, and it is about using these relationships to empower students and their families so they can be successful in school and in life.

Culturally responsive practice is simple, but it does *not* mean it is easy. This chapter provides a foundation for culturally responsive practice with four Rs: reflexivity, relationships, responsiveness, and relational empowerment. We highlight how these four concepts are woven together to enhance a practitioner's ability to provide culturally responsive school-based services (see Figure 1.1). First, we will introduce the concepts of reflexivity and cultural humility. Then, we will discuss

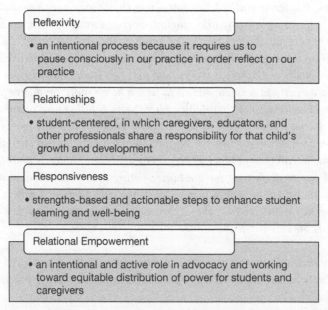

Reflexivity
- an intentional process because it requires us to pause consciously in our practice in order reflect on our practice

Relationships
- student-centered, in which caregivers, educators, and other professionals share a responsibility for that child's growth and development

Responsiveness
- strengths-based and actionable steps to enhance student learning and well-being

Relational Empowerment
- an intentional and active role in advocacy and working toward equitable distribution of power for students and caregivers

Figure 1.1. Culturally Responsive Practice for Supporting the Mental Health and Learning of Culturally and Linguistically Diverse Students.

how critical it is to cultivate relationships with students, families, community members, educators, and fellow practitioners, and the importance of earning trust to cultivate those relationships. We will then introduce how responsiveness—the deliberate, actionable steps to support students—can lead to effective educational and mental health services in schools. Finally, we define and discuss how we can use relational empowerment to foster relationships and empower students to be successful. Throughout our discussion, it is important to provide some context for and definitions of concepts, so we also highlight some key terms (e.g., "cultural competence," "cultural humility") as they relate to providing school-based services. These foundational elements will then lead to discussion of specific practices and strategies in the upcoming chapters of this book.

REFLEXIVITY

In culturally responsive practice, practitioners use critical reflexivity, an intentional process of reflection and self-critique (Cunliffe, 2016). Derived from qualitative methodologies, critical reflexivity is a useful tool prior to delivering school-based services because it allows us to engage and question our beliefs and knowledge as they relate to our practices. For example, it is about asking: *What do I know? How do I know it?* (Bettez, 2015). Reflexivity is an *intentional* process because it requires the individual to pause consciously in their practice in order to *reflect* on their practice. The process allows for time and space to consider their beliefs and actions, and how they may have an impact on their work with CLD students and families. It requires them to provide a critique of themselves in this process, recognizing that this process is an uncomfortable, but necessary, task so they can be sure that their beliefs and actions do not have a negative consequence when working with students and families.

To begin engaging in critical reflexivity, let's do a quick activity. If you have a backpack or bag next to you, take a look inside. Choose five items that you believe represent your cultural background. Reflect on the item and ask yourself: *What do I know about this item? How does this reflect my cultural values? In what ways does this represent my family or me?* In our professional trainings, we find that a common item that participants choose is the cell phone, so let's dive deeper. The participants often use the cell phone for the calendar function—how does this represent their cultural values? For one, the calendar is most likely based on the Christian calendar, which highlights the underlying religious beliefs that guide the sociopolitical system in the United States. Further, the calendar often includes a 5-day workweek from Monday to Friday. In other cultures, such as those based on Muslim calendars, the workweek may be Sunday to Thursday. Secondly, schedules and time also represent cultural values. In schools, "being on time" is a highly valued norm. In fact, being late to a meeting may reflect poorly on the practitioner, and they may even get reprimanded, and students who are frequently late are disciplined. In other cultures, however, schedules are more flexible, and there is not a sense of unprofessionalism or concern for arriving at

Table 1.1. DOMAINS OF CRITICAL REFLEXIVITY

Domain	Questions for Engaging in Critical Reflexivity
Cognitive	• What is your identity (e.g., social, cultural, racial, professional, gender, etc.)? How does your identity affect your work with diverse students and colleagues? • What are some examples of the injustices occurring at your school? How do they affect students and families? • Are you consciously or unconsciously contributing to these injustices? If so, how? • What are the causes of these injustices? • What are strategies or approaches that can help reduce or eliminate these injustices?
Social-Affective (Attitudes)	• How do you feel about the injustices that you have encountered or experienced? • Do you feel any personal responsibility for addressing these injustices? • Are you motivated to take action against injustices? If not, why not? • Do you feel confident in your ability to affect change? What areas do you feel most confident about? What growth areas should you focus on? • Do you have the social support system to assist with change?
Procedural (Skills and Process)	• How do you discuss issues regarding racism and social change, and with whom? • How do you effectively navigate through systems to promote change? • How do you make formal changes in educational or school-related policy? • How do you receive professional development on these topics? • How do you promote advocacy and accountability at school?

different times during the day. By reflecting on the underlying cultural values of the items you chose, you are engaging in critical reflexivity (see Table 1.1 for additional questions).

The process of critical reflexivity is a core component of *cultural humility*. Practitioners who embrace cultural humility have "an accurate perception of their own cultural values, as well as maintain an other-oriented perspective that involves respect, lack of superiority, and attunement regarding their own cultural beliefs and values" (Hook et al., 2017, p. 29). In schools, embracing cultural humility requires practitioners to engage in self-awareness, develop skills, and obtain knowledge while cultivating relationships (see Figure 1.2; Goforth, 2016; Pham et al., 2021). Importantly, this process is lifelong—practitioners will always be learning about themselves, always developing skills, and always obtaining knowledge about others' cultures.

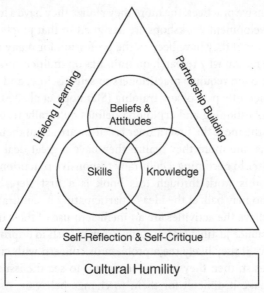

Figure 1.2. Cultural Humility Model of School Psychological Practice.
SOURCE: Goforth, A. N. (2016). A cultural humility model of school psychology training and practice. *Trainer's Forum, 34*(1), 3–24. Reprinted with permission.

There are intrapersonal and interpersonal aspects of cultural humility. The intrapersonal aspect is related to the practitioner's sense of their own biases, assumptions, strengths, and limitations. When working with students, culturally humble practice means that the practitioner is focused on understanding their biases and assumptions and thus continuously engaging in critical reflexivity. Because everyone has biases, it is about asking themselves: *What are my cultural values? How do I know?* Asking these questions allows the practitioner to be attuned to their cultural beliefs and values, and to encourage them to determine how they play out in professional relationships and in educational decision-making.

The interpersonal aspect, in contrast, is related is being open to others and engaging with them in a humble way. This engagement involves having the practitioner be open to the student's and family's perspectives, and moving away from being an expert within that relationship. That is, as a practitioner, they become attuned to the student's culture, beliefs, and perspectives, and they approach the relationship with the student and their family with openness and respect. Embracing the interpersonal aspect of cultural humility, therefore, means that they relinquish their position and power as an expert or authority figure.

Reflexivity and cultural humility are key to culturally responsive practice, yet many practitioners may find the process difficult or may believe that these activities are not worthwhile in their work. Engaging in cultural humility requires practitioners to recognize that although they have advanced education and relevant training experiences, they continue to have areas for growth. The challenge of culturally responsive practice is that the more a practitioner learns about providing culturally responsive practices, the more they realize they have a lot more to learn! Professional development workshops are designed so that practitioners can continue to learn, even if they have been in the profession for many years. This challenge is also the reason why research on trainings on multicultural competence is so difficult, as it often requires practitioners to self-disclose, and the ability to be self-aware is inherently part of any training (Stanhope et al., 2005). Nonetheless, this process of questioning and critiquing defines culturally responsive practice. In other words, the more the practitioner is self-aware about their culture, biases, and assumptions, the more they realize they have a great deal to learn, which moves them closer to becoming a culturally responsive practitioner.

Engaging in this work through this book is a first step, but what about practitioners who may balk at the idea of participating in cultural responsiveness because they believe the activities are an inefficient use of their time? Is their reluctance or resistance justifiable? Practitioners may wish to improve their skills or better themselves if they likely see a problem or concern with current practices. When people resist, then they may be likely not to see the issues as a concern, which would make it difficult for them to change behavior. As we mentioned earlier, these efforts require lifelong self-critiques, and for some, the ability to improve or change one's behavior can be emotionally exhausting given the amount of stress and work they do in schools already. Other practitioners may employ the bystander effect: "If others are doing it, why should I?" We argue, however, that these efforts will aid in both prevention and intervention for students and developing innovative practices so that, over time, practitioners' efforts to engage in cultural responsiveness will not require as much cognitive load, energy, or even discomfort as they experienced initially. The effort is worth it.

Understanding Ourselves to Understand Others

To engage in critical reflexivity, practitioners must give time and space to understand themselves. The research on multicultural competence, as discussed by Derald Wing Sue and colleagues (e.g., Sue et al., 1982; Sue & Torino, 2005), shows that understanding ourselves to understand others, or *awareness*, is one of three components of practice: (a) awareness, (b) cultural skills, and (c) cultural knowledge. In this model, *awareness* refers to practitioners being able to understand their own biases, stereotypes, and culture; *cultural skills* refer to practitioners obtaining the necessary skills to provide culturally competent practices to diverse individuals; and *cultural knowledge* refers to practitioners gaining knowledge on specific cultural groups, including understanding the groups' history, values, and norms (Sue, 2001).

Awareness is key during critical reflexivity. Practitioners may expect that when working with a student from a different ethnic, cultural, or religious group from their own, their first task is to explore that student's particular ethnicity, culture, or religion. They may explore resources online on the student's history or soak up articles that provide best practices for that particular group. Learning about a particular group is certainly important; in fact, we encourage it. We notice, however, that practitioners often jump to that stage; instead, we encourage practitioners first to explore *themselves.*

This process of self-exploration can be quite uncomfortable, since practitioners may or may not have interacted with individuals from cultures different from their own; yet, practitioners are encouraged not only to lean into that discomfort, but also to explore why they experience discomfort in the first place. Practitioners must have awareness about their personal values and biases, and how these values and biases may shape their perception of the student and caregiver, the student's concerns, and their professional relationships (Sue, 2006).

As the adage goes, "Culture is to people as water is to fish." As people, we need culture to survive, yet it is often invisible to us unless someone points it out. We define *culture* similarly to Whaley and Davis (2007) in that it is a "dynamic process involving worldviews and ways of living in a physical and social environment shared by groups, which are passed from generation to generation and may be modified by contacts between cultures in a particular social, historical, and political context" (p. 564). We appreciate this definition because it highlights the dynamic and fluid nature of culture, in which norms, traditions, and values are learned across multiple generations and sometimes changes based on the current sociopolitical context. That is, the sociopolitical context, such as issues being discussed by individuals within the society (e.g., racial injustice, social media use, climate change) can influence a practitioner's worldview. Similarly, their norms, traditions, and cultures are influenced by the individuals within those groups (e.g., family, peers, religious leaders), but may be invisible to them. For example, some White Americans may not be aware that they have certain traditions, norms, or values until they compare them with those of another cultural group (this often happens quickly when visiting a new country). All of a sudden, they might realize that eating with knife and fork, celebrating Halloween, or using particular idioms (e.g., "It's raining cats and dogs") is an exemplar of the larger cultural norms. For those who are not White Americans (e.g., immigrants), they often would view these traditions as the standard or norm that they perceive as ideals, whether to attain or to adapt as part of their own culture.

These values, norms, and traditions shape practitioners' worldviews, perspectives of others, and behavior. For example, as highlighted in the vignette, Catherine was raised with certain values, particularly religion, that shaped her identity and culture. Although she does not recognize herself as following a particular faith, and identifies herself as an atheist, her religious upbringing continues to shape her personally and professionally. As a social worker, Catherine can reflect on these values, norms, and traditions, which is particularly helpful when working with students who were raised outside of the United States or who identify as a person of color. Without understanding our underlying culture, it is difficult to understand the culture of others. By understanding the culture of others, we can cultivate rich and rewarding relationships.

[Reflexivity Activity] As a way to dive deeper into exploring your culture, consider these reflexive questions:

- *In your family, what is "happiness"?*
- *Why do these values exist?*
- *For you, what is "happiness"?*

For many practitioners, these questions are surprisingly difficult. It requires them to consider the norms, traditions, and values in their own family, and whether they are similar to or different from their own. In some families, *happiness* can equate to *success*, sometimes defined as obtaining an education degree or a job. Sometimes, *happiness* can equate to *having a family*. At other times, *happiness* equates to having *a life well lived*. By understanding how your family perceives being happy, you also explore your family's underlying values. If happiness means success, then obtaining a job and having money may be an important value. If happiness means having a family, the continuation of the family and extending the generations may be a value. It may be interesting to ask your own caregivers this same question—are their responses similar to what you had initially guessed?

RELATIONSHIPS

Relationships are the bedrock of culturally responsive practice. Our relationships with fellow practitioners, educators, families, and students are critical in providing educational and mental health services successfully, because without those relationships—without trust—we cannot conduct assessments, develop interventions, or provide consultation in any meaningful way. Indeed, this can be used within a social justice framework, which is defined as the process and goal of ensuring the protection of the educational rights, opportunities, and well-being of all children (Shriberg et al., 2013). It is important for decision-making on mental health, and education is not only conducted by educators or administrators, but also through strong family, school, and community partnerships (Jones, 2013).

We define *family-school relationships* similarly to Clarke et al. (2009) and use the term *family-school-community partnerships* (we discuss this in more detail in Chapter 3). These relationships are student centered and ones in which families in the home, educators and other professionals in the school, and stakeholders in the community share a responsibility for that child's growth and development. We also extend that definition to where that shared responsibility is based on deep trust, which is earned through cultivating relations and connections through cultural knowledge. It can be difficult to establish and maintain these partnerships because there may be competing beliefs, values, and opinions. These competing ideologies are not a bad thing. If there is a common or shared goal among all stakeholders, then these conversations may be necessary to ensure that actions and practices are culturally responsive.

Earning Trust, Cultivating Relationships

One of the foundational elements of healthy family–school relationships comprises *trust* (Clarke et al., 2009). Families, students, and educators must see practitioners as not only trustworthy, but also *worthy* of trust. That is, they must see them as compassionate, understanding, and respectful. Clarke and colleagues also emphasized that trust in this family–school relationship is related to confidence that each individual within that relationship will act in a way that benefits that relationship. Both the practitioner and the student's caregiver must trust that each of them will make decisions and take actionable steps to support the student's well-being. Trust can take time to establish within the relationship when each individual knows that the other person will act in ways that will benefit the student (Clarke et al., 2009). We devote Chapter 3 to discussing strategies for cultivating relationships through trust.

Earning trust is especially important because there may be imbalances of power within the family–school relationship. Caregivers, such as parents, may perceive that they do not have much to contribute within school decisions, or teachers may not realize that parents are heavily involved in the student's education. Clarke and colleagues (2009) use the term *equality* as an important element in healthy family–school relationships because conflict can occur when the power dynamics between the family and school are unequal. Thus, for effective culturally responsive practice, families and school staff must cultivate relations where trust is developed and the power balance becomes equalized. Caregivers coming into a school may already be on unequal footing, as they may be unfamiliar with school district policies regarding special education evaluations compared with educators or other school staff. In order for the student to be supported in school, both the practitioner and the caregiver must have similar levels of power in the decision-making process. Trust must first be established so that they can work effectively together, but there must also be shared power so that each person's voice can be heard.

[Reflexivity Activity] Consider a time when you worked closely with a family that was successful in supporting a student's well-being and learning. Ask yourself:

- *How was that relationship cultivated? How did I earn the family's trust?*
- *What actions did I take to ensure that trust was maintained during the decision-making process?*
- *If I could turn back time, what would I have done differently?*

Now, consider a time when you worked closely with a caregiver that was not successful. Ask yourself:

- *What aspects of the relationship were similar between these two families? What aspects were different?*
- *What were some actions that I could have taken to cultivate that relationship more effectively?*

- *What were some contextual or systemic issues that contributed to the lack of trust or difficulty cultivating that relationship?*

During this critical reflexivity activity, what do you notice about your feelings and thoughts? Sometimes, reflecting on difficult situations can be uncomfortable, but it is often that discomfort that pushes us to learn and consider ways to provide more effective mental health services.

Overall, it is the effort and work that practitioners put into those relationships that earns trust from families and community members. We provide specific strategies for earning trust and cultivating relationships with caregivers, families, and community members in Chapter 3.

Connections Through Cultural Knowledge

In addition to earning trust and cultivating relationships, practitioners can work to establish relationships through *cultural knowledge*. Learning about different cultural groups, whether the groups are students, families, educators, or fellow practitioners, can be an important component of culturally responsive practice. Understanding the traditions, norms, and beliefs of others can be helpful in reducing misunderstandings and misinterpretations that arise through cross-cultural social interactions and communication. By asking families about their needs and goals, a practitioner may notice that differences between their beliefs, values, and norms exist if they are working with a family that may have recently immigrated to the United States, and it is a cultural group with which they have had no prior experience. Working to understand the unique aspects of the student's culture can highlight their compassion, respect, and caring.

In the third component of the Sue (2001) model, cultural knowledge relates to the practitioner's ability to gain information about the student's and family's cultural values, norms, worldview, and expectations. Practitioners who are multiculturally competent aim to learn about the cultural and linguistic groups of the students and families they serve. However, learning about culture is complex: There is great heterogeneity within cultural and linguistic groups. Thus, there must be a balance between wanting to learn about a particular cultural group and recognizing that there are significant variations within most cultural groups. In fact, we purposefully did not organize this book to cover different cultural groups (e.g., one chapter on Black Americans, one chapter on Indigenous peoples) because it can easily evolve in brushing people with broad strokes. There is great potential for stereotyping and inaccurate assumptions or biases.

That being said, it would also be inappropriate for a practitioner to neglect learning about the cultural and linguistic groups of students with whom they may work for fear that it would be too broad. For example, Catherine started working with a Pakistani American student, but she had never worked with this population in the past. Thus, she may want to take proactive steps to learn about Pakistani culture. She may read about the history of Pakistan and learn about the customs and traditions of Pakistanis to understand the student's background; however, Catherine also must take steps to get to know *that family's* cultural heritage ("Are they Sindhi or Punjabi?") or the student's acculturation process (e.g., "Is the student a third-generation Pakistani American?"). Diving deeper into that family's and student's culture, norms, and traditions also shows the care that the practitioner has in providing culturally responsive assessment or intervention.

RESPONSIVENESS

The third component of culturally responsive practice is using strengths-based and actionable steps to enhance student learning and well-being. It is about leveraging students' strengths and applying *evidence-based practice* (EBP) to the mental health and learning needs of culturally and linguistically diverse students and families. Responsiveness encompasses being proactive and accountable, rather than reactive, in promoting student's strengths. Proactive efforts may include creating relations with a community center that provides services to all students and families, including access to information, resources, or supports.

There are many similar terms to *culturally responsive practice*, such as *multicultural competence* or *cross-cultural competence*, that are used across the field of mental health. Cultural competencies are used, for example, by the American Counseling Association (2015) whereby counselors are expected to obtain specific competencies associated with working with culturally and linguistically diverse populations. Some Indigenous scholars, however, have noted that such cultural competencies may be problematic because they could be associated with psychological and cultural essentialism (i.e., perceptions that social distinctions are associated with biological foundations) and do not address the complex cultural process across ethnic and racial groups (Wendt & Gone, 2011). In other words, they argue that even the construct of psychotherapy is based on Eurocentric notions of wellness and may not adequately reflect approaches to supporting certain minoritized groups (e.g., Indigenous students).

Thus, we use the broader term *culturally responsive practice* because it encapsulates the *active* component of practice; practitioners should work toward responding to the strengths, values, norms, and needs of students and their families. It also means to be attuned to the social, political, and cultural aspects of racism and oppression. We use the term *culturally responsive* because we believe practitioners should be proactive and be guided by the student's and family's expectations, worldviews, and values, rather than be guided by their own perceptions of what is best for the student. Hook et al. (2017) have critiqued the use of the term *culturally responsive*, suggesting that practitioners are being reactive to the student's culture. We understand this argument, but in our view, it enables the student and family to take the lead in informing the practitioner about their goals regarding student success. It is the practitioner's role to respond respectfully, thoughtfully, and intentionally to the student and family in how they describe their culture or identify themselves. Each student's identity, beliefs, values, and norms may vary, even within the same ethnic or cultural group, and being culturally responsive means following the student's and family's lead. The proactive and responsive approach to school-based services means that students' and families' cultures guide the assessment and interventions. Our responsiveness to a student's and a family's needs is something we would need to understand, evaluate, and most importantly, be held accountable for.

Additionally, responsiveness also means conceptualizing the strengths, intersectional identities, and historical and contemporary realities of each student from a systems-level perspective. We emphasize that practitioners should provide culturally responsive services from a systems-level or ecological perspective. Each student is surrounded by multiple systems (e.g., classroom, home, community) that are interrelated and interact in the student's development (Bronfenbrenner, 2005). Culturally responsive practitioners recognize that these various systems are likely affecting students' ability to be successful, and that these systems also have strengths and support for a student's well-being. Culturally responsive practitioners, therefore, avoid deficit views of students (e.g., "What's wrong with Nadia?") and, instead, focus on the systems that support students (e.g., "What aspects of Nadia's family can help her thrive in school?").

Culturally responsive practice also means acknowledging a student's intersectional identities (see also Chapter 2). On a basic level, intersectionality theory emphasizes a student's multiple, intersecting identities that may impact the student in different ways (Crenshaw, 1989). School policies, legislation, and other systems-level factors may seek to oppress those with intersecting or minoritized identities. Thus, a student who is Black and gay would have multiple, intersecting identities, and focusing on only one aspect of the student's identity would not allow for a complete picture of the student's life. Responsive practice would mean that the practitioner is taking actionable steps in understanding, respecting, and supporting each of these identities that the student holds, where systems have often sought to diminish or not recognize these identities explicitly as equal.

Further, culturally responsive practice is about understanding the student's historical and contemporary realities. Also called *culturally sustaining practice* (McCarty & Lee, 2014), practitioners who work with CLD students must recognize the historical landscape that has shaped particular groups, and how these social, political, and historical forces may shape the student's current reality. For example, working with Indigenous students requires an understanding of how White colonial settlers and the U.S. federal government have impacted their communities, including their community's genocide and cultural erasure. At the same time, practitioners also recognize the contemporary realities of Indigenous students, where an urban Indigenous student may or may not closely identify with their tribal heritage. Practitioners must recognize that the student's experience of Indigeneity may not align with the stereotypical notion an Indigenous person. Each student's contemporary reality should be acknowledged and respected.

It is important, however, to acknowledge that being responsive cannot happen without reflexivity or relationships. To be responsive, we must be able to self-critique and be reflexive in our work as practitioners. When we critique, we are held accountable for our behaviors—whether positive or negative—to determine whether change in our behaviors is needed if outcomes are not achieved. Additionally, we cannot take concrete actions if those with whom we work do not trust us. It is about being humble, and recognizing our own weakness or ignorance. Responsiveness is woven within relationships and reflexivity.

Utilizing Evidence-Based Practices and Practice-Based Evidence

Responsiveness also incorporates the use of EBPs and practice-based evidence to support students. Culturally responsive practices must be scientifically grounded and must also be specific to that particular student's needs and culture. We define the term *evidence-based practices* similarly to other scholars (e.g., Hoagwood & Johnson, 2003) in that it characterizes practices (e.g., assessment, therapy) that have been rigorously tested and found to be effective both in laboratory settings (e.g., university clinics) and within naturalistic settings (e.g., schools). To be considered an evidence-based intervention, the intervention must follow a set of rigid criteria (Kratochwill & Stoiber, 2002; White & Kratochwill, 2005) and must demonstrate both efficacy (success when implemented under controlled conditions) and effectiveness (success when implemented in other contexts, e.g., a classroom). We emphasize the use of science and data to guide the practices with students—practitioners should not be providing services that have not been shown to be effective.

We emphasize in Chapter 9 the importance of adapting practices as needed given the complexity of needs and strengths of CLD students. Culturally responsive practice also requires an understanding that all mental health interventions (e.g., psychotherapy, counseling) are based on Eurocentric ideas of wellness and are often tested with primarily White people (Wendt & Gone, 2011). EBP, therefore, becomes problematic because it may focus on using scientifically supported interventions that are based on Eurocentric theoretical models of interventions and because adaptations of these interventions may only be superficial, rather than deep restructuring, in addressing specific ethnic and racial groups.

In addition to using practices that have been scientifically supported, it is almost as important to use practice-based evidence. *Practice-based evidence* is characterized as information that is gathered through intervention (e.g., progress monitoring data) to ensure that it is meeting the needs of that individual student. Although research suggests that cultural variables are important to examine when planning, designing, and implementing evidence-based interventions, the challenge remains of maintaining a balance between program fidelity (implementing the intervention as developed) and adaptation (making sure the intervention meets the needs of a specific student or group; Castro et al., 2004). Although interventions may have been tested with that particular student's racial or ethnic group, it does not mean that it would necessarily work for that student due to variability in skills, strengths, and attributes. As a result, it is critical that data are gathered throughout the implementation of an intervention to ensure that the specific intervention is effective for that particular student. These progress monitoring data are essential in confirming that an intervention (whether adapted or not) aligns with the students' needs.

Developing Cultural Skills

Being responsive to student's strengths, and thus taking deliberate, actionable steps to leverage those strengths, requires practitioners to develop *cultural skills*. Sue (2001) emphasized that practitioners need specific skills in implementing interventions, conducting assessments, or providing consultation. When implementing interventions, for example, a practitioner may need a specific skill set in adapting interventions to the student's needs (Bernal, 2006) or using assessment tools that align with the student's ethnicity, language, or culture (Ortiz, 2014). Practitioners may need to learn specific intervention approaches or assessment tools that are culturally relevant to the student. For example, a cognitive-behavioral treatment may be adapted by modifying the parent psychoeducational pamphlets to be written in Spanish or when the examples within the treatment are changed to be culturally specific. Practitioner's cultural skills can also be related to the use of assessment tools. Practitioners may need to choose a measure or questionnaire but would need to consider whether it is appropriate for the students' ethnic, racial, or language group. Some assessment tools have not been normed with certain populations, and thus the measure's validity would be problematic. We explore this further in Chapters 4, 5, and 6, discussing the complexity of conducting culturally responsive assessments for special education, interventions, and counseling. In sum, culturally responsive EBPs should guide the provision of school-based mental health services for students and their families. Practitioners must use scientifically supported approaches while simultaneously being responsive to the student's identity, beliefs, values, and norms.

RELATIONAL EMPOWERMENT

The final component of culturally responsive practice is relational empowerment. Within a social justice framework, relational empowerment involves practitioners (1) playing an intentional and active role in advocacy, and (2) working toward equitable distribution of power for students and caregivers. In general, empowerment has been conceptualized as a process in which there is respect, care, and group participation in the local community, and where there is shared access and control of resources (Cornell Empowerment Group, 1989).

In our cultural humility model in Chapter 2 (Pham et al., 2021), we describe relational empowerment as a part of focusing on individual and community strengths. Our role as practitioners is not only to provide educational and mental health services, but also to engage with the families and students so they are empowered to make decisions to ensure student success. Empowering students and their families is an important part of safeguarding that they have a voice in the decision-making. Empowerment is ceding power in order to have family's voices more involved in the process in schools. In her book on decolonizing trauma, Linklater (2014) describes how "community empowerment must come from within. Empowerment can be achieved when the detrimental power structures in communities become flattened and the natural leaders and community workers are able to bring forward ideas for growth, healing, and sustainability" (p. 91). This "flattening" of power structures is essential in order to foster relational empowerment.

Practitioners have an important role in empowering students and families so they can advocate for the student's mental health care in school. Empowerment cannot happen, however, without established trust and relationships. Questions that can be asked include:

- What do the family and student need?
- What are resources the family needs to feel "empowered"?
- As practitioners, what can we do to ensure that the family is empowered (e.g., change systems, develop skills, sustain trust)?
- How do we know when communities feel empowered or attain power?

Practitioners who engage in empowerment participate in the community with respect and intentionality and ensure that they are doing so in ways that the community (families, religious leaders, etc.) can access and in which the community can control resources for the betterment of students. Indeed, empowerment is also defined as providing supports to make changes in people's lives, as well as the transferring of power, whether it be a gain in rights, knowledge, or goods (Weidenstedt, 2016). This "transactional aspect of empowerment" is what we discuss here, where one party (the practitioner) may empower someone else (e.g., the student) (Weidenstedt, 2016, p. 2).

Relational empowerment extends this idea in that practitioners recognize that relationships and connections are critical in transferring power and social capital (Christens, 2012). These relationships and connections with families, students, community members, educators, and administrators can be critical in having shared leadership, promoting wellness, and reducing oppression (Prilleltensky, 2008). There is a shared leadership and, thus, active membership in the redistribution of power.

Nonetheless, it is important to consider that there is a fine line between empowerment and taking on a role as a "White savior." The act of empowerment does not occur, as sociologist Weidenstedt (2016) stated, in a total social vacuum. The sociopolitical context of that dynamic is important to consider. There is a long history of White educators believing that their role is to "save" minoritized students (see films like *Freedom Writers*), and White practitioners can easily fall into this role, even with good intentions.

[Reflexivity Activity] As a practitioner, ask yourself:

- *Why am I helping? What are my intentions?*
- *How do I feel about giving away the power that I have?*

With critical reflexivity and cultural humility, practitioners should also have established trust and cultivated relations with students, families, and community members. Practitioners who engage in relational empowerment have already established trust with that caregiver and would work closely with them so that their voices can be a part of the decision-making in ways that align with their beliefs, values, and norms. For example, let's say the student assistance team referred Maria, a Latina second-grade student, because of concerns related to attention in class. Maria's mother, Elena, is a single Latina mother of three children and has been unable to attend meetings with her child's teacher. Within culturally responsive practice, the school psychologist would already have earned trust and cultivated a relationship with Elena, Maria, and their family. With this in mind, the school psychologist could visit with Elena, listening to her story. Elena may believe that it is not her role to make decisions about Maria's education; instead, her role is to support Maria and her siblings at home. Elena is concerned that Maria is not focusing on her schoolwork, and these concerns have been ongoing since kindergarten. The school psychologist may engage in relational empowerment by writing down Elena's needs and goals, asking her what steps she'd like to take next, and connecting her with the school social worker to be sure that she is accessing all the necessary resources she requires (e.g., access to day-care supports for her other siblings).

Overall, relational empowerment aligns with the social justice model. Increasing equity for CLD students and their families is essential so that they do not continue to be marginalized within the school system. It also means understanding the barriers that exist within the educational system as well as the community in which the school exists. In what ways can practitioners support students who have been marginalized and who do not have access to mental health care? In what ways can practitioners ensure that all students in their schools have their needs met, and that they are working toward equity?

IS ADVOCATING FOR CULTURALLY RESPONSIVE PRACTICE AND SOCIAL JUSTICE A LIBERAL BIAS?

The topics and issues discussed in this book can be viewed by some as controversial or politically biased, which can lead to divisiveness. Anti-immigrant discourses, recent waves of violence against marginalized populations, and the history of discriminatory or nativist policies in the U.S. toward maintaining White supremacy are reasons why culturally responsive practice and social justice are needed. However, questions and critiques have been raised about teaching or employing social justice and related topics (e.g., critical race theory) in K–12 schools and higher education, particularly as it relates to political neutrality and educator bias. Teachers who bring up issues regarding privilege, power, and injustice are seen as "political," imposing a one-sided, liberal ideology, whereas those who dismiss such issues apparently are not. *Liberal ideology* is characterized as a system of ideas, attitudes, and values that emphasize change, equality, and government action to improve human welfare (Steele et al., 2014). *Conservatism* is characterized as a system of ideas, attitudes, and values that support stability, tradition, and restricted government involvement in domestic social interests (Dunn & Woodard, 2003). Those who identify as conservative question fairness due to demands for being neutral or balanced in perspectives and cultivating intellectual diversity.

Therefore, one might wonder: *Is teaching or implementing culturally responsive practice considered a liberal bias? If so, is it unfair? Can we be neutral but also socially just?* We do acknowledge that these are thought-provoking questions, as this issue opens up discussion and a space to be critically reflexive on the processes and aims of social justice. Whether teaching social justice in the classroom or advocating for diverse students, there is an assumption that bias equates to partiality or discrimination. Years ago, a school-based team probably would not think much if a teacher provided a reading list in an English course consisting of nearly all White male authors, and his instruction would not be considered biased. However, if they were provided a reading list that highlights perspectives from scholars of color who focus on oppression and power in literature, they might encounter resistance by some families and fellow teachers. In the latter example, privileged students may feel silenced, not because they have been excluded, but because they are used to having their ideas go unchallenged, whereas other students may feel liberated and welcomed to express ideas more openly that they would not have been able to in the past. Applebaum (2009) suggested that under conditions in which education reinforces oppression, demanding neutrality from teachers is similar to being color-blind; that is, being neutral does not mitigate bias but sustains it. Thus, neutrality does not necessarily equate to balance but, rather, functions as a way to normalize and perpetuate social dominance, especially when the status quo is not questioned.

Social justice issues can be, and often are, controversial and will be further explored in Chapter 2. Some purport that social justice can be a form of propaganda and indoctrination. Students and families may be more likely accuse a teacher of liberal bias if they did not welcome a conservative viewpoint. These students or families would believe they have been silenced because their voices are not being heard as the dominant view and would refuse to be critically reflexive about their power and privilege. In this case, we do not believe the teacher is indoctrinating or imposing his or her views but, instead, is attending to student viewpoints that have been historically unheard or undervalued by the system (Applebaum, 2009). The goals of social justice can therefore be considered biased but fair when taking a position on the existence and the meaning of injustice.

Political and educator neutrality is therefore virtually impossible when advocating for a socially just society. Emerging studies have found that school-based professionals with liberal ideologies were more likely to engage in social justice advocacy than those who were conservative (Linnmeyer et al., 2018; Parikh et al., 2011). Despite potential disagreements people may have about social justice, schools want to ensure that the students are successful. Lastly, we believe the goals of diversity, equity, access, inclusion, and the common good are not partisan issues but, rather, the values needed for a safe and healthy society.

SUMMARY

As practitioners, we may worry about offending, unintentionally harming, or not protecting CLD students and families, and these feelings can sometimes overwhelm us to the point of inaction. Nevertheless, it is our ethical and moral responsibility to equip ourselves with the appropriate skills to prepare to support students' mental health and learning. The intentional practice of reflexivity, relationships, responsiveness, and relational empowerment come together to create comprehensive, culturally responsive practices. The concepts of reflexivity and cultural humility come together as the result of trust between a practitioner and the students, families, and communities they serve. Relatedly, relationships (specifically family–school relationships) can serve as a keystone in fostering communication and trust. When building these relationships, however, it is important to consider making connections through cultural knowledge and understanding other cultures' perceptions of mental health.

Throughout all this, it is important to adapt practices as needed given the complexity and individuality of CLD students. The combination of using EBPs and a strengths-based approach will highlight student strengths and bring empowerment to those involved in the intervention. Importantly, this chapter is just the beginning of exploring reflexivity, responsiveness, relationships, and relational empowerment. In the upcoming chapters, we will outline specific practices and strategies when working with CLD students.

DISCUSSION QUESTIONS

1. In what ways have you noticed yourself or others utilizing one (or more) of the components for culturally responsive practice?
2. Which parts of culturally responsive practice (reflexivity, relationships, responsiveness, and relational empowerment) do you believe will be easiest to implement? Which one(s) will be more difficult to implement? Why?
3. Latasha is a Black middle-school student who was recently referred to the school counselor (who is White) to address emotional concerns. The school counselor sees a lot of potential in Latasha and is eager to talk to her about how Latasha can think of things differently. What concerns come up when considering the school counselor's plan and perspective? What would you recommend the school counselor do prior to beginning counseling sessions with Latasha?

APPENDIX 1
CRITICAL REFLEXIVE ACTIVITY: I AM . . .

Write down the first things that come to mind (don't ponder—just write!).

I am _____.

I am _____.

I am _____.

I am _____.

I am _____.

Reflect on your responses:

1. What feelings or thoughts did you have that were associated with each of these responses?
2. How do these responses align with the culture, traditions, or norms of your family and/or society? How do these responses *not* align with the culture, traditions, or norms of your family and/or society?
3. What do you wish your responses had been, if any?

Social Justice, Privilege, and Oppression

VIGNETTE

Luc is a high school student who identifies as a bisexual male from Thailand, speaks fluent English, and resides in a middle-class neighborhood. His teacher Ms. Porter overheard two students call Luc "gay" and "tranny" because of the way he dressed. Mr. Rowe, the assistant principal, called the two students into his office and required them to apologize to Luc. Mr. Rowe and Ms. Porter later informed the school counselor of the incident and stated that Luc should stop "dressing gay" and "not make trouble," otherwise other students would continue teasing and bullying him. The counselor is reluctant to propose a program to support Luc and other students who may have witnessed or experienced similar events. After school, Mr. Rowe found Luc vandalizing the exterior of the school building.

- How could the situation have been handled?
- What do you believe are the reason(s) for the counselor's reluctance?
- What, if any, are examples of implicit bias or microaggressions in this scenario?
- What social justice issues are at play here?
- What ecological factors contributed to these events?

Social justice requires us to contemplate: What is fair? What is just? These are fundamental questions when working with students whose identities, experiences, and cultures have been historically oppressed. Unfortunately, some students experience more challenges or hardships than others, often from injustices happening in society that are beyond their control, including economic disparities, racism, or intergenerational trauma. Social justice thus represents a multifaceted approach to helping at the individual, community, and societal levels. As practitioners, we strive to resolve inequities and promote human development and success by attending to issues at all levels. In order to do so, practitioners must understand factors that contribute to these inequities and consider ways to support marginalized students.

Accordingly, culturally responsive practices that focus on social justice must leverage student strengths to address issues of privilege, power, and oppression in society. Although social justice and culturally responsive practice are related, they are not entirely the same. *Culturally responsive practices* includes several important components in which practitioners (1) acknowledge and respect students, families, and communities' cultural identities, (2) collaborate with fellow school professionals to create equitable and optimal learning environments, (3) engage in cultural humility where personal beliefs, attitudes, and biases are regularly examined, (4) interrogate institutional policies and procedures, and (5) achieve social justice through proactive efforts. We believe that culturally responsive practice can be a means for achieving social justice goals.

The aim of this chapter is to describe the frameworks and strategies to promote social justice for practitioners who provide services to support students' mental health and learning. First, we define the concept of social justice and contextualize it within culturally responsive practice. Second, we describe forms of systemic oppression, such as cultural and structural oppression, and its relevance when it comes to intersectionality. Third, we discuss the cultural humility model, a framework that can aid in promoting social justice at the individual and systemic levels. Importantly, this chapter provides an initial focus for engaging in social justice efforts; practitioners should not expect that positive change will occur immediately, as these efforts will require planning, patience, support, and time.

DEFINING AND INCORPORATING SOCIAL JUSTICE IN SCHOOLS

[Reflexivity Activity]. Reflect on the following. When you work with culturally, ethnically, racially, and linguistically diverse students in schools, the question starts with examining and recognizing the injustice:

- *Are these situations due to actual cultural differences, or are there structural or institutional factors that contribute to these inequities?*
- *How would we engage in these discussions with students, educators, administrators, legislators, and mental health professionals, while ensuring that social injustices are sufficiently remedied?*

Inequities arise from social injustices and, therefore, have significant implications in students' overall development, identity, and well-being. Minoritized students experience higher rates of mental health problems and lower rates of using school-based mental health supports (Bear et al., 2014; Coker et al., 2017), along with higher rates of school expulsions and referrals to special education than White students (NCES, 2019; Sullivan & Bal, 2013). Students with disabilities are more likely to experience bullying, social ostracism, and depression (Young et al., 2012). Sexual- and gender-minoritized students in schools (e.g., lesbian, gay, bisexual, transgender, queer, or questioning [LGBTQ]) report feeling unsafe and distressed due to verbal and physical harassment, bullying, and stigmatization from their peers (Kosciw et al., 2020). Preschool suspensions and expulsions for young boys, particularly Black boys, can lead to loss of early educational placement and access to educational opportunities (Gilliam et al., 2016). Structural inequities, such as racism and discrimination, have contributed to not only negative psychological outcomes (e.g., suicide ideation, substance abuse, depression; Sutter & Perrin, 2006), but also physical health inequities (Trent et al., 2019). Considering that the risk is higher among minoritized youth, these actions committed by adults can be considered a form of bullying. In Luc's scenario, the injustices he experienced are caused not only by his peers, but also by adults, whereby these individuals acted on their own biases, based on the student's appearance and actions. These injustices occur not only in schools, but also in public settings, the workplace, and throughout society. Striving for social justice may feel like a constant struggle, because not all individuals or groups realize the impact of their actions or inactions.

As mentioned in Chapter 1, social justice has become a critical topic in education and mental health in recent years. It is an abstract term with interpretations across multiple disciplines, including education, psychology, counseling, and philosophy, all of which have a central theme: to promote equity for those who have been marginalized. Generally, we define *social justice* as an aspiration that recognizes diversity and equity of social, economic, political, and educational rights through redistribution of resources, opportunities, and privilege, and through representation of diverse people, thoughts, and ideas. Specifically, social justice can be viewed as both as a process and a goal. The *goal* of social justice is to ensure that all individuals have equitable participation in, and access to, resources and supports that promote learning and well-being, regardless of their race, ethnicity, culture, language, age, sexual orientation, gender, socioeconomic status, religion, (dis)ability, or other characteristics (National Association of School Psychologists [NASP], 2020; Shriberg et al., 2013). That is, the goal of social justice is for all students to have the necessary opportunities and resources for successful learning and well-being.

The *process* for attaining this goal may involve isolating factors contributing to social injustices and oppressive environments, and demonstrating proactive efforts to promote change (Theoharis, 2007). Social justice also requires understanding of our position within the broader social-economic-political and cultural contexts that contribute to inequities. Systemic changes require continuous actions and alliances by families and communities. Most importantly, accountability is required, so that any systemic changes that lead to positive outcomes are sustained, and any continued injustices would continuously be addressed.

Social justice has also been used synonymously with anti-oppressive education and multiculturalism (Kumashiro, 2015), and therefore serves as a foundation for implementing strategies that promote egalitarian practices. These strategies can be described as interventions to solve real-world problems, to increase opportunities, and to improve circumstances for those who have been oppressed by systems (Lopez, 2016), or as a means of addressing and eliminating marginalization in schools (Theoharis, 2007).

In one paradigm of social justice, Fraser (2008) outlines multiple dimensions that are interconnected with culturally responsive practice, including recognition of injustices and equitable redistribution of resources. Social justice involves being reflexive of values and cultural identities of others, along with self-realization of actions that may contribute to injustices. Thus, practitioners identify and respect the cultural norms, beliefs, values, and identities of students and their families and are aware of how their own behaviors may intentionally or unintentionally contribute to injustices (Fraser, 2008). For example, educators can reflect on cultural biases that may influence disproportionate referrals for special education. They must not only start to examine school-level data, but also to listen to colleagues, students, and families who have been underestimated or misjudged, along with reviewing existing educational placement policies and practices.

Secondly, redistribution implies that existing systems are not equitable and requires reallocation of resources (responsiveness), positive alliances with community (relationships), and transformation of structures to ensure equity (Fraser, 2008). A practitioner may try to change existing systems and redistribute resources within those systems (e.g., funds to support educational and mental health programs, personnel). Lastly, representation (relational empowerment) allows for inclusion of and respect for diverse individuals, ideas, and perspectives. Collaboration with administrators and educators is key to ensuring that families and community members have equal voice in decision-making, and to capitalize on existing strengths.

Social Justice as an Ethical and Moral Obligation

Social justice goals are often tied to ethical guidelines outlined in many professional associations. Ethics represent the moral principles, aspirational goals, or ideal set of standards for conduct within a profession. The American Psychological Association ([APA], 2017a), for example, identifies justice as one of the core principles, "entitling all persons to access to and benefit from the contributions of psychology and to equal quality in the processes, procedures, and service." Similarly, the National Association of Social Workers (NASW) and the American Counseling Association (ACA) outline social justice as a core professional value, with ACA (2014) defining social justice as, "the promotion of equity for all people and groups for the purpose of ending oppression and injustice affecting clients, students, counselors, families, communities, schools, workplaces, governments, and other social and institutional systems." Finally, the National Association of School Psychologists ([NASP], 2020) recommended taking a proactive role in advocating for social justice by (a) understanding the impact of culture and biases in service delivery, (b) recognizing equitable practices for diverse student populations, (c) speaking up for the rights and welfare of students and families, and (d) striving to reform systems-level patterns of injustice. Ethical principles are needed for considering how our professional behavior contributes to or impedes social justice goals.

Although ethical principles from professional associations guide practitioners on how they should work toward social justice, they may still face dilemmas when implementing social justice initiatives. For example, as a practitioner, you may be expected to examine your own biases and cultural values that may interfere in your professional work. As we discussed in Chapter 1, critical reflexivity is a key aspect of culturally responsive practice. Thus, when you discover your beliefs and values (e.g., political, religious) that are different from those of the community members with whom you work, how do you navigate these differences? Would you compromise your own belief system? Would you request to have another colleague take your place instead to avoid the issue? These questions may challenge practitioners to consider personal morals, along with the best interests of students. Thus, ethics allow us to be more introspective and to weigh multiple options, but they are often unclear as to the extent of our responsibility in our ongoing efforts to achieve social justice.

Remedying Injustice in Schools

Social justice involves actively changing and remedying injustices that affect all students. Fraser (2008) discussed two distinct approaches, affirmative and transformative approaches, that can assuage social injustices. The *affirmative approach* addresses the end state outcomes of injustices, without changing structures that create and reproduce them. That is, to remedy injustices using the affirmative approach, a practitioner may focus on fixing the *outcome*, rather than the *root of the injustice*. In the vignette, Luc's school may implement a disciplinary policy, which prevents any bullying or aggressive behaviors toward another student by suspension or expulsion. Although this approach may lead to decreases in negative behavior, the underlying issues surrounding prejudice and school climate would still be present. The school counselor may engage in the affirmative approach by focusing on the bullying behavior (outcome) rather than the systems in place that are perpetuating the harm (prejudice or school climate).

The *transformative approach*, on the other hand, aims to correct social inequities by challenging institutions, processes, and ideologies that lead to disparate outcomes. This approach focuses on the systems and structures (e.g., curriculum restructuring, reducing cultural biases, etc.). Luc's school counselor may integrate lessons and examples that promote LGTBQ awareness within existing social-emotional curricula. Despite the value in this approach, it may unintentionally convey that there is one central, normative culture, whereas the other cultures are fortunate to be included, which does not present a culturally responsive or inclusive perspective. A deeper-level approach can incorporate educator professional development to engage in culturally responsive teaching (e.g., discussing LGTBQ leaders or history in academic content areas), administrative support, or peer advocacy. Although these initiatives may take time to implement, transformative approaches are preemptive to ensure safety where individuals and systems do not violate human rights of others.

Using this transformative approach in addressing the root causes of injustice, there are a number of steps that the practitioner may consider: (1) assessing the specific unjust actions and review policies, (2) gathering information and data about unjust actions or policies, and (3) creating a safe space or opportunities for dialogue, all of which can lead to development of an action plan. First, practitioners must assess what the specific unjust actions or policies within the institution are through discussion with colleagues and school leaders. Reviewing existing practices or policies can be helpful to understand if there is previous history of similar incidents and whether any corrective actions or consequences occurred as a result. These issues may be brought up in department meetings and with other administrative personnel. Second, tangible data are needed to understand better the inequities that are occurring. School outcomes, feedback from students and families, or individual student data can be used when determining which unjust actions or policies are worth pursuing and changing. Practitioners may need to engage in careful planning, obtain buy-in from those in power, and navigate various systems in order to address the inequities effectively. Not every person may see eye to eye, particularly among those who have benefited from the existing system, yet data using graphs and tables can be compelling to display, as inequities can be intangible or invisible to many.

Third, creating safe spaces and opportunities for dialogue provide better understanding of the urgency of the situation and what can be done to remedy the injustice. These discussions should involve teachers, practitioners, school leaders, families, and/or community members. Voices from students who have experienced inequities should be included. Similarly, classrooms can promote awareness and civic engagement by addressing related issues with students, which can serve as authentic opportunities (in particular, in middle and high school) through discussion, reflexivity, and collaboration. For example, when Ms. Porter overheard the slurs directed at Luc, she could have worked with several students and the school counselor to hold a "peace circle," or a safe space for conflict resolution, healing, and communication. Ms. Porter can ask the classroom to share meaningful stories to encourage relationship building, while also addressing the use of slurs that were directed toward Luc. The school counselor along with Ms. Porter can then provide strategies for students to use that encourage empathy, emotion regulation, and safety. Action plans include having students assist in setting rules and consequences for promoting a supportive school climate and to increase accountability.

Practitioners often are well positioned to lead schools in tackling injustices. They can develop infrastructure by taking steps to discuss these issues openly, developing team-based action plans, and monitoring outcomes regularly. Motivating colleagues and the school community to develop and sustain socially just practices is not an easy endeavor. Practitioners may likely still find themselves leading these efforts, while still witnessing the injustices committed by others. In order to develop skills to lead schools toward the goal of social justice, they will need to question, discuss, and collaborate with school and community leaders, check in with teachers and students, and continually evaluate effectiveness from implemented programs to ensure that these efforts are sustained.

In sum, social justice represents a multifaceted approach in which practitioners strive to promote equity for students, families, and within systems. From a social justice perspective, it is insufficient for practitioners to engage only in work between individuals without also working to change oppressive policies and institutions that contribute to inequity (Vera & Speight, 2003). Thus, most social justice agents work in both interpersonal and structural levels.

Systemic Oppression in Schools

Oppression is broadly defined as an act to exploit differences and establish dominance over different groups and individuals (Sue, 2010). Minoritized students and families may experience compounding effects of historical and contemporary political and economic discrimination, exclusion, and marginalization, leading to negative student outcomes. For example, Indigenous students have been systematically oppressed by colonialism that began when settlers arrived in North America. The federal government's policies of genocide of Indigenous culture and language, and forced attendance of children in residential boarding schools, have subsequently led to intergenerational trauma, high rates of suicidality, alcohol use, and poverty in Indigenous communities (Campbell & Evans-Campbell, 2011). The practitioner's role, therefore, is to ensure that policies and practices that are enacted in schools do not perpetuate oppression.

In schools, marginalized groups have experienced structural and cultural oppression for the longest time. *Structural oppression* consists of ways in which systems, institutions, laws, and policies all work together to marginalize a subordinate group (Diemer et al., 2009). For example, structural oppression in schools can be understood as a lack of funding for mental health services for immigrant youth or disproportionate disciplinary practices that have a negative impact on students of color. These students may have limited feelings of agency, competence, and control, negatively affecting their academic or social development.

Another type of oppression, *cultural oppression*, consists of shared societal values and norms that allow people to see oppression as typical or right (Sue & Sue, 2013). For example, cultural oppression in school can involve the belief that a Language Arts class would include only White authors, but any non-White authors are considered "special." This curriculum decision implies that the works of minoritized authors are not in the norm, legitimizing Eurocentric teaching and knowledge. This type of oppression has short- and long-term impacts on marginalized students, such as on their sense of belonging, community, and identity (Sue & Sue, 2013). Both structural and cultural oppression can negatively affect academic outcomes and well-being of these students.

Another form of oppression is *colonialism*, a practice that privileges one group (e.g., non-Indigenous) over another (e.g., Indigenous) by domination and removal of the others' cultural heritage, identities, and resources (Alfred & Corntassel, 2005). Colonialism is embedded within U.S. education, demonstrated by low expectations of Indigenous students from teachers or microaggressions related to Indigenous peoples shown in textbooks (Holter et al., 2019). Indigenous families have also experienced historical trauma, whereby the impact of traumatic events by settlers has continued effects across generations (Brave Heart, 1998). These issues have a profound and negative impact on Indigenous youth, resulting in poorer student behavior (Gion et al., 2018) and higher school dropout rates (McFarland et al., 2020). It is not uncommon for schools to have different layers of oppression (structural, cultural, colonialism) that exist within multiple systems.

Privilege as Power

Oppressors often view power as not something they already possess or distribute, but as a way for them to benefit from subordinating others through economic exploitation, racial segregation, or cultural imperialism (Tew, 2006). Power, however, can also be used to influence individual or social change, open opportunities for accessing resources, or renegotiate relationships. In many organizations, complex power dynamics and power imbalances can easily occur when there is hierarchy based on social group membership (e.g., gender, age, language) and legitimate power (Wellman et al., 2020). Legitimate power refers to the formal title or role held within an institution (e.g., principal, assistant principal, student) and can be dependent on educational level, rank, or years of experience.

Privilege is a form of power and comes from inherent or unearned social advantages, benefits, or degrees of prestige and respect due to belonging in a specific social identity, status, or group. One of the ubiquitous forms of privilege, *White privilege*, is often unrecognized and invisible, particularly to those who have benefited the most (McIntosh, 1989). Scholars have discussed some of these unearned benefits associated with systemic White privilege, such as membership in the norm (Wildman, 1996), feelings of superiority (Ostrander, 1984), reinforcement of discrimination and inequality (Mindrup et al., 2011), the power to ignore race, or objection to the notion of privilege.

Like colonialism, White supremacy culture is embedded within U.S. society, including the education system. This social ideology, for example, is a component of the myth of the Protestant work ethic, in which hard work leads to success, rather than acknowledging the biased social structures that impede certain people's ability to succeed (Roberts & Rizzo, 2020). Another example is when White people claim that they "don't see color," where not acknowledging race means they cannot be racist, when in fact, this color-blind philosophy is indeed racist (Bonilla-Silva, 2006). These ideologies and beliefs are passed from generation to generation, perpetuating White supremacy (Roberts & Rizzo, 2020). Sue (2006) suggested that Whiteness would not be problematic if it were not predicated on

Table 2.1 EXAMPLES OF PRIVILEGED AND OPPRESSED GROUPS IN THE UNITED STATES

Categories	Privileged	Oppressed
Gender	Male	Female, nonbinary, transgender, queer
Age	Adults	Children, elderly
Ability	Individuals without impairments	Individuals with impairment
Social class	Middle and upper class	Poor and working class
Religion	Christianity	Buddhism, Hinduism, Judaism, Shintoism, Islam, Taoism, Confucianism, Rastafarianism, etc.
Ethnicity	European	People of color
Sexual orientation	Heterosexual	Lesbian, gay, bisexual, queer, questioning
National origin	North American born	Immigrant or refugee
Language	English	Other than English

NOTE: Adapted from *Addressing Cultural Complexities in Practice: Assessment, Diagnosis, and Therapy* (2nd ed.), by P. A. Hays, 2008. American Psychological Association.

White supremacy, and a failure to recognize either has led to normalization of biased policies and practices.

Those who claim to value social justice may unknowingly continue to participate in systems of White hegemony to maintain their dominant position in a racialized social system (Boatright-Horowitz et al., 2013). As long as White privilege remains invisible and is equated with normality and superiority, people of color will continue to feel oppressed. Table 2.1 provides some examples of the differences between privileged and oppressed groups in the United States, adapted from Hays' framework (2008).

Cultural Appropriation

Consider this scenario: *A Black female college student confronted a White male student over his dreadlock hairstyle, accusing him of cultural appropriation. The male student asks, "Why can't I wear a hairstyle because of your culture? Why?"*

Recently, instances of cultural appropriation have surfaced within the media as well as in schools and college campuses (e.g., Blackface, wearing feather headdress as a costume). *Cultural appropriation* is an unacknowledged or inappropriate adoption of a non-dominant culture by a dominant group of people or society. Typically, cultural appropriation occurs when a person or group reproduces facets of a culture from which it has not been socialized and thus does not fully understand (Fryberg et al., 2008). For example, studies have found harmful social repercussions for Indigenous students when schools use mascots at sporting events, leading to increased stereotyping and discrimination, and decreased student self-esteem and academic aspiration (Davis-Delano et al., 2020).

The main factor for identifying cultural appropriation is the unequal social context that occurs between dominant and non-dominant cultures (Lenard & Balint, 2020). Immigrant populations, for example, adopt or assimilate specific aspects of the dominant culture, known as *cultural assimilation* (Berry, 2005). Students may be given messages that to succeed, to belong, or to be taken seriously in the United States, one must adopt practices of the dominant culture and conform to White standards. Overall, diverse cultures are often celebrated and shared across and between communities, but primarily at a surface-level, including art, fashion, or food. Deeper-level or structural differences, such as history, values, identities, and belief systems, should be recognized as part of cultural responsiveness. Privileged societies, on the other hand, have had a long history of seizing aspects of other cultures through colonization. Thus, cultural appropriation enables the dominant culture to be rewarded for taking advantage of oppressed communities by disregarding the meaningful history of the non-dominant culture; it also insensitively uses the products of a culture by reinforcing or ignoring the prejudice experienced by the people who created them.

With the example earlier, if a White student wishes to wear dreadlocks from another person's culture, it becomes necessary for the student to learn about the historical context and understand reasons for opposition if they choose to wear the hairstyle. The White male may believe that wearing dreadlocks is the latest fashion trend, showing preference to the ability to do "whatever they want" or showing power. For others, the hairstyle symbolizes continuation of historical iterations, representing opposition to sociopolitical structures. When people of power and privilege decide to validate customs and traditions from oppressed people who have long been disenfranchised, then it is considered cultural appropriation.

Distinguishing Stereotypes, Prejudice, and Discrimination

Stereotypes, prejudice, and discrimination are also important concepts that often contribute to systemic oppression in schools. *Stereotypes* are overgeneralizations that people hold about characteristics of a group, and they may be either positive or negative. For example, in the 19th century, there was the stereotype that Asian immigrant laborers were lazy and dirty (Wu, 2003), yet as Asian Americans' academic and socioeconomic statuses improved, a "model minority" stereotype evolved in which they were perceived as having higher intelligence, diligence, and success. The latter stereotype is problematic because it masks the inequities within a heterogenous group and discounts the challenges of other racial and ethnic minoritized groups.

Although some may be inclined to use positive stereotypes to counter negative stereotypes, there are drawbacks. Emphasizing positive characteristics may represent a coping strategy for dealing with stigmatization of negative stereotypes (Sue et al., 2007). Black students, for example, may select an identity or career more consistent with athletics in reaction to negative stereotypes related to Black students pursuing a STEM career (Dubrow & Adams, 2010). Research has found positive stereotypes generally attributed to lower-status groups tend to be associated with subordination (Becker et al., 2011) and are endorsed by higher-status groups so as to flatter group members into accepting their lower status (Czopp et al., 2015). Moreover, positive stereotypes can lead many to view the system as already socially just and fair, so they are less likely to become motivated to engage in change. Positive stereotypes do influence the way individuals choose educational and career goals and have implications for students' cultural identity development (Czopp et al., 2015). Therefore, positive stereotypes may lead to adverse effects on students' well-being and mental health, particularly for those who value personal distinction.

Prejudice and discrimination are also important considerations in understanding how systemic oppression is developed in schools. *Prejudice* refers to attitudes, opinions, and judgments of others based on perceived group membership (Devine et al., 2012), such as "I get frustrated when Hispanic students are disruptive." Most, if not all, people have implicit biases rooted in racial and cultural stereotypes, and the persistence and power of these biases have become associated with lack of personal awareness. Thus, when we become consciously aware of how our social position and privilege have shaped our values and experiences, we are less likely to make faulty assumptions or stereotypes about others.

Discrimination refers to prejudicial behaviors and unjust treatment of individuals or groups based on group membership (e.g., verbal harassment, social exclusion of students based on race). Due to variations within subgroups and the presence of multiethnic identities (e.g., Asian-Black), practitioners should take precautions not to make broad generalizations or discriminate when working with families and students. Exposure to racial discrimination is a risk factor for negative student academic outcomes and well-being; however, not all youth respond to discrimination in the same way (Neblett et al., 2006). Individual differences in the development of racial identity, coping strategies, or the sense of belonging have helped explain the variation in racial- and ethnic-minoritized students' adaptive responses to discrimination (Leath et al., 2019).

Mitigating Racism and Microaggressions Using Microinterventions

Racism is a form of oppression against individuals or groups based on beliefs about one's own racial superiority (Salter et al., 2018). The social construct of race consists of a set of federally sanctioned categories and labels, which promotes generalizations and associations that inherently leads to prejudice (Roberts & Rizzo, 2020). When public policies, institutional practices, cultural representations, and norms reinforce or perpetuate inequity, then racism is systemic. It can be perceived as intentional or unintentional, subtle or egregious, explicit or implicit, interpersonal or institutional. It is a spectrum of acts and behaviors that all of us have displayed to some degree. Children experience the effects of racism through place (i.e., where they live), education (i.e., where they learn), economic status (i.e., what they have), and legal means (i.e., how their rights are violated).

Critical race theory (CRT) is a lens through which to understand the degree to which racism is embedded within institutions, as well as to consider ways to engage in antiracism. Proponents of CRT have supported the notion that racism is a pervasive and vast system that structures our relationships, and that it is not merely an individual pathology (Delgado & Stefancic, 2001). In the context of education, CRT focuses directly on the effects of race and institutional or societal racism in the school system, while simultaneously addressing the hegemonic system of White supremacy (Ladson-Billings & Tate, 1995). Due to its many manifestations, racism adapts to changes within the system by altering its form or expression, so it never fully diminishes or disappears.

One reason why racism is pervasive is the implicit associations we learn in our environment. Racism can take the form of beliefs, judgments, and perceptions of racial groups that stem from *implicit bias* (Sue & Sue 2013). Implicit biases are unconscious beliefs that arise from organizing patterns and establishing associations about a social group. Implicit biases have been known to influence educators' beliefs about student discipline and decisions regarding student behavior (Girvan et al., 2017). What is harmful about implicit biases is that we unknowingly make decisions based on these associations of student attributes. That is, our biases may lead to racist, sexist, classist, or heterosexist prejudiced behavior (Levinson et al., 2017), as often these biases generally favor a socially dominant group. It is important to maintain ongoing awareness of how our privilege and power might instigate or recreate prior experiences of injustice, to minimize oppressive actions.

Microaggressions are an outgrowth of implicit bias and are described as verbal, behavioral, and environmental indignities that communicate derogatory or negative slights and insults to the target person or group (Sue et al., 2006). The term *micro* is associated with the brief or commonplace nature of these types of aggressions, but the impact is just as powerful as explicitly racist statements. Further, the *intent* of the speaker does not matter—what matters is the impact on the statement on *the recipient*. For example, a statement of "You speak English very well" to a Thai American woman may be intended as a compliment, but the underlying meaning is that a person of Asian descent is not truly American. This microaggression magnifies the cultural differences in ways that put the person's identity into question, often causing stress and alienation since it perpetuates a worldview of White superiority.

When a microaggression is committed, recipients may point out the stereotypic nature of the compliment and its negative effect in an attempt to change the perpetrator's future behavior (Czopp et al., 2006). Perpetrators, either through their own self-awareness or another person's suggestion, may realize the comment is inconsistent with their personal standards and regulate their future behaviors (Monteith et al., 2002). Importantly, the expectations we hold for students should not depend on stereotypes, even if those group-based expectations are positive. High expectations are useful and can be motivating, but they could have the opposite effect if the student knows these expectations are present because of their group identity ("You are Asian, so you study a lot."). Thus, greater awareness and discussions related to microaggressions and positive stereotypes are necessary for people to acknowledge individuality and diversity of students within the same culture.

Fortunately, there are methods to disarm microaggressions at school through *microinterventions* (Sue, 2019). If a practitioner is in a situation where they hear a parent say a microaggression, they need to discuss it with the parent about how or why specific statements may be perceived as harmful by asking for clarification or educating the parent. For example, if a parent says, "Asians study a lot," a practitioner can try to undermine the statement (e.g., "Not all Asian students study a lot."), challenge the statement, (e.g., "Many of our students who are not Asian also study a lot."), or disempower the statement by naming it (e.g., "That is a stereotype."). The example activity may be useful when preparing to talk about microaggressions with peers, colleagues, and parents (Box 2.1).

[Reflexivity Activity] To make implicit associations more explicit, consider the following questions:

- *What specific features do you look for when finding a place to live, or when sending your kids to school? What makes certain communities or neighborhoods less desirable than others?*
- *What jokes do we find humorous that play on stereotypes? Are we prejudiced if we laugh at jokes that involve stereotypes?*
- *Do you believe positive stereotypes to be beneficial or harmful? How does this apply to the education profession?*
- *What does the American Dream mean to you? Does your success depend on others' failures?*

As an example of how implicit biases may play out, consider the first question. A White school counselor is looking to purchase a home, ideally a three-bedroom house in a safe neighborhood. How would she define "safe?" How was she taught this definition? She may feel more comfortable searching in neighborhoods that includes mostly White families and perceive these communities as "safe." The counselor does not explicitly recognize this bias; however, due to the structural discrimination that overrepresented families of color reside in impoverished neighborhoods, she eventually developed an implicit association between people of color and risk, or Whiteness and safety. The associations can come from her own lived experiences, the news, or other media venues, which can make stereotypes more salient.

Intersectionality Is Key to Diversity, Equity, and Inclusion

All students have intersecting identities. *Intersectionality* recognizes that all aspects of one's identity need to be examined as simultaneously interacting and affecting one's perception within a society (Crenshaw, 1989). For example, Luc is a 16-year-old who identifies as a bisexual male from Thailand, speaks fluent English, and resides in a middle-class neighborhood. He has multiple, intersecting

Box 2.1.

MANAGING MICROAGGRESSIONS ACTIVITY

Microinterventions Activity

1. Brief Introduction to Microaggressions
   - Begin the activity with foundational information on implicit biases, microaggressions, and stereotypes (Sue, 2019) most relevant to the participants. The facilitator can provide a brief presentation, discussion, or survey about prior knowledge of the concepts or show videos on the topic.

2. Role Play Activity
   - In groups of four, participants should brainstorm examples of microaggressions based on the initial discussion and within groups.
   - Participants can role-play responding to various microaggressions. This can also be adapted to work in groups of three.
   - The facilitator will distribute sample microaggressions written on pieces of paper, prepared in advanced.
   - Two participants will act out the conversation using the scripted microaggression.
   - The third participant will describe the *intent/assumption* and the *impact* of that microaggression: What did the perpetrator *intend* to get across? What was the message *actually* received and perceived by the target, and the impact of that?
   - Finally, the fourth participant will respond to the situation using an appropriate strategy/microintervention (Sue, 2019).
   - Group members will switch/rotate roles until everyone has a chance to be the intent/effect identifier and the responder.

3. Debrief and Discussion
   Once the role-playing activity is done, the facilitator will lead participants in a whole-group discussion about the scenarios discussed today.

   - In what ways did they respond to each scenario provided?
   - Which microintervention strategies or techniques did they use? Were they effective?
   - Are there better ways one might respond?

This would be a great opportunity to go over additional strategies or personal experiences/encounters regarding microaggressions in various settings (e.g., schools, workplace, social) and how they could have intervened or prevented the situation.

Note. Credit goes to Renee Bastian for developing this activity.

social identities. As shown in Figure 2.1, these identities do not exist in a vacuum; rather, his various social identities are intimately connected to how the world perceives him. Intersectionality is therefore a concept that, on one hand, considers the differences between co-occurring identities and, on the other, considers the power structures and the social inequality that results from them.

Power dynamics also can become complex when the intersection of identities confer differing levels of privilege (Cole, 2009). If particular students from certain groups succeed while others do not, then as professionals and educators, we need to examine whether oppression (e.g., stereotypes, microaggression, implicit bias) explains these differences in how they perceive their identities and their outcomes. Luc, for example, experienced bullying as a form of cultural oppression due to his social identities. Institutional policies, social norms, and socioeconomic status often reinforce cultural oppression, making it difficult for Luc to feel a sense of belonging at school. The school counselor, a White cisgender female, might understand how Luc can be dually stigmatized due to his sexual orientation and ethnic identities. Certain identities may be more or less salient in specific situations, and awareness of intersecting identities and shifting power dynamics

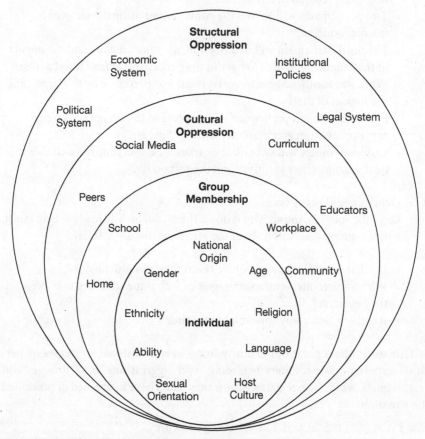

Figure 2.1. Circles of Intersectionality and Oppression.

is important. Therefore, when engaging with a student who shares aspects of their identity (e.g., ethnicity, gender, sexual orientation), practitioners should consider how their shared identity might obscure important differences between their own and the student's life experiences.

At a structural level, several social groups are subject to continued marginalization via policies and practices that restrict rights and privileges, and by extension, opportunity and well-being. Practitioners should be aware of the intersections of non-dominant social identities in compounding disenfranchisement and marginalization (e.g., multiple disadvantages experienced by an undocumented immigrant student who identifies as transgender). For many children, prejudice and discrimination serve as chronic stressors and threats to their well-being (Sanders-Phillips, 2009). Environmental (e.g., positive school climate) and individual protective factors (e.g., coping skills) can serve to buffer negative effects of oppression. By examining how cultural and structural oppression interact in a society, we can see how privilege functions.

PROMOTING ANTIRACISM AND SOCIAL JUSTICE IN SCHOOLS

Dialogues on racism, oppression, and marginalization should be an integral part of culturally responsive practice, particularly in schools. As we have highlighted, these issues are embedded within the school system, and continued discussions among educators, administrators, practitioners, and community members is essential in working toward antiracism and social justice efforts.

Difficult dialogues with our colleagues can elicit feelings of discomfort and distress, for which reason many will avoid such discussions by engaging in *intellectualization* (Leonardo & Porter, 2010), a defense mechanism whereby individuals use reasoning to protect themselves from discussing personal or controversial topics by focusing on facts or logic (Gladding, 2016). For example, a person may list reasons for why they may not be a racist, rather than discussing their feelings, beliefs, or actions about how they may contribute to racism. Avoiding uncomfortable emotions perpetuates the notion that racism is not a concern and thus invalidates minoritized students' experiences, perspectives, identities, and lives. If some members do not wish to engage in dialogue, then they should be encouraged to listen to others first before sharing.

Antiracism is an active effort and process of countering racial inequity that is created and maintained by a dynamic interplay of psychological factors (e.g., feelings and actions) and sociopolitical factors (e.g., laws, policies, and practices; Roberts & Rizzo, 2020). Transformative approaches include working with school leaders and stakeholders in discussing racism, reviewing and updating nondiscrimination policies, and providing psychoeducation and mental health promotion to students, staff, and families. Antiracism efforts also require practitioners to engage in critical reflexivity—to reflect and rethink their own education and training, while being willing to learn from those who are different from themselves. Because there is scarce guidance regarding implementing social justice or antiracism efforts in education, we propose a model of cultural humility as a starting point for changing our behaviors and our interactions with others.

Cultural Humility as a Framework for Social Justice

Cultural humility can provide a foundation for social justice efforts for school-based mental health practitioners. As we discussed in Chapter 1, *cultural humility* is a process for individuals to move away from a position of superiority, and to engage openly and respectfully with diverse students, families, and communities through self-reflection, lifelong learning, and partnership building (Tervalon & Murray-Garcia, 1998). To be an effective agent for social justice, accountability is key; thus, compared with cultural competence, cultural humility directly addresses issues relating to personal discomfort stemming from power and unearned privilege (Pon, 2009). Those who are not honest about their limitations might feel anxious and might try to avoid appearing "incompetent," rather than embracing their discomfort, which is essential for professional growth and accountability. Overall, cultural humility challenges practitioners to re-envision who they are in the context of a larger system, and to proceed toward changing the status quo.

A cultural humility framework (see Figure 2.2) includes actions that reflect ongoing learning, advocacy, and accountability at both the individual and systems

Figure 2.2. Model of Cultural Humility.
SOURCE: A. V. Pham, A. N. Goforth, L. N. Aguilar, I. Burt, R. Bastian, & D. M. Diaków. (2021). Dismantling systemic inequities in school psychology: Cultural humility as a foundational approach to social justice. *School Psychology Review*, 1–18. https://doi. org/10.1080/2372966X.2021.1941245. Copyright © National Association of School Psychologists, Inc., reprinted by permission of Taylor & Francis Ltd., http://www.tandfonl ine.com on behalf of National Association of School Psychologists, Inc.

level (e.g., Fisher-Borne et al., 2015; Goforth, 2016). The relation between practitioner and the individual (e.g., student) starts with openness and critical reflexivity (Domain 1) and considers the multiple contexts in which they function in a system. The curved arrows indicate that these processes of reflexivity are continuous throughout their interactions. Additionally, understanding their own privilege and power, along with oppressive factors, can help with determining systemic factors that affect the individual's functioning (Domain 2). After demonstrating these domains of awareness, efforts to become an ally or advocate for social justice can start (Domain 3). As indicated by up-down arrows, when oppression increases, then the strengths of the individual and community decrease, suggesting an inverse relationship. However, when anti-oppression (or antiracism) increases, then individual and community strengths should also increase. Positive alliances or partnerships with other stakeholders, family, or community are also required (Domain 4) to leverage individual strengths through relational empowerment (Domain 5).

CRITICAL REFLEXIVITY

As discussed in Chapter 1, engaging in critical reflexivity is key in providing culturally responsive practice. The goal of critical reflexivity, or the intentional process of self-reflection and self-critique of one's identity (e.g., race, gender, etc.) and existing structures, is to question how one's role reflects different levels of power and privilege, and how it has shaped the system (Cunliffe, 2016). This personal work begins with first recognizing that we live in a society where inequalities and injustices exist and are interwoven with social structures and norms. Socially just individuals must allow themselves to feel vulnerable yet motivated about implementing change. The process also brings out implicit knowledge, skills, and unconscious attitudes into conscious awareness.

Critical reflexivity and social injustice operate both intrapersonally and interpersonally, as a practitioner's actions and inactions affect others directly or indirectly. This process requires openness to others' beliefs systems, values and perspectives, and willingness to improve.

UNDERSTANDING AND TRANSFORMING POWER, PRIVILEGE, AND OPPRESSION

Those who engage in critical reflexivity acknowledge their relationship with power and privilege and recognize areas for growth. At the interpersonal level, practitioners must be curious about others' culture and intersecting identities within the larger socioeconomic-political context to develop trusting alliances (Hook et al., 2017). Further, they must seek out guidance from colleagues and professional development, while staying attuned to how their own privilege and/ or experiences affect those with whom they work. Cultural humility can also be demonstrated at a collective level, which can assist in addressing cultural and structural barriers that have oppressed not only individuals but also communities. The following activity can help assess and understand how systemic (i.e., cultural and structural) oppression can influence others.

[Reflexivity Activity] Refer to Figure 2.1, and ask:

1. Identity—*Do you have privilege or power at your school? Why or why not? How does the individual (e.g., student, parent, or colleague) with whom you work describe their identity?*
2. Group Membership—*How does the particular setting (e.g., home, school, community) support or oppress the individual's identities? Does the individual feel a sense of belonging in that setting?*
3. Cultural Oppression—*Is there cultural oppression? If so, what are some examples (e.g., persistent microaggressions, harassment, Eurocentric curriculum, implicit bias). How has cultural oppression influenced the individual's identities, behaviors, or outcomes? How can I use my power and privilege to change this?*
4. Structural Oppression—*Is there structural oppression? If so, provide some examples (e.g., racial discrimination, school policies negatively affecting transgender students, disproportionate student outcomes). How has structural oppression influenced the individual's identities, behaviors, or outcomes? How can I use my power and privilege to change this?*

SOCIAL JUSTICE AS ADVOCACY

The negative impact of oppression prompts the need for advocacy, which is an essential part of cultural humility. Advocacy can be described as actions and efforts to promote social change by navigating power dynamics at the individual and systems levels (Oyen et al., 2019). Advocacy for social justice can occur at the individual, institutional, or community level (Na & Fietzer, 2020).

Often, interventions focus on changing the individual exclusively, rather than changing institutional or structural factors that lead to these inequities. For example, if a practitioner pathologizes Luc's vandalism as a conduct or behavior disorder, then they may be reinforcing the idea that his difficulties were based on deficits, rather than attributing them to the interplay of personal (e.g., intersecting identities) and environmental factors (e.g., bullying, oppression). Therefore, we define social justice advocacy as intentional and sustained actions to remove structural and institutional barriers contributing to oppression, and to ensure equity, respect, and fairness for the individual, whose rights have been violated. Although Luc was at fault for vandalizing the school, it might have been easily avoided if the school system implemented prevention efforts that offered him a means for healing or coping, particularly since he endured disproportionate levels of distress from bullying. Thus, social justice advocates should embrace positive prevention as a means to end injustices and oppression by fostering individual strengths (Albee, 2000). When advocating for students, we provide several steps along with a sample template for creating an action plan (see Appendix 2).

1. *Goal Orientation:* Collaboratively identify the need(s), strengths, and measurable goals.

2. *Level of Advocacy:* Determine what level of advocacy is needed (e.g., individual, institutional, community).
3. *Initial Plan:* Develop an initial plan of action for confronting these barriers in consultation with stakeholders and ensuring that the plan is consistent with the individual (e.g., student, family) goals.
4. *Resources:* Determine resources needed to carry out the plan (e.g., stakeholders, financial support).
5. *Communication:* Communicate the plan with the individual, administrator, or stakeholders, including rationale and possible outcomes of advocacy.
6. *Implementation:* Implement the plan of action.
7. *Evaluation:* Evaluate the effectiveness of advocacy efforts.
8. *Alignment with Goal Orientation:* Reassess needs based on unmet goals and revisit the initial step of goal orientation.

ALLIANCE BUILDING (ALLYSHIP) AND SCHOOL–COMMUNITY PARTNERSHIP

Another domain of the cultural humility framework is alliance building or school–community partnerships. We define allies as those individuals who (1) recognize power and privilege, (2) seek to dismantle structural barriers, and (3) do so in collaboration and in partnership with the advocate, other allies, and the student or family who has been systematically oppressed and marginalized. Importantly, allies also engage in cultural humility and critical reflexivity to ensure that they understand the deep structures of oppression, commit themselves to dismantling structural barriers, and engage in ongoing learning and accountability. They can be stakeholders within the school, within the community, and with other students or families. Some individuals may claim to be allies with good intentions, but their actions, efforts, and lack of cultural humility may lead them to perpetuate social injustice without their awareness or understanding. Consider the following statements:

> *I want the students of color to feel welcome in our school, just like the White students.*
> *I want him to do well in his job interview next week, so I will work with him so that he appears less gay. He will be successful.*

Statements that reinforce positive stereotypes or are microaggressions may seem to be complimentary on the surface but still reinforce White supremacy as the accepted standard. This attitude not only demonstrates lack of awareness of student diversity and intersectionality but also sees them as recipients of charity or as *being saved*, which may harm students and perpetuate oppressive systems. The goals of improving student outcomes and success may be more difficult to achieve if the means or process puts them in a less empowering position. Positive alliances can be fostered by understanding the cultural values and worldview of the individual and family, minimizing comparisons of performance of minoritized students with the majority, avoiding pathologizing groups of people, while collaborating effectively toward meeting their goals.

RESILIENCE AND EMPOWERMENT

Through cultural humility and by establishing alliances, it is the goal for students and families to demonstrate liberation from oppressive forces to achieve positive outcomes. Culturally humble practitioners enhance and reinforce culturally relevant strengths, such as racial identity (Leath et al., 2019) and critical consciousness (Watts et al., 2011), which can empower individuals from oppressed groups to cope with and resist internalization of cultural and structural oppression. Moreover, they promote radical healing, which acknowledges and promotes active resistance from oppression, as well as a vision of possibilities for freedom and wellness (French et al., 2020). Seeking liberation from oppression is necessary for radical healing.

Empowerment, which is often characterized across various levels and contexts, promotes resilience while working toward social change (Prilleltensky, 2008). At the individual level, empowerment occurs when individuals exert control of the environment to better their own lives and decision-making, while at the community or institutional level, collaboration and alliance building are critical for improving community outcomes (Peterson & Zimmerman, 2004). Although the intent of empowerment may be to give control, it can still become oppressive if allies and advocates do not understand their own unearned privilege. As discussed in Chapter 1, *relational empowerment* provides recognition and acknowledgment of student strengths, collaborative relationships, and healing when successfully redistributing social capital and transforming power (Christens, 2012). The following are a few ways to promote relational empowerment.

- *Create safe spaces to interrogate and resist cultural and structural oppression.* Schools make time to discuss oppression and inequity that students see on the news, in social media, and in their communities. Students can learn about ways to engage in social justice and share their ideas and reactions on addressing injustices in small groups or through reflective journaling.
- *Cultivate radical healing, emotion regulation, and coping strategies for students to deal with challenges.* Practitioners can teach students to use various strategies that promote well-being and resilience when feeling oppressed. For example, students can share personal narratives that give voice to experiences of oppression, create meaning for their individual and collective experiences of oppression, and envision future possibilities and goals.
- *Involve students in advocacy.* Students learn skills for how to prevent and/or respond to microaggressions, stereotypes, and discrimination. School-based professionals, administrators, and students learn to participate together in local and state-level advocacy, which can contribute to policy change and improved student outcomes.

SUMMARY

The education and mental health professions are political and ideological activities that inherently involve ideals, power, and opportunity. This creates unavoidable conflicts, particularly in school systems where biases, prejudice, and discrimination are likely to occur and escalate. Mitigating these concerns requires cultivating cultural humility and establishing positive relationships with colleagues, families, and students who have been historically marginalized. It also requires our efforts, energy, and additional resources to create systems-level change. We do not expect change to occur overnight, and often conflicts will continue, or perhaps worsen, before positive change occurs. However, these initiatives should be at the fore-front, not only in school systems, but also in educator preparation programs to ensure that culturally responsive training and supervision occurs for aspiring educators, practitioners, and leaders. It can be a long road ahead with bumps along the way, but it can lead to long-lasting and meaningful outcomes.

DISCUSSION QUESTIONS

1. What social injustices do you face at your school? What do you believe are the causes?
2. What steps would you take to bring about change when dealing with social injustices or oppression?
3. Should educators be concerned with White supremacy and advocacy? Why or why not?
4. What are the advantages or disadvantages of having token members or cultural brokers from a community?
5. Consider the following scenario: A Virginia elementary school teacher opposed a new policy that would allow transgender students to use their preferred names and pronouns outside their legal names. He indicated that his reason for opposing the policy was that it went against his religious faith. Discuss your stance if you were the school principal, fellow teacher colleague, and/or caregiver of a student who attends the school.

APPENDIX 2
SAMPLE ADVOCACY ACTION PLAN

1. *Goal Orientation:* Provide a brief context and analyze the situation, explaining the problem. Why advocate on the issue?
   - Define the problem:
   - Describe needs, strengths, and measurable goals:

2. *Level of Advocacy:* Determine what level of advocacy is needed (e.g., individual, institutional, community).
   - Who has the power to make the necessary changes?
   - Who influences those people?

3. *Initial Plan:* Develop an initial plan of action for confronting these barriers in consultation with stakeholders, ensuring plan is consistent with the individual (e.g., student, family) goals.
   - List activities needed to complete the plan:
   - Describe roles and responsibilities:
   - Determine potential barriers for implementation:

4. *Resources:* Determine resources needed to carry out the plan (e.g., stakeholders, financial support).
   - List potential allies and partners:
   - Describe budget restraints:

5. *Communication:* Communicate plan with the individual, administrator, or stakeholders, including rationale and possible outcomes of advocacy.
   - Describe the intended audience:
   - Describe any strengths and weaknesses of the proposed plan:
   - Include suggestions for improving the plan:

6. *Implementation:* Implement the plan of action.
   - Include detailed timeline:
     - Short-term goal(s):
     - Long-term goal(s):
   - Describe opportunities for greatest influence:

7. *Evaluation:* Evaluate effectiveness of advocacy efforts.
   - Describe outcomes based on data:
   - Determine whether outcomes meet the goals of the plan:

8. *Alignment with Goal Orientation:* Reassess needs based on unmet goals and revisit initial step of goal orientation.
   - Describe any additional goals or resources needed to attain any unmet goals.
   - Seek and summarize input from stakeholders regarding outcomes, successes, and challenges with the plan:

Creating Positive Relationships
with Children and Families

VIGNETTE

The Huerta family has two children in your school: Antonio is in kindergarten and Elena is in third grade. The parents, Lucas and Francisca Huerta, own and operate a convenience store in town. The family lives with Francisca's parents and single brother. This multi-generational home is often vibrant with activity, and the children's grandparents and uncle sometimes care for the children when the store is busy. Elena and Antonio speak both Spanish and English at home and attend an elementary school of primarily English-speaking teachers and students. For the past year, Elena had been receiving reading intervention support. Her reading skills improved substantially. However, Lucas and Francisca are concerned about Antonio's behavior at school, since Antonio is often very energetic and easily distracted at home. He has run into tables and knocked over lamps or bruised other members of his family; while at school, he often gets up from his seat to wander around the classroom. Antonio's teacher shared that he gives Antonio more redirection and prompting than other students in class to stay focused on the lessons.

- *What would be some factors that would be contributing to Antonio's behavior?*
- *In what ways might a practitioner develop authentic relationships with Antonio's family?*
- *What might be some challenges that the practitioner might consider?*

The connections that practitioners have with students and their families often inspire them to continue to do the work that they do, even when they are fatigued or face challenges that naturally come with working in schools. They care deeply about their students and families, putting in the time and effort that it requires to make sure that their students get the educational and mental health support they need.

Practitioners also know that engaging with families and encouraging their involvement in their children's education is important for their children's success in school. *Family-school partnerships* have a positive impact on children's behaviors, academic achievement, and social-behavioral competence (Smith et al., 2020). A related, yet distinct concept, *family involvement* in their children's education has been shown to be associated with improved academic performance, as well as positive social, emotional, and behavioral outcomes in early elementary education (Ma et al., 2016) to secondary levels (Jeynes, 2007). Thus, family-school partnerships and family involvement are critical for children's educational success and well-being in school.

To engage with families and encourage their involvement, though, can be challenging. Connections with students and their families are not always easy, particularly when a practitioner's skills or resources are limited, or when encountering conflict or misunderstandings with families. Cultural or linguistic mismatches often occur that can make establishing or maintaining relationships between the school and family difficult. Acknowledging and understanding these cultural differences is particularly important because practitioners may make assumptions about a family's behaviors or actions without realizing their own privilege. Other systemic factors may have a greater impact on how families interact with the school. For example, schools may perceive a mother who does not attend parent-teacher conferences as not caring about her child's education; however, the mother's decision not to attend the conference could be explained by an evening work schedule that overlaps with the school or lack of daycare for her other children. Like any relationship, conflicts can be difficult to navigate, but can motivate practitioners to connect and collaborate with families, while also demonstrating greater understanding and empathy for them.

In this chapter, we will provide specific, culturally responsive strategies for developing authentic school-family-community partnerships. We emphasize that although there is a great deal of focus on family-school partnerships, including community members is essential to ensure that relationships are sustained. We also believe that centering the family in this partnership is vital; it is the school's responsibility to include families in decision making, to foster these partnerships, to provide meaningful resources, and to create supports to ensure families are comfortable with being part of the process. Importantly, we use the term *family* to represent any adult that provides care (physical, social, emotional) to a child, and we choose to use the term *caregiver* when describing those adults.

First, we will summarize the current theoretical models describing family engagement and involvement, particularly highlighting sociocultural factors. We will then explain why we use the term *authentic partnerships* when considering culturally responsive practice with culturally and linguistically diverse students and their families. Then, we will describe a series of steps to foster family-school-community partnerships: (1) engage in critical reflexivity, (2) develop partnerships through trust and reciprocity, (3) create an action team for school-family-community partnerships, (4) understand strengths and

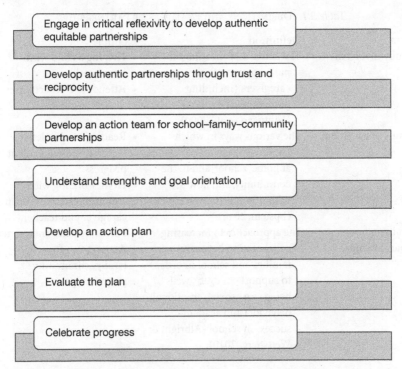

Engage in critical reflexivity to develop authentic equitable partnerships

Develop authentic partnerships through trust and reciprocity

Develop an action team for school–family–community partnerships

Understand strengths and goal orientation

Develop an action plan

Evaluate the plan

Celebrate progress

Figure 3.1. Steps in Authentic and Equitable School–Family–Community Partnerships.

goal orientation, (5) develop an action plan, (6) evaluate the plan, and (7) celebrate progress (see Figure 3.1).

AUTHENTIC AND EQUITABLE PARTNERSHIPS WITH FAMILIES

Engaging with families and encouraging their involvement in their children's education are important components of supporting student learning and well-being. Various terms are used to describe this interaction, such as *family involvement, family engagement,* or *family-school partnerships* (see Table 3.1). In general, these definitions are driven by ecological systems theory (Bronfenbrenner, 2005), which emphasizes multiple systems that interact and affect families and child outcomes directly or indirectly. *Family involvement* has been conceptualized as the active and meaningful participation of relevant caregivers (including parents) in school-related activities (Fantuzzo et al., 2000). For example, this participation could include a father being involved in their child's homework, reading aloud to the child's class, or attending parent-teacher association (PTA) activities. *Family engagement,* in comparison, is defined as the various ways in which families engage with activities at home, school, and in the community,

Table 3.1. DEFINITIONS AND EXAMPLES OF PARTNERSHIPS

Term	Definition	Example
Family involvement	The active and meaningful participation of relevant caregivers (including parents) in the school (Fantuzzo et al., 2000)	• Helping a child with homework • Attending PTA activities
Family engagement	The various ways in which families engage with activities at home, school, and in the community, and how the school supports those efforts (Epstein, 2010)	• Reading teacher letters to parents about student progress. • Homework log with communication between caregiver and teacher.
Family–school partnerships	The approaches to increasing collaboration between families and school in order to support children's well-being (e.g., social, emotional, behavior) and academic success in school (Albright & Weissberg, 2010).	• Parent–teacher conferences • Action team for school–family–community partnerships

and how the school supports those efforts (Epstein, 2010). An example can be the school providing opportunities for caregivers to volunteer to read to their child's class. Further, *family-school partnerships* has been conceptualized as the approaches used to increase collaboration between families and school to support children's well-being (e.g., social, emotional, behavior) and academic success in school (Albright & Weissberg, 2010). For example, caregivers may provide input and share decision making with schools in promoting literacy at school or in the community.

We focus in this chapter on *family–school partnerships*, a component of family-school relationships, which has been defined as a "child-centered connection between individuals in the home and school settings who share responsibility for supporting the growth and development of children" (Clarke et al., 2009, p. 61). We particularly appreciate this definition because it emphasizes the collaborative relationship and its goal: to mutually support the student's learning, needs, growth, and well-being. Further, this definition highlights the *shared* responsibility within this relationship. The family and the school have a commitment within this relationship to ensure that both parties recognize and provide shared effort and support to foster the student's development (Christenson & Sheridan, 2001). Although these terms have subtle differences, ultimately, the goal is the same: to have close, authentic connections between families at home and in the community, and professionals/educators at school in order to benefit children's learning and mental health.

[Reflexivity Activity] Provide examples of family involvement and family engagement in your school. Review these examples and rank them based on what you value and believe is important. What do you notice about these examples?

Healthy Family–School Relationships

Like any relationship, the family–school relationship should be healthy. Clarke et al. (2009) highlighted that healthy family–school relationships are comprised of three key elements: *trust, sensitivity,* and *equality.* In order for the relationship to be successful in supporting the student's learning and well-being, trust must occur between the family and the school, where each party is willing to see the other's perspectives. Although trust is essential in this relationship, research has shown that parents tend to trust teachers more than teachers trust parents, perhaps because teachers have little at stake compared with parents (Adams & Christenson, 2000). Further, there is socioeconomic variability across families in their degree of trust of teachers, with parents of students eligible for a free or reduced lunch being less trusting of teachers and the school compared with those parents whose students do not participate in free or reduced lunch (Santiago et al., 2016). Although the research is unclear about why this association exists, one possibility may be that some lower-income and economically marginalized parents have had negative schooling experiences from less resourced schools. For instance, a parent may have had negative interactions with teachers in their own schooling experience and thus is unlikely to trust their child's teachers compared with parents who have not had those experiences. Practitioners may therefore need to make the first step and initiate the relationship after putting aside any preconceived notions about caregiver's behaviors in order to develop trust. Establishing and maintaining trust between families and schools is important, as research studies have shown that the more parents trust teachers, the more their child has increased prosocial behavior, decreased peer problems, and decreased overall difficulties (Santiago et al., 2016).

The second element of a healthy family–school relationship is *sensitivity,* particularly when there are cultural and linguistic differences between the family and members of the school (Clarke et al., 2009). Clarke and colleagues emphasized that within this relationship, sensitivity begins with an understanding of the family's cultural and linguistic background. Caregivers will have their own expectations about how they want to involve themselves in their child's learning that may differ from the expectations of teachers. Some caregivers may perceive teachers as experts in the school and allow the teacher to make decisions. Alternatively, some caregivers may expect to have considerable input into educational decisions. These differences in perceptions should be shared and valued by the school, as an initial step to foster a meaningful partnership.

There are indeed variations in family–school relationships across cultural and linguistic groups, and there are many ways that caregivers can be involved in the student's education. Schools may need to make concerted efforts to communicate with parents who do not speak English by providing various resources and posting messages in hallways in multiple languages. Family involvement in schools across different racial or ethnic groups has been shown to predict children's academic achievement (Jeynes, 2007). Yet, it is important that practitioners acknowledge the many ways for caregivers to be involved, regardless of whether they are physically present in the school. For example, in one study, parents of Black adolescents who are involved in school-based activities (e.g., volunteering at school) were positively associated with their child's academic performance. For parents of Latinx students, a combination of home-based (e.g., providing a learning environment at home) and school-based involvement was associated with higher academic outcomes (Day & Dotterer, 2018). These different approaches to involvement suggest that practitioners should recognize and respect how caregivers are choosing to be involved in their child's education, even if they contrast with the practitioner's perception of involvement.

We extend the concept of sensitivity and also suggest that *reflexivity* and *cultural humility* (see Chapters 1 and 2) are essential within a healthy relationship. These skills allow the families and school professionals to be open (or sensitive) to differences, humble in their approach to establishing and maintaining relationships, and recognize that errors can lead to misunderstandings or conflict. An intentional process of reflecting on errors made, taking accountability, and repairing harm can be used to earn trust in these relationships.

The third element for a healthy relationship is *equality* between family and school (Clarke et al., 2009). In this context, it is about equality in power within the relationship, and recognizing that each party within the relationship has equal responsibility (i.e., families and school are responsible for the student), equal values (i.e., some values are not viewed as better than others), and equal respect (e.g., reciprocal trust). Further, the family and the school should have equal voice in the decision-making related to the child's learning and mental health. For example, in the vignette, the Huerta family has voiced concerns with their son Antonio's behavior at school and at home. Practitioners may wish to work with the family to identify behavioral goals that could help Antonio be successful. Through active listening, it may become apparent that body awareness could improve how often Antonio gets out of his seat in the classroom, as well as how often he injures himself at home by running into the furniture or other members of the household. A practitioner can then work with the Huertas on strategies to help build body awareness for Antonio. This demonstrates *equality* by allowing the family to voice their concerns and linking their observations at home with the circumstances that teachers and practitioners are aware of in the school.

Race, Ethnicity, Privilege, and School Involvement

The existing school system in the United States is based on Eurocentric ideas of learning and advantages some students over others. In fact, there is great inequity across schools, where educators interact with parents or caregivers differently based on ethnicity and race (Wilson, 2019). As one example, there is a "paradox of minority parental involvement," in which teachers complain that parents are not involved in their child's education, yet if parents are involved, then teachers complain that parents are too aggressive (Shannon, 1996). In another study, teachers perceived that they are interacting with parents in a neutral way to address their students' achievement, and they expected parents to trust their judgment and be continuously positive and supportive, rather than to provide critical feedback to teachers (Lareau & Horvat, 1999). Among Black families, Wilson's (2019) research suggested that teachers may perceive parents who are highly active or assertive in schools as "angry and counterproductive," rather than acknowledging that these families "love, cherish, and behold their children with the same wonderment, hope, joy and belief in their potential, and desire for their happiness, achievement, and success as other families" (Wilson, 2019, p. 54). In other words, race, ethnicity, and privilege play an important, yet complex, role in the family–school relationship.

[Reflexivity activity]: School and caregiver's perceptions of each other can vary, from positive to negative, as highlighted in the research described earlier. Consider the following questions:

- What has been your experience as a practitioner? And if relevant, as a caregiver?
- In what ways do you hold some of these views?

Additionally, within this power structure, social capital can play a role in family–school relationships. Social and cultural capital are the resources, opportunities, and privileges that people have accumulated through social ties and networks (Wilson, 2019). For example, research has found that students who were first-generation Asian, Hispanic, and third-generation Black had lower levels of parent–school involvement (Kao & Rutherford, 2007). Further, eighth grade students' GPAs and standardized test scores were positively associated with higher parent–school social capital (Kao & Rutherford, 2007). The current school systems, therefore, may privilege some students (and families) over others. Caregivers who have accumulated social and cultural capital may be able to navigate the school system to benefit their children's learning. These resources, in turn, provide an opportunity for them to secure themselves within the social class hierarchy, which often matches that of the school. As Wilson (2019) put concisely, "Power dynamics and cultural norms influence families' experiences in educational spaces" (p. 56).

There are also divergent experiences of families of color compared with those of White families in terms of their interactions with the schools. Wilson (2019) noted that Black families, for example, may view schools as spaces that neglect or even deny the Black experience in the curriculum, such as ignoring contributions to history. Culturally responsive pedagogy (as discussed in Chapter 9) may allow more inclusive instruction by integrating the cultural histories of families and students in content areas. As another example, Indigenous parents reported they felt discomfort in interacting with the school because of the legacy of residential schools, resulting in distrust of their children's schools (Milne, 2016). These power structures, racism, and lack of representation in the curriculum may affect the degree to which families are involved in school.

Given that school structures and organization are such that some voices are heard over others (Olivos, 2019), it is imperative that culturally and linguistically diverse families be given social capital and power to level the playing field. This could be done by engaging with the community so families can utilize various community resources, welcoming family input in promoting inclusive climate, celebrating and highlighting family or student successes, or connecting families with other families to form additional support systems. In Florida, Parent to Parent of Miami organizes various in-person and virtual workshops to empower families. These workshops include topics on the rights and protection of children with disabilities, advocacy for educational supports and services, financial planning, and transition support from preschool to elementary school. Moreover, annual events, such as all-day picnics, connect families who may be experiencing similar challenges, and holiday drives encourage family engagement and support those with financial hardships. This redistribution of power then reinforces equitable relationships. Developing authentic equitable partnerships with families requires understanding the role of inequities within schools (see Chapter 2), along with providing meaningful resources and opportunities for families to network with other families.

[Reflexivity Activity]. Consider the following prompts:

- *Reflect on those families with whom you've interacted in the school compared with those who have not been to your school. Have there been some assumptions about why some families may come to the school (e.g., participate in parent–teacher conferences, school events) compared with other families who do not?*
- *What social capital do you and/or your family hold, if any? How do you know?*
- *Considering the ideas of trust, sensitivity, and equality, how can a school promote communication to caregivers?*
- *In what ways can you demonstrate that you are open to communication with families?*

FACILITATING AUTHENTIC AND EQUITABLE SCHOOL–FAMILY–COMMUNITY PARTNERSHIPS

We suggest that *authentic and equitable partnerships* between schools, families, and communities are healthy when there is trust, sensitivity, and equality. In order to have authentic and equitable partnerships, there must also be acknowledgment of the history and contemporary realities that shape the school and community, including the racial and power structures. Indeed, Olivos (2019) emphasized that engaging with caregivers in schools is inherently a "political act" (p. 15). School systems are based on power, and the positionality of educators and parents within that power structure matters. Healthy partnerships between the school, family, and community requires a solid foundation of trust, equity, and sensitivity.

Researchers have developed several models of family–school–community partnerships. For example, Epstein (2010) recommended developing what she calls *Action Teams for Partnerships* (ATP), which provides a series of steps to facilitate partnerships, which is discussed in more detail later in the chapter. Similarly, Bryan and Henry (2012) recommended a model of school–family–community partnerships that can be established by leveraging "democratic collaboration" to empower families to have equal voice in the decision-making. In this partnership process model, they describe seven stages: (1) preparing to partner, (2) assessing needs and strengths, (3) coming together, (4) creating shared vision and plans, (5) taking action, (6) evaluating and celebrating progress, and (7) maintaining momentum. Here, we have integrated these models for a culturally responsive approach to authentic and equitable family–school–community partnerships. In particular, we encourage practitioners to work toward relational empowerment with families through collaborative decision-making. In this process, schools intentionally work with families and communities who have been traditionally marginalized to understand the key issues that are affecting their children and use resources to support them.

Engaging in Critical Reflexivity to Develop Authentic Equitable Partnerships

Developing effective family–school relationships requires practitioners to engage in critical reflexivity of (1) their own positionality within the school structure, (2) the intersection of education and history, and how this intersection has an impact on students and families, and (3) cultural and linguistic differences among families and within the community.

First, practitioners should engage in critical reflexivity on their positionality, power, and social capital as it relates to family engagement and involvement. A practitioner's positionality encompasses not only their formal position in the school (e.g., their job as a mental health professional), but also their position within the power structures of the school and the community. Although their position as a school-based mental health professional, for example, may imply that they have power in decision-making regarding students in the school (e.g., providing recommendations for programs, collaborating with educators to screen for mental health), the degree of power they have depends on a number of factors. These factors include how practitioners seek family input in decision-making, how they perceive their competence and skills, and how they identify with a particular cultural or ethnic group. Their positionality, as a person, not just as a professional, is important to consider as they cultivate relationships with families.

Additionally, practitioners must also consider the positionality of the school within the community. Sometimes, the school is the center of the community, where the actual physical school building hosts community events (e.g., farmers' markets, art fairs) and the school sports teams bring together members of the community, even when they may not have children in the school. Other times, the school and community may not be aligned, and there may be distrust among community members about the school. For example, some school policies do not allow Indigenous students to wear traditional regalia during high school graduation ceremonies (e.g., Shilling, 2019). These policies sometimes create tension between the community's desires (seeing tribal culture and identity represented in graduation).

[Reflexivity Activity] Some questions to consider:

- *Based on my race and ethnicity, what power (or lack of power) do I have within the community? Does this power look similar or different from the power that I have within the school?*
- *In what ways can I leverage the power that I do have to advocate for students and families?*
- *How does my positionality within the school structure allow me to foster relational empowerment for students and families?*

Second, practitioners should examine the intersection of education and history of the school and community in which they work and determine how this intersection has impacted the students and families within this community. To engage in reflexivity, practitioners could work to understand and reflect on the role of racism and colonialism in the education system, particularly as it relates to their school and community. For example, they can first understand the history of their school by speaking with elders and community members. They can ask:

- *When and why was this school established?*
- *Who were the students who attended this school, and has this changed across history?*

They can also research the school district lines, and whether these lines were changed to include or exclude certain students. For example, some school districts were designed to exclude Black students, and practitioners could ask:

- *Have the school district lines changed to ensure that the students in the school adequately reflect the community?*

Assessing the sociocultural and political context of education in general, and the schools in which they work specifically, is essential because they can have a deeper understanding of the factors that affect families' perception of the schools and leverage strengths to enhance partnerships in authentic and meaningful ways.

Additionally, to earn trust and cultivate relationships with families, practitioners should also engage in critical reflexivity about the cultural and linguistic differences among families and within the community. Their own culture and values shape understanding of parenting practices (they often learn about what positive or negative parenting looks like from their own families); thus, engaging in critical reflexivity can help assess parenting practices as well as the values held by families with whom you work. A review of the literature has found that authoritative parenting, a form of parenting consisting of high warmth and high control, is associated with positive academic outcomes seen across many ethnic groups in the United States, particularly in non-Hispanic, White families. However, authoritative parenting (i.e., low warmth and high control) of parenting may be also seen as tolerable in very few cultures (Pinquart & Kauser, 2018).

[Reflexivity Activity] Some questions to consider:

- *What is a "good" parent? How do I know?*
- *In what ways have the values of my own parents or caregivers shaped my perception of others?*
- *What are my thoughts and feelings when I encounter parents with disciplinary practices that are different from those of my own parents, or the parenting of my children?*
- *What if their practices differ from what research says related to positive parenting or parent training?*

Using a cultural humility approach, establishing authentic partnerships begins with taking steps to develop cultural knowledge of students and their families. One aspect of this cultural norm would be parenting and disciplinary practices. For example, among Asian immigrant populations, there are differences in cultural expectations related to parenting practices and child obedience to elders. In particular, parents are expected to be highly involved in their children's education, and children are expected to have deference to their elders, which ultimately impacts the family–school relationship (Li & Sun, 2019). Additionally, there may also be different belief systems in pedagogy. Among Asian immigrant parents from Confucian backgrounds, parents perceive that learning should entail drills and practices, in comparison with Western perceptions of pedagogy that is more meaning based (Li & Sun, 2019). These different pedagogical approaches have shown to lead to less parental participation among Asian immigrants in school classrooms but, instead, participating in or engaging with their child's learning at home.

Further, as we described in Chapter 2, racism and White supremacy are deeply embedded within the U.S. public education system. We argue that ignoring how racism and White supremacy have shaped schooling would not only be neglectful, but it would even be harmful to students and families of color. It is important to understand that colonialism is endemic within education and continues to impact communities, particularly tribal communities (Brayboy, 2005). As one example,

Garcia (2019) encouraged critical and culturally sustaining engagement with Indigenous families and communities in which practitioners discuss the history of Indigenous peoples as it relates to education. Historically, the U.S. federal government removed children from their families to attend residential boarding schools, where they were forced to abandon their culture, spirituality, and language. These experiences led to significant historical trauma across generations, leading to (a very warranted) distrust of the government-funded school systems (Campbell & Evans-Campbell, 2011). In some communities, elders may perceive school systems as an extension of the erasure of their culture. Thus, by acknowledging how our education systems have been molded by sociocultural and political context, we can better understand the perceptions of Indigenous families related to school involvement.

When discussing Indigenous family involvement, Garcia (2019) emphasized that in order to work effectively with families and increase their involvement in the school system, we must fully determine how colonialism is integrated, and embedded, within education. Culturally sustaining engagement with families, therefore, means acknowledging and then disrupting the legacy of colonialism, and revitalizing education so that it aligns with the culture and language of families, particularly those who are Indigenous (Garcia, 2019). In order to connect and collaborate with families, practitioners need not only to consider how racism and colonialism may impact family's involvement in school but take also action in eradicating racism.

As a form of restorative justice, Wilson (2019) emphasized the importance of facilitating "critical care" with Black families, acknowledging that Black parents have experienced racism and inequity in their own educational experience, and that they have a desire to protect their own children from racism within the school. Indeed, when interacting with teachers, some Black parents may shape their own behaviors to "diffuse the risk of racial discrimination," and "educators may not even be aware that the parents are concerned about racism within the school setting" (Lareau & Horvat, 1999, p. 44).

In sum, cultivating relationships and increasing family involvement require critical reflexivity on one's positionality within the school, the historical and political context of the school (particularly as it relates to race and colonialism), and the cultural and linguistic demographics of the families and community. Although we highlight this as a first step, in practice, critical reflexivity should be an ongoing process.

Developing Authentic Partnerships Through Trust and Reciprocity

The next step in the process is working to develop authentic and meaningful partnerships with families. In this stage, practitioners must consider *why* this partnership is important. Answering this question will be helpful in challenging a school's own vision about the purpose of the partnerships. Based on some of

Bryan and Henry (2012) suggestions, these questions may require cultural humility and vulnerability:

- *What are your beliefs, attitudes, and values about the families? What is the school's vision?*
- *Which kinds of families have power within the school and community?*
- *What historical and contemporary experiences or events have led to these families having more power?*
- *Is your goal to appear as a savior? To facilitate better communication? To ensure that families have voice in their children's decision-making?*

Once these questions are addressed, practitioners can then begin working on establishing family–school partnerships. As leaders in the school, practitioners can play a really important role in facilitating family–school relationships that are healthy, authentic, and equitable. Practitioners can support educators and administrators in this process, as well. Authentic partnerships between families and schools are more than "coffee with the principal" or bake sales for the PTA; rather, they include respectful alliances through dialogues and discussion on difference, and sharing power and social capital (Auerbach, 2010). As one concrete example, a public school located in a tribal nation includes an end-of-the-year powwow celebration for graduates and a pancake breakfast for families. The celebration is hosted by an elder, and the high school Indigenous club facilitates the honoring of the graduates. This connection between school and community fosters authentic partnerships, trust, and reciprocity, and subsequently work toward social justice.

Respectful alliances among families, community members, educators, and administrators are built through *trust* and *reciprocity*. Trust must be earned: We cannot assume we have trust from families without showing effort and following through with activities. Indeed, it is important that the school should be setting the tone for respectful alliances, taking the time and space to visit with families in order to establish that trust.

One approach is to cultivate trust through reciprocity, or the process of give and take. *Reciprocity* has been defined as equitable or comparable exchanges between individuals and within society, and it can include material or financial exchanges, as well as expressive or relational exchanges (Izuhara, 2010). Relationships and reciprocity are core for many culturally and linguistically diverse families. For example, in families descended from Japan, the value of reciprocity may involve having adult children support aging parents (Izuhara, 2010). Engaging with Indigenous families, for example, requires understanding the network of relationships in Indigenous families and communities, such as the Hopi (Garcia, 2019).

Schools can cultivate trust through reciprocity by using strategies to improve communication and collaboration with families (Tran, 2014). These strategies include inviting a cultural liaison or facilitator to the school to whom parents can direct their questions, regular meetings to consider solutions to support students, or home visits where teachers and other school professionals aim to understand the home environment, routines, and parents' goals (Tran, 2014). Social media, monthly newsletters, and email announcements can be used to reach out to parents about various events that are happening in classrooms. An example of a welcome letter is provided in Appendix 3.

A practitioner providing school-based mental health care can use active listening skills to develop these respectful alliances. Similar to therapeutic alliances, respectful alliances can include personal attributes such as trustworthiness, confidence, and enthusiasm (Ackerman & Hilsenroth, 2003). A practitioner can leverage their active listening skills, similar to therapeutic techniques. For example, effective alliances have been found to be associated with techniques such as exploration, depth, reflection, expression of affect, affirmations, and attending to the person's experiences, which can be beneficial across cultures (Ackerman & Hilsenroth, 2003).

In order to establish alliances, expressing and sharing enthusiasm with families can go a long way. During community events, for example, they can show enthusiasm in getting to know families through authentic means. From the vignette, a practitioner may wish to engage with the Huerta family through a visit to their neighborhood or work. Learning about their livelihood, whether stressors from their workplace or positive ties in the community, shows willingness to support and advocate for the Huerta family and to understand better the types of support that the school can offer. Additionally, getting to know the other caregivers in the Huerta household, such as the grandparents and uncle, may provide a more authentic connection to the family. A visit to their home could offer a chance to see how the family operates and provide common ground when discussing challenges that the family is facing.

From the vignette, a practitioner can use therapeutic techniques with a caregiver, such as motivational interviewing (Miller & Rollnick, 2013). One approach, OARS, begins with asking Open-ended questions that can evoke information about Antonio's behavior at home that the parents may want to address. Then, it includes Affirming the real difficulty of managing their businesses and raising children, which demonstrates empathy and allows for trust to develop with the family. Thirdly, Reflection about the emotional quality of what the parent is sharing can show active listening and the desire to learn about their personal experience. Finally, Summarizing what they share can convey to the family the compassion and trust needed to establish a positive and respectful alliance (Miller & Rollnick, 2013).

In addition to establishing respectful alliances, discussing similarities and differences in expectations between families and school (Auerbach, 2010) can prevent future miscommunication and misunderstandings. Engaging with families and establishing authentic partnerships requires honest dialogue and challenging traditional notions of parent involvement (e.g., PTAs). As we discussed in Chapter 1, it is about developing connections through cultural knowledge, understanding the beliefs, traditions, and values of the families with whom you work. It requires not only talking, but also *listening* and *learning*.

Finally, for authentic equitable partnerships to develop, there should be relational empowerment and strengths-based decision-making. As discussed in Chapters 1 and 2, relational empowerment involves being intentional in advocacy as well as working toward an equitable distribution of power for students and families. Empowerment is about leveraging strong relationships in order for families to build power. In the context of these partnerships, empowerment should include (1) recognizing and acknowledging the differences in power, (2) taking steps to reduce the practitioner's power within the relationship, and (3) honoring the families' knowledge and expertise in order to support the student (Holcomb-McCoy & Bryan, 2010). Through relational empowerment, families' voices can be heard.

Develop an Action Team for School–Family–Community Partnerships

Once the practitioner has earned trust with families, the next step is to develop a formalized team to facilitate more effective, culturally responsive family–school–community partnerships. Sometimes called Action Team for Partnerships (ATP; Epstein, 2010), the team creates a goal of evaluating existing approaches to family–school partnerships (if any) and works toward developing programs that foster long-term partnerships. Epstein (2010) recommended that the team include at least one administrator, school staff, and educators who represent different grades and specialties. Practitioners' experiences and perspectives could be vital not only in encouraging team membership, but also in taking a leadership role. The leader should have the trust and respect from both families and administrators/educators. In addition to this membership, we would also encourage the team to include a community or cultural liaison who has a deep knowledge of the families within the community.

Understanding Strengths and Goal Orientation

The team should review any historical data on existing family–school–community partnerships and involvement (Epstein, 2010) in how these partnerships were formed, and perceived effectiveness of the partnership. Solution-focused processes within these partnerships can be a useful approach to do this (Christenson & Sheridan, 2001). For example, the Huerta family has some experience with academic supports from their experience with their oldest child, Elena. Building on this history, you can discuss how behavioral supports for Antonio may be similar and different. Asking questions about what their experience was like in the past (what went well or could be improved) can help establish a starting point for addressing the concerns that the parents have about Antonio.

Data can be gathered through formal (e.g., brief questionnaires for educators to complete) or informal (e.g., conversations with parents) methods. We emphasize that the focus should be on strengths, thus asking, *What is needed to have strong partnerships between families and school?*, versus asking, *Why aren't families getting involved in the school?* Further, it is important that data be analyzed and interpreted with a culturally responsive lens.

During this stage, the team should assess the needs and strengths in order to identify the goals of the partnership (Bryan & Henry, 2012). Through a needs assessment (e.g., surveys, interviews), as well as through attending community-based events (e.g., church picnics), practitioners can take steps to engage with families at the community level. Connecting with religious leaders in the community, such as imams or pastors, can be a helpful way to learn about the major topics of discussions. Local events, such as powwow or harvest festivals, can also be ways to engage with the community. Similarly, attending school-based social activities such as sports, concerts, or community dinner nights are great ways to engage with families. Bryan and Henry (2012) encourage practitioners to ask:

- What existing partnerships are already meeting identified needs?
- How will you get buy-in from staff?
- How will you overcome any perceived barriers and challenges when implementing your plan? (p. 412)

The process of developing goals should also include discussions about the barriers to forming or continuing school–family–community partnerships. Increasing authentic partnerships also means increasing opportunities for interactions between schools and families. Immigrant parents, for example, may have work requirements that reduce the likelihood that they can interact with their children's teachers (Li & Sun, 2019). Further, some parents, like those from East Asian cultures, may prefer informal, in-person communication with teachers rather than formal parent–teacher conferences (Ji & Koblinsky, 2009). Thus, to increase opportunities for interaction, the schools could consider videoconferencing, increasing transportation options (e.g., having school buses take parents to the school), providing day care, or having teachers go to the community or participate in home visits with parents. Practitioners, teachers, and the caregivers could collaboratively develop a plan to be able to increase the opportunities for interactions.

As stated earlier, there should be increased opportunities to engage in the families' language. These efforts are particularly important because language can be a significant barrier to developing authentic partnerships. For example, Li and Sun (2019) highlighted that among Asian immigrant parents, limited English proficiency can lead to lower school participation. School personnel can also ensure that they increase interaction by asking families for their ideas and opinions in regard to the child's learning (Christenson & Sheridan, 2001).

Develop an Action Plan

Once the team has a true sense of the existing strengths and perceived barriers within the school and community, as well as the vision among families, then the team should develop an action plan. In this plan, it is important that there be a shift in the school's perspective: Instead of families having to reshape their behavior to fit the school, it is about gradually reshaping the behavior of the school to fit the families (Olivos, 2019). This action plan should directly align with the vision or goals that were developed collaboratively and should leverage the existing strengths of the families, school, and community. Epstein suggested developing a one-year action plan where the team considers how to develop a program that fosters family–school partnerships and provides a plan for implementing the program. Epstein emphasized that that this plan should include (1) details of the program, (2) responsibilities of those who will be developing and implementing the practices, (3) the costs associated with the program, and (4) evaluation of the practices and activities.

Epstein (2010) described six ways that families can be involved in school, and these components may be a part of the action of plan. *Parenting* involves the school providing families with parenting skills and facilitating a home environment that can support children's learning. *Communicating* involves continuous interaction between families and schools about the child's progress and the curriculum. *Volunteering* involves inviting and encouraging parents to participate in school activities during their free time. *Learning at home* involves supporting parents in monitoring or aiding children with homework and other academic tasks. *Decision-making* allows involvement of parents in advocacy, governance, and school management. *Collaborating with the community* involves seeking and utilizing resources within the community to support parenting and children's learning at school.

Conjoint behavioral consultation is a form of service delivery that has been shown to foster home–school collaboration. A trained consultant facilitates a partnership between families, teachers, and support staff (Sheridan & Kratochwill, 2008). Relational approaches (e.g., semi-structured interviewing) as well as structured approaches (e.g., collecting data) during the consultation process support positive student behavior at school or at home. This approach consists of four stages: (1) Conjoint Needs Identification Interview, (2) Conjoint Needs Analysis Interview, (3) Plan Implementation, (4) Conjoint Plan Evaluation Interview. In the vignette, collaboration between teachers and the Huerta family can help to identify and prioritize the children's needs. The parents articulated that this is important for Antonio both at home and at school; thus, the practitioner could use conjoint-behavioral consultation to design an intervention plan. Monitoring Antonio's progress by collecting data that the family perceives as efficient and meaningful is important for the success of the intervention. Emerging research has also shown promise in delivering consultation via remote videoconferencing, particularly to schools and families in underserved communities (Witte et al., 2022).

One approach to an effective partnership is to center the family's goals and aspirations for their child. For example, Li and Sun (2019) highlight that Asian immigrant parents care deeply about their child's future; thus, you could leverage their educational aspirations for their child by asking questions or including prompts such as, *What goals do you have for your child in school? What are the most important skills you hope your child will learn in school?* Similarly, when working with Indigenous families, it is helpful to acknowledge and respect that their Indigenous ways of knowing should be integrated into their children's education (Garcia, 2019).

Another approach to partnering with families to is to develop a family resource center where a family consultant serves as a liaison between the home and school (Stormshak et al., 2009). The liaison would be someone who works in and understands the school system while working to serve the best interests of the family and student. Further, they can attend meetings, such as for student behavioral support, that can facilitate conversations with parents, answer questions, and ensure that they and their child are receiving the necessary resources. This action plan should be done collaboratively, focusing on the student's needs.

Evaluate the Plan and Celebrate Progress

In the final stages, practitioners evaluate and celebrate the progress. Importantly, collecting meaningful data throughout the process would ensure that decisions are being made based on reliable information, rather than "gut feeling." Bryan and Henry (2012) suggested asking, *"How will you measure and evaluate each partnership to show results/outcomes? What difference did the partnership make?"* (p. 412). These questions are really important because the goal is about not just collecting data about the outcome of the program, but also collecting data about the *process of partnership.* Celebrating progress of this partnership is really important for sustaining relationships and keeping the momentum of those partnerships. If the plan was not considered effective, then further discussion between parties is helpful for reviewing and revising the plan as a shared goal.

SUMMARY

Partnerships between families and schools are crucial for children's overall success in school. Engaging with families can be especially challenging when cultural differences are present. Ultimately, collaboration is the foundation for these partnerships to be authentic and successful. Healthy family–school relationships are built on trust, sensitivity, and equality. These elements can be brought to each of the following steps in forming partnerships between schools and families.

First, engaging in critical reflexivity means considering personal values, the history of the community, and cultural differences among families. Cultural values of families will often shape the way they approach relationships with the school and may prompt families to be more or less involved with educational planning and support. Second, developing partnerships through trust and reciprocity means taking the first step in developing relationships with families and the community. It is important to consider *why* this partnership is important and *how* schools can facilitate various forms of involvement from families. Third, creating an action team for school–family–community partnerships means using school resources to establish a team committed to these partnerships. Fourth, understanding strengths and goal orientation means striving for solutions-focused discourse about perceived problems or areas of possible improvement. Creative solutions should be encouraged to increase staff buy-in and accessibility for families. Fifth, developing an action plan means that details of the program should be established, responsibilities for implementation assigned, costs of the program evaluated, and practices for evaluation of the program created. Finally, evaluating the plan and celebrating progress go hand in hand. Evaluation procedures include specific methods of collecting data or information about the effectiveness of the program.

DISCUSSION QUESTIONS

1. What does an authentic partnership mean to you? How can you tell if you are being authentic when working with caregivers?
2. In what ways do you show parents and families you are interested in establishing and maintaining collaborative partnerships?
3. How can you improve your school's process for collecting and responding to caregiver concerns?

APPENDIX 3
SAMPLE WELCOME LETTER

Hello Guardians and Parents,

Welcome to Cherry Elementary School! We strive to meet students and families each year and work together to achieve educational, social, and developmental goals. I wrote this letter to introduce myself as the school psychologist at your child's school.

My name is Alex, and I grew up in the community around Cherry Elementary. I am passionate about helping children and families achieve their personal and educational goals. I earned my degree at State School and specialized in reading disabilities and anxiety disorders. I work with families, teachers, and students to discover ways to boost a child's strengths at school. Sometimes this includes interviews, standardized testing, and other ways of collecting information.

If you are concerned about your child's learning and mental health, reach out using the online referral system on our school's website. I can also be reached during the week via phone or email using the contact information below.

Come meet me in person at the Parent Open-House before the school year begins, on Friday, August 11th.

Thank you for being part of our community at Cherry Elementary!

Sincerely,
Alex Baker, NCSP

Conducting Culturally Responsive Assessment

With the foundations in culturally responsive practice in place, practitioners can then gather information on students' socio-cultural factors and ecological systems to inform interventions. In this section, we highlight the *Culturally Responsive Strengths-based Assessment to Inform Intervention* model to effectively assess students' learning and mental health. Then, we provide strategies for conducting a culturally responsive assessment that is strengths-based and uses multi-method and multi-source approaches. An ecological assessment of students' knowledge, skills, and abilities is important because learning is often the result of the environment and systems in which the student functions. Thus, we specifically provide strategies to assess acculturation, literacy, and language, as well as how to assess intelligence of students from culturally and linguistically diverse backgrounds. The section ends with strategies to assess mental health and traumatic stress, with an emphasis on how mental health is grounded in cultural understanding and perspectives of wellness.

Culturally Responsive Approaches to Traditional Assessment

VIGNETTE

Juan is a Black second-grade cisgender boy who speaks Creole and English. Juan's parents immigrated from Haiti to the United States because of a technology-related job position for Juan's father. He lives with his parents and maternal grandmother. They told Ms. Gonzalez, his teacher, that he has been attending school since he was 6 years old. Ms. Gonzalez has noticed that Juan is "quite disruptive" in class. He playfully pokes at his peers, yells answers to questions, and purposefully throws pencils and other objects. These behaviors become more disruptive when he becomes frustrated, crying or screaming when he does not get what he wants. Ms. Gonzalez tried to ignore these behaviors and reinforce Juan positively when he is calm and uses an "inside voice." Most of the strategies she has used in the past have not been effective. Similarly, Juan's parents are becoming increasingly concerned about his behavior at home.

- *What sociocultural factors might be considered during an assessment of Juan?*
- *In what ways would it be important to engage in critical reflexivity throughout this assessment?*

In schools, assessment of students' academic performance and behavior is important for obtaining a clearer understanding of the student's strengths and areas of concerns. Traditionally, best practices in conducting a comprehensive assessment include gathering information from multiple sources using multiple methods to understand the specific problem and subsequently to inform appropriate interventions to address that problem (Tilly, 2014). Culturally responsive assessment practices incorporate this multi-method, multi-source approach within a problem-solving process while recognizing that not every problem is due to a deficit within the student.

The purpose of this chapter is to provide strategies for conducting high-quality, culturally responsive assessment to inform interventions. We will first provide an overview of the Culturally Responsive Strengths-Based Assessment to Inform Intervention model, and culturally responsive approaches can be integrated within this model to assess students' learning and mental health effectively. We will then provide strategies for conducting a culturally responsive assessment that is strengths based using multi-method and multi-source approach. This chapter will focus more specifically on using a sociocultural and ecological framework for students referred for a broad range of concerns, while other chapters will focus specifically on assessing literacy and language (Chapter 5), cognitive abilities (Chapter 6), and mental health and traumatic stress (Chapter 7).

CULTURALLY RESPONSIVE STRENGTHS-BASED ASSESSMENT TO INFORM INTERVENTION

The Culturally Responsive Strengths-Based Assessment to Inform Intervention is a model used to develop goals collaboratively, gather information to understand the student's strengths and areas of concern, and implement and evaluate an intervention to improve desired skills. Traditionally, there are four steps of the problem-solving model: (1) problem identification, (2) problem analysis, (3) implementing the intervention, and (4) evaluating the intervention (Tilly, 2014). This problem-solving model has been integral in the work of many school-based professionals, such as school psychologists. The model provides a structure for conceptualizing and addressing learning and social-emotional problems for students, with an emphasis on gathering data to inform whether the individualized intervention is effective for that student.

One of the challenges we find with this type of conceptualizing, however, is that it assumes that there is something inherently problematic with the student. Is the student the problem? Or are there contextual variables at play that contribute to the student's problem? This is often what distinguishes between a disability and a difficulty. Although this framework allows school-based professionals to brainstorm and develop solutions, it can also lead to or reinforce implicit biases, particularly for minoritized students as we discussed in Chapter 2. Therefore, we suggest reframing this model to enhance a more culturally responsive approach to assessment and intervention with culturally and linguistically diverse (CLD) students. There are five steps in the Culturally Responsive Strengths-Based Assessment to Inform Intervention (see Figure 4.1). In the upcoming section, we will first describe the five steps, and in the following section, we will dive deeper into assessing sociocultural and ecological factors.

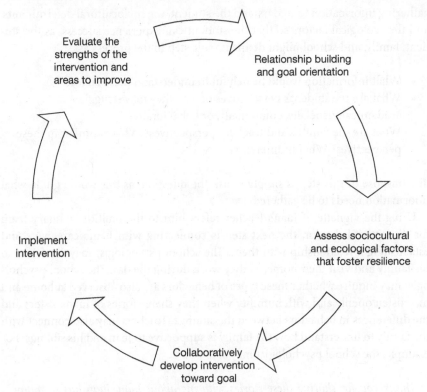

Evaluate the strengths of the intervention and areas to improve

Relationship building and goal orientation

Implement intervention

Assess sociocultural and ecological factors that foster resilience

Collaboratively develop intervention toward goal

Figure 4.1. Culturally Responsive Strengths-Based Assessment to Inform Intervention.

Relationship Building and Goal Orientation

When beginning the assessment process, the most important step is to develop strong relationships with the student's family. As described in Chapter 3, practitioners need to put forth efforts toward developing—and sustaining—authentic school–family–community partnerships. These partnerships should be developed early, when the practitioner is earning trust and building relationships with the student and their caregiver.

During this step, the practitioner is also describing the assessment process, the caregiver's role in this process, and obtaining informed consent. Caregivers may not be clear about the rationale for an evaluation of their child, or what is required of the family when they provide consent to participate, especially if the referral concern involves potential eligibility for special education services. Thus, the practitioner can visit with the caregivers and listen to their story (see Chapter 7 for discussion on relational interviewing).

By listening to their story about their child's strengths and areas of concern, the practitioner can then explain the assessment process. The term *goal orientation* characterizes the process by which the student, family, and multidisciplinary team collaborate to determine what the goal is for the assessment. Assessment is simply gathering information to understand the student, the sociocultural determinants, and the ecological factors so that the student can experience success, as the student, family, and school might define it. This step in the process asks:

- What information would be helpful to understand these factors?
- What are the student's perspectives of why they may struggle academically, socially, emotionally, or behaviorally?
- What are the family's and teacher's perspectives? What is similar in these perspectives? What is different?

The purpose of this step is simply to ask the question, as this would guide what information needs to be gathered.

Using the vignette, if Juan's teacher refers him to the multidisciplinary team for disruptive behavior, the next step is connecting with Juan's caregivers and establishing a relationship with them. The school psychologist may reach out to his family and visit their home, as they work during the day. The school psychologist may inquire whether these types of behaviors are also observed at home and may listen openly and with humility when they share stories of Juan's sisters and the differences in behaviors between the siblings. Teachers may also connect with the family to understand how the family is supportive to Juan and his siblings. For example, the school psychologist may say,

> Thank you for sharing these stories with me about Juan. Juan has so many strengths, and together, I hope that we can figure out a way to support him at school and use these strengths to address some of the concerns you've shared. One of the steps that we're going to take together is to figure out whether Juan needs support or accommodations so he can be successful in school. We are a team of educators and professionals, and importantly, you are a member of the team too. As a team, we will gather lots of information—through interviews, observations, and some testing—to figure out whether Juan has a disability and whether he qualifies for special education services. Your voice in this process is really important. Let me answer any questions you have at this point.

In this model, we emphasize the collaborative component of assessment to inform intervention. Assessments, including those to determine special education eligibility, should be directly tied to intervention. If a teacher is worried about a student who is struggling in school, a culturally responsive strengths-based assessment can be helpful in developing interventions that meets the student's needs. This strengths-based assessment includes closely investigating the sociocultural factors and ecological systems that encircle the student and that reflect the student's resilience. In other words, the question is *not* "What is wrong with the student?" but, rather,

- "What cultural strengths does the student have that facilitate success as defined by the student and family? What other strengths related to academic, familial, neighborhood, school, community, region, interests are relevant?"

- "How can the caregivers and teachers collaborate to understand the student's strengths and areas to improve?"
- "What can we do together to support their child best?"
- "What are some changes we can make in the classroom that can promote student success?"

Studies have shown that teachers often describe behavior of racial- and ethnic-minoritized students as more severe and are more likely to see a pattern of negative behavior after one or two minor incidents (Okonofua & Eberhardt, 2015). Teachers also have used less positive language when speaking with minoritized students (Tenenbaum & Ruck, 2007). Given the disproportionate number of minoritized students who receive special education services or who are disciplined with expulsions or suspensions (Morgan et al., 2018), this model reframes how schools discuss the student in meetings while considering socio-cultural factors and strengths within the assessment, and while also refraining from developing and reinforcing implicit biases that may further contribute to disproportionality.

Then, a goal should be developed for the assessment. To clarify, this is not to develop the goal of the intervention; rather, it is about determining what information needs to be gathered to understand best the student's strengths and areas of concern. This step clarifies the purpose of the assessment. It is also about determining what data already exist and what data need to be gathered. Do not underestimate the importance of this step: gathering data for the sake of gathering data is inefficient and time consuming for students, families, and practitioners. Intentional and purposeful gathering of data will not only be more efficient, but it may also lead to improved outcomes because the data would help in the implementation of the intervention and ultimately lead to better progress monitoring.

For Juan's case, if the family is similarly concerned about his behavior, then the next step is to develop a goal for the assessment collaboratively. The teacher may define "disruptive behavior" as yelling, throwing objects in the classroom, crying, and banging his hands and feet against the floor. These behaviors are different from those of other second graders, and Juan's family also notices that his behaviors are different from his sister's at the same age. Many may believe that because Juan is male, the teacher may easily associate boys with disruptive behavior. However, Juan throws objects at his mother, in particular, but also yells and cries at home when he wants an object or food that he cannot have. As a collaborative team, the family, practitioner, and teachers may determine that the goal of the assessment is to understand additional factors or circumstances that contribute to Juan's behavior and understand when Juan is behaving as expected in the classroom and at home without making swift assumptions regarding gender or another's culture. Ultimately, this assessment would help choose an intervention.

Assess Sociocultural and Ecological Factors That Foster Resilience

The second step in the process is to assess the sociocultural determinants and ecological factors that help understand the student's strengths and areas of concern. By gathering explicit information from the family in relation to their situational context, this may help avoid imposing implicit bias in the assessment and decision-making process. Building the relationship with the family will facilitate this stage in the assessment. The purpose is to collaborate with the student, family, and other relevant people in the student's life (e.g., favorite teacher, counselor, spiritual advisor) in the process, which will help cultivate a genuine relationship for student success.

Importantly, this stage should include multiple methods and multiple sources to understand the various sociocultural and ecological factors that foster the student's strengths and what may be impeding their well-being. Such multi-method assessments align with diverse students, including Indigenous students (Johnston & Claypool, 2010). This multi-method, multi-source approach may include (1) reviewing medical records, (2) conducting interviews, (3) observing the student at home and school, and (4) administering and interpreting tests (Sattler, 2018). Although the process of integrating the data is common in traditional approaches to assessment, culturally responsive assessment in this case entails working with families to ensure accuracy of information, providing an ecological context to understanding behaviors, and relying on students' existing skills to foster new skills, while determining an acceptable plan for all parties in moving forward.

Using these methods, Aganza and colleagues (2015) suggest a cultural asset approach to assessment that incorporates the values, norms, and attitudes within the student's culture. In their research, they focused specifically on Latinx students, but the suggestions may be broad enough and applicable to other culturally and linguistically diverse students. Particularly, they suggested considering the cultural assets in the home that would help the student learn at school. Through the record review, interviews, and observations, the practitioner gathers information about home- and culture-based activities that help in understanding the student's strengths. These activities may include the student's interactions with elders, their contribution to the household (e.g., chores), and language, and these can inform what strengths the student has that would be used as part of the student success plan.

In Juan's case, the practitioner may conduct interviews with his grandmother and other elders in his life about Juan's family relationships, skills, and behaviors. For example, "Tell me some things that Juan does well at home that you have seen"; "What do you say or do to encourage good behavior?"; "What are some skills you would like to see improve with Juan and/or with his parents?" Through this process, the practitioner learns that he does have the knowledge and skills to be respectful to elders (i.e., he listens to his grandmother when spoken to, follows her instructions for chores). The practitioner could utilize these cultural assets to foster positive behaviors at school as well as with his parents and teacher.

The assessment of sociocultural determinants and ecological factors should be comprehensive, and it may take the most time. This helps to minimize implicit bias by understanding the environmental or ecological context of the student from others' knowledge and perspectives. In fact, efficiently, accurately, and comprehensively collecting information from caregivers and teachers during this stage will actually save time in the long run. There should be enough information to understand fully the student's strengths and areas to improve so that an intervention can be developed. On the other hand, gathering data for the sake of gathering data is not only inefficient; it is also inappropriate. Data should always be gathered for the purposes of fully understanding the primary issues affecting the child's mental health and learning. Overall, this process of assessment should help in informing interventions, regardless of whether the student qualifies for special education.

Collaboratively Develop an Intervention Plan with the Goal

Once the strengths-based assessment has been conducted, the next step is to collaborate with the student and their family in developing an intervention that builds on the student's existing skills and is aligned toward a specific mutual goal. The previous three steps should clearly lead to a decision about what social, emotional, and behavioral factors the intervention should address. The information or data that were gathered should be shared with all team members, and the intervention goal should be collaboratively determined.

Progress monitoring of the student's well-being is essential to ensure that the intervention is effective and addressing the concerns. This stage should also include discussions about the details of the intervention:

- Who should be implementing the plan (e.g., school counselor, general educator, multiple members)?
- Where and when should the plan be implemented (e.g., 2 days a week for 30 minutes in the office)?
- How are the data for progress monitoring going to be collected?
- How will the implementation fidelity be monitored?

Implement an Intervention Plan

In this step, the intervention can be implemented. Throughout this stage, the practitioner should be in continuous contact with the student's family to update them about the student's progress, and also how they may contribute to the plan (e.g., providing rewards at home for improvement in skills or behaviors in school). Furthermore, the intervention plan should be implemented as designed (i.e., with fidelity), particularly because the intervention was specifically designed in collaboration with the family.

Evaluate Strengths Within the Intervention Plan and Areas to Improve

The student, family, and practitioner, and any other important members of the team, should meet to discuss the effectiveness of the intervention plan by determining if the student reaches their predetermined goal(s). Specifically, they should document and review the progress monitoring data (in graphs, tables, or charts) to ascertain whether the intervention outcomes meet or exceed the goal that was set initially. Schools should also consider the barriers of the intervention plan and whether there are aspects of the intervention plan that need to be modified, if the concerns have not been adequately addressed (see Chapter 9).

CONDUCTING A CULTURALLY RESPONSIVE ASSESSMENT

In the previous section, we outlined the model of Culturally Responsive Strengths-Based Assessment to Inform Intervention. In this section, we elaborate on one of these steps from the model: assessing sociocultural and ecological factors. In order to conduct a culturally responsive assessment, the practitioner should focus the assessment on the student's strengths as well as the student's sociocultural and ecological context using a variety of sources (e.g., caregivers, educators) and methods (see Figure 4.2). We discuss four methods: (1) reviewing psychological, educational, and medical records, (2) school and home observations, (3) interviews, and (4) tests and measures. We wrap up the section by discussing how to share results of the assessment through feedback and reports.

Reviewing Psychological, Educational, and Medical Records

In most schools, reviewing records can be a very useful source of information for understanding the student's psychological, educational, and medical history. It also can be characterized as the least intrusive, and these data are accumulated and stored each year at the student's school or in district. In this section, we will discuss the process by which records could be reviewed, as well as factors that professionals should consider when working with students from CLD backgrounds.

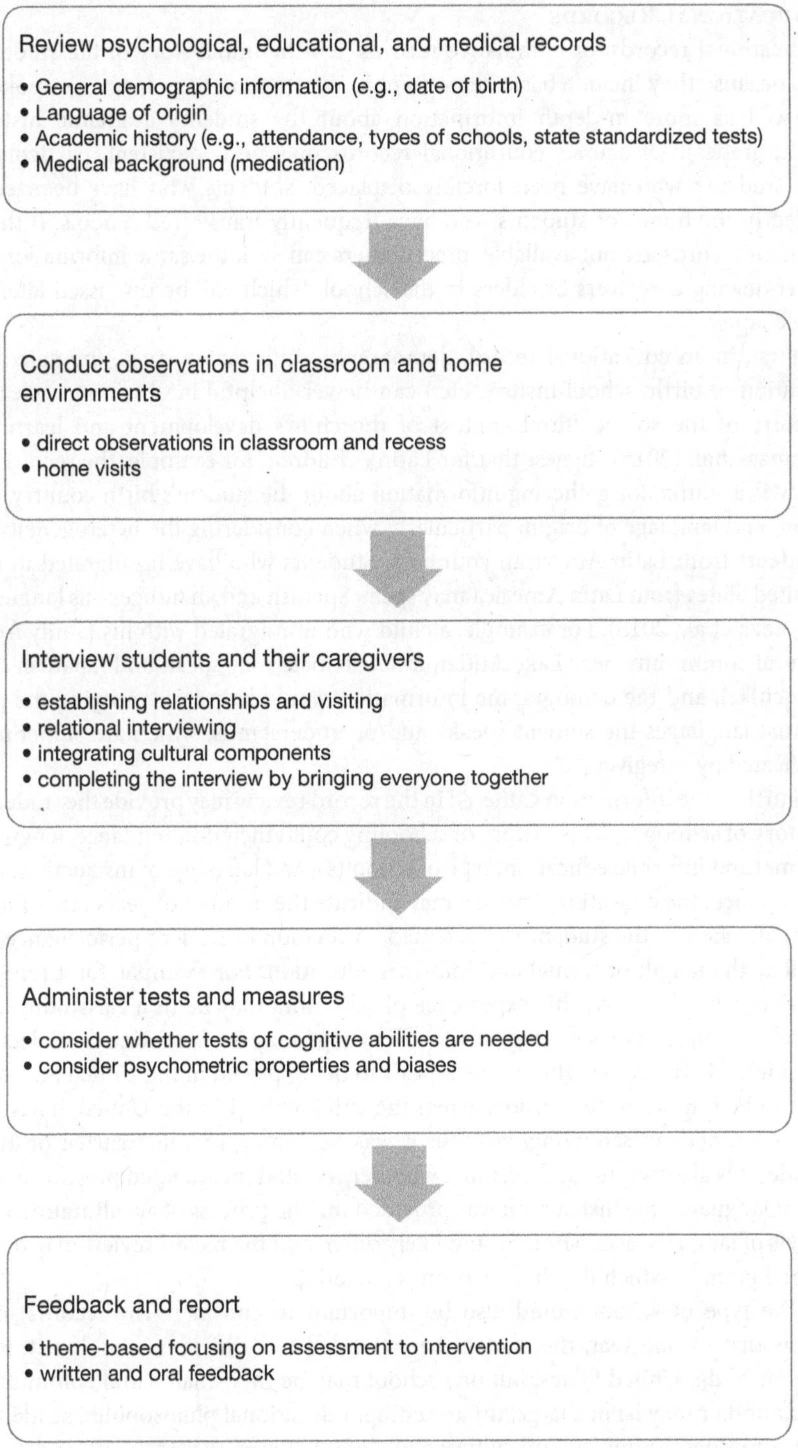

Review psychological, educational, and medical records

- General demographic information (e.g., date of birth)
- Language of origin
- Academic history (e.g., attendance, types of schools, state standardized tests)
- Medical background (medication)

Conduct observations in classroom and home environments

- direct observations in classroom and recess
- home visits

Interview students and their caregivers

- establishing relationships and visiting
- relational interviewing
- integrating cultural components
- completing the interview by bringing everyone together

Administer tests and measures

- consider whether tests of cognitive abilities are needed
- consider psychometric properties and biases

Feedback and report

- theme-based focusing on assessment to intervention
- written and oral feedback

Figure 4.2. Culturally Responsive Assessment of Sociocultural and Ecological Factors.

EDUCATIONAL RECORDS

Educational records, or cumulative records, tell the initial story of the student's life because they include basic demographic information (e.g., language spoken) as well as more in-depth information about the student's academic history (e.g., grades). Of course, educational records may be nonexistent, particularly for students who have been forcibly displaced, students who have been educated in the home, or students who have frequently transferred schools. If these written records are not available, practitioners can seek the same information by interviewing caregivers or elders in the school, which will be discussed later in the chapter.

First, in an educational record, demographic information (e.g., the date and location of birth, school history, etc.) can be very helpful in obtaining a clearer picture of the sociocultural context of the child's development and learning. Aganza et al. (2015) suggest that for Latinx children, for example, the record review is a source for gathering information about the student's birth country, region, and language of origin, particularly when considering the heterogeneity of students from Latin American countries. Students who have immigrated to the United States from Latin America may speak Spanish and an indigenous language (Aganza et al., 2015). For example, a child who immigrated with his family from a rural community near Lake Atitlán in Guatemala may speak both Spanish and Kaqchikel, and the demographic information would help in identifying the potential languages the student speaks and/or understands, which are sometimes indicated by caregivers.

Further, the information gathered in the record review may provide the student's history of schooling. This history of schooling could include attendance, length of formal and informal education, type of school(s), and language of instruction. For attendance, the educational record may indicate the number of years attending a school, whether the student was retained, evaluation of student performance, as well as the length of formal and informal education. For example, for a refugee student who fled Syria, his experience of schooling may be in a classroom in a refugee camp in Greece. Thus, his first language may be Levantine (a dialect of Arabic), and he was taught in Greek prior to being placed in the United States. It would be important to consider when the child arrived in the United States for formal American schooling, whether it was beginning in kindergarten or 10th grade. It is also helpful to determine whether the student attended preschool and what languages the instruction was provided in. The process of acculturation and levels of language acquisition would likely differ, and the record review may be an initial point in which that information is gathered.

The type of school would also be important to consider. The records may show that in one year, the student has attended two different schools within a region of the United States, but one school may be in a small, rural community and another may be in a large, urban setting. Educational philosophies, academic opportunities, resources, and culture may differ between these schools, and, thus, the student's experience in each school may also differ. Similarly, the student may have been homeschooled, and the expectations of schooling may differ, as well.

For example, a student who was educated using a religious homeschool curriculum may have different cultural values and expectations than the mainstream public education system does. States may have different educational requirements for what information they need for a homeschooling curriculum.

Importantly, educational records also serve as a place to review the child's learning and behavioral performance. Class grades, report cards, standardized tests, and office discipline referrals are likely to be included. Although grades are helpful in understanding the students' academic performance, there is great variation in how teachers deliver grades. For example, if students retake a class test and the average score is used in a grade, it may not accurately show the student's current abilities. If grades are unknown or if they are coming from a school system outside of the United States, Rhodes, Ochoa, and Ortiz (2005) suggest that comparing the student's academic performance with those of siblings may be helpful. Further, report cards may include standards-based grading, which allow for practitioners to understand the student's proficiency compared with other students.

Educational records can also provide information and understanding of the family context. Members of the family who are involved in the student's education may be revealed in the record. The student's biological parents, grandparents, aunts, or uncles may all be included as caregivers in the child's life. Importantly, the term *aunt* may not describe the child's father's sister; rather, it may be an important member of the extended family or a member of the community. Among some indigenous communities, for example, members may raise children who are not directly biologically related to them.

PSYCHOLOGICAL AND MEDICAL RECORDS

Psychological and medical records can also be a rich source of information to understand the sociocultural and ecological context of a student's well-being and learning. Records from mental health providers (e.g., psychologists, therapists), as well as medical providers (e.g., psychiatrists, pediatricians), can be helpful in understanding the history of the student's health, previous evaluations, and information on any school-based interventions or school services used. Practitioners can ask caregivers, with a signed release of information, to access these records, highlighting that only the necessary information will be included in the assessment.

One of the first steps in reviewing the student's mental health records is asking about the family's perceptions of mental health overall, particularly the origins and outcomes of mental health in their culture or country (Schlosser & Ninnemann, 2012). The family's cultural background and religion are likely to shape their perceptions of their child's mental health problems. The concept of "wellness" may be conceptualized differently within that family, and the records (e.g., progress notes from therapists), may highlight that variation (see Chapter 10).

When gathering a student's mental health history, practitioners can ask about how the family describes the student's current behaviors, any behaviors that may be of concern to the family, and their perceived understanding of and explanations for these behaviors. The purpose is not to invalidate their beliefs, especially if their explanations contradict research on these issues, but their views may help in understanding what interventions or approaches to take (e.g., consultation) when alleviating these concerns. For example, family members from Puerto Rico may describe anxiety symptoms as *ataque de nervios* (Guarnaccia et al., 2003), or family that is Native American may describe their child's behavior in terms of wellness and spirituality (Portman & Garrett, 2006). These descriptors reflect underlying values of the family that may need to be considered within a broader assessment.

The family's approach to treatment may also be helpful in determining their own or the student's willingness to participate in school based support. For example, some families' religion or beliefs may not value medication as a treatment option. Although professionals in schools are not involved in prescribing medication, it is important that they understand the family's beliefs. Practitioners should note any underlying religious views or belief systems related to previous support given to the student. The family's perceptions of medication, such as psychostimulants, may be important to consider when examining the child's history of symptomology. Some families from diverse cultural backgrounds, such as Latinx, may perceive non-pharmacological approaches as more acceptable than medication (Pham et al., 2010).

Observations in School and Home Environments

School observations can provide important information on whether the student can apply knowledge or demonstrate the desired skills in different contexts. Although less common, practitioners (e.g., school psychologists) can conduct observations in the home, with caregiver permission. From a sociocultural perspective, a student's behavior in each environment may differ, and this can be important in considering ways to intervene to address mental health or learning problems. Johnston and Claypool (2010) particularly emphasized the importance of observations with a multi-method assessment because it aligns with the traditional experiential learning of Indigenous communities. Specifically, they emphasized that observations of children during an experiential learning exercise or task would be particularly useful (e.g., creating a cultural artifact such weaving a blanket or basket). Further, by understanding the student's behavior in multiple environments, educators and school professionals can more effectively collaborate with caregivers to determine any discrepancies in the observed behaviors based on environmental context. For example, when working with Indigenous communities, sporting events (e.g., basketball games) or cultural/community centers may be important environments to observe, while for forcibly displaced students, a housing complex garden or central area may also be important, as they may be areas that foster the family's safety or sense of belonging.

Some professionals may argue that conducting a behavior observation, particularly a systematic direct observation, does not align with a culturally responsive model of practice. That is, some might suggest that considering cultural context would diminish the value of the behavior in its "purest" form—that it is measurable and observable and focuses on contingencies and reinforcements. We argue that observing behavior is essential within a culturally responsive assessment because *behavior is culture* and *culture is behavior*. A student's behavior is shaped by the cultural context in which they live. For example, eye contact with adults may be polite in one culture (shows respect to an elder by looking at them) while avoiding direct eye contact with adults may be polite in another culture (shows respect to an elder by looking slightly away). Similarly, Fong and colleagues (2016) emphasized that "an individual's unique set of distinguishable stimuli and response classes are collectively referred to as an individual's cultural identity" (p. 84). Without understanding the student's sociocultural context, we may miss key behaviors that are contributing to the student's difficulties with mental health and learning or, conversely, understand the student's strengths to know how best to support them. In this section, we provide specific strategies and suggestions for conducting systematic, direct observations as well as unstructured or anecdotal observations in the student's school and home environments.

SCHOOL-BASED OBSERVATIONS

Culturally responsive school-based observations should incorporate a number of different methods and settings. Practitioners can use both systematic direct observations (e.g., momentary time sampling) and unstructured/anecdotal observations (e.g., narrative format) of the student's behavior across various school settings (e.g., classroom, playground, bus). Systematic direct observations are helpful tools within culturally responsive assessment because they provide an objective measure of student's behavior, which may reduce bias when observing student behaviors and facilitates observing cultural assets (Aganza et al., 2015). As Volpe and McConaughy (2005) described, it allows for an assessor to operationalize and measure a specific target behavior and to be able to follow a standardized coding procedure that provides a quantitative score, and it can be tested for reliability and validity across different observers, settings, and time periods. When conducting observations, Fong et al. (2016) suggested that practitioners consider the language of assessment by avoiding behavioral jargon with families and examine nonverbal (e.g., personal space, body language) and verbal language.

There are a number of systematic direct observation methods that can be used in the school. These methods include event, duration, latency, and interval recording, and each type of observational method has its advantages and disadvantages. An in-depth discussion is beyond the scope of this chapter (see LeBlanc et al., 2016), but it is important to consider the target behavior when making decisions about the observation method. These systematic direct observations should also be conducted in multiple settings in the schools, such as the classroom setting during both structured (seat work) and unstructured (free choice time) activities to analyze patterns in a student's behavior.

In addition to systematic direct observations, anecdotal or narrative observations can also be helpful within a culturally responsive assessment. These types of observations can facilitate the goal orientation using strengths-based approaches. Similar to systematic direct observation, these observations should be conducted in multiple settings where the student's behavior could be observed in both structured and unstructured contexts. These observations of children in the school can also allow for spontaneous behaviors. For example, when assessing preschool students, McGoey, McCobin, and Venesky (2016) suggested that the student may not show their skill in drawing when prompted because of emerging second language acquisition; however, when observed in the classroom, the child may spontaneously draw a sun or a wheel of a bike. They noted that observations may show that children have the skill, just not the opportunity.

HOME-BASED OBSERVATIONS

Although it can be logistically difficult for school-based practitioners, conducting a home-based observation is a critical aspect of culturally responsive assessment. Initial conversations with the family are necessary to establish rapport and clearly explain the rationale for a home observation. Some families may be uncomfortable with a school professional being in their home; therefore, it would be very important to develop a positive relationship with the student's family prior to conducting a home observation. Indeed, this observation should be conceptualized as an invitation, whereby the student's family sees the value of your involvement in the process of understanding the student's strengths and areas of concern to support their well-being.

Once invited to the home, practitioners should learn and respect the cultural norms in that family. For example, if the family are of Cambodian heritage, they may expect guests to take off their shoes before entering the home, as it is polite to go barefoot in one's home. Similarly, if the family is Eritrean American, they will offer food and drink to a guest in their home, and it would be polite to accept this offer. Be prepared to be in the home for longer than anticipated, as the family may expect to visit with the practitioner prior to doing a formal observation. This visit can be a rich opportunity to connect with the family, by learning from their experiences and their goals for their child.

After a visit with the family, a more formal observation can take place. A first step may be to observe the student's interactions with each member of the family and particularly with siblings. With elders, in what ways is the student showing deference? How is this behavior similar to or different from behaviors with teachers or administrators at school? With siblings, how is conflict being addressed, both by elders and between siblings? Similarly, how is spirituality or religiosity expressed in the home? In some families, religious symbols such as the Star of David or a Buddha statue with fruit and flowers may be visible.

The practitioner can ask the family to go through their daily routine, recognizing that having an outside observer (a stranger) may influence their behavior. During this daily routine, notice the parents or elders' discipline practices and family expectations. Are children supposed to make direct eye contact with an adult or are they expected to look away? These observations can be helpful in understanding the student's sociocultural context. The practitioner can ask the family to share a video if a student does not demonstrate a behavior at school but can do so at home.

Another important area to observe is how literacy and language are used in the home. Are the caregivers modeling behavior to enhance literacy in the first or second language (Geva & Wiener, 2015)? Are there books in the home in different languages? What kinds of activities are the children involved in? Additional information on supporting students' language and literacy is further discussed in Chapter 5.

Interviewing Students, Caregivers, and Educators

Interviewing students and the adults in their lives (e.g., caregivers and educators) is a critical aspect of culturally responsive assessment. Not only does interviewing provide information about the student's sociocultural context or ecological factors, but it can also facilitate relationships and foster trust between the practitioner, student, and family. An important consideration is the power dynamics between the practitioner and the person they are interviewing. Although we often think of interviews as simply dialogue between two individuals, there is in fact, dominance and power (Kvale, 2006). The relationships and dynamics between the practitioner and the caregiver, for example, are shaped by the power the practitioner holds as a person within the school as well as what they may represent. As discussed in Chapter 3, providing time and space for developing relationships with students and caregivers can allow for a stronger, more effective assessment to understand the strengths and areas of growth. Interviewing can facilitate strong relationships.

There are a number of components of interviewing that should be considered within a multi-method, multi-source assessment, including (1) establishing relationships and visiting, (2) relational interviewing, (3) integrating cultural components, and (4) completing the interview by bringing everyone together. The focus of this chapter will be interviewing students and families within culturally responsive assessments for a broad range of referral questions while Chapter 7 provides strategies for interviewing within an assessment of mental health and traumatic stress.

VISITING AND CREATING A RELATIONALLY SAFE SPACE

When conducting interviews with students and families, an initial step is to visit with them and create a relationally safe space. *Visiting* is a common practice in most societies, including American society. Often, people visit each other to establish connections and share stories about their lives. It is an opportunity for building relationships and developing trust. A component of visiting may also be to offer food and drink to the student or family. Offering food and drink in itself is a powerful symbol of reciprocity across many cultures. It represents connection and giving to others, and it is often simply polite to do. It could be as easy as offering tea and cookies. When working with students, it may also be important to consider the types of food, such as fruit or granola bars (taking into consideration food allergies and the family's preferences). Not only does this interview serve to build a relationship with the student; it also serves to take care of their basic needs (Sommers-Flanagan & Sommers-Flanagan, 2014).

During a visit, the practitioner should also be creating a *relationally safe space* that affirms their culture. This culturally affirming space should be a space where the student feels safe and comfortable in the meeting. The physical office should be warm and inviting, with furniture that is arranged in a way that creates an open space, such as in a half-circle (Cook-Cottone et al., 2014). In the office itself, there should also be images that reflect the cultural and linguistic groups of the students and families in the school and community. The practitioner can provide a warm and comfortable physical environment in the office, or perhaps the student and practitioner will choose to go outdoors and find a private area with trees and in nature.

When interviewing the student, creating a relationally safe space may also mean providing opportunities to develop relationship through play. Sommers-Flanagan and Sommers-Flanagan (2014) provide a number of recommendations for engaging in play during a clinical interview, such as using arts and crafts (e.g., drawing, Play-Doh), or playing with action figures, Lego, or Jenga to facilitate more conversation. These activities can be particularly helpful if the student is feeling anxious about being involved in an assessment.

When visiting, it is also the time for the practitioner to introduce themselves, their sociocultural identities (e.g., their age, gender identities, race), and discuss the process of the interview or assessment. Importantly, the introduction may need to be modified depending on the student's age or developmental level. For example, when interviewing caregivers, an introduction could be:

> I am grateful that you came here today. I recognize that we have not met before this, and I thought it may be helpful to share a bit about myself. As a school psychologist, my role is to really understand your child's strengths and the concerns that you and the teachers may have, so that we can come together to support your child. I am a White woman whose background may be different from yours, and I acknowledge that these differences may shape my perspectives. This is why I want to speak with you. Your perspectives and knowledge are valued and important.

In this introduction, the school psychologist is opening the conversation about identity and culture and acknowledging that these identities may affect the lens through which they work together. Although it may initially feel awkward or uncomfortable, these types of introductions are particularly important when the practitioner's culture may be different from the student's or their family's culture. In addition to this introduction, it is also helpful to describe the assessment process. For example, the practitioner working with Juan might say,

> I am excited about working with Juan, as I had heard from his teachers that he really works hard and enjoys math. I know he is struggling with his behaviors in the classroom, and I am eager to work with you and his teachers to figure

out how best to support him. I want to explain a bit about what I'll be doing with him. As a school psychologist, I tell kids that I'm a detective, looking for lots of different clues about how to help kids learn and feel better. No one clue is going to give me a full picture of Juan. I will look at different information to help me understand his strengths and to think about ways to support his areas of growth. So, I will be speaking with you, his teachers, doing an observation of him in the classroom, as well as doing some testing of his cognitive abilities and his academic skills. Can I answer any questions about this process?

RELATIONAL INTERVIEWING

There are different types of interviews, including structured, unstructured, and informal interviews (Dombrowski, 2015). Structured or semi-structured interviews are a series of questions a practitioner asks that are organized in a particular way and followed systematically. Examples of semi-structured interviews include the Cultural Formulation Interview (discussed more in Chapter 7) in which specific sociocultural variables are explored through an organized series of questions. The disadvantage of this approach is that it may be perceived as more formal and less authentic than back-and-forth conversation.

Unstructured interviews, on the other hand, are designed to "go with the flow" of the conversation with the student, family, or educators. It allows for the practitioner, for example, to follow the family's lead in what they want to address as part of the assessment. The disadvantage is that it may mean that certain information is not gathered because certain topics may not be covered during the interview process.

The type of interview structure may depend on the cultural and linguistic background of the student and their caregiver, as well as the type of information gathered through the interview. For example, when interviewing African American students and families, Zink, Lee, and Allen (2015) recommended *not* using unstructured interviews because there is a high risk that biases and misperceptions about African Americans would influence practitioners' judgment and interpretation of the student's behaviors, if practitioners are not adequately skilled in interviewing. They also recommend that there be discussion about racial identity to contextualize the behaviors and reduce the chance that practitioners may misinterpret the answers to questions. Practitioners should be honest, and even vulnerable, when bringing forth these conversations. For example, they could talk with caregivers and say, "One's identity, and particularly racial identity, is an important aspect of children's development. I want to make sure that my personal judgment does not affect my understanding of your child's behaviors."

Further, when conducting an interview with Asian American children and their families, Thaler, Allen, and Scott (2014) suggested that the practitioner consider the relationships between adults and children (and the degree of hierarchy that is embedded within those relationships). Thus, children are expected to respect adults, including minimizing eye contact and ensuring that there is limited emotion and social interaction. Similarly, when working with Latinx families,

Zamarripa and Lerma (2013) recommended that practitioners consider the cultural values of *familismo*, which is related to the obligation and connectedness to the family. Thus, it may be important to conduct interviews with other members of the family beyond the parents.

Relational Interviewing with Students and Caregivers

Structured, semi-structured, and unstructured interviews can be helpful approaches. We suggest also considering using relational interviewing. We are storytellers by nature, and our relationships are often fostered when we share and narrate our own histories and experiences. Similarly, *relational interviewing* is storytelling—allowing for the caregiver, student, or educator to share stories. Derived from qualitative research studies (e.g., Hydén, 2014), relational interviewing within culturally responsive assessment is characterized by using stories to gather information.

When conducting relational interviewing with students and their caregivers, it is important to consider the self-introduction as well as the prompts for questions. These prompts should elicit stories. For example, the prompts and questions below loosely based on Hydén (2014) are intentionally broad to allow for flexibility on what is important for the family.

- *I would like to share a story about your child. May I share a story?*
- *I would like to hear a story about your child.*
- *Keep telling me, does this remind you of something you've experienced before, or is there something more to say about this?*
- *Is it possible to give me an image, or color, or scent, that could express what you're talking about?*
- *Parents often talk about . . . . Is this something that's familiar to you?*

In addition, the interview should also integrate sociocultural variables and ecological factors, such as intersectional identities, acculturative stress, perceived discrimination, beliefs about mental health and wellness, and immigration history (see Appendix 4). For example, to understand the student's cultural identities and intersectionality, the practitioner could ask:

- *There are many aspects of our identities that are meaningful to us. Share with me some of your identities.*
- *In what way does your identity shape your daily life?*
- *I am curious to learn about what aspects of your identity are important to you.*

Similarly, if the student or caregiver is a recent immigrant, and potentially an undocumented immigrant, the practitioner could ask:

- *You mentioned that you recently arrived in this community. Tell me the story about this journey here.*

- *There are lots of parents in our community who have recently immigrated to the United States. In what ways has this journey shaped your child's life?*

Further, asking about the family's perceptions or beliefs about healing can also be helpful in developing intervention plans.

- *Describe to me what you and your family have done to support your child's well-being or health.*
- *Some parents are comfortable with counseling while other parents are not. Tell me about your thoughts on counseling for your child?*

These types of questions can be helpful when working with CLD students. For example, in Juan's case, it would be helpful to know whether his parents see counseling as a potential intervention to address his behavior.

In addition to Western and Eurocentric approaches for interviews, Johnston and Claypool (2010) suggest that talking circles may also be a helpful method to foster trust and belonging. Talking circles have been used with Indigenous students to provide opportunities to share their experiences. Importantly, this approach is based in Indigenous knowledge and systems, and it should be acknowledged as such and care taken not to culturally appropriate this assessment methodology (indeed, Elders should be involved in integrating this approach). Talking circles can be an important tool for Indigenous and non-Indigenous students alike because "the Circle by its very nature creates a safe space where people can rapidly work through or lean into their discomfort and share at a very deep level" (Brown & Di Lallo, 2020, p. 371). The talking circle should be organized in a specific way: (1) students should be sitting in a circle, (2) a brief ceremony is carried that may include mindfulness breathing exercises, (3) a facilitation of the values and guidelines is co-created by the students, (4) a "talking piece" or an object is passed around, (5) communication occurs between students that fosters empathetic relationships, and (6) there is a closing ritual (Brown & Di Lallo, 2020).

Interviewing Educators

In addition to the student's and caregiver's perspectives, the educator's perspectives are also really important within a culturally responsive assessment. Geva and Wiener (2015) suggested that interviewing classroom teachers helps in understanding the student's functioning within the classroom compared with other students, particularly if they have taught other students from the same cultural group. Educators are a rich source of information about the student's social interactions with peers, classroom behaviors, and academic performance.

Bringing Everyone Together (Completing the Interview)

Once the stories are shared and sufficient information is gathered from the caregiver, student, or teacher, then concluding the interview is also about bringing everyone together. In the beginning of the interview, visiting was an important aspect of relationship or rapport building. The practitioner can think about the interview as simply a beginning of an ongoing relationship with the student and caregiver, and when concluding the interview, the practitioner can create a space where they can return to ask questions and provide additional information as needed.

It is also an opportunity to share next steps in the process. When the interview is complete, the practitioner can use the opportunity to discuss the additional steps that will be occurring in the assessment. For example, the practitioner can state,

> *Juan and I had really good conversations about how he is doing at school and home. I appreciated you sharing some stories about Juan at home. When you shared a story about how he and his brother would play together, I could tell they have a special relationship. Thank you for giving me so much information that will help the school team figure out how best to support him. Now, the next step in this process is that I'm going to do some testing with him and give some questionnaires to you and his teachers. I know some of the questions may be unclear or may be not relevant—let's talk through those questions specifically. This testing will help me understand his cognitive skills, or his ability to solve problems, his memory, and verbal skills. I'm going to reach out soon to check in. Do you have questions about this next step?*

This final step in the interview is also helpful when interviewing a student. If the interview is part of an evaluation, it would be helpful to visit with the student and have opportunities to discuss the process, and how their voice can play an important role in the evaluation. It's also a chance to connect with them and open the conversation for topics they may want to discuss.

Tests and Measures

In addition to record review, observations, and interviews, administering tests and measures can also be an important aspect of culturally responsive assessments. Traditional standardized assessments, such as norm-referenced tests (e.g., Wechsler Intelligence Scale for Children, Woodcock–Johnson Tests of Academic Achievement), can be helpful in comparing students' cognitive abilities, academic achievement, and social, emotional, and behavioral skills with those of other students their age. Sattler (2018) emphasized the utility of tests because they can provide information about the student's current functioning, particularly when compared with that of the student's peer group, can help in determining the specific student strengths and areas of improvement, and can be helpful as a way to measure progress (comparing baseline to post-intervention).

However, there has been a great deal of critique of norm-referenced, standardized measures as the primary method for gathering information about academic achievement or cognitive abilities for minoritized students.

Johnston and Claypool (2010), for example, highlighted that current measures are grounded in Eurocentric curricula and knowledge, and thus they are inappropriate for Indigenous students because these measures focus specifically on learning deficits rather than strengths, fail to account for systemic factors, and do not consider the holistic and experiential learning that occurs across their lifetimes. The use of a norm-referenced test also perpetuates a hierarchical system that ranks students using a comparison group. Additional information regarding strengths and limitations of standardized IQ tests, in particular, is further discussed in Chapter 6.

Thus, if tests and measures are used within a culturally responsive assessment, it is important that is in the context of multiple methods and multiple sources. Geva and Wiener (2015) emphasized that the use of standardized tests of cognitive abilities should be done on a case-by-case basis. Further, we agree with their advice that such tests should not be administered to a recent immigrant or refugee. Geva and Wiener recommended that practitioners consider a number of factors: (1) the age at which the immigrant arrived, (2) the degree to which the student had an opportunity to learn the second language (i.e., English) as well as the culture, norms, and values within the host culture, (3) educational experiences, and (4) the cultural differences between the home (heritage) culture and the new, host culture.

Similarly, when working with Asian American students, Li and Wang (2014) recommended that when testing with standardized tests, the practitioner should assess the student's English and native language proficiency and acculturation levels. Specifically, language proficiency may be particularly important because research has shown that English language skills predict academic performance (Lindsey et al., 2003). As a result, sometimes practitioners may seek to administer tests of cognitive abilities that are nonverbal; however, while these tests may require less language, they are not language free (Ortiz, 2002). Practitioners should be intentional about which tests, if any, are needed.

Additionally, when administering and interpreting tests (e.g., for attention issues) among Asian American children, it is important to consider that language in specific subtests may affect the results (Thaler et al., 2014). For example, research has shown that speakers of certain Asian languages (e.g., Mandarin) are expected to perform better than speakers of languages with longer pronunciations (e.g., Malay; M. E. Chan & Elliott, 2011). There may be similar differences in performances of tests of processing speed (Kuwabara & Smith, 2012).

Another consideration is the measure of adaptive functioning. Among some cultural groups, adaptive functioning may look different. For example, Li and Wang (2014) emphasized that among Asian Americans, it is important to consider whether the expectations for independent living actually align with the home expectations. That is, some children may be expected to live with their families (multigenerational home) and, therefore, the expectation of living by oneself, independently, is not culturally appropriate. It may be helpful to refer to the *Standards for Educational and Psychological Testing* (2014), which provides technical information about educational and psychological tests.

Indeed, an important consideration is whether the tests or measures are needed at all—did the record review, observation, or interviews provide sufficient information about the student's learning or social-emotional skills? Is the test necessary? It may be that there are other methods to gather information. Johnston and Claypool (2010) emphasized the use of rubrics and portfolios within a multi-method assessment to provide a holistic view of the student's skills. They argue that "authentic forms of assessment must start with authentic tasks" (p. 132). They suggested that Elders and community leaders be involved in developing the rubrics or portfolios, asking:

- What activities and knowledge do they feel are most important?
- In what ways might they participate or initiate instruction?
- Are there opportunities for urban students to visit rural reserves on a regular basis? (p. 132)

PSYCHOMETRIC CONSIDERATIONS

Different types of psychometric bias exist in testing that should be considered within a culturally responsive assessment: construct bias, method bias, and item bias. In *construct bias*, the items may not completely cover the domains of the instrument (Sattler, 2018). For example, the concept of well-being can differ across cultural groups, with some groups focusing heavily on mood or negative emotions, while others focus on somatization (Beirens & Fontaine, 2010). Further, psychological tests, for example, may have been translated into different languages, but they may not have conceptual equivalence (Okazaki & Sue, 1995). That is, the instrument itself may have been translated, but the underlying meaning may not be the same.

In *method bias*, however, there may be a number of variables that affect the response to items in an instrument that may differ across cultural groups (van de Vijver & Poortinga, 2020). This may include excluding different cultural groups in the instrument norming, test administration issues of the instrument (i.e., the practitioner's training, skills, or interactions with respondents), or the creation of the items themselves (van de Vijver & Poortinga, 2020). For example, when administering standardized tests to Asian American children, Thaler et al. (2014) suggested that practitioners consider normative comparison because tests that have been developed and tested with the broad population may not include sufficient samples of Asian Americans, such as including South Asians and not solely East Asian populations.

Finally, *item bias* refers to the individual items within the instrument (van de Vijver & Poortinga, 2020). How an item is worded may affect how the item is interpreted by different people. For example, there may be issues with the translation of the items, or there may be specific expressions that are culturally bound (e.g., the Xhosa term *amafufunyana*, "ants from the grave;" Mzimkulu & Simbayi, 2006). As a personal example, when Anisa (author) was living in Brazil as a second grader, she was administered a standardized academic test and recalls being asked the question, "Where would you find a pig?," with a few options: (1) a farm, (2) the beach, (3) the street, and (4) none of the above. Although she recognized what the answer was *supposed to be* (given that she attended an American school), she saw pigs in her neighborhood, on the beach, and at farms. Thus, the validity of the item is taken into question because of the student's environment.

Practitioner bias may also influence educational decision-making. For example, Black youth were rated higher on externalizing behaviors and lower on internalizing behavior domains, while White and Latino youth were rated higher on internalizing behaviors and lower externalizing behaviors (Minsky et al., 2006). These discrepancies in ratings may exist because practitioners are using their own cultural framing in problem behaviors, or due to practitioner bias of Black students (Chin et al., 2020).

Finally, it is important to note that there may be discrepancies between informants on certain measures. Information is typically gathered from multiple informants, such as teachers, caregivers, or therapists. Although it is important to gather information from multiple sources to capture the student's experiences across environments, there are differences in how each informant shares information about the child. For example, in one study, parents' reports of White adolescents showed that they have more internalizing and externalizing problems compared with minority adolescents, but according to teacher reports, Black adolescents had fewer internalizing problems while Asian/Pacific Islander youth had fewer externalizing problems (Lau et al., 2004).

Sattler (2018) argued that there is insufficient evidence that intelligence tests have a cultural bias, as defined by mean differences between groups, profile analyses, single-group or differential validity, and differentiated construct validity. Although psychometrically, the research studies he cites (some of which are from the 1970s and 1980s) may not suggest that intelligence tests specifically are culturally biased, we emphasize that the utility and interpretation of such tests warrant caution. Indeed, Sattler stated, "Verbal tests should never be used alone to estimate the cognitive ability levels of children whose primary language is not English" (p. 163). The results and interpretation of a standardized test, whether it is for cognitive abilities or academic achievement, should be contextualized within a student's ecological system. That is, if a standardized test of intelligence is chosen, the results are only one, small component of a larger multi-method and multi-source assessment. Further, the intelligence score (i.e., IQ) must be contextualized within the sociocultural factors and ecological systems of the student. For example, if an Indigenous student is given an IQ test, it is imperative that the practitioner consider the historical and contemporary systems that have impacted Indigenous communities, and how the governmental public educational institutions (e.g., residential boarding schools) have negatively impacted Indigenous communities. A score on an IQ test does not sit alone—it is embedded within a larger system. It is irresponsible, and we argue, unethical, to fail to consider this history when administering an IQ test.

Feedback and Reports

Once all the information is gathered from the record review, interview, observations, and testing, the information should be interpreted and summarized through (1) a written report that is disseminated to relevant team members and the family, and (2) a feedback session with the family. First, when integrating and summarizing the information gathered through the multi-method, multi-source assessment, the report should be written in a way that a caregiver could understand. The practitioner should consider the language and literacy of the family, and if a bilingual practitioner speaks and writes in the same language as the family's preferred language other than English, a briefer version summarizing the report could be written in that language. Specifically, we recommend using a question-driven, theme-based report format (Rahill, 2014) in which the focus of the results is on *the student*, rather than the scores of the test or measure. Some examples of questions could be "What supports are necessary to help Madison make adequate progress toward classroom expectations?," "Is Juan demonstrating disruptive behavior because of difficulties with learning the material?," or "Is Cassandra's placement in a special day class meeting her educational needs?"

The goal of theme-based based reports is to link results to themes that arise from the assessment (Rahill, 2014). Each identified theme is conveyed in one to two paragraphs within the report. The initial sentences of the paragraph should be child oriented, and not test oriented. Subsequent sentences then provide all of the evidence from the assessment that supports the identified theme. The written report can integrate the stories that highlight the results of the evaluation, as well as within a feedback session. For example, when integrating findings from interviews, observations, and testing, the school psychologist can share the following:

> Juan is experiencing frustration with attention and recalling details at school and at home. His family described that when they give him instructions to do something, they often have to repeat those instructions several times. For example, Juan's mother shared a story that when they were preparing dinner, she asked Juan to get the butter, milk, and eggs. Juan only remembered to get the butter, and she had to remind him twice to get the milk and eggs. His teachers and school psychologist also observed similarly in the classroom and during testing when asked to remember vocabulary and details of stories.

The report should also clearly outline practical recommendations based on the theme and questions from the beginning of the report. The goal of the recommendations is to relate the assessment findings to assist the child in becoming successful. These recommendations should include sections related to home, school/classroom, and community, and with the student. We believe it is important for each student to understand the results in a developmentally appropriate way, which may be done either at a one-on-one meeting with the practitioner or in conjunction with the family. Children are more willing to take ownership of their education once they have a fuller understanding of their strengths and identified areas of need (P. E. Chan et al., 2014).

SUMMARY

In this chapter, we described strategies for conducting culturally responsive assessment that fosters collaboration with families to develop goals and school-based supports for students. The Culturally Responsive Strengths-Based Assessment to Inform Intervention includes five steps: (1) relationship building and goal orientation, (2) assessment of sociocultural and ecological factors that fosters resilience, (3) collaborative development of intervention aligned toward goal, (4) implementing an intervention, and (5) evaluating strengths within intervention and areas to improve. The most comprehensive approach to assessing sociocultural and ecological factors is through a multi-method and multi-source approach. Specifically, practitioners can gather information from (1) reviewing psychological, educational, and medical records, (2) school and home observations, (3) interviews, and (4) tests and measures. Finally, we briefly provided suggestions for summarizing and synthesizing this information in a written report and sharing the results with the student and their caregivers. We continue to elaborate and discuss important issues related to standardized testing in Chapter 6.

DISCUSSION QUESTIONS

1. Reflecting on this chapter, what would be some aspects of a culturally responsive assessment in which you would feel the most comfortable? The least comfortable? What steps do you need to take to continue your professional development in that area?
2. We stated that "behavior is culture and culture is behavior." Think of a student with whom you have worked. How has the student's behavior reflected their culture? How has culture reflected their behavior?
3. Mr. Davidson is a monolingual school psychologist who currently has a referral for Carmen, a second grader who mostly speaks Spanish. Carmen is referred by her teacher because of concerns with reading. What steps can Mr. Davidson take to foster authentic relationships with Carmen's caregiver and begin to develop goals for the assessment? How can he use relational interviewing to gather information?

APPENDIX 4
RELATIONAL INTERVIEWING FOR CAREGIVER

1. Visiting
Welcome to space, offer food, coffee/tea (if appropriate)

Self-introduction and purpose of the assessment
I am grateful that you came here today. I recognize that we have not met be-fore this, and I thought it may be helpful to share a bit about myself. As [JOB], my role is to really understand your child's strengths and the concerns that you and the teachers may have, so that we can come together to support your child. I am [SELF-IDENTIFIERS: RACE, GENDER, ETC.], and my background may be different from yours, and I acknowledge that these differences may shape my perspectives. This is why I want to speak with you. Your perspectives and know-ledge are valued and important.

2. Relational Interviewing

Initial Strengths and Concerns

- Share with me a story about a child that makes you proud.
- Tell me about some of your worries about your child.
- When did you begin to worry? When did you notice the changes?
- Share with me some of the things you have done so far to support your child.

Sociocultural Factors

- There are many aspects of our identities that are meaningful to us. Share with me some of your identities.
- I am curious to learn about what aspects of your identity are important to you.
- Spirituality and religion can play an important role in many families' lives. Tell me about your family.
- You mentioned that you recently arrived in this community. Tell me the story about your journey here.
- There are lots of parents in our community who have recently immigrated to the United States. In what ways has this journey shaped your child's life?
- Tell me about the important adults in the child's life.

Developmental History

- Tell me a story about your child when they were really young. What were they like?

- When your child was a baby, did they have any trouble with
  - Motor Development: Crawling/Walking/Running?
  - Sleeping: Difficulties Falling Asleep, Night Waking, Apnea, Sleepwalking, Terror?
  - Feeding: Refusal to Eat, Compulsion to Eat, Picky Eating, Vomiting/Purging, Obesity?
  - Toileting: Bedwetting, Soiling, Smearing, Regression to Diapers, Constipation?
- Any concerns during the mother's pregnancy? During pregnancy, how many times did the mother smoke? Drink?
- Was your child born prematurely? If yes, by how many weeks? Was neonatal care needed?
- Language Skills
  - Expressive Language: Cooing/Babbling/Words/Phrases/Sentences
  - Receptive Language

Education History

- Did your child attend day care or preschool? If yes, at what ages? How often?
- What are the child's skills associated with
  - Reading: Phonological Awareness, Decoding, Fluency, Comprehension?
  - Mathematics: Calculation, Concepts, and Applications?
  - Writing: Handwriting, Grammar, Sentence Structure, Fluency, Essay Composition?

Medical and Psychological History

- Describe to me what you and your family have done to support your child's well-being or health.
- What serious medical issues has your child had? Has your child ever been hospitalized? Had any operations? Had any accidents?
- Tell me about any mental health concerns.
  - Internalizing Symptoms: Low Energy, Hopeless, Sad, Helpless
    - Self-Harm: Cuts, Hits, Kicks, Burns Self, Bangs Head, Risk Taking
    - Suicidal Ideation, Attempts
  - Externalizing Symptoms:
    - Attention Issues: Inattention, Distractible, Can't Concentrate
    - Activity Level: Overactive, Hyperactive, Out of Control, Inactive, Passive
    - Disruptive Behaviors/Tantrums
    - Friendship Issues/Bullying
    - Cruelty to Animals
    - Damaged Property

- o Trauma: Victim of Sexual/Physical/Emotional/Verbal Abuse, Accident, Injury
- o Sexual: Preoccupation, Intrusive Ideas, Exposing Self, Touching Others, Role Confusion
- Some parents are comfortable with counseling while other parents are not. Tell me about your thoughts on counseling for your child.
- Tell me about any medical problems in your family. Mental health problems in your family?

Additional Prompts Throughout:

- I would like to share a story about your child. May I share a story?
- I would like to hear a story about your child.
- Keep telling me, does this remind you of something you've experienced before, or is there something more to say about this?
- Is it possible to give me an image, or color, or scent, that could express what you're talking about?
- Parents often talk about. . . . Is this something that's familiar to you?

Literacy, Language, and Acculturation of Diverse Students

VIGNETTE

Josef is a seventh-grade male student who recently enrolled in a new school in southern Florida. He is receiving some academic support in spelling, vocabulary, fluency, and reading comprehension. His Language Arts teacher, Ms. Randall, expressed that Josef frequently becomes distracted and looks over and copies his peers' assignments and exams. Josef and his family relocated to Florida when he was in sixth grade. He has not had contact with his father. Due to immigration concerns, Josef's father was unable to enter the United States. Josef's mother indicated that her son becomes stressed when completing homework assignments. He is classified as an English Speaker of Other Languages (ESOL) at Level 2, indicating low-to-intermediate skills in English. His older sisters assist Josef with homework assignments because his mother is unable to due to not being able to speak English fluently. His mother noted that he was doing "OK" before moving to Florida in his previous school, although he seldom attended school to help his family work at their farm.

- *What stressors might Josef encounter or experience? How might they affect his learning and well-being?*
- *How would you communicate with the family?*
- *How would you determine the best way to support Josef in school?*

Every student who enters a new classroom brings their own educational and family history, language background, and life experiences. It can be very easy to overlook how important these cultural elements are when understanding a student's past, current, and future learning. Practitioners, however, often encounter difficulties in assessing and supporting the academic achievement of culturally and linguistically diverse (CLD) students. Limited knowledge on this topic, historical shortages of CLD professionals in schools, and the complex diversity within the

CLD population can make it difficult to address individual student needs consistently or adequately. Although bilingual practitioners and teachers may be able to communicate with students in a language other than English (e.g., Spanish), we argue that the issues discussed in this chapter are relevant for all school-based practitioners to acquire knowledge pertaining to acculturation, second-language acquisition, and literacy even for those who do not speak languages other than English. Of course, to deliver services or communicate with families in a different language requires both language fluency and culturally responsiveness.

Immigrant students and refugees like Josef are likely exposed to very different curricula, expectations, and viewpoints of learning. Students must continually adapt to succeed in school. They may encounter a number of stressors prior to or during integration in a new school environment; they must learn new sociocultural norms, often a new language, and new classroom expectations that are different from home and previous learning environments. When looking further into his situation, Josef has difficulties completing assignments at home and at school. His emerging English language skills, however, compounded by his complex family situation, would likely present as barriers to his success in his new classroom environment. Without understanding these details, it can be easy to think that Josef may have a learning disability or behavioral problem, unless one explores further his history and even use of his current knowledge.

As practitioners, understanding literacy development and culturally responsive assessment of literacy and language is critical in ensuring that schools are providing adequate supports for CLD students. "Culturally and linguistically diverse" is an education term to define students enrolled in education programs who are "English language learners" (ELLs) or dual language learners (DLL), students of color, and students living in poverty. For the purposes of this chapter, we use CLD to recognize that the needs of diverse students are broader than just learning English. The purpose of this chapter is to bring cultural factors to light when conducting assessment of academic learning and language of CLD students. First, we discuss enculturation, assimilation, and acculturation as factors to consider in assessment. Then, we discuss the reasons for achievement and opportunity gaps, curriculum and instructional considerations, and considerations for assessment of language and literacy. Importantly, practitioners should have a strong foundation of ecological assessment of knowledge, skills, and abilities because learning is often the result of the environment and systems in which the student functions.

ENCULTURATION AND ACCULTURATION

Teachers play a significant role in guiding students through the process of integrating into the school culture and environment. Yet, teachers' assumptions, biases, and culture can influence the student–teacher relationships and peer–student relationships. Teacher expectations can lead to over- and under-identification of language and literacy problems, which are complex issues for many CLD students due to the diversity of home and school experiences that affect learning outcomes

(Goodrich & Namkung, 2019). Thus, when considering culturally responsive approaches, practitioners must learn about enculturation and acculturation first, as this knowledge will help determine whether student outcomes are typical given adjustment to the new environment and not student deficits.

Enculturation

[Reflexivity Activity] Consider the following questions below and discuss them with a colleague or in a group of peers:

- *Is it better to be intelligent or attractive?*
- *Is it better to be independent or to be a team player?*
- *When parents get older, is it the children's responsibility to take care of them by living with them?*
- *Is it the teacher's fault if a student is not learning in school?*
- *Is it important to find a job that you love even if it does not pay well?*

In reflecting on answers to these questions, ask: Where did these views come from? How are they reinforced or perpetuated? Do you agree with your colleagues' responses, or does the post-activity discussion eventually change your response?

This exercise prompts understanding of how social norms are developed and reinforced in one's culture (e.g., home, school, neighborhood, etc.) through enculturation. *Enculturation* enables people to adopt behaviors, beliefs, and values that are deemed socially acceptable to become successful members of society (Kim, 2009). Many people born in the United States learn about their own culture, values, social norms, and etiquette through enculturation. Social norms sometimes influence major life decisions, such as how to treat students, what career path to pursue, how one should act in different settings, or what is desirable behavior. For example, prior to arriving in the United States, Josef learned various customs, ate specific foods, wore specific clothes, or engaged in religious practices aligned with his faith. Family, teachers, peers, and mentors influenced his social behavior, belief systems, and attitudes.

Additionally, enculturation provides individuals with a cultural lens through which they interpret the behaviors and interactions of others and recognize whether inconsistencies in our expectations are considered problematic (Kim, 2009). Practitioners, for example, have learned certain expectations for behavior. They have learned that social norms include expecting students to sit quietly in school, to do well in college, and/or to have a successful career. Yet, the school's (and the larger society's) expectations may not necessarily align with the expectations from the student's family or community. These issues also have an impact on student learning and success in schools, particularly when expectations or norms differ in the new school environment. For Josef, if he is not achieving or conforming to classroom expectations, then teachers would likely view his behaviors as problematic, regardless of his previous school experiences.

Reviewing one's own enculturation can be an eye-opening experience in how we teach, interact with, or impose our expectations on students. Individuals who are able to identify their own cultural lens, or way of viewing the world, are generally much better able to recognize how that lens colors or distorts their perceptions of other people and events. They often will address and judge students more carefully and responsibly. As an example, from the school's perspective, assumptions and responses to student concerns would lead Josef's teacher to form implicit biases and potentially damage the relationship with him. Ms. Randall may believe erroneously that Josef is cheating, is hyperactive, or has a learning or language disability. As Josef becomes more accustomed to his new academic and social environment, Ms. Randall should be mindful of assumptions and biases that may differ from Josef's experiences. Schools can utilize students' existing knowledge, skills, and strengths as a foundation to new learning so that their cultural backgrounds and identities are valued.

Assimilation and Acculturation

Immigrants and refugees often speak of experiences that require them to leave their heritage culture to fully absorb into the American way of life, a process known as *assimilation* (Knight et al., 2016). The United States has sometimes been described as a "melting-pot," a metaphor to describe society as the unity of diverse cultures; yet, dominant social norms and standards of the White, middle- and upper-class are pervasive, which leads to immigrant or refugee students and families to believe they need to "give up" their heritage culture (Gleason, 2019). Thus, some perceive that society may be better described as a "pressure-cooker," where CLD students and families feel the need—or pressure—to assimilate by learning to speak English and abide by social norms, philosophies, and practices of the host culture (Gleason, 2019).

On the other hand, many students or families experience *acculturation* by maintaining aspects of their heritage culture while adopting aspects of the dominant culture (Berry, 1992). For Josef, he may be accustomed to peer interaction or group learning in his previous school compared with independent seatwork at his current school. Acculturation involves successful navigation of the school environment, understanding new teacher expectations, a grading system, homework expectations, and socialization. Students do not have to be born in a different country to experience acculturation; how they adopt, adjust, and integrate both their past cultural experiences and new ones broadly characterizes acculturation.

Additionally, acculturation is a two-way process. It entails both a student's adaptation to a new culture as well as the process of the new school culture to accommodate and accept the student's cultural identity and assets (Kim, 2009; Pham et al., 2017). It focuses not only on the important role of the student's learning about the host culture, but also on the role of the school, classroom, or society in acknowledging and incorporating the student's heritage in instruction (Ward

Box 5.1.

CRITICAL REFLEXIVITY: EDUCATORS AND PRACTITIONERS' FUNDS
OF KNOWLEDGE

Economics	Currency used, financial resources
Agriculture	Gardening, farming
Technology	Use of technology during the day, Internet, cell phone
Geography	Travel, landmarks of heritage country, rurality
Religion	Organized religion, spirituality, connection to place
Family	Values, traditions, outings, relationships with family
Politics	News, current events, local or national government, tribal council
Language	Preferred language to speak, write, and read
Scientific Knowledge	Health, mechanics, physical sciences
Sports/Hobbies	Sports teams, individual or group activities

& Geereart, 2016). For many students, however, acculturation can be stressful if they perceive it as a unidirectional process, whereby the student spends more effort selecting and determining what aspects, if any, of the host culture to adopt. This process may lead some students to question their cultural or ethnic identity, or their knowledge, cultural beliefs, and values, if students experience conflict or dissonance with the host culture.

To lessen students' levels of stress related to acculturation, schools should draw upon the student and family's historical and cultural knowledge and experiences, also known as their "funds of knowledge" (Moll et al., 1992; Moll, 2019). Gonzalez and colleagues (2005) developed a taxonomy of 10 categories of funds of knowledge. These categories can be used to guide instruction, enhance student learning, and improve family engagement. Some categories include economics, agriculture, scientific knowledge, and family occupations (see Box 5.1). When teachers shed their role of expert, they can come to know their students and tailor their approaches to working with them. Otherwise, students may believe that all they have previously learned in their heritage culture was meaningless and futile.

[*Reflexivity Activity*] *With your colleagues or group of peers, complete the table in Appendix 5A regarding the funds of knowledge related to you and your family. Skip any categories that do not pertain to you or your family, and you may add a new category based on your culture. Within your small group, share the aspects of your funds of knowledge that you have completed. Consider the following questions:*

- *What similarities did you notice among the funds of knowledge shared in your small group? What differences did you notice?*
- *How might you gather the funds of knowledge of children and families in your classroom or program?*

Schools can directly ask and gather information questions about the students' and families' funds of knowledge (a sample interview is provided in Appendix 5B). Once this information is collected, educators or practitioners can identify which categories of funds of knowledge best apply to support the student's learning. Academic activities or instructional considerations can subsequently be developed and applied in classroom lessons and instruction. Using the vignette of Josef, here are some ways to consider his funds of knowledge:

> *Funds of Knowledge #1 (Economics):* Josef's family lived in Nicaragua, and the currency was different, with the *córdoba* rather than U.S. dollars.
> * *Instructional Strategy Consideration:* In math, students can learn to convert money of different currencies. The class can discuss why there are different values across countries.
> *Funds of Knowledge #2 (Agriculture):* Josef's family was active in gardening and would give vegetables to neighbors and friends.
> * *Instructional Strategy Consideration:* The class can read about and discuss types of fruits, vegetables, and plants that can grow in different climates.

MEASURES AND SCALE OF ACCULTURATION

Because acculturation is a complex and multidimensional construct, it can be difficult to assess in students. Acculturation scales are often constructed for specific populations (e.g., Mexican Americans; see Kim & Abreu, 2001). Schools seldom use these scales but may gather similar information using home language surveys from caregivers regarding the student's proficiency in their heritage and host language and number of years residing in the United States.

Nonetheless, assessing acculturation can be useful within a broader culturally responsive assessment of language and literacy for CLD students. There are few published measures of acculturation that are used in schools, especially as a self-report for adolescents, but items in Table 5.1 can help assess concrete behaviors and preferences related to cultural identification. Kim and Abreu (2001) suggested including four dimensions for assessing acculturation and enculturation: (1) behavior (e.g., participation in cultural activities, English language use, food choice),

Table 5.1. SAMPLE ITEMS RELATED TO ACCULTURATION SELF-REPORT FOR ADOLESCENTS

Host	Heritage
Culture Identity	**Culture Identity**
I like to participate in (host culture) celebrations.	I like to participate in (heritage culture) celebrations.
I like to have (host culture) friends.	I like to have (heritage culture) friends.
I spend a lot of time with (host culture) friends.	I spend a lot of time with (heritage culture) friends.
I prefer speaking (host language).	I prefer speaking (heritage language).

(2) values (e.g., attitudes and beliefs about social relations, familism, gender roles, independence/collectivism), (3) knowledge (e.g., culturally specific information such as names of historical leaders), and (4) cultural identity (e.g., attitudes toward one's cultural identification). These dimensions can be assessed using interviews with caregivers and the student themselves.

Students like Josef, and other young children, however, might not comprehend concepts such as values and customs of their heritage culture, because their cultural or ethnic identity may be developing. Their acculturation status might be defined more by their behaviors and preferences, such as their choice of friends, music, or food, than by their attitudes and philosophies. For example, if Josef demonstrates preference of his Nicaraguan culture, then the school should continue fostering his heritage and identity, as research shows that their cultural identification serves as a protective factor for CLD students (Shin et al., 2007). Ultimately, students integrate and value both cultures; more specifically, they selectively retain aspects of their heritage culture and selectively adopt aspects of the host culture.

Overall, culturally responsive assessment of enculturation and acculturation can be helpful in supporting CLD students. It is an approach to discovering any challenges that the student is experiencing due to acculturative stress, previous schooling experiences, or situational circumstances that make it difficult for them to achieve optimal outcomes.

EDUCATIONAL DISPARITIES: REASONS FOR THE ACHIEVEMENT AND OPPORTUNITY GAPS

There are persistent educational disparities between CLD and White students that are reflected in standardized test scores, gifted education proportions, office discipline referrals, and school dropout rates. According to the Grade 4 NAEP Reading Assessment (National Center for Educational Statistics, 2019), 23% of White students performed below basic level compared with 52% of Black students, 50% of American Indian/Alaska Native students, and 45% of Hispanic students. In contrast, 19% of Asian/Pacific Islander students performed below basic level. Although overall school dropout rates have decreased in 2010 to 2019, Hispanic and Black students had higher dropout rates than White students. Closing these gaps was one of the major goals of the No Child Left Behind (NCLB) legislation in 2001, which required schools to report achievement data disaggregated by race and ethnicity (Paige & Witty, 2010).

These gaps are due to systemic issues in schools that include structural racism (Crutchfield et al., 2020). Due to what are better described as *opportunity gaps*, many CLD students are likely to fall behind in reading due to (1) inequitable opportunities stemming from socioeconomic or ecological risk factors, (2) pedagogical or curricular practices that do not center or value students' culture and identities, and (3) biased testing and assessment practices.

First, socioeconomic risk factors pertain to poverty and limited access to economic and educational resources. Studies have found that economic segregation and poverty predict gaps in academic achievement between White and Black or Hispanic students (Reardon et al., 2015). Moreover, racial segregation and economic inequality are often intertwined, as families of CLD students often reside in high-poverty neighborhoods and attend less-resourced schools, where access to high-quality teachers and educational programs may be limited (Fall & Billingsley, 2010). Also, higher percentages of Latinx and Black students dropped out of school compared with White students (De Brey et al., 2021).

A second reason for the opportunity gap is that pedagogical or curricular practices do not center or value students' culture and identities. States develop curricular frameworks, guidelines, and blueprints to ensure accountability of what is taught in public schools. Educators use these standards to plan and deliver the core curriculum to all students; however, instruction and curricula can introduce bias, stereotypes, and generalizations that would become barriers to inclusion. For example, in a history class, White inventors, explorers, authors, and other prominent historical figures tend to be the most visible, yet limited time is devoted to Asian or Black explorers, who thus would be considered "invisible" from history. Another example is the use of specific terms, such words as "forefathers," "mankind," and "grantsmanship," which deny the contributions of females. Curricula may present one side or interpretation of an issue and may omit different perspectives.

Finally, a third reason for the opportunity gap is the potential for bias in testing and assessment practices. Classroom tests, such as teacher-designed tests or exams that include cultural bias of content area knowledge, may potentially lead to inappropriate interpretation of results. For example, a teacher decides to administer a classroom exam that includes concepts related to standard U.S. measurement (e.g., miles, feet, inches), yet some students may have specific cultural or background knowledge of the metric system (e.g., meters, grams). This exam would disproportionately affect students who are recent immigrants and may not accurately assess their current knowledge of measurement. Indeed, this exam not only inaccurately assesses their knowledge but also may perpetuate student's feelings of inadequacy in the classroom. Thus, if the educator is trying to determine student's knowledge of U.S. measurement, then it may be more beneficial to determine prior knowledge of these concepts before evaluating them on mainstream concepts.

When evaluating student knowledge, practitioners should also take into account the cultural validity of a test or assessment. *Cultural validity* refers to the effectiveness with which the test or assessment addresses the sociocultural factors that influence student's prior and current learning and the ways in which students make sense of test items and respond to them (Trumbull & Nelson-Barber, 2019). Determining the test's cultural validity can be especially difficult, as culture is a complex and dynamic construct with multiple interpretations. Test items, questions, tasks, activities, prompts, and instructions should be carefully evaluated for wording and clarity. Tests used in various academic domains (e.g., math, sciences) should also consider how students rely on their funds of knowledge and experience that match content, instruction, and observations (Moll, 2019).

For example, schools should consider the student's prior educational experiences, communication patterns, teaching and learning processes, and language proficiency inherent in the students' cultural and language backgrounds, along with the format and modality of test administration and delivery of student responses (Trumbull & Nelson-Barber, 2019). Table 5.2 provides an outline of a sample questions that can be used to encourage cultural validity of classroom tests.

Table 5.2. SAMPLE QUESTIONS FOR PROMOTING CULTURAL VALIDITY
OF CONTENT IN CLASSROOM TESTS

Activity	Sample Questions/Issues
Identify the content of the test.	• What is the purpose of the testing? • Is it a formative assessment or summative assessment? • Does the content from the test match what is taught? • Does the content from the test relate to any prior knowledge or experiences of the student?
Review language used in the test.	• What language(s) is used during instruction? At home? • What language(s) is the student is most proficient in (e.g., reading, writing, speaking, listening)? • Do the instructions and test items avoid any complex grammar or unfamiliar vocabulary that is not relevant to the content?
Determine testing format.	• What format of testing (e.g., forced-choice, essay, true-false) is most appropriate for determining whether the child demonstrates knowledge of the content? • What modality is used to understand the test instructions (e.g., reading, listening, observing) and for the student to respond in (e.g., speaking, writing, performing)? • Does the child type out the responses or handwrite freely? • Would a group/collaborative project or performance-based assessment be more appropriate? • What are the advantages and disadvantages for these modalities?
Determine test arrangement.	• Is the test administered on a particular day/time? • Is it administered individually, in small groups, or in classroom? • Is the test timed? • What accommodations, if any, can be provided?
Determine ways to observe qualitative indicators of performance.	• How did the student approach the test? • Did the student demonstrate effort to complete it? • Did the student employ strategies to answer? • Did the student plan, check, or review responses before completing the test?
Set guidelines for evaluating or scoring responses.	• How is the child's response evaluated? • How is a response given in a different language evaluated? • Would there be any interrater reliability for evaluating performance? • What are alternative explanations if a student responds incorrectly?

(continued)

Table 5.2. CONTINUED

Activity	Sample Questions/Issues
Determine use of testing information.	• How are scores or evaluation used in decision-making (e.g., grades, placement, graduation)? • What other information is needed to make these decisions? • How are the results of the testing communicated to the student? What feedback is given to the student/caregiver? • When compared with other peers, what potential reasons or biases may explain differences in performance?

NOTE: Adapted from "The ongoing quest for culturally-responsive assessment for Indigenous students in the US," by E. Trumbull & S. Nelson-Barber, 2019, in *Frontiers in Education,* 4(40) (https://doi.org/10.3389/feduc.2019.00040).

Importantly, assessment processes can either reinforce a sense of belonging or add to students' belief that they do not belong because their prior learning or experiences are inconsequential. Learning is frequently intertwined with culture; thus, student difficulties adapting to a new environment are often due to differences in cultural expectations. For example, if parents do not reinforce speaking English at home, do we place fault with the family when students receive ESL support? When possible, schools should encourage developing the heritage language while promoting English language support, so heritage language, culture, and experiences are assets on which to build when they enroll in school (Han, 2012). Thus, the goals of these assessments are not only to inform instructional planning, but also to acknowledge and minimize gaps between previous and current expectations, while finding ways to incorporate and value the student's cultural experiences into the classroom.

STRATEGIES FOR CULTURALLY RESPONSIVE ASSESSMENT OF LANGUAGE AND LITERACY

Using elements of the Culturally Responsive Strengths-Based Assessment Model introduced in Chapter 4, we highlight specific approaches to assessing and monitoring progress of language and literacy. In many schools, students are identified through universal screening and receive data-driven interventions designed to address enhance strengths and mitigate difficulties through Multi-Tiered Systems of Support (MTSS; Hoover & Soltero-Gonzalez, 2018). Although standardized tests are likely to be used, we recommend using universal screening, progress monitoring, and ecological approaches that consider student context and provide multiple opportunities for students. Further, culturally responsive assessment for language and literacy should include informal and formal methods using a number of different sources. Information should be gathered about the student's knowledge, strengths, and challenges, while considering the role of culture, language, acculturation, curriculum, and prior schooling experiences in their current academic environment. In this section, we outline a series of assessment methods for practitioners to use for culturally responsive assessment of literacy and language: (1) direct observations of students, (2) self-monitoring checklists, (3) curriculum-based assessments, (4) curriculum-based measurements, and (5) performance-based assessments for understanding students' language and literacy. Assessment approaches can more accurately capture students' skills and achievement within the context of everyday natural activities and link students' needs with appropriate placement or support.

Direct Observations of the Student

Before any direct testing of student skills, conducting an observation of the student is a very useful method for recording and monitoring achievement, language, and performance across multiple settings. Observations provide the practitioner with useful information on how students learn in the classroom context, as well as information about how they can demonstrate and/or generalize skills over time compared with other peers. Additional advantages include documenting data such as (1) classroom expectations, (2) student learning strategies and skills, (3) goals during response to instruction, and (4) changes in student learning. Observations can be used as a formative assessment (i.e., progress monitoring), which can yield useful information in multiple contexts within a natural setting regarding a student's academic strengths and difficulties, and a student's expression and understanding of language and content areas. Such observations enable teachers to provide students with support to build their confidence in language and literacy skills while fostering student engagement.

When conducting classroom observations, structured observation checklists are commonly used to document student's learning and behaviors and compare across children or settings. Checklists are especially helpful when educators observe students in action, working collaboratively, or exhibiting unpredicted or spontaneous evidence of skills. Appendix 5C provides an example of an observation form on guided reading that emphasizes the learning of reading strategies. Documentation of the conditions in which a behavior occurs, as well as those in which it does not, can be instructive in the design of future learning environments, activities, and interventions.

Self-Monitoring Checklist

In addition to classroom observations, educators and practitioners should provide explicit instruction regarding strategies for students to engage in self-monitoring and *self-regulation*, or the ability to monitor, assess, and manage one's learning and behavior through setting goals (Kim & Linan-Thompson, 2013). Many of us can

Table 5.3. SELF-MONITORING CHECKLIST

Goal (Day #): How many words can I learn today?	Words Mastered: Highlight the words I know.	Evaluation: How many words do I know?
1	technology	1
2	maximum	2
3	moral	3
4	sequence	4
5	durable	5
6	observe	6
7	channel	7
8	irritate	8

NOTE: The student selects the goal under "Goal (Day #)." After the lesson, the educator revisits the checklist and asks the student, "Do you understand the word? Highlight the words you understand." The student highlights the word(s) in the "Words Mastered" column. The student circles the number of words in the "Evaluation" column.

provide examples of students engaging in negative behaviors by watching or mimicking others, but this tendency to learn by observation can also be drawn on positively during classroom instruction. This is particularly potent for CLD students who are going through periods of acculturation, but who may learn better initially through observation of peers and educators.

In Table 5.3, an example checklist is provided for understanding definitions of target words during a vocabulary review. In the beginning of lesson, a student can establish a learning goal with the educator: "Today we will learn eight words. . . ." The student can select the goal under "Goal (Day #)." The educator can encourage the student to set a higher goal if it is reasonable to attain. After the lesson, the educator revisits the checklist and asks the student, "Do you understand the word? Highlight the words you understand." When the student understands the question and directions, the student can highlight the word(s) in the "Words Mastered" column from the checklist. Once complete, the student can count the number of highlighted words and circle the number in the "Evaluation" column. The student can complete this activity daily or weekly to monitor the number of words learned over time.

Curriculum-Based Assessment

Curriculum-based assessment (CBA) is a type of assessment that directly evaluates student performance in learning content to address students' learning needs (Gravois & Gickling, 2008). Many classroom assessments can be described *as curriculum based,* where content is determined by curriculum standards. As stated previously, curricula and instructional delivery should be carefully reviewed to ensure that they are sensitive to the student's culture, language, and prior learning history (Notari-Syverson et al., 2003).

First, books and other literature that address race, ethnicity, class, and/or disability should be embedded within the content and assessment. Second, when conducting a CBA, the practitioner can observe student behaviors and teach various strategies to the student during the assessment. When assessing reading decoding or blending skills, for example, a practitioner can use a book chapter to observe the student's current reading skills directly; however, if there are gaps in student learning, strategies can be implemented such as breaking up the words into syllables. Third, since various information can be gathered through reading CBA (e.g., fluency, comprehension), interrater agreement between evaluators can be used to establish reliability of the assessment. Lastly, data collected from the CBA does not lead to any particular reading score but provides the practitioner with both qualitative (student's use of reading strategies) and quantitative (e.g., accuracy rate, words read correctly per minute) data, while determining which explicit teaching and learning strategies were most useful for the student. Information gathered from the CBA reflects directly on what is being taught in the classroom and can be useful for making instructional decisions.

Reading CBAs are common ways to assess multiple reading skills. They can also be used to assess expressive language skills, listening comprehension, and metacognitive awareness (Martines & Rodriquez-Srednicki, 2007). A sample reading CBA is provided in Appendix 5D, which assesses a student's (a) listening comprehension, (b) word recognition and decoding skills, (c) oral reading fluency, and (d) comprehension, while making any content adjustments based on student skill level. To assess listening comprehension, the practitioner reads a passage aloud for the student to listen to. The practitioner asks a series of unaided questions prepared in advance for the student to respond initially without assistance (e.g., "Tell me about the story"). If the student responds accurately, the practitioner asks additional unaided questions. Questions can be translated to allow ELLs to respond in their heritage or preferred language. If the student does not respond accurately, then the practitioner asks aided questions prepared in advance to assist the student in conveying understanding. Aided questions (e.g., "What is the name of the main character?") require the student to provide a more targeted answer without the need to elaborate. If the student continues to struggle or answer incorrectly, the practitioner can assist by providing multiple choice questions, which allow the student to select the answer from several options (e.g., "Is the character's name Carlos, Lindsay, or Antoine?"). The last option, visual questions, allows the student to look back to the text for the answer. Unlike norm-referenced achievement tests where questions often increase in difficulty, this method enables the student to engage with the text at their instructional level, while providing strategies to assist the student in developing language concepts, using receptive and expressive language, and activating prior knowledge.

When assessing the student's word recognition and decoding skills, the practitioner conducts a *word search* by pointing to various words throughout the text in isolation and asking the student to identify the word. The selection should be not in any particular order but can be chosen as a mixture of easy and more challenging words. The purpose of the word search is to determine the student's readiness to read the passage. If the student struggles to recognize or decode majority of words, then content adjustments or word-reading strategies can be modeled to ensure that the student is proficient enough in reading the passage. However, if the student continues to struggle even after these adaptations, then an easier book (or a book selected by the child in advance) can be used for the word search, and the process can continue with similar directions. Practitioners can make note of errors, but not penalize, if students mispronounce words due to dialect, articulation delays or impairments, or accents from speaking a first language other than English. Penalizing will likely develop negative perceptions of students and low expectations for their achievement.

To assess the student's independent reading, the student then reads aloud the same passage by themselves. The practitioner observes and records the student's reading fluency (e.g., words read correctly per minute) and comprehension skills. If a student struggles with the passage, the practitioner can introduce reading strategies and allows the student to reread the passage again to determine improvement. Similar to the word search, practitioners should not penalize or correct the student mispronunciations due to dialect, articulation, or accents. Reading comprehension is assessed from the student's retell, similar to the listening comprehension task with the preplanned questions, and the student responds to each question with or without assistance. The practitioner can model reading comprehension strategies to the student to learn and to develop reading motivation. Overall, curriculum-based assessments are helpful and provide a wealth of information for understanding the student's language and literacy while being mindful of any cultural and linguistic differences.

Curriculum-Based Measurement

Although CBAs can be useful for gathering information on student's learning at one point in time, regular monitoring of student progress is necessary to determine whether reading goals are achieved. Curriculum-based measurement (CBM) is a tool within CBA that is most useful for universal screening, monitoring academic progress, and evaluating effectiveness of instruction or intervention (Deno, 2003). CBMs specifically assess a student's speed and accuracy of skills across academic domains (e.g., reading, math, and writing). While a CBA is a broad assessment based on curriculum, a CBM is a brief probe that can be used as a formative assessment. Thus, these probes can be given more frequently to provide continuous feedback.

Reading-Curriculum Based Measurement, or Reading CBM, is often used in schools to screen for reading difficulties (e.g., Deno, 2003) and has been established as a valid measure of reading for ELLs and bilingual students (Gersten et al., 2007; Kim et al., 2016). Reading CBMs have been proved useful in examining student performance from an intercultural perspective, such as oral reading for

Hebrew students (Kamintz-Berkooza & Shapiro, 2005) and Spanish speakers who are learning multiple languages (Ramirez & Shapiro, 2007). Additionally, reading CBMs are valid measures when predicting reading outcomes for Black and White students (Hintz et al., 2002). Findings from these studies are important given little attention in research regarding a cultural perspective in validating the effectiveness of CBMs with CLD students. Reading CBMs can also be used to determine when students have developed sufficient language skills to support the transition to English instruction, and to monitor the progress of CLD students on reintegration into general education instruction.

Several examples of reading CBMs include Dynamic Indicators of Basic Early Literacy Skills ([DIBELS]; Good & Kaminski, 2002), now known as Acadience Reading, as well as AIMSweb (Pearson, 2010) and EasyCBM (Alonzo et al., 2006). Because CBMs provide consistent feedback on student progress, these measures may be helpful in determining whether instructional accommodations for CLD students are effective. Research has shown that teachers who reflect on and self-monitor their use of CBMs tend to modify their instruction more than those who do not self-monitor or do not use CBMs (Allinder et al., 2000; Förster & Souvignier, 2015). In other words, teachers who use CBM were more likely to attend to students' learning needs by adapting instruction, leading to greater gains in students' reading achievement.

Performance-Based Assessment

Another method for assessing student knowledge is developing a *performance-based assessment* (sometimes called alternative assessments), which center students' learning and experiences on authentic projects. Some examples of performance-based assessments in literacy or language arts include responding to an open-ended response question, developing an analysis in an essay, journaling, creating a portfolio of student work, and completing self-assessments. Performance-based assessments can provide a critical space for students to reflect on and share their experiences and identities as learners, similar to a self-assessment. Teachers can engage students by providing them opportunities to demonstrate their knowledge and skills in various modalities (e.g., orally or written), while also sharing more in-depth information on students' academic needs.

For ELLs, performance-based reading assessments are a better alternative to traditional standardized reading tests, while also improving student engagement (Darling-Hammond et al., 2019; Lenski et al., 2006). In performance-based assessments, students' actual performance, rather than their expressive language, may more clearly convey the knowledge being assessed. For example, students not only hear the instruction to the task but also see it in a demonstration. Therefore, these tasks should employ multisensory modalities, so that language is not the only way to present the performance-based assessment or obtain student responses. These open-ended assessments improve the chances for students to engage with language production and learning, offering unique opportunities for students to express their knowledge in a broader sense than in the limited linguistic opportunities given to them in traditional standardized, multiple-choice tests.

Using the vignette with Josef, Ms. Randall decided to implement a performance-based reading and writing assessment for Josef and the entire seventh-grade class. She selects a fiction text the class has not read, a story with a significant theme, a clear problem and resolution, well-developed characters, and high interest. Ms. Randall then creates a few writing prompts that encourage students to contemplate the story in their own way (e.g., connecting to prior knowledge and experiences). Ms. Randall provides the class with story maps, a type of graphic organizer, that allow the students to plan their ideas and provide enough time to complete the performance-based assessment. Students complete the story map by outlining essential parts of the story and then retell the story in concise paragraphs or an essay. To assess the quality of the product, Ms. Randall created a rubric that provides information on the students' performance level (rating of 0 to 3) and brief descriptions for all score levels. As seen in the Appendix 5E, to receive full credit of 3, a student's response must be complete, indicating good understanding of the story and its problem, and providing accurate and relevant examples, details, and supportive reasoning.

UNIQUE NEEDS OF ENGLISH LANGUAGE LEARNERS

Immigrant students in U.S. schools may be in a family that speaks a language other than the majority language (Hussar et al., 2020) and may have unique needs compared with monolingual students, depending on fluency of the host language (Lenski et al., 2006). Cross-sectional studies have shown that ELLs may encounter academic difficulties across age levels (e.g., National Center for Education Statistics, 2019), in addition to encountering socioeconomic risk factors and challenges as a result of the immigration process.

Although not all ELLs demonstrate learning problems, evidence suggests that there has been a 30-point reading gap between ELLs and non-ELLs since 2002 (National Center for Education Statistics, 2019). This disproportionate representation of ELLs is likely due to schools not having a consistent or accurate identification system across states, where policies have been designed for monolingual student populations. For example, ELLs have been traditionally defined as *at-risk* if they perform below specific cutoff scores (e.g., performance at or below the 16th–25th percentiles) on standardized reading or math tests (e.g., Brandenburg et al., 2017; Geary et al., 2012). Further, while some studies have found that ELLs are overrepresented in special education (e.g., Artiles et al., 2005), others have found that ELLs are less likely to receive special education services (e.g., Morgan et al., 2018). Specifically, under-identification tends to occur when ELLs are in the lower grades, and over-identification is more likely to occur in upper-level grades (e.g., Artiles et al., 2005).

Further, an overwhelming majority of assessment tools are in English only, presenting a potential threat to the utility of assessments that may prevent ELLs from understanding test instructions or items. Despite these challenges, these students represent important assets in a multilingual society; attaining fluency in more than one language increases access to a generally higher-paying job opportunity. These opportunities can go unrealized when schools lack knowledge to respond to unique student needs.

Studies have shown that preservice teachers who are bilingual are more likely to adopt an asset-based perspective of ELLs' linguistic diversity (Carley Rizzuto, 2017), while monolingual educators tend to perceive ELLs' heritage languages as obstacles (Svalberg, 2016). Due to systems prioritizing English as at the standard in U.S. schools, teachers may perceive student difficulties in academic performance as due to language delays. Often many teachers faced with this situation turn to English support or special education services because they may be unsure of how to adapt their curriculum to address ELLs' cultural and linguistic skills.

Dual Language Development as Fluid, Dynamic, and Flexible

Learning languages is a dynamic process that does not follow a predictable sequence, which makes assessment of typical second-language acquisition difficult (Claussenius-Kalman et al., 2021). More specifically, some researchers have described bilingualism as a construct that occurs on a spectrum rather than as a unitary or categorical variable. Because of the diversity of ELLs in schools, several types exist: (1) newly arrived students who have adequate formal schooling, (2) newly arrived students with limited formal schooling, (3) students exposed to two languages simultaneously (e.g., at birth), and (4) long-term dual language learners (Freeman & Freeman, 2003; Lenski et al., 2006). Students with formal schooling tend to demonstrate good progress in ESL programs and often are integrated into classrooms after a few years. Students with limited formal schooling, on the other hand, may encounter more challenges in learning a second language, and learning academic knowledge and skills in school. Students who learned two languages simultaneously may have varying academic outcomes but are more likely to have acquired listening comprehension in their heritage language first and not to have learned to read or write in that language. Long-term dual language learners may require ongoing language and literacy support to succeed in school. As they experience acculturation, ELLs go through *academic socialization*, learning about academic expectations, behaviors, and attitudes from parents, which can affect students' language development and their cultural identities (Cho, 2016; García-Sánchez, 2010). An ELL can be perceived as high achieving in one language context but not in another, due to differing expectations home, school, and community environments (Souto-Manning, 2016).

There is growing consensus that learning more than one language from an early age affects brain plasticity (Mechelli et al., 2004), which refers to the brain's ability to reorganize and create new connections as a result of experience. Contrary to what many believe, language learning in early ages does not lead to confusion, language delays, or disorders (Hoff & Core, 2015). Although described as "mixing" of languages, dual language learning should be viewed more holistically (i.e., not as separate languages), whereby teachers and practitioners can build on students' *translanguaging* practices to enrich and nurture learning (García & Wei, 2014). Translanguaging can allow ELLs to draw on all their linguistic resources, their full repertoire, to learn academic content in a new language in multilingual classrooms. The following are steps that multilingual or ESL classrooms can use to encourage students to use their heritage language as a scaffold when learning academic content in the new language.

1. *Preview the topic/text in the heritage language (L1).* Bilingual teachers facilitate a reading activity (e.g., share book reading; Pontier & Gort, 2016) by brainstorming, making connections, and sharing prior knowledge on the topic/text in their heritage language. Students can complete graphic organizers and organize their writing in L1.
2. *View the topic/text in the new language (L2) while making connections to the heritage language preview (L1).* Students are presented with the topic/text in the new language. Bilingual teachers can present content by a reading passage, charts/tables, or video or audio clips individually, with peers, or with the entire class. The teachers can make connections between what students previewed in their heritage language and new content they are learning in the new language.
3. *Review the topic/text in the heritage language (L1) and go back to the new language (L2).* Students can then actively discuss, analyze, or summarize the text/topic back in the heritage language. With support, they can then restate the summary back to the bilingual teacher or class using all their language resources, including the new language.

When providing instruction using translanguaging, bilingual teachers leverage their expertise by introducing new words, checking for understanding, modeling, providing feedback, and drawing on their students' bilingualism and strengths by requesting or confirming translation. Teachers thus can engage students as emerging experts to foster sociocultural integration during these classroom practices (Pontier & Gort, 2016).

Balanced-bilinguals is a term frequently used in research to describe students with similar fluency in two languages; however, the majority of students rarely achieve this (Grosjean, 2008), as they typically have a dominant or preferred language. Many bilingual and ELL students are likely to develop cognitive and linguistic strengths, such as *code-switching*, which refers to alternating elements of two languages when speaking or writing within a phrase or sentence. For example, "I'll begin a sentence in English y termino en español [and finish it in Spanish]."

Code-switching often indicates a high level of metalinguistic awareness (Gort, 2012), where students are likely to follow grammatical rules when integrating more than one language. However, this skill is often not captured in many standardized or norm-referenced achievement tests. Some researchers propose that assessments of a bilingual or ELL student's language skills should not be compared with the same trajectory or norms used for monolinguals, which historically has been a mainstream standard (Altman et al., 2021; Hoff, 2013).

Issues Related to Assessment of ELLs

Dual language development often does not follow a consistent trajectory, which makes it challenging to determine typical language development when assessing ELLs, as English proficiency can change over time, is domain specific (e.g., reading, writing, listening, and speaking), and is contextual (e.g., home, school) (Rojas & Iglesias, 2013). If a student is not exposed to a particular language in multiple settings, the student would be less fluent and more restricted than if they hear and use another language in multiple environments. Like, Josef, some ELLs may only speak one language at home and have limited exposure to another prior to preschool or kindergarten. Others may be exposed to both languages by one caregiver and a second language (e.g., English) by a second caregiver, although the student may prefer responding in the heritage language.

These complexities and variable trajectories in language development make it difficult for practitioners to distinguish language delays or differences, particularly when using standardized tests that have been traditionally normed for monolingual students. When standardized achievement tests are administered in English only, ELLs may score substantially below their peers due to their (1) limited English proficiency or (2) differences in cultural knowledge rather than a deficit in the construct being assessed (Artiles et al., 2005). However, tests that assess students' English language proficiency should be conducted to determine proficiency in English as L2 before administering any other tests. For example, the majority of U.S. states are part of the WIDA Consortium (2020; formerly World-Class Instructional Design and Assessment), which develops and implements proficiency standards and assessments (e.g., ACCESS) for ELLs in Pre-K through 12 grades.

Bilingual practitioners should assess the student's language proficiency in both the L1 and L2, while taking into consideration the academic, social, family, and schooling histories. Some experts reported that students should be assessed using the language of instruction (often L2) for the skill being assessed (Kieffer et al., 2009), while others recommended using the language for which the student scores higher in *cognitive-academic language proficiency* (CALP; Cummins, 1979). Because CALP is a complex skill required for academic learning, low performance on CALP may be due to lack of formal instructional support or opportunity to develop academic skills, or inconsistent learning experiences in the previous school, rather than a disability. Additionally, a student's difficulty in acquiring a second language (L2) can also be attributed to insufficient development of (L1).

Traditional approaches to assessing ELLs' language skills have primarily focused on evaluating the two language systems separately and then comparing the results (Hopewell & Escamilla, 2014). Because ELLs rarely achieve the same level of proficiency in all the languages in their repertoire, it is common to find lower performance in one language compared with the other when using standardized bilingual tests (Grosjean, 2008). Barrueco et al. (2012) reported that most English assessment tools have been carefully developed and validated, but they found that there was limited information about the development and validity of the forms in other languages (e.g., Spanish). For example, many Spanish versions are often translated from English tests, with varying levels of attention given to ensure comparability of the conceptual, linguistic, or semantic content, and/ or level of difficulty of the translated items across languages. Therefore, validity may not be the same for the Spanish as for the English version of the same test. Additionally, translating an existing English language test to the child's heritage language may not eliminate test bias (Abedi et al., 2004). Caution should be taken when comparing ELLs' performance using norms from monolingual English populations. To ensure that culturally responsive assessments demonstrate cultural validity, it is important to assess the child's language repertoire holistically and not separately.

CULTURALLY RESPONSIVE LANGUAGE ASSESSMENT OF ENGLISH LANGUAGE LEARNERS

A proposed framework for assessing ELLs should entail a dynamic and ecological systems perspective. Schools should not rely only on standardized test scores but involve other informal assessments (as indicated for literacy) to obtain the overall picture of the students' abilities. Guzman-Orth et al. (2017) proposed a framework that emphasized a holistic assessment of language knowledge, skills, or abilities in lieu of separate distinct language pathways. As stated earlier, ELLs develop proficiency in multiple languages by learning how to negotiate the relationships between them. Thus, schools should consider how to conduct a culturally responsive assessment of ELLs by: (a) relationship building and goal orientation with caregivers, (b) examining curriculum and instructional practices, (c) using multiple informal and formal assessments, (d) engaging students in the assessment process, and (e) carefully interpreting of results from all assessment data.

Relationship Building and Goal Orientation with Caregivers

Partnering and building relationships with caregivers are an essential component of culturally responsive assessment of ELLs. Through this partnership, caregivers can work alongside school teams, including educators, speech-language pathologists, school psychologists, reading specialists, and other practitioners to determine the goals of the assessment. School teams collaborate with caregivers to gather information regarding acculturation, which includes language history, development, skills, and previous schooling experiences. Translators may be brought in if school team members do not speak in the parents' heritage language. Information gathered through this meeting may serve as a starting point for analyzing the ecological context and history of the student's literacy and language development. Some information may include:

1. Demographic characteristics (e.g., where student was born, where student has lived, length of time in the United States, where the parents or extended family are from)
2. Language experiences (e.g., language[s] the student has been exposed to, how the child uses the language[s], the language[s] of the adults and other children in the household, use of language outside of home or school)
3. Literacy experiences (e.g., types of reading activities practiced at home, reading activities practiced at school)
4. Formal and informal educational experiences (e.g., preschool experiences, peer interactions, technology, and media)

Culturally responsive assessments require that classroom and test materials (e.g., texts, illustrations, contexts, topics) acknowledge diversity across cultures, gender, ethnicity, and race. They also should not require that students have prior knowledge of American culture or familiarity with U.S. school contexts (Padilla, 2001). When gathering this information, practitioners should exercise caution, as these behaviors often represent a Eurocentric, mainstream approach to literacy and language activities and may not be entirely reflective of the activities at home.

Examining Curricula and Instructional Practices

In classrooms and social settings, practitioners should review content, activities, and curricula that are relevant to the students, while also encouraging classrooms to use translanguaging, when possible, as ways to be inclusive. These practices include providing opportunities for students to demonstrate their knowledge by taking into account all the languages to which they have been exposed and have learned. Classroom language tasks or tests can be examined using a self-assessment questionnaire (Appendix 5F). The following suggestions are examples of using the curriculum to assess ELLs:

1. *Create an inclusive and safe space for ELLs to interact not only with the content, but also with peers and teachers, in either home or school language:*
   • When conducting a CBA, select a book chapter or reading topic with a clear title and allow the student to share prior knowledge and make connections in his heritage language.
   • Allow the student to preview the reading passage and have the student continue to share knowledge on the topic/text in their heritage language and English.
   • Allow educators and peers to read aloud the directions or passage first so the student can listen to how the chapter can be read accurately. Modeling these behaviors can help improve language development.

- When the student reads the passage orally, provide assistance as needed (e.g., at the word, phrase, or sentence level). Reward for effort and accurate reading.
- When assessing reading comprehension, allow the student to use their heritage language and English when responding to questions related to the passage. Reward for effort and accurate responses in either language.
- Allow the student to ask questions and to refer back to the passage if they do not know the answer. Reward for effort and accurate responses in both languages.

2. *Provide opportunities for ELLs to demonstrate knowledge and skills in content by drawing on all languages the student knows.*
   - Allow the student to use their heritage language (when possible) or English for oral and written responses. Code-switching should be allowed.
   - Allow the student to apply learned skills and knowledge from the classroom in common social and daily situations (e.g., interpreting tables/charts).
   - Allow the student to use written language, oral language, nonverbal language, and visual representations to help them understand content and communicate information.
   - Use the observation form to keep a record of language skills and development.
   - Use performance-based or alternative (e.g., portfolio) assessments to capture student strengths and successes over time.

Using Multiple Formal and Informal Assessment Data

Gathering multiple sources of information is essential to providing context of assessment results. We recommend that the previous assessments discussed should be included and incorporated in school-based evaluation processes or MTSSs. Interviews with caregivers must be planned out with particular attention given to culture and linguistic background (Ortiz et al., 2008). Together, these multiple sources facilitate a comprehensive profile and understanding of the student's strengths and needs and provide a foundation from which to interpret assessment results and develop an intervention or success plan.

Engaging Students in the Assessment Process

Students are able to showcase their knowledge and skills when given opportunities to learn, practice, and apply strategies in everyday learning. Standardized tests may not necessarily capture their academic strengths. Moreover, students may be reluctant to show their language skills if they are not familiar with unfamiliar tasks or the language. Encouraging students to use other languages as resources in a context engages them and provides them with opportunity to express what they know. If the student has persistent reading and writing difficulties, the examiner must not make the assumption that a disability is present. Instead, other factors, such as proficiency in L1, second-language development support in family, and MTSS implementation (interventions at each tier) must be considered before determining a language disability. If interventions and support are implemented yet students demonstrate little growth or progress, then a disability evaluation may be used to consider additional accommodations, services, or placement.

One way to engage ELLs during the assessment process is to use *contextualized tasks*, which are a series of related items that allow students to use multiple language skills (Lopez et al., 2016). For example, a contextualized task may require students to listen to a short story being read aloud in one language and then retell the story to the teacher or a peer in the same or different language. Further, using technology as a means of instruction, assessment, or even as reward can help students become more engaged. When designing technology-enhanced tasks, special attention should be paid to students' level of experience with the relevant technology. Particularly during COVID-19, technology use can be an asset for some families, although it can be barriers for other families, particularly depending on socioeconomic status, education level, age, immigration status, and geography (Kim & Padilla, 2020).

When assessing students' language repertoires, the interactions between the ELL student and the bilingual practitioner should reflect common translanguaging practices that are used in classrooms (e.g., García & Wei, 2014). The practitioner assists the students to navigate through the assessment and the relationship between all the languages in the student's repertoire. Because many schools or classrooms have language practices that may allow students to use their entire repertoire, the practitioner should encourage them to use all their languages, to demonstrate their language and literacy skills. The practitioner and the student should also use a wide range of modalities, such as reading, writing, and speaking. This wide acceptance of cultural and linguistic knowledge and skills may help, in turn, foster a comfortable and non-threatening environment for young ELLs to demonstrate what they know and are able to do.

Interpreting Test Results with Care

When conducting a culturally responsive assessment, practitioners should interpret the results of multi-method, multi-source data with care. That means that practitioners should be mindful in examining sources of information and the entire assessment process, as they all influence student performance, test results, and practitioners' interpretation. When practitioners gather information on the student's acculturation and family history, they can begin to examine individual student data through individual assessment. Questions to ensure careful consideration and interpretation of results include:

1. Does the content of the assessment reflect the student's prior learning or current classroom expectations?
2. Are the results of the assessment similar to or different from the student's performance in the classroom? If so, why do the discrepancies exist?
3. Have the knowledge, skills, and concepts assessed been taught in a comprehensible manner?
4. Does the assessment allow opportunities for the student to use multiple languages throughout?
5. Is student performance compared with that of peers who are ELL or non-ELL? How is progress monitored over time?
6. How might a student's acculturation level or task familiarity have affected performance on the assessment?

One of the biggest challenges when conducting assessment of ELLs is that it requires a practitioner (or assistant) to be bilingual or multilingual, as well as have knowledge of second language acquisition and development. Although there are multilingual practitioners in some schools, this may not always be the case. Thus, collaboration with bilingual professionals or interpreters and collecting information from multiple sources require a collective effort. Even when school professionals share the same home language as their students, they also need to be biliterate in the subject area taught in the classroom. Further, monolingual practitioners will likely need to use interpreters. Interpreters should maintain neutrality and confidentiality, while also being familiar with technical terms related to assessment concepts or content area. They also must be aware of the procedures, rationales, and process of standardized assessment.

In schools, ELLs are a heterogeneous group that are distinguished by their cultural experiences (i.e., funds of knowledge), and the environments in which they hear, use, and express language. Moreover, the literacy experiences that these students have had in their heritage language will influence their ability to acquire literacy in the host language. Because the range of literacy knowledge and skills may be quite vast in any classroom with ELLs, traditional testing formats may be insufficient for the evaluation of English literacy as a second language. School teams, including teachers, practitioners, and families, must collaborate to ensure enrichment and capitalizing of current language knowledge and skills, while also filling gaps that may occur from lack of opportunities.

SUMMARY

Given the myriad issues related to assessment of CLD students, understanding the relationship between language exposure, literacy development, and acculturation experience will help inform culturally responsive decision-making and collaboration between home and school. Multiple assessments across the day and during authentic tasks will make it possible for students to show more accurately what they know and can do. Although supports and instructional practices may be different for each student, schools must ensure that students feel supported and must value the child's heritage culture, particularly if they strongly identify and engage in traditions and customs that the family views as important. Simultaneously, they can use some of this knowledge to integrate into the classroom or school culture. As they adapt into our multicultural and multilingual society as adults, they will ultimately decide on how and what cultural aspects to retain and adopt.

DISCUSSION QUESTIONS

1. What are the languages, cultures, and educational backgrounds of your dual language learners at school?
2. To what extent does your language program leverage your dual language learners' experiences and cultures in the classroom or during special education evaluations?
3. What performance or alternative assessments would be most beneficial in capturing students' knowledge and skills? How would you evaluate student performance or product (e.g., rubrics, qualitative feedback)?
4. In addition to academic progress, how would your school monitor or support social-emotional well-being, particularly for immigrant students like Josef?
5. To what extent do dual language learners connect their personal interests and their home/community life to your school?

APPENDIX 5A
USING STUDENT'S/FAMILY'S FUNDS OF KNOWLEDGE
TO INFORM PRACTICE

Funds of Knowledge	Home/Community Practices (Student/Family)	Classroom Application/ Instructional Practices
Economics		
Agriculture		
Technology		
Geography		
Religion		
Family		
Politics		
Language		
Scientific Knowledge		
Sports/Hobbies		

APPENDIX 5B
GUIDING QUESTIONS FOR ASSESSING STUDENT'S/
CAREGIVERS' FUNDS OF KNOWLEDGE

1. What do you remember about your own schooling experiences?

2. What kind of support did you have at home when you started reading and writing?

3. What did you like or dislike about learning in your native language?

4. Tell me about your experiences learning to read and write in your second language.

5. Tell me about when your child first began to read and write.

6. Describe the kinds of experiences that your child has with reading and writing at home.

7. Please tell me some examples of things you do at home to help your child with reading and writing.

APPENDIX 5C
GUIDED READING OBSERVATION FORM

Goals to be addressed in this lesson:

Preparation	Observations
☐ Identify reading strategy. ☐ Select culturally relevant text that will give students opportunities to practice. ☐ Develop comprehension questions.	
Before Reading (few minutes)	**Observations**

☐ Book Introduction (quick statement)
☐ Discuss any prior knowledge that connects student experiences with the book/chapter topic.
☐ Name the reading strategy (make it specific).
  • Model strategy.
  • Explain strategy and give an example.
  • Guided practice
☐ Address potential challenges in text (vocabulary, concepts, format/structure).	

During Reading	**Observations**

☐ Students independently apply strategy
  • Coach students individually/as needed.
  • Take notes on reading behaviors used/not used (can be used for teaching point after reading).
  • Reward for attempts, effort, and accurate reading.	

After Reading	**Observations**

☐ Begin a conversation on student's comprehension.
  • Have the student retell the passage/story.
  • Ask comprehension question(s)—factual, inferential, critical.
☐ Review areas that proved difficult or challenging for student—prompt as needed.
  • Opportunity to follow up on anything observed during reading
  • Reward for attempts, effort, and accurate reading.	

APPENDIX 5D
SAMPLE READING CURRICULUM-BASED ASSESSMENT

Student: _____ Date: _____

Steps and Procedures	Notes/Strategies
1. Build relationship with student	
2. Select culturally relevant reading material (begin with grade level). Text used:	
3. Read aloud to student	

Steps and Procedures			
4. Retelling by student		Main Idea	Details
(a) *Unaided* (e.g., *Tell me what you know about . . . Tell me more about . . .*)	Unaided		
	Aided		
	Forced		
(b) *Aided Questions* (e.g., *Who, what, when, where, why*)	Visual		
(c) *Forced Choice* (e.g., *Who was speaking, the mother or daughter?*)	Listening comprehension:		
(d) *Visual Questions* (e.g., *Look back in the text: Who did it say was speaking?*)	Prior knowledge: Language concepts:		

5. Word Search	Known:
What does the student know? (a) Sight words (b) Word attack drills (c) Known and unknown words (d) Prior knowledge (e) Language concepts	Unknown: Skills: Words taught:

Decision: Does the student possess the language and/or word recognition skills to be able to comprehend the selection?

___ Yes = Go ahead to Step 7.   ___ No = Go ahead to Step 6 to make content adjustments.

6. Content Adjustments
   (a) Teach
     (e.g., Pocket words for accuracy; breaking words into syllables; chunking; looking for patterns—"ed," "ing," etc.)
 	
   (b) Ask students what strategies they use and apply them.
 	
   (c) Provide background knowledge
 	
   (d) Select different material and do another word search.
	How does the student respond to instruction?

7. Student Reads Aloud
   Text used:
   (a) Fluency timing
   (b) Running record
   (c) Self-corrections
   (d) Known/unknowns
   (e) Word analysis skills
   (f) Sight words
	Words read correctly (WRC) per minute:
	_____
	
	( ) Instructional level
	( ) Independent Level
	
	Word study skills observed:
	
	| Word
		Strategy |
		|---|---|
		| | |
		| | |
		| | |
		| | |
		
		Are fluency strategies needed? Yes or No
		If yes, strategy used:
		• WRC per minute (after first practice) ____
		
		• WRC per minute (after second practice) ___

8. Retelling by Student
   (a) Unaided
       (e.g., *Tell me what you know about . . . Tell me more about . . .*)
   (b) Aided Questions
       (e.g., *Who, what, when, where, why*)
   (c) Forced Choice
       (e.g., *Who was speaking, the mother or daughter?*)
   (d) Visual Questions
       (e.g., *Look back in the text: Who did it say was speaking?*)

	Main Idea	Details
Unaided		
Aided		
Forced		
Visual		

Comprehension:
Prediction:
Sequencing:
Self-questioning:
Metacognition:

APPENDIX 5E
SAMPLE RUBRIC FOR READING COMPREHENSION

Task	0 point	1 point	2 points	3 points
Character Point of View or Main Idea	I said something about the character(s)	I describe the character(s), including actions, traits, and emotions. I talk about my own actions, traits, and emotions.	I share the point of view of the character(s). I also share how the character has changed or developed. I may make connections to my own experiences or background in relation to the character	I made a clear claim about the character's perspective and point of view. I provided my perspective and made connections to the examples from the story that explained the character's perspective and point of view.
Inferences and Predictions	I describe an event in the story without prediction or inferences.	I can make inferences or predictions based on the events in the story but with prompting.	I can make one inference or prediction based on the events in the story without prompting.	I can make several inferences and predictions based on the events in the story without prompting.
Connection to Reader's Experiences or Other Texts	I describe an event in the story without connecting to my experiences or other readings.	I can make a connection to my own experiences or other readings with prompting.	I can make a connection to my own experiences or other readings without prompting.	I can make connections to my own experiences and other readings without prompting.

APPENDIX 5F
SAMPLE SELF-ASSESSMENT QUESTIONNAIRE FOR REVIEWING LANGUAGE-RELATED TASKS FOR ENGLISH LANGUAGE LEARNERS

1. Are the oral and/or written directions of the task comprehensible to the student?	☐ YES ☐ NO ☐ Uncertain
2. Are the levels of vocabulary, grammar, and syntax of the task align with the student's current level of language proficiency?	☐ YES ☐ NO ☐ Uncertain
3. Does the task adequately align with the student's social and academic language proficiency?	☐ YES ☐ NO ☐ Uncertain
4. Do the instructions of the task have multiple steps? Does the student understand each of those steps?	☐ YES ☐ NO ☐ Uncertain
5. Are resource materials and tasks (i.e., internet resources, textbooks, reference books, additional readings, handouts) at the student's appropriate instructional and language proficiency levels?	☐ YES ☐ NO ☐ Uncertain
6. Are response modalities for the task (e.g., oral/written responses) adapted to the student's level of language proficiency and competencies?	☐ YES ☐ NO ☐ Uncertain
7. Are tasks provided in which students can demonstrate a variety of skills (e.g., content knowledge vs. language competence in writing)?	☐ YES ☐ NO ☐ Uncertain
8. Are tasks accompanied by tools such as concrete stimuli, models, and pictures to provide students with contextual support?	☐ YES ☐ NO ☐ Uncertain
9. Are tasks accompanied by modeling, demonstrations, and experiential activities that provide students with contextual support?	☐ YES ☐ NO ☐ Uncertain
10. Are tasks and materials used are of interest to the students in the classroom?	☐ YES ☐ NO ☐ Uncertain

Assessing Intelligence
of Diverse Students

VIGNETTE

Henrietta is an African American second-grade student who was evaluated for gifted education at the request of her mother. She resides with her parents in a low-income and economically marginalized neighborhood. Henrietta's teacher, Ms. Matheson, described her as "doing well" compared with her other students but believes she would not qualify for gifted evaluation. A school psychologist administered a brief cognitive ability test as part of the evaluation. Henrietta's test scores are described as "above average" but was one point lower than the school district cutoff score. The school team decided that Henrietta is deemed ineligible for gifted education.

- *What additional information could have been considered as part of the Henrietta's evaluation? What are the advantages and/or disadvantages of providing gifted education services in schools?*
- *Are intelligence or IQ tests adequate measures to determine whether a student is gifted or intelligent? Why or why not?*

The vignette of Henrietta highlights a common occurrence in schools, where test scores play a prominent role in educational decision-making. Specifically, intelligence tests (also known as IQ tests or cognitive ability tests) are common tools for school professionals, particularly for school psychologists, when completing evaluations to determine a student's eligibility for educational services, such as gifted education. These tests purport to determine a child's general intelligence or an overall level of cognitive ability compared with other students in their peer group. These tests often measure traits that are not directly observable and are measured only on a relative scale (Reynolds et al., 2021). Teachers and other professionals nevertheless rely on these scores to inform caregivers about students' learning potential; however, they generally provide limited utility regarding instructional planning when compared with tests that assess academic learning or achievement.

Historically, psychological tests and assessment of intelligence have been fraught with controversy. Since the American eugenics movement in the early 20th century, a number of psychologists, including Lewis Terman and Robert Yerkes, have used intelligence tests to claim innate differences between White and Black people (Turiel, 2020). Court cases such as Larry P. *v.* Riles (343 F. Supp. 306, 1972; 495 F. Supp. 976, 1979), involved allegations of cultural bias in intelligence tests that resulted in the underestimation of the intelligence of Black children and subsequently led to disproportionate placement in special education programs. Thus, there have been long-standing inequities related to the utility of intelligence tests for assessing culturally, linguistically, and racially diverse students in school settings. Some argue that intelligence tests are indeed culturally biased (Ford et al., 2014), while others believe that tests may not necessarily be the primary cause for the disproportionate rates of referrals for special education or gifted education programming (Reynolds et al., 2021).

There are many important questions within these debates. What is the reason for these disproportionate rates in educational placements? How do different cultures define intelligence? For what purposes have IQ tests been shown to be useful, and for whom? Overall, the purpose of the chapter is to try to elucidate these complex issues in testing the intelligence of CLD students. We first provide an overview of assessment and testing to provide a foundation for understanding how to assess for intelligence in CLD students. Then, we define intelligence and the different conceptualizations of these terms across cultures. We discuss why intelligence is assessed in many schools, and how to use information from testing effectively and appropriately to make culturally responsive decisions. Intelligence testing requires extensive training, so this chapter is not meant to substitute for any formal training in psychological testing or assessment coursework; rather, the chapter can serve as a supplemental resource for training or practice. We also anticipate that other professionals who may be involved in observing student learning outcomes, competencies, or skills would find this chapter relevant. All professionals would benefit in having awareness and sensitivity to these issues, and to discuss the historical and contemporary problems associated with intelligence testing and assessment of CLD students.

ASSESSMENT, TESTING, AND EVALUATION IN SCHOOLS

Assessment, testing, and evaluation are important aspects of practitioners' roles in supporting student's learning. This section provides a brief overview of how assessment and testing fit within the broader process of evaluating CLD students. Importantly, assessment should not be confused with testing or evaluation, although these terms have been used interchangeably in practice. *Assessment* is a comprehensive data collection process, whereas *testing* is part of the assessment process that involves administering a series of predetermined questions, items, or tasks to obtain a score (Salvia et al., 2016). *Evaluation*, on the other hand, is a method of interpreting all assessment data to make a professional judgment regarding instructional needs. Assessment and evaluation, therefore, often go hand in hand; the former focuses on methods of collecting data, while the latter focuses on how to use the data when making decisions. Both have the end of goal of improving educational outcomes for students.

Standardized tests often use *norm-referenced* interpretations, which are designed to compare the performance of one student with others within a norm or comparison group. They also involve scripted procedures for test administration and scoring because the adherence to protocol allows fair comparison between students. There are some drawbacks, however, to norm-referenced tests. For example, practitioners who overrely on national norms may subsequently undervalue students' skills, attributes, and knowledge. Thus, using national norms may lead practitioners to favor a general ability score or a narrow set of abilities over other sources of data (e.g., observation, work products). Further, comparing scores between peers can also lead to decreased academic expectations for minoritized students, English-language learners (ELLs), migrant populations, or students with disabilities. For example, students who are viewed as less able than their peers are often provided fewer opportunities and limited learning experiences, contributing to a self-fulfilling prophecy of underachievement (Rubie-Davies, 2010).

Another drawback to using norm-referenced interpretations is that they can perpetuate deficit-based thinking, rather than thinking about their strengths. Practitioners, for example, may emphasize students' difficulties with the school curriculum or instructional tasks, rather than emphasizing areas in which students were successful. Nowadays, there has been interest in examining both student strengths and difficulties over time. Tests that use *criterion-referenced* interpretations, for example, allow comparison of a student's performance to a fixed set of standards or predetermined criteria. Although norm-referenced interpretations can be useful in comparing performance with other peers, they do not always provide detailed information about the learning strategies of the student, the growth that a student is achieving, or the skills that should be incorporated into the student's educational plan. A majority of contemporary intelligence measures (e.g., Wechsler scales) use norm-referenced scores and interpretation.

Despite its limitations, standardized testing has played a long-standing and significant role in assessment for many education professionals as a basis for determining eligibility for school-based services. For example, 95% of school psychologists reported administering an intelligence test as part of their job responsibilities (Benson et al., 2019) and spend about half of their professional time engaged in eligibility determination and, specifically, individual assessment (Farmer et al., 2021). School psychologists, along with other professionals who are part of an interdisciplinary team, should use multiple methods and sources to make educational decisions for students. Importantly, the team also includes caregivers, who are often the best sources of information about how a student uses skills in the home and community (IDEA, 2004). Having an interdisciplinary team that includes caregivers ensures that there are multiple perspectives across multiple contexts during a psychoeducational evaluation, gifted evaluation, and/ or development of an Individualized Education Program (IEP).

On the other hand, these perspectives may highlight the challenges of comparing students with peers. Caregivers, for example, may react strongly when test scores are used to make comparisons with other children, particularly if it makes their child appear inferior. Unwanted results from tests lead to questions about the tests' technical adequacy, the skills or behaviors the test purports to measure, the selection of tests, the tests' use and interpretation, and the cutoff scores (Ford et al., 2014). Our obligation as practitioners is to understand and meet the needs of students as they come to us—with their strengths, academic skills, varied learning experiences, cultural backgrounds, and socioeconomic circumstances. Schools cannot—and should not—use one test, or one piece of data, to deny opportunities to children. School teams should continuously review or revise schoolwide evaluation procedures, provide reasoning for using particular cutoff scores, and deliver training on implicit bias whenever it comes to administering and interpreting data from standardized tests.

In sum, assessment is a comprehensive data collection process, and within this process, standardized testing has become an integral part of educational decision-making. The movement to educate CLD students in more inclusive settings has created a greater need for practitioners to learn culturally responsive assessment practices, including recognizing and mitigating individual and systemic factors that contribute to disproportionality in special education and/or gifted education programs, which most likely require an intelligence test.

CULTURAL CONCEPTUALIZATIONS OF INTELLIGENCE

Intelligence is defined differently across cultures, and specific terms for intelligence or cognitive ability often do not translate directly across languages (Serpell, 2011). Definitions of intelligence may also vary based on experiences in the social and cultural environment. Scholars in Western cultures (e.g., United States and Europe) tend to agree that intelligence reflects cognitive components, such as problem-solving, knowledge acquisition, abstract reasoning (e.g., Neisser et al., 1996), and how quickly individuals mentally process information (e.g., Sternberg, 2004). Other countries, however, may conceptualize it differently, defining intelligence as having social, moral, and/or emotional components. For example, in communities in Zambia, for example, they emphasize social responsibility, cooperativeness, and obedience, although contemporary Westernized schooling in many African countries highlights development of cognitive skills and knowledge acquisition (Serpell, 2011).

Western cultures also conceptualize emotional intelligence as distinct from, but interrelated with, cognitive abilities. *Emotional intelligence* is the capacity to recognize, manage, and express one's emotions to others to foster personal growth (Salovey & Mayer, 2004). For example, children who are able to regulate or manage emotions in a way that facilitates adaptive functioning also demonstrate higher cognitive ability and perform better on standardized tests (Graziano et al., 2007). Some Eastern cultures (e.g., Asia) consider family and community, discipline, politeness and respect for elders, and strong social relationships as important components of emotional intelligence (Sung, 2010).

Some scholars proposed common elements of intelligence across cultures, such as general cognitive ability or Spearman's g (Warne & Burningham, 2019); however, many caregivers and teachers would not likely be familiar with these concepts or how they can be used in their student's individualized education program. Thus, one way to explain the purpose of testing intelligence is to contextualize intelligence as it relates to a variety of skills, attributes, or behaviors needed to be successful in different facets of life.

Indeed, many everyday tasks require at least some cognitive ability, which would explain why adaptive behavior is correlated with intelligence (Alexander & Reynolds, 2020). *Adaptive behaviors* are essential skills necessary for a student to function in home, school, or community environments. Some examples include self-care, communication skills, social and interpersonal skills, activities of daily living, application of academic skills, planning, and self-regulation. For example, many societies place importance on developing language skills so that children are able to communicate with peers and teachers about their wants and needs. Caregivers can share additional examples of skills they believe their children need to demonstrate to do well in school (e.g., attention, applied learning), to get along with peers and adults (e.g., communication, problem-solving), and to be successful at home (e.g., following directions).

Individuals achieve academic, social, or occupational success in a variety of ways. For example, people may have achieved success through the blending of specific abilities, skills, and external supports that may be different compared with another individual. It provides not only a broader understanding of intelligence outside of a testing situation or school environment but also allows for meaningful and individualized discussion on essential skills that are valued in society and the conditions needed to ensure an individual's success. Sternberg's (1997) triarchic theory or *successful intelligence* conceptualizes intelligence as context dependent and consisting of three dimensions: *analytical* (the ability to evaluate information and solve problems), *practical* (the ability to adapt to different environments), and *creative* (the ability to invent and develop novel ideas), which can be demonstrated outside the classroom. This information can be useful for caregivers to consider as additional examples of when and how students demonstrate these skills. The components of intelligence may be universal, but their manifestations may be different for each student and in different environments.

Since culture and knowledge of content are inextricably woven into language, culture-free testing does not exist. Even nonverbal tests can have cultural assumptions embedded in them and thus are not entirely removed of language. Moreover, issues surrounding the nature and definition of intelligence, the contributions of heredity and environment to intellectual performance, and the accuracy and appropriateness of cognitive ability tests for diverse groups have led to continuing debates regarding the utility of these tests in schools (Ford, 2014). Although current intelligence tests have improved over the past few decades with regard to their validity and technical adequacy (i.e., tests measure what they intend to measure), they are still controversial because intelligence involves a variety of knowledge and skills that may not be easily captured in a test.

Despite its complexity, the elusive construct of intelligence has been frequently shown to predict academic achievement (Roth et al., 2015; Sternberg & Grigorenko, 2002a). From an ecological-systems perspective (e.g., Bronfenbrenner, 2015), a student's intelligence is a construction based on student ability and potential (individual), home resources, school policies and opportunities (microsystem), social and cultural values (macrosystem), and state-level or federal legislation (e.g., exosystem). Cognitively stimulating environments enhance abilities of students, whereas environments in marginalized communities may affect the development of intellectual potential, based on the IQ tests used (Christensen et al., 2014). Because environmental and economic opportunity are not equally distributed across all subgroups in our society, socioeconomic factors (e.g., family income, financial resources) and oppression (e.g., racism) likely contribute to observed differences in test performance between subgroups (Gillborne, 2016; von Stumm, 2017). Culture and intelligence are closely interrelated, and thus any assessment of intelligence must carefully consider culture.

ASSESSMENT OF INTELLIGENCE IN SCHOOLS

School professionals may describe intelligence in different ways, such as a student's learning potential, a student's creative ability to solve novel problems, or a student's use of knowledge to adapt to new situations (Sternberg, 2007). Schools are often interested in determining student's levels of intelligence to understand the best ways to support the student's learning as well as their likelihood to do well in classrooms. Therefore, many schools have specific policies and practices related to assessment or testing of intelligence.

Assessment of intelligence in schools is typically conducted via individual or group-administered standardized tests. These types of tests involve measuring particular cognitive abilities using novel tasks that assess reasoning, knowledge, and behavior. One of the most well-known measures, the Wechsler Individual Scale for Children (WISC; Wechsler, 2014), is a standardized test that measures skills such as verbal comprehension, visual-spatial ability, working memory, and processing speed, to name a few. Although many of these tests conceptualize intelligence as one global ability score or overall "general intelligence," other theories (e.g., the Cattell–Horn–Caroll theory; McGrew, 2005) have described intelligence as comprising of multiple cognitive abilities. The challenge of having a general intelligence score is that it will not explicitly explain why a student struggles with math or reading, or if the student has special skills and talents in art, music, or learning a foreign language. More importantly, because an overall IQ score cannot explain a student's specific learning strengths and difficulties, it is not useful for drawing conclusions about *how* a student learns (Fletcher & Miciak, 2017).

Other theories of intelligence, such as Gardner's (1993) theories of multiple intelligences, challenged the traditional notion of general intelligence or *g*. This conceptualization of intelligence proposed several different types of intelligence (e.g., linguistic, logical/mathematical, spatial, bodily-kinesthetic, musical, interpersonal, intrapersonal, and naturalist). Despite its popular use in schools, Gardner's theory has very limited empirical support (Waterhouse, 2006). Further, educators have conflated this theory with *learning styles*, which suggest that matching materials to a student's preferred method (e.g., auditory, visual, tactile/kinesthetic) will enhance learning. Although students may have a preference for how material is presented, many research studies have shown that teaching based on learning styles is ineffective (e.g., Pashler et al., 2008). Instead, providing students with multiple methods to access content and demonstrate knowledge, rather than just one method, improves learning and engagement (Hattie, 2011). Nevertheless, Gardner did believe that intelligence is defined within the context of culture, so what is intelligent for one culture may not be so for another. Therefore, assessment of intelligence at least should consider the cultural contexts as essential sources of information, while considering their application in and outside of school.

[Reflexivity Activity]: Reflect on your experiences with intelligence testing and answer the following questions.

- *How would you define intelligence? Is it a skill or ability that can be developed? What are the strengths and limitations of your definition?*
- *What factors in your cultural background or experiences have led to this definition?*
- *How does your school determine if a student is intelligent?*
- *What are the strengths and limitations in the testing of intelligence in determining educational placement?*

SYSTEMIC FACTORS AND BIAS IN INTELLIGENCE TESTING

Complex, systemic factors contribute to the disproportionality in intelligence test performance across cultural, racial/ethnic, and linguistic groups. For example, research has highlighted that fewer Black and Latinx students are performing at advanced levels compared with their White and Asian American peers (Peters et al., 2019). We describe four explanations in our current systems that contribute to disproportionately lower test performance among particular CLD students: (a) unsupportive learning environments, (b) racism and deficit thinking, (c) poverty and socioeconomic status, (d) cultural or test bias, and (e) educator/examiner bias.

Unsupportive Learning Environments

Learning environments that promote discriminatory policies, referral practices, and evaluation procedures hinder opportunities and experiences for marginalized students. For example, only 2% of Black fourth-grade students achieved an advanced level and 3% of Latinx/Hispanic students, as opposed to 12% of White students and 23% of Asian American students (NCES, 2019a). These disparities between subgroups of students (e.g., race, disability, ethnicity, income levels) performing at the highest levels of achievement have been described as the *excellence gap* (Plucker et al., 2017). The National Association of Gifted Children purported that students in these subgroups have the potential to achieve more than minimum competency. If students were assessed and identified for gifted education on the basis of a score on this test or similar measures of achievement, fewer Black and Latinx students would be identified than White students (Ford, 2014). For those students who are from low-income and economically marginalized groups, 3% of fourth-grade students achieved advanced levels in math, while for those who are not eligible for free/reduced lunch programs, 15% achieved advanced levels (NCES, 2019a). These excellence gaps have been thought to be the result of discriminatory practices, such as inconsistent referral rates, and not due cultural differences in aptitude or child-centered abilities (Plucker et al., 2017).

Unsupportive learning environments include limited resources allocated to low-income and economically marginalized communities (Knight, 2019), poor teacher–student relationships (Redding, 2019), and lack of attention to and knowledge of issues surrounding diversity, equity, and inclusivity in classrooms (Bonner et al., 2018). For example, if a middle school teacher fosters a climate that lowers expectations for particular subgroups of students, they may be more susceptible to negative stereotype threats, or the fear of confirming a stereotype (e.g., subgroups performing low on standardized tests) that may impede test performance. A nonnative English speaker may score lower on an intelligence test than a White, English-speaking student who was not threatened with the stereotype (Steele & Aronson, 2004). They may also be more likely to be referred for special education or less likely to be recommended for enrichment programs.

Assessment practices have long been shaped by a variety of forces, trends, and challenges, including controversies related to intelligence testing and the use of a medical model of assessment for students with disabilities that prioritizes student deficits. Addressing the causes and persistence of excellence gaps would involve systems-level change and advocating for diverse students. These barriers can be addressed via the following steps: (a) demonstrate awareness of excellence gaps or disproportionality in the school population, (b) update referral and assessment practices to include cultural responsiveness, (c) revise practices in classrooms and create intervention plans that take into account family culture or the student's cultural identity, and (d) review data of referred children disaggregated by race and ethnicity. Additionally, other common challenges when it comes it educational placement, such as stigma due to potential disability, can have long-lasting consequences to the student's emotional well-being and future career goals.

Racism and Deficit Thinking

Structural inequalities, including racism and deficit thinking in educational settings, contribute to disproportionately lower test scores among CLD students. These inequalities are products of privileged systems that are deeply embedded within society and difficult to change. Historically, researchers have attempted to explain group differences in test scores between White students and students of color by suggesting that they are due to inferiority or pathology of students of color (Sue et al., 1992). Even on the most recent version of the Wechsler Intelligence Scale for Children - Fifth Edition (WISC-V; Wechsler, 2014), White children had a mean standard score of 103.5, which is higher than that of Latinx/Hispanics (mean score of 94.4), and Black/African Americans (mean score of 91.9) on the Full Scale IQ (FSIQ). Asian Americans outperformed the other three groups with a mean standard score of 108.9 (Weiss et al., 2015). These observed differences in test performance do not necessarily indicate actual differences in intelligence. In fact, studies suggest that only 50% of the variance in individual intelligence can be attributed to genetics or heritability (Plomin, 2018), which means that environmental or contextual influences, including parent education, acculturation, socioeconomic status, and academic expectations for students, also explain variations in test performance between subgroups (Weiss & Saklofske, 2020). However, some may still believe that the difference is evidence of heredity or genetic inferiority, which is highly problematic and perpetuates racism. Although intelligence testing is widely used in cross-cultural contexts, it can be easy for practitioners to make sweeping generalizations based on average performance, leading to discrimination.

Additionally, teachers may believe they must help students to overcome cultural disadvantages and deficits that result from "inadequate" family and cultural experiences, when in fact, marginalized students may have lacked the social and cultural capital necessary to succeed in school (Ford et al., 2014). This perspective harms CLD students in a number of ways. It pathologizes students and families based on their cultural, social, and economic status. Further, it suggests to CLD students that the only way to success is to assimilate into the majority culture. It also places blame on families, rather than on the underlying social structures that contribute to these disparities. This type of deficit thinking goes against culturally responsive practice because it hinders meaningful change, reform, and accountability; yet, some schools may unknowingly continue to perpetuate this view (Ahram et al., 2011). This simplistic and dangerous explanation ignores the role of systems, such as educational policies, teacher training, and opportunities to learn, on student outcomes.

Poverty and Economic Marginalization

Other structural inequalities, such as poverty, have been associated with discrepancies in intelligence test scores (e.g., Weiss et al., 2020). Several validity and factor-analytic studies of common intelligence tests, including the Kaufman Assessment Battery for Children - Second Edition (KABC-II; Kaufman & Kaufman, 2004), and Differential Ability Scales (DAS-II; Elliott, 2007) did not find strong evidence of test bias for racial- and ethnic-minoritized groups (Scheiber, 2016; Trundt et al., 2018). Since there is no identified set of biological markers for race or ethnicity, these constructs have been most aptly described as socially derived and may be considered inappropriate for use as independent variables to explain psychological outcomes (Helms et al., 2005). According to this view, race and ethnicity are more likely proxies for socioeconomic status (SES), such that families with greater income and parental education perform better on intelligence tests than students from lower-SES families. A variety of potential environmental mechanisms linking SES in childhood and cognitive abilities include SES-related differences in parenting and interactions with caregivers, exposure to toxins, poor nutrition, exposure to violence, and stress (Hackman & Farah, 2009). Thus, differences in test scores may not necessarily be due to the ethnicity or culture but may more likely be related to poverty, opportunity, and socioeconomic status.

Access and Target Skills

Students must have *access skills,* which refer to skills necessary to demonstrate knowledge and competency on a test (Dembitzer & Kettler, 2018). For example, many intelligence tests require that students listen and follow directions in English (e.g., attention and language), point to responses (fine motor skills), and persist through difficult tasks (e.g., motivation) in order to complete a processing speed subtest. In other words, access skills are necessary to engage with the test items and content but are not the target constructs being assessed. Access skills should be identified for students who complete any form of testing.

To level the playing field for students with disabilities, accommodations can be made to provide them with access skills (Kettler, 2012). These accommodations remove barriers for them so they can demonstrate their problem-solving skills and reasoning ability. Furthermore, students with disabilities have the right, and trained practitioners have the obligation, to adapt the testing situation to minimize the effects of these access skills on test outcomes. For example, providing translations of test instructions or providing breaks in between subtests can increase motivation and effort to complete the test.

Target skills refer to the knowledge or competencies that are being measured (Kettler, 2012). In this case, students would not use test accommodations for target skills because such accommodations would be considered unfair, as they would potentially inflate the student's IQ test scores relative to those who did not have accommodations. For some intelligence tests, some examples of target skills may include defining words, recalling sequences of numbers (e.g., working memory), problem-solving, or visually discriminating pictures. Practitioners must ensure that any testing accommodations should not directly affect target skills.

Cultural or Test Bias

Another factor that contributes to disproportionately lower test performance among CLD students is cultural or test bias. *Cultural or test bias* is the observed differential performance among student subgroups, where test items or procedures penalize or disadvantage particular subgroups but benefits others (Reynolds & Suzuki, 2012). Kwate (2001) argued that these differences can be traced to the adherence of Eurocentric, middle-class value systems of these tests. An example: A student may not likely perform well on an intelligence test if there are pictures (e.g., snow, tractor, typewriter) that a student has not seen before due to their cultural experiences and background. Moreover, the student may have migrated to the United States recently and may not be familiar with the process of individualized testing and thus may perform worse compared with students raised in the same neighborhood as the school. Therefore, any test items or procedures may penalize or disadvantage the student to a greater degree compared with students who have been exposed to these cultural experiences. Box 6.1 provides an example of two checklists, which can be used to evaluate a test or instrument, as well as practical suggestions for minimizing bias.

Although contextual information (e.g., language proficiency, acculturation, prior educational history, etc.) helps us to understand how students will likely perform on the test, to date, there lacks a consensus on the most effective approaches to assess CLD students. Options include providing the student with a translated test (e.g., testing in the student's native or primary language), administering an adapted test (e.g., nonverbal IQ or alternative score), including an interpreter during administration, or incorporating test accommodations (Figueroa, 2000). Although these options are common alternative test procedures when English-speaking tests may not offer valid results for CLD students, caution should still be taken when making interpretations, as their scores may continue to be an underestimation of their actual abilities. For CLD students, multiple methods are needed to obtain a broad estimate of intelligence or abilities.

One consideration for assessing CLD students using IQ tests is to select tests that have reduced cultural loadings and linguistic demand. Flanagan et al. (2013) developed the Cultural-Language Interpretative Matrix (C-LIM), which provides an interpretive framework for understanding IQ test scores of individual students and determining whether results are influenced by cultural or linguistic variables. If so, the test scores would be considered invalid and should not be interpreted because they reflect cultural and linguistic experiential differences between the student and those in the normative sample. However, several studies (e.g., Styck &

Box 6.1.

CHECKLIST FOR EVALUATING ASSESSMENT BIAS

Part 1. Checklist for Evaluating Assessment Tools

1. Description of the measure
2. Type of measure (norm-referenced, criterion-referenced, checklist, rating scale, etc.)
3. Content area assessed (description of each domain and, if applicable, list of subtests)
4. Requirements for completion successfully
   a. Presentation of items
   b. Language
   c. Response modality
   d. Individual or group administration
   e. Time factors
5. Examiner requirements
   a. Necessary training
   b. Administration time
   c. Ease of use
6. Standards of test
   a. Reference type (e.g., individual progress, norm groups, curricular goal)
   b. If applicable, description of norm group
      • Age, grade, gender
      • Method of selection
      • Representation of sample (e.g., race, ethnicity, language, gender)
      • Size
      • Recency of norm sample
   c. If available, technical adequacy—validity and reliability (if none available, why not?)
7. Reliability
   a. Test–retest reliability
   b. Internal consistency
   c. Interscorer validity
8. Validity
   a. Content validity
   b. Construct validity
   c. Criterion-related validity (predictive, concurrent)
9. Considerations for cultural fairness in assessment
   a. Is the norm sample appropriate for the student?
   b. Are there any items that may lead to cultural bias?
   c. Is the language of the measure appropriate for the student?
   d. Does the measure consider strengths of the student?

Part 2. Checklist for Minimizing Bias when Interpreting Results

1. Examine characteristics of the *student* that might influence test results or performance, such as:
   - Language spoken at home
   - Age, health, nutrition
   - Disability or accommodations
   - Mode of communication
   - Motivation, persistence, effort
2. Examine characteristics of the *test* that might influence the results, such as:
   - Purpose of the test/assessment
   - Mode of communication (student–examiner; student response to items)
   - Norms
   - Technical adequacy (e.g., reliability and validity)
   - Relevance of items
   - Scoring criteria
   - Type of scores (e.g., standard scores, percentiles, raw scores)
3. Examine characteristics of the *examiner* that might influence results, such as:
   - Training and competence (e.g., previous experience)
   - Knowledge of and attitudes toward the child's background and context
   - Behaviors during test administration (e.g., penalizing for controversial responses)
4. Examine conditions with the *environment* that might influence performance.
   - Time of day
   - Environmental distractions
   - Testing materials (e.g., accessibility)
   - Length of session
   - Antecedents prior to testing session
   - Order of assessment activities or tasks
5. Examine relation between *examiner and student* that might influence performance.
   - Rapport
   - Attention
   - Response to success or failure
   - Maintaining motivation, persistence, and effort
   - Communication
6. Determine if student's performance is representative of actual behavior or potential. If not, why not?
7. Compare and contrast findings with other tests and assessment tools.

Watkins, 2013) have found limited support for the clinical utility of the C-LIM to produce accurate decisions with the WISC-IV. Further research is needed to validate the utility of this framework and its ability to distinguish typically developing individuals from those with disabilities in diverse populations (Pham et al., 2017).

Educator and Examiner Bias

The potential for bias in assessment still remains, even after selection of the most valid tests. In addition to cultural or test bias, educator and examiner bias may contribute to disproportionately lower test scores among CLD students. *Examiner bias* refers to any systematic errors in the testing or assessment process or the interpretation of its results that are attributed to an examiner's attitudes, preconceived beliefs, expectations, or behaviors. For example, if Henrietta demonstrated a thick accent when responding to verbal test items, would it negatively bias the examiner's perception and judgment of Henrietta and her verbal abilities? Would this lead to a lowering of expectations, and consequently, result in a lower scoring of the test responses?

To mitigate educator or examiner bias, greater responsibility and accountability are now placed on the professional, and there is emphasis on cultural fairness in testing or assessment. *Cultural fairness* entails judgment of whether the test and test scores are truly reflective of the student's abilities, and treatment; this may entail selecting the most appropriate test measures, reviewing the norm sample of the test, and understanding limitations when reporting and interpreting test scores (Pham et al., 2017).

Teachers may have implicit or explicit biases and attitudes about student ability (Ricciardi et al., 2020). These biases may lead to differing nomination rates for gifted education or referrals to special education. Practitioners who fail to consider their own biases, perspectives, and subjectivities may perpetuate unfairness in the assessment process. Addressing and making meaning of cultural and examiner bias, for example, can lead to the development of more critically conscious and equity-minded assessment strategies, which will be highlighted later in the chapter. Reynolds and Suzuki (2012) had outlined additional examples of potential cultural and examiner bias in testing. We provide potential solutions when addressing examiner biases:

1. *Item content.* Tests items are geared to majority experiences and values (e.g., "Who is George Washington?").
   Potential solution: Avoid asking the test item or select a different test. Administer the test item but interpret results with caution.
2. *Underrepresentation in standardization samples.* Specific minority groups may not be adequately representative in norming samples (e.g., Are immigrant students reflected in sample?).

Potential solution: Select a different test that uses norms reflective of the student's background or consider using local norms. Administer the test items but interpret results with caution.

3. *Examiner and language bias.* A majority of tests are developed and administered in English and thus may not be valid when used to assess CLD students (e.g., assessing a student's cognitive ability in Russian).

    Potential solutions: Review and repair individual- (e.g., examiner beliefs and behaviors) and systems-level factors (e.g., evaluation guidelines) that contribute to bias. Select a different test or method of assessment. Translate items and directions to student's native language and interpret results with caution.

4. *Inequitable social consequences.* CLD students, some already disadvantaged because of stereotyping and past discrimination, continue to perform poorly on tests due to inequality of educational opportunities.

    Potential solutions: Review and repair individual- (e.g., examiner beliefs and behaviors) and systems-level factors (e.g., school policies) that contribute to lack of opportunity. Assess and reallocate funds to increase educational opportunities for students, and professional development for staff training.

5. *Measurement of different constructs.* Tests largely based on a White majority or Eurocentric culture are measuring different characteristics of CLD students, rendering them invalid (e.g., Is the construct of verbal ability the same for ELL students?)

    Potential solutions: Review norming sample and technical adequacy of the test (e.g., construct validity, reliability). Select a different test that uses norms reflective of the student's background or consider using local norms.

6. *Differential predictive validity.* The criteria that tests are designed to predict, such as achievement in White, middle-class schools, may be biased against minoritized students (e.g., Are there differences in outcomes between Whites and Latinx students based on the test scores?).

    Potential solutions: Review norming sample and technical adequacy of the test (e.g., predictive validity, reliability). Select a different test that uses norms reflective of the student's background or consider using local norms.

CONSIDERATIONS FOR CULTURALLY RESPONSIVE ASSESSMENT OF MINORITIZED STUDENTS

We described the issues related to testing of cognitive abilities of students from CLD backgrounds, the cultural conceptualization of intelligence, and the systemic factors and biases associated with the testing of intelligence. This foundational knowledge is important for practitioners to conduct culturally responsive assessments of intelligence responsibly. In this section, we provide recommendations that practitioners can use as supplemental considerations for assessing intelligence.

Reassessing Assessment Skills

Practitioners may first want to reassess their training and experiences in assessment in light of the topics discussed earlier. Using cultural humility, practitioners should engage in critical reflexivity as individuals within a larger educational system (Pham et al., 2021). They may need to reflect on their roles in assessment more broadly, and how their cultural beliefs and values, as well as educational background, training, and experiences, shape the lens by which they use intelligence tests as a way to support student's learning. They may want to consider how they were taught to think about and assess intelligence in their current practices, and how those practices may differentially affect minoritized students or CLD populations.

[Reflexivity Activity]. Consider the following questions.

1. *We all have implicit biases. What biases might you have about intelligence? How were you taught about who is "smart"?*
2. *How were you trained in understanding intelligence? How do you think your professor was trained?*
3. *What are your skills in assessing students who are ELLs? Students with visual impairments? Students who are deaf or hard of hearing?*

Reviewing or Revising Schoolwide Assessment Practices

Practitioners should review data and procedures related to school-based evaluation outcomes. For example, school-based teams could review referral rates, along with any schoolwide data collected from implementing multi-tiered systems of support (MTSSs). Reviewing these data is helpful for determining trends on an annual basis. The school team should work toward equitable identification of students, making sure that minoritized students are not disproportionately referred. Further, the school-based team should review vulnerable decision points and implicit biases that lead to referral processes. For example, when individuals (e.g., teachers, practitioners) experience stress and frustration, they are more likely to be susceptible to implicit bias, which influences educational decision-making (Girvan et al., 2021).

If there are suspected disproportionate referral rates, for example, then the team would need to discuss, analyze, and potentially update schoolwide or district-level procedures. These procedures include: (a) past and current assessment practices that involve intelligence tests, (b) types of tests and measures used to determine eligibility for various programming and services (c) processes and guidelines for decision-making (e.g., cutoff scores), (d) the interpretation framework of the practitioner or as required by the state or district, and (e) monitoring of student outcomes.

When reviewing past and current assessment practices, the team can examine disaggregated data of student outcomes by race, ethnicity, language, and/or gender to determine if there is overrepresentation or underrepresentation by subgroup. If there is disproportionality in gifted education, what changes may need to be made to ensure that intelligence scores are not the dominant factor? One school district highlighted by Card and Giuliano (2016), for example, provides two routes of eligibility (Plans A & B) to ensure equity in screening and identification of CLD students for gifted education. Students in Plan A, for example, go through a standard process and must achieve a specific IQ score threshold. For students in Plan B who are economically disadvantaged (e.g., receive free and reduced lunch), less emphasis is placed on the IQ test to be considered eligible for gifted education. They are required to use additional documentation, including parent and teacher rating scales that examine creativity or leadership strengths.

Overall, by reviewing the existing school policies, the school-based team can consider whether there are equitable practices for all students to access educational programming. The goals of these practices are to (a) promote ongoing awareness of implicit or examiner bias; (b) ensure that the interests, needs, abilities and culture of every student and family are valued and respected; (c) maximize learning opportunities for every student; and (d) empower students and parents in the assessment process. These goals can be used as part of a sustained plan for ensuring success of students who have been traditionally underserved.

Approaches to Culturally Responsive Assessment of Intelligence

Despite its limitations, the use of intelligence tests will likely continue in many schools. Given the diverse educational and life experiences of children; however, these tests may not always capture child's intellectual potential. Employing multimethod assessment approaches can be useful to ensure that CLD students are able to demonstrate knowledge and skills in different yet meaningful ways. Some approaches may require more extensive training (e.g., dynamic assessment; Lidz & Macrine, 2001) than others. Culturally responsive assessment allows practitioners to go beyond traditional assessment, while ensuring students display their best effort while respecting their learning histories and cultures.

AWARENESS OF ASSESSMENT CHALLENGES

Practitioners are likely to encounter various questions and dilemmas on how best to assess CLD students using norm-referenced intelligence tests. Besides the time needed to construct and develop these tests, students' intersecting identities (e.g., a student who is biracial and economically marginalized) should also be considered, making it virtually impossible to create norms to address this diversity of students. Practitioners should therefore rely on reflexive approaches related to test and examiner bias and use adaptations or translations of existing tests developed for specific contexts and communities. For example, for the Block Design subtest on the WISC-V, a student's visual-motor skill can be described as the target skill. On the other hand, verbal ability may be described as an access skill for the subtest, since the task requires understanding that the blocks should be constructed as quickly as possible. Providing opportunities to demonstrate the task can help moderate this effect while checking the student's understanding. Appendix 6A provides additional questions to promote cultural awareness in intelligence testing.

We outline three approaches to intelligence testing that enable practitioners to assess a student's intelligence holistically and contextually. First, the assessment of diverse students should involve a nondiscriminatory process that examines student skills from an ecological perspective, or how systems and environmental contexts influence student's intelligence. Second, the strengths-based approach is critical when promoting students' development and school belonging by creating high expectations, and it avoids deficit thinking. Third, practitioners can assess how students adapt and employ strategies that facilitate learning as part of a dynamic perspective, which allows students to demonstrate knowledge or skills in multiple ways, rather than a single approach. Table 6.1 outlines the differences between each approach.

ECOLOGICAL ASSESSMENT

The goal of ecological assessment is to gain information about the interplay between students and environments rather than making comparisons with other students (Armour-Thomas & Gopaul-McNicol, 1997). The student's *ecology* or *ecosystem* is an inclusive term describing the sociocultural and environmental context that influences child development (Bronfenbrenner, 2005). These procedures (as discussed in Chapter 5) include a review of educational records and developmental history; observations of the student in various settings (e.g., classroom, home); interview with parents, teachers, and other professionals involved with the student; work samples (e.g., homework, seatwork assignments, class tests); and measures of adaptive behavior.

Another purpose of an ecological assessment is to examine how the student functions in a given setting by examining the match between student outcomes and environmental expectations. In the classroom or testing situations, an ecological assessment may include the student's understanding of instructional demands, rapport and interactions between student and teacher, or even the physical layout of the room. For example, when conducting an ecological assessment of a student, a practitioner may look beyond the student-specific behavior. If a student is demonstrating lack of motivation during the testing, it may be because the they do not understand the task directions or may not be familiar enough with the environment or the examiner for them to feel comfortable giving their best effort.

During an ecological assessment, cultural factors should also be considered due to potential differences in expectations between home and school settings, along with strengths of the student. Familial factors (e.g., family values, goals, language)

Table 6.1. ECOLOGICAL, STRENGTHS-BASED, AND DYNAMIC ASSESSMENT

	Ecological	Strengths-Based	Dynamic
What is it?	An approach to observing and gathering information on the child across multiple settings in which he or she routinely operates	An approach that recognizes student assets that can be used to maximize opportunities for success	An interactive approach to understanding how the child can maximize performance during assessment
What is the goal?	To assess instructional and environmental supports and demands needed to ensure a match (or mismatch) between the student and the environment	To foster motivation self-efficacy, self-control, resilience, and academic achievement	To determine the child's ability and potential to acquire skills or knowledge after explicit teaching or modification of testing procedures
How is it done?	Observations across settings, structured parent/teacher or student interviews	Interviews or rating scales that assess interests, well-being, and resilience. Gathering information regarding environmental protective factors.	Uses "test-teach-retest" model or "testing of limits" to see if the child adapts and learns
What are its limitations?	More research is needed to link assessment with intervention.	Limited research support, lack of standardized measures for creativity as part of school-based assessment and intervention	Limited standardization, validity and reliability evidence unavailable. Requires significant experience and knowledge of testing

and sociocultural contexts (e.g., acculturation, immigration experiences, traumatic stress, previous testing experiences) can influence performance on intelligence tests (Sternberg, 2007). Practitioners should consider the stressors the student may experience when adapting into a new environment and attempt to address these stressors prior to testing. Critical questions to ask in an ecological assessment include:

- Is there a difference as to how the student functions in a structured testing environment versus classroom testing or seatwork?
- What behavioral characteristics does the student exhibit when approaching a novel task? Does the child ask for assistance? Does the student approach the task using any strategies)?
- What differences exist between the environments or interactions where the student manifests the greatest and the least difficulty?
- How does the examiner establish a trusting relationship with the student before testing? Does it take as long as several minutes, days, or weeks?
- How does the family perceive the child's strengths and challenges?
- What environmental stressors is the child experiencing?
- What is the match/mismatch between the curriculum and what is being tested?
- What are the instructional practices provided in the classroom? Are they effective? Are these practices more effective in small groups or one-on-one settings?

STRENGTHS-BASED ASSESSMENT

A second approach is utilizing a strengths-based assessment. Not all evaluations in schools are conducted to understand student problems or concerns, such as in the case example of Henrietta. Nevertheless, it can be easy for practitioners to talk and write about problem behaviors or pathology, especially when there are persistent concerns. As an outgrowth of positive psychology, strengths-based assessment is often a preferred approach when working with CLD students (Jimerson, 2004). It recognizes that ability and disability are not extremes of the same scale but instead coexist, and each provides important information about the student's functioning within their learning environment (Gilman & Huebner, 2003).

Although strengths-based assessment is not a new idea, it may be seen as lesser goal for most psychoeducational evaluations, particularly when identifying students for special education. Informed by resilience literature, a strengths-based assessment examines how to identify critical protective factors within students and their environments (Climie & Hemley, 2014). This type of assessment allows the practitioner to recognize both student assets and challenges, to promote excellence in education opportunities, and to increase student motivation and engagement. A strengths-based assessment would evaluate a broader range of outcomes such as subjective well-being, life satisfaction, optimism/hope, motivation, cultural identity, self-esteem, or self-efficacy (Terjesen et al., 2004). Students have the capacity to learn and demonstrate strengths when providing a supportive environment. Thus, a student's failure to demonstrate a particular skill does not necessarily indicate a deficit; rather, it is about changing the perspective to see that the student simply requires further experience, instruction, or opportunity for mastery. Lastly, focusing on student strengths and resources will likely motivate the student to learn and use these skills, and to include in IEPs (Terjesen et al., 2004). The approach can inform strengths-based intervention practices specifically tailored to the student.

A strengths-based assessment of students can be conducted in a number of ways. The practitioner may simply ask the teacher, parent, peers, and student, *What does the student do well and what are the student's areas of strengths?* This information would be helpful in understanding student assets across multiple contexts and from multiple information. Further, practitioners can gather information through self-reports, parent and teacher rating scales, work products, and observations. Additionally, measures of adaptive behavior can be used to assess strengths related to resilience. The assessment would explore how a student is currently coping with the challenges he or she is facing, as well as protective factors, contexts, and supports that facilitate the child's best performance (Rhee et al., 2001). For instance, information regarding self-perceptions across learning domains (e.g., *How does student feel about reading?*) as well as the quality of the student–teacher relationship would be explored, with attempts to identify any other existing positive relationships (e.g., peers, siblings, adults, counselors, extended family) that might be used to facilitate growth.

Some additional recommendations during the assessment of intelligence include:

- Gather information about the student's goals for their life, as well as their likes and dislikes.
- Examine any current positive relationships the students have, such as with caregivers, educators, faith leaders, or mentors.
- Determine what protective factors may be in the student's systems (e.g., classroom-level, school-level, or community-level) as well as how the student adapts to their environment.
- Review other areas that may be student strengths, including creativity, motivation/self-efficacy, hope/optimism, persistence/resilience, problem-solving, social and interpersonal skills, self-care, achievements, and leadership.

When it comes to gifted evaluations, strengths are often described in the form of high test scores. Many states reported intelligence and creativity as two domains of giftedness but also indicated others: academic ability, performing arts, leadership, visual arts, music, psychomotor ability, and task commitment (Rinn et al., 2020). These domains can apply to any student. Similar to intelligence, creativity is multifaceted and comprises different conceptions and definitions, including divergent thinking, which involves novel generation of ideas and solutions. Creative skills can be assessed through open-ended measures, such as writing short stories based on a prompt, drawing and providing a title, or oral storytelling in response to a series of images. Formal measures of creativity include the Torrance Test of Creative Thinking (Torrance, 1974) and the Williams Scale (Williams, 1980).

Overall, the strengths-based assessment can be advantageous in fully understanding the student's skills and abilities as well as contribute to an increased sense of trust and empowerment from families. By creating a vision for the student, such as present and future goals, practitioners and families can communicate attainable goals based on a more comprehensive view of the child (Terjesen et al., 2004), while also improving the family's perceptions and acceptability of interventions and supports (Nickerson & Fishman, 2013).

DYNAMIC ASSESSMENT

A third approach to assessment of intelligence is dynamic assessment. Generally, intelligence tests are often described as static tests, which reflect a student's level of performance(s) at one point in time without any attempt to intervene to change, guide, or improve the student's performance (Lidz & Macrine, 2001). This static testing assumes that all children have had the same cultural and learning experiences and opportunities prior to testing. This assumption is undoubtedly not the case in today's diverse school systems.

In response, *dynamic assessment* is a process-oriented assessment that allows for intervention as a method for determining a student's intellectual potential instead of prior knowledge (Lidz & Macrine, 2001). Indeed, there is increasing interest in a developing an interactive approach to administering standardized tests that focuses on the student's response to instruction, or capacity for change and improvement. Specifically, dynamic assessment aims to understand mediated learning processes and maximize performance for the purpose of success, rather than ending a test after failure (Lidz, 2009; Sternberg & Grigorenko, 2002b). The dynamic assessment component involves paying close attention to how the student approaches the task, or mediating learning, during the testing and how this information can be used to optimize student outcomes. Repeated exposure to testing items may reduce the influence of culture on performance, for example, by compensating for differences in familiarity with the test, learning opportunities, or language (e.g., Van De Vijver, 2008). Qualitative data can be collected from the student during the assessment to understand how they adapt to challenging or novel tasks and regulate learning. Importantly, before using any dynamic approaches, practitioners should understand the potential impact of these modifications in relation to the original purpose and intention of the test. When deciding decisions based on these approaches, careful judgment should be exercised when determining whether additional points should be given for aided responses, or if data should be collected qualitatively and reported.

There are two methods of dynamic assessment that have been primarily described for standardized tests: testing the limits and test-teach-retest. *Testing the limits* is a common technique that involves determining the highest level at which a child can respond under alternative or modified conditions. Several examples include (a) removing time limits, (b) providing additional prompts or clues, (c) re-administering failed items, (d) changing task/stimuli modality, and (e) reconstructing the child's errors and asking them to find and correct their errors by providing additional information (Sattler, 2001). In practice, scores determined after testing the limits are not necessarily reported if the question is how the student performed compared with peers. However, if the question is what the student's optimal performance is, then describing the conditions and performance of the student in a narrative format is appropriate when testing the limits.

The *test-teach-retest* method (Lidz & Pena, 1996) assesses the student's ability to acquire the skills and knowledge tested after being exposed to instruction. Teaching items are common in most intelligence tests where the student is given guidance and feedback about whether the response is accurate to ensure understanding of the task expectations. For example, when administering the test item as intended (i.e., test), if the student responds incorrectly, instruction and guidance on how to complete the task accurately are provided (i.e., teach) while keeping detailed notes about any strategies the student uses or their responses. The test item is then re-administered (i.e., retest) to determine improvement (i.e., how student approaches the task, how student responds to feedback). For example, many current intelligence tests have teaching items to ensure that students understand the initial instructions of the task. However, this method can be used for more difficult test items or questions to determine whether they can complete more challenging tasks with limited assistance.

There is strong utility of dynamic assessment for students who are identified as gifted (Lidz & Elliott, 2006), students with disabilities (Al-Hroub & Whitebread, 2019), and students with language impairments (Petersen et al., 2017). Figure 6.1 outlines the overlap of the three approaches; however, the dynamic approach has not been implemented widely in school districts due to limited guidance and procedures regarding on how aid or feedback should be given to students, which is often contingent on their testing performance or behaviors. Testing-the-limits and other process-oriented approaches facilitate understanding of how students

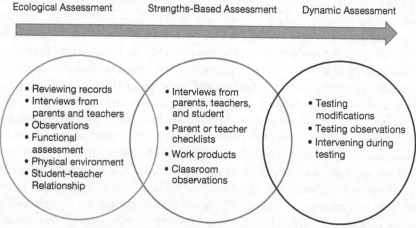

Figure 6.1. Three Assessment Approaches and Their Overlap.

learn, optimal performance, and factors that support learning. Until there is more research and guidance on dynamic assessment in schools, practitioners may refer to current tests for specific suggestions on accommodations or modifications of test materials. Nonetheless, dynamic assessment can be a useful approach for assessing intelligence of CLD students.

Culturally Responsive Feedback Regarding Intelligence Testing

One of the most important aspects of assessing intelligence is to convey results of the assessment meaningfully to the family and teachers, as well as to discuss how best to support the student's future school and life success. People read psychoeducational reports to shed light about the students' strengths and challenges. We believe that caregivers are the most important consumers of this information because assessment results are often given directly to caregivers during feedback sessions or in team meetings. Unfortunately, some of the main points regarding the student's abilities can easily get lost in lengthy reports or in meetings when technical jargon and statistical concepts are emphasized. Practitioners should thus write and verbally explain assessment results of intelligence testing in a purposeful way that should be cogent yet understandable to the audience.

More often than not, many reports will provide a listing of tests and explain test scores with little explanation or relevance to the referral question. Many practitioners are likely to summarize their assessment findings in a structured report, which often includes a plethora of standard scores, percentile ranks, and their interpretation of the results. When working with caregivers of ELL students, it is often not necessary to have a second full report in the parent's language, but practitioners may provide a brief version of the report in the parent's heritage language if possible, along with the full report in English. Practitioners should demonstrate confidence in their test results, describe how they assessed the student's skills, outline any modifications made, and provide the reasons for these adaptations. They should also indicate when results are interpreted with caution, which are often determined if procedures are not standardized. Conducting culturally responsive assessments may often go beyond standardization but requires thoughtful and sensitive approaches to interpret test data that captures the strengths and needs of CLD students.

When communicating assessment results during feedback sessions, strengths and challenges should be conveyed clearly to students, teachers, and caregivers. For any approach, families and teachers should understand that students' learning is dynamic, complex, and malleable, and that students demonstrate their success in different ways, which are cultivated by the home and school environments. Students should be commended on their efforts, and any other observed behaviors (e.g., attention, cooperation, improvement in skills over time) prior to discussing strengths and challenges. All students have inherent strengths and skills. Culturally responsive practices involve not only identifying what strategies works for the student, but also how they work so that are used when necessary to compensate for any challenges. When conveying results to students, discussion of their strengths is conveyed in concrete terms and is developmentally appropriate. We have provided an example of a child letter that can be given to the student after completing the evaluation (see Appendix 6B). It provides practical recommendations that the student can use that help the student engage in advocacy and self-monitoring of skills.

We recommend using a thematic approach using headings while providing data and interpretation under each theme. A few examples are described next using ecological, strengths-based, and dynamic approaches.

ECOLOGICAL

A variety of methods are used to gather assessment data to understand a child's intelligence. A comprehensive assessment requires a record review of the child's history, interviews, and observations to contextualize testing results and to understand the child's learning and behavior under varied conditions and environments (e.g., home, school, community). Data should go beyond performance in a testing environment by assessing the ecology of the student. For example, using the vignette with Henrietta, may summarize the results of an ecological assessment:

Henrietta's Educational Background

Henrietta's background and adaptive skills were assessed through review of records, teacher reports, interviews, and observations. Henrietta has been enrolled in three different schools over the past 2 years. She continues to excel in reading and visual arts and demonstrates strong attachment to her family's cultural heritage through her family's stories and songs. Henrietta expressed wanting to be a veterinarian and shared her love of learning and talking about animals. She has regularly read stories to her classroom on a weekly basis and is a peer tutor for a first-grade student. Her parents have both indicated that she is articulate, responsible, and hardworking. Her test scores from testing indicate high abilities, and she would benefit from differentiated instruction to support her areas of strengths.

STRENGTHS-BASED

Communicating students' strengths and challenges after a comprehensive evaluation facilitates greater participation from caregivers in the assessment process and subsequent interventions. It also enables all team members to understand when student strengths are shown during the testing environment or across different settings. Strengths should be gathered from different sources of information and not just from a single test (see Table 6.2). When using a strength-based assessment for Henrietta, we may write:

Strengths in Language and Recalling Information from Text

Henrietta showed exceptional skills when learning names of animal pictures, and retelling stories with specific details. Although she was a bit distracted

Table 6.2. STUDENT STRENGTHS CHECKLIST

Motivation and Self-Efficacy
    Learns quickly outside of school
    Enjoys new experiences
    Makes good choices
    Feels pride in cultural heritage
    Ambitious or has drive
    Follow rules well
    Self-starter
    Sticks to things they are interested in
    Independent/self-helper
    Finishes projects

    Solves problems quickly
    Has high self-esteem

Creativity
    Creative, has new ideas
    Recognized for a talent they do well
        (list):
    Artistic
    Sports/activities (list them)
    Makes creative ideas happen
    Hobbies/crafts (list them)
    Interests (circle): music, dance, video
        games, movies
    Builds and constructs things
    Musical talents (list):
    Computers/board games (circle)

Hope/Optimism
    Takes moments for self-reflection or
        prayer
    Has a good sense of humor
    Hopeful and positive attitude

Self-Care
    Grooms and clothes self well
    Cares for belongings
    Cares for/repairs things
    Takes care of self
    Can summarize events of the day
    Good hygiene

Persistence/Resilience
    Tolerates challenges well
    Willing to ask for help
    Recovers well from challenges/bounces
        back
    Stands up for self when needed
    Handles stress well
    Willing to ask for help
    Tolerates challenges well
    Calms down in stressful situations
        (list):

Social and Interpersonal Skills
    Joins activities and plays well with peers
    Shares feelings
    Friendly and outgoing
    Caring to small animals and/or children
        (circle)
    Good manners and social skills
    Shares or cooperates with others
    Trusting
    Helpful
    Liked by others (babysitter, teacher,
        others)

Other Interests (list):

NOTE: Instructions to place at beginning of the checklist would read: Below is a list of positive or good behaviors. Please rate on a scale of 0 to 5 (0 = not at all, 5 = very much) in each area. Some items may not be applicable to all grades/ages. Questions to ask include: (1) What is the child's best subject in school?; (2) What is the child's proudest achievement?; (3) What are your hopes/dreams/expectations for your child's life?

with the test materials, she followed simple and complex directions well and responded well to verbal praise. Parents also indicate that she listens well, completes chores, and cleans her room when asked.

This will also aid in developing concrete recommendations that capitalize on strengths to compensate for any challenges or to use as positive reinforcement.

Dynamic

The process of dynamic assessment may be more difficult for caregivers to understand, as it involves divulging details of specific cognitive tasks. Similarly to the previous discussion, this process should include multiple sources of information from the home or classroom rather than from a test-taking situation. However, if tasks are clearly and cogently described, then the practitioner can focus on discussing observed strategies or explicit teaching and instructional procedures used during the testing as recommendations for improving school performance.

> Henrietta's Current Strategies to Plan and Learn New Information *Henrietta talked aloud while completing a timed task that assessed her visual and spatial skills. She continued to use self-talk while completing tasks that were unfamiliar to her. On another timed task searching for animal pictures, Henrietta initially appeared distracted as she talked about her favorite ones on the page. However, when given the opportunity to plan before starting, she completed the task efficiently while talking through the steps of the task.*

SUMMARY

Assessment of intelligence in schools has its share of controversies, particularly as they relate to their use in assessment and educational decision-making with students from CLD backgrounds. Thus, culturally responsive assessment entails learning the strengths and limitations of current and widely used intelligence tests in terms of what information they tell us, and what they don't tell us. Ethical and culturally responsive practitioners should also be mindful of the history, assumptions, cultural biases, and research when using intelligence tests, as they have led to educational inequities. Although intelligence tests will likely continue to be widespread in school systems, norm-referenced interpretations do not necessarily provide contextual information on individual learning strengths and weaknesses unless conveyed meaningfully with additional information from the assessment. Alternative approaches to traditional assessment will need to be further researched to substantiate their use with CLD students, since standardized administration will likely yield underestimates of the student's intelligence and abilities.

DISCUSSION QUESTIONS

1. What are the strengths and challenges of current evaluation processes for special education? For gifted evaluation? How is intelligence used in these processes?
2. Describe the various systemic factors and biases in intelligence testing. What are some specific strategies that you could use in your school to address these factors?

3. Alina is a first-grade Ukrainian refugee student who has excelled in reading and is highly creative. Her teacher believes she may qualify for a gifted evaluation. As a practitioner, consider the three approaches for culturally responsive assessment of intelligence: ecological assessment, a strengths-based approach, and dynamic assessment. How would you conduct an assessment? What factors should you consider during the assessment?

APPENDIX 6A
CENTRAL QUESTIONS TO PROMOTE CULTURAL
RESPONSIVENESS IN INTELLIGENCE TESTING

Practitioners must be reflexive and inquisitive in their practice of interpreting test performance and scores for decision-making. The following assumptions can help guide the development of culturally responsive assessment to minimize cultural bias in intelligence testing.

1. The purpose of the IQ test in the large part of assessment.
   a. Is it to determine the likelihood they will do well in school?
   b. Is it to determine access to educational services?
   c. Is it used to rule out any disabilities or dysfunction?
   d. Perhaps a reason is not known, only that the IQ test is stated as a requirement by the district? In that case, this may raise questions as to the purpose of inclusion in a policy.
2. Practitioners must be mindful and reflexive about strengths and limitations of such tests. They should acknowledge what they do not know and be willing to adapt based on new evidence.
3. Validity is not only a property of the test itself but also a property when making interpretations of test scores.
4. Intelligence tests measure the student's prior knowledge and thus do not typically determine their optimal learning potential. The content of all tasks, whether described as verbal or nonverbal, are culturally embedded.
5. Intelligence tasks assess samples of behavior and skills demonstrated in a controlled testing environment. Additional information (e.g., observations, interviews, work products) must be collected to develop an understanding of the child's strengths and skills that are cultivated in other settings.
6. Strengths-based approaches should be emphasized to minimize deficit thinking when assessing diverse students.

APPENDIX 6B
SAMPLE LETTER TO STUDENT

Dear (Student Name),

You should be very proud of yourself! I can tell you enjoy learning at school, making friends, and reading! I know there are times when it is hard for you to focus and pay attention, but I could tell you were always trying your best. Your hard work paid off because I was able to find out a lot about you! I can tell that you are bright and hard-working. I was really impressed!

When you came to see me we did all kinds of thinking and remembering and all kinds of school work. You read some words, did some spelling and math, listened to stories, looked at different pictures, and you did a lot of things that helped me understand how you remember information.

Well, guess what? I found out that there are some things that come really easily to you! (Student name), you have many great ideas, and you can solve really difficult problems—especially when answering questions about stories and hearing different sounds in words. I was amazed to see how much you can remember! You remember a lot of stories, and having something you can relate to makes it easier for you to remember. That is so important for your mother and teachers to know about you.

I learned a few more things from the work that we did together. The next thing I would like to talk to you about is your attention. (Student name), sometimes you pay attention well, especially on things you found interesting. When things take a long time to do, sometimes it is hard for you to focus, but we took breaks to help you focus again, and that helps!

(Student name), I noticed sometimes reading and writing can be difficult for you, because you have to remember a lot of words on paper and to write things down. I can tell you have a LOT of great ideas, and if you practice reading and writing every day, you will do great!! I can also let your parents and teachers know about ways to help you with reading.

Lastly, I am so glad you have made so much improvement the past few years. You are a very kind and thoughtful, and you always try your best. I am glad you have great friends and that you enjoy school! I hope things go well for you in third grade and beyond! Thanks for all your hard work!

Sincerely,

James Smith, Ed.S.

School Psychologist

Cultural Perspectives of Mental Health and Traumatic Stress

VIGNETTE

Alejandra is a Blackfeet cisgender female and a seventh grade student in Ms. Fiore's class. Ms. Fiore has noticed that Alejandra's demeanor recently has changed. She no longer participates in class, does not turn in any homework, is very tired, and often misses school. In a writing assignment, Alejandra has shared that she had witnessed a teenager die by gunshot in her neighborhood, located in a large city. Ms. Fiore reached out to Alejandra's parents as well as to Ms. Smith, the school psychologist. During a meeting with Ms. Fiore and Ms. Smith, Alejandra's father responded by saying, "I don't think there's anything wrong. She just doesn't want to go to school." Ms. Smith asked whether she could check in with Alejandra and provide her with some support. Alejandra's father agreed, although reluctantly.

Many students in schools experience mental health issues and traumatic stress. According to the Substance Abuse and Mental Health Service Administration (SAMHSA, 2020) more than 2 out of 3 students reported at least one traumatic event in the past year, including community violence, sexual and physical abuse, national disasters, or the violent loss of a loved one. The effects of traumatic stress can include anxiety, difficulty concentrating, alcohol or drug use, or becoming involved in risky sexual behavior. Symptoms can worsen over time if left unaddressed. One study showed a nearly 8% increase in diagnoses of anxiety or depression in children in 2011–2012 (Bitsko et al., 2018). The COVID-19 pandemic also exacerbated mental health issues for children and adolescents, leading to an advisory from the U.S. Surgeon General (Department of Health and Human Services, 2021), highlighting statistics that death by suicide have increased by 54% among the 10–24 age group in 2020. Clearly, these statistics are concerning.

The pandemic has also exacerbated systemic inequities, with the U.S. Surgeon General's report showing that American Indian / Alaska Native, Black, Latinx,

Asian American, Native Hawaiian, and Pacific Islander youth are at higher risk for mental health challenges compared with White youth. These challenges have led to persistent mental health disparities among children across racial and ethnic minoritized groups, although the patterns of disorders are similar (Liang et al., 2016). For example, the prevalence of ADHD differs between White (4.33%), Hispanic (3.06%), and Black (5.65%) children (Cuffe et al., 2005). Black children, however, have lower a prevalence of mood disorders and substance use compared with White children (Roberts et al., 2006). These mental health disparities are due to a wide range of factors, such as differing parent perceptions of what constitutes a disability (Pham et al., 2017), historical and contemporary racism (Neblett Jr., 2019), and difficulties accessing mental health services (Lyon et al., 2013).

These disparities also occur in the context of special education, where schools are 2–3 times more likely to label African American students and Native American students with emotional disturbance (Bal et al., 2019). Researchers (e.g., Sullivan, 2017) have emphasized that there are a number of systemic factors that contribute to disparities in diagnoses and misdiagnoses, such sociocultural and contextual factors (e.g., beliefs about the etiology, acculturation, referral rates) or inappropriate or unreliable assessment approaches.

The purpose of this chapter is to provide specific strategies to conduct culturally responsive assessment of students who are experiencing mental health difficulties. Specifically, we focus on assessing mental health, including traumatic stress, for students who may need more individualized support. Importantly, best practices suggest that mental health should be screened for all students, particularly given the increased rates of mental health difficulties. First, we will highlight cultural perspectives of mental health and traumatic stress. Then, we will discuss several steps within culturally responsive assessment: (1) engaging in critical reflexivity, (2) developing relationships and earning trust with the student and family, (3) obtaining background information, (4) conducting interviews with caregivers, (4) administering tests and measures, and (5) writing the assessment report and collaboratively planning for the intervention.

CULTURAL PERSPECTIVES OF MENTAL HEALTH AND TRAUMATIC STRESS

[Reflexivity Activity]: Reflect on your and your family's perspectives of mental health. How do you define mental health? How does your family describe "mental health"? How do members of your community perceive mental health?

As practitioners, we may have been trained in providing mental health services to students, where concepts are actually grounded in cultural understandings and perspectives of wellness. This reflexive activity may have highlighted the differences in how you, as a school-based mental health practitioner, may conceptualize mental health compared with members of your family or community. Further, the construct of "mental health" is shaped by the values our society places on what is "normal" behavior. In this section, we discuss cultural understandings of "mental health" and "trauma," and how these understandings affect how practitioners can provide services and supports to students.

Mental Health and Wellness

Often, in the mental health profession, practitioners may perceive psychological well-being or wellness to be universal; however, this concept is defined by the values that are shared within a culture. To be "well," "happy," or have a "fulfilled life" may be conceptualized differently across cultures because to have a "life well-lived" is defined by the values that are shared within the family and cultural group (Christopher, 1999). For example, for one person, to have a fulfilled life may be to have a large family with many children, yet for another person it is to have a partner with no children. The values associated with having a family, therefore, are connected to the idea of what constitutes a "a life well-lived."

The concepts of "mental health" and "wellness" are similarly based in culture and are connected to how someone's behavior is related to, or compared with, others in that society. When specifically focusing on mental health, how people conceptualize whether the symptoms are discrepant from typical or normal ones, as well as its etiology and severity, is based on culture. Indeed, labels for disorders (e.g., "mental retardation" or "intellectual disabilities"), how symptoms are described, and additions (e.g., gender dysphoria) and removal (e.g., Asperger's disorder) of mental health disorders from the *Diagnostic and Statistical Manual of Mental Disorders - Fifth Edition* (DSM-5; American Psychiatric Association, 2013) highlight how mental health is deeply rooted in culture and is a social construct. In fact, the entire concept of a mental health illness or disorder is based on cultural ideas and norms (e.g., what is normal vs. abnormal) and subsequently may impact how these behaviors are treated or how one is treated in society. The Lakota, for example, do not have any language to define mental illness and describe it as "life forces" (Todd-Bazemore, 1999, p. 141). Thus, traditional healing practices, such as magical thinking, rituals, and ceremonies, may be more appropriate to enhance wellness (Trimble, 2010).

As an example of the link between culture and wellness, there may be differences in *distress thresholds*, or the degrees to which a student or their family may consider certain symptoms problematic. Specifically, differences in how mental health problems are recognized, how they are conceptualized, where the problems are derived from, and the severity of the symptoms play a role in whether families will seek services (Cauce et al., 2002). Chinese Americans, for example, were more likely to seek mental health services when there were somatic or physical symptoms compared with symptoms associated with anxiety or depression (Kung & Lu, 2008). This somatic distress may be more socially acceptable. Further, non-Hispanic White parents may have a lower threshold for seeking mental health supports for their children's emotional and behavioral problems because they tend to have knowledge about the Western, Eurocentric ideas about disorders and symptoms (Lau et al., 2004). The cultural norms about "distress" influence parental behavior related to conceptualizing mental health and seeking services.

Further, the idea of wellness is connected to how we understand the self and our relationship with others. Although some cultures value individualism while others value collectivism (Markus & Kitayama, 1991), the idea of wellness moves beyond these simple dichotomies. Rather, it is much more of a spectrum of understanding ourselves in the context of others. For example, Adams et al. (2006) suggested that the ways we measure psychological concepts such as "self-esteem" need to be expanded to understand collectivist cultures, such as those from Indigenous communities. They highlighted that some items on measures of self-esteem (e.g., "I am worried about what other people think of me") may be perceived as an "'unhealthy' concern about the social environment that limits elaboration and enhancement of the individual self," when in fact, it may be a cultural strength in which Native Americans have connections of self to others (p. 505). In other words, these measures of self-esteem suggest that, in fact, being worried about what others think is socially and culturally appropriate, depending on the overarching values within that society. Thus, the perception of what is unhealthy or healthy, or well or unwell, is a cultural concept that must be taken into consideration when understanding culturally and linguistically diverse (CLD) students' experiences.

EXPRESSIONS AND EXPLANATIONS OF DISTRESS AND WELLNESS

Another way that mental health or wellness is culturally constructed is in how students and their families express their distress. Sometimes called *culture-bound syndromes*, expressions and experiences of distress and wellness may vary. For example, in Western Africa, "brain fag" characterizes a number of different symptoms, including visual disturbances (pain in the eyes) and cognitive impairment (e.g., inability to concentrate) and is considered a coping response to stressful or overwhelming situations (Ebigbo et al., 2014). Further, there are also specific idioms, for example, that highlight cultural conceptualizations. Among some Latinx communities, idioms like *nervios a flor de piel*, which is directly translated as *exposed nerves*, can mean intense anxiety (Arredondo et al., 2014). As another example, Cambodian refugees in the United States describe their experiences of trauma as "*khyâl* overload," associated with somatization of trauma and with the Pol Pot genocide (Hinton et al., 2010). Thus, although practitioners may rely on diagnostic criteria and labels from the DSM-5 (American Psychiatric Association, 2013) or the Individuals with Disabilities Education Act (IDEA) for determining whether a student has mental health issues, these disorders or disabilities may not adequately capture the experience of some CLD students.

Families are likely to have different explanations for etiology, or the cause, for mental health issues across cultures (Pham et al., 2017). Faith or religion can drive the underlying beliefs for some families. Muslim students and families, for example, may perceive that mental illness stems from supernatural forces (El-Islam, 2008). Further, the Islamic tradition suggests that their lives are based on God's will, and thus illness may be perceived as punishment (El-Islam, 2008). As another example, families descended from the South African Xhosa culture may align with traditional healers' perspectives that the etiology of psychosis is related to supernatural causes, particularly as a result of spell cast to deliberately hurt that person (Mzimkulu & Simbayi, 2006). These explanations of distress or disorder are important to consider when working with students from culturally and linguistically diverse backgrounds.

BELIEFS ABOUT HELP SEEKING

Students and their families may also have different beliefs about seeking mental health support. Cultural norms, beliefs, and attitudes influence the degree to which some students and families may have stigma related to seeking mental health supports. There are three types of stigma associated with help seeking: (1) *self-stigma*, which is associated with internal feelings and attitudes toward seeking mental health supports, (2) *social stigma*, which is associated with expectations from others, such as family or friends, and (3) *public stigma*, which is associated with expectations from the larger public (Corrigan, 2004). Stigma and cultural norms may cue whether a person is experiencing mental health problems and how others may perceive the reason for those problems (Abdullah & Brown, 2011). If a student is experiencing a mental health issue, for example, their attitudes or perceptions of that issue are likely shaped by the community's attitude, beliefs, cultural history, and values. Indeed, there has been a great deal of harm caused by the mental health field on minoritized groups, as highlighted by the American Psychological Association (2021) resolution, apologizing for their role in perpetuating racism against people of color. The history of racism and harm against minoritized groups may contribute to their reluctance to pursue mental health care, and their distrust of mental health professionals. Multilingual practitioners are also limited, resulting in difficulties with communicating between families and practitioners. Unless culturally responsive practitioners demonstrate skills to understand and incorporate their perspectives during outreach and consultation, the likelihood of families to seek out mental health supports is low.

Acculturation or enculturation also has been thought to be associated with the degree of help seeking, but it varies across family members. In a meta-analysis using racial and ethnic minoritized groups as the sample, a person's orientation to their heritage culture was found to be associated with public stigma, but not social stigma, for psychological help seeking (Sun et al., 2016). Thus, for some immigrants, maintaining their heritage culture was related to worries stemming from public perception, rather than from family or friends, which plays a significant role in their willingness to seek mental health services.

Finally, another consideration related to help seeking includes the role, dynamics, and structure of the family. In some Arab cultures, for example, the family system, rather than an individual, is the primary system that makes decisions about ultimately seeking mental health supports (El-Islam, 2008). The role of family in mental health supports is not new to most school-based practitioners, but it is helpful to conceptualize "family" as more than simply the immediate family members (e.g., biological mother, father, sibling). For some Indigenous families, for example, not only are grandparents involved in raising the children, but also extended family members or other relatives may be providing care on a daily basis. Similarly, community members (e.g., faith-based leaders, barbers, etc.) may also serve as social supports for families.

Culture and Traumatic Stress

Culture is also important to consider when providing supports to students who are coping with trauma and traumatic stress. Traumatic stress is the reaction that a child or individual has to a particular event that is considered dangerous to or violent in their life (The National Child Traumatic Stress Network [NCTSN], 2021). Sometimes described as adverse childhood experiences (ACEs), events can include child abuse, disruptions in caregiving, or violence in the home. The NCTSN (2021) lists a number of events or experiences that potentially cause traumatic stress:

- Physical, sexual, or psychological abuse and neglect, such as trafficking
- Natural and technological disasters or terrorism
- Family or community violence
- Sudden or violent loss of a loved one
- Substance use disorder (personal or familial)
- Refugee and war experiences, including torture
- Serious accidents or life-threatening illness
- Military family-related stressors, such as deployment or parental loss or injury

Broadly, factors that contribute to a student's reaction to a stressful event can include type and intensity of the event, the student's characteristics (e.g., age, developmental level), and the student's background (e.g., family, culture, support network; Nader, 2008). When the event involves an actual or threatened death or serious injury that causes a substantial psychophysiological response (specifically, intense fear, helplessness, or agitation), then the child may develop symptoms of post-traumatic stress disorder (PTSD; American Psychiatric Association, 2013). For children, PTSD symptoms include being exposed to such events, re-experiencing those events (e.g., intrusive thoughts, dreams, or distress in response to reminders), persistent avoidance of those reminders, increased arousal (e.g., sleep disturbance, feeling detached from others). These symptoms occur longer than one month and cause functional impairment in the child's life (American Psychiatric Association, 2013).

Further, trauma and traumatic stress are specifically highlighted in the IDEA (2004) through Title 1, Part C (Infants and Toddlers). Specifically, it states that disability can be determined by a "substantial case of trauma due to exposure to family violence"; however, it is not explicitly included in the broader special education disability categories. Nonetheless, a trauma-informed approach to an Individualized Education Program (IEP) is possible and can include specific goals related to family engagement, trauma-informed assessment, and strategies to promote the child's emotional regulation (Rossen, 2018).

Approximately one-fifth of school-age children who were exposed to a traumatic event met the criteria for PTSD (Woolgar et al., 2021). Further, trauma exposure has been associated with a number of other mental health concerns, including conduct disorder (Bernhard et al., 2018). Additionally, children's exposure to traumatic events can lead to negative developmental trajectories, including physical and psychological difficulties (Copeland et al., 2018; Felitti et al., 1998). In the vignette from the beginning of this chapter, Alejandra witnessed a death by gun shot and thus could potentially experience traumatic stress. Her physiological, emotional, and adaptive functioning were affected by witnessing the violence; she was experiencing fatigue, was missing school, and was not participating in class. Thus, trauma exposure can have both short- and long-term deleterious effects on children and adolescents.

HISTORICAL TRAUMA

In addition to discrete traumatic events, practitioners may also need to consider the legacy of trauma across generations in a community. Historical trauma, or sometimes called intergenerational trauma, is defined as the collective, generational trauma of a large group who share the same culture or community. Those who have been inflicted by historical trauma may experience significant emotional and psychological distress (Brave Heart et al., 2011). This type of trauma is associated with historical and contemporary colonization of many communities, such as Indigenous communities in the United States. The legacy of colonization, as well as of forced settlements, residential boarding schools, and genocide, continues to affect Indigenous people, with higher rates of mental health challenges among Indigenous youth, compared with Black and Hispanic youth (DPHHS, 2021).

Further, historical trauma and colonization are not exclusive to Indigenous communities. For example, research has found that the colonization and oppression of Puerto Rico have ramifications on self-image and identity among Puerto Rican high school students (Varas-Díaz & Serrano-García, 2003). Students' emotions associated with being colonized by the United States were both positive (pride in their identity as Puerto Ricans) and negative (shame associated with perceptions from U.S. nationals). Thus, practitioners need to discuss, carefully and sensitively, with the student and family the role of historical trauma and the subsequent impact that colonization may have on the student's cultural or ethnic identity development during mental health assessments.

RACE-BASED AND IMMIGRATION-RELATED TRAUMA

In addition to historical trauma, minoritized students and their families may also experience race-based and/or immigration-related trauma. Race-based trauma is characterized as traumatic stress associated with the effects of racism and discrimination and has been found to be negatively associated with individuals' emotional and psychological well-being (Carter, 2007). Specifically, race-based traumatic stress can occur from individual-level or systems-level racism and discrimination, and research has shown that incidents of racism and discrimination can cause great distress for individuals from 2 months to over a year after the incident (Carter & Forsyth, 2010).

Similarly, students and their families may experience immigration- or refugee-related trauma. In recent years, the sociopolitical context in the United States and perceptions about immigrants and refugees have caused traumatic stress for many people. There have been significant impacts of racism, ethnocentrism, and nativism on Latinx individuals, families, and communities (Chavez-Dueñas et al., 2019). In particular, the increase in immigration enforcement has caused great distress for many Latinx families, with 68% of Latinx fearing that they themselves, a family member, or a close friend would be deported (Lopez & Minushkin, 2008).

For many refugees and forcibly displaced peoples, traumatic stress can occur at all stages of migration. There are three stages of migration for individuals who have been forcibly displaced: (1) pre-migration, in which the individual is encounters oppression, prosecution, poverty, famine, and other types of life-threatening events, (2) migration, in which the individual is in transit (e.g., living in refugee camps), and (3) post-migration, in which the individual has reached their destination country (Bhugra & Jones, 2001). Forcibly displaced individuals and families may be exposed to trauma prior to leaving their home country (e.g., witnessing or experiencing violence as a result of war), as well as during or after involuntarily fleeing their homes and seeking safety (e.g., witnessing or experience violence within refugee camps; Sullivan & Simonson, 2016). Children and adolescents who experienced war or political violence also experienced higher prevalence of traumatic loss, and community and domestic violence (Betancourt et al., 2012). This trauma exposure can subsequently affect their general well-being, with refugees having higher rates of mental health disorders (American Psychological Association, 2010; Arnetz et al., 2013).

It would also be important to consider intersectionality of these identities when considering traumatic stress. Minoritized students who are oppressed due to race, birthplace, documented status, and/or refugee status are more likely to be oppressed by other systems (e.g., economic marginalization) in society. Subsequently, these students may experience other types of trauma (e.g., physical, sexual, or psychological abuse), neglect (including trafficking), exposure to family or community violence, sudden or violent loss of a loved one, substance use disorder (personal or familial), serious accidents or life-threatening illness (The National Child Traumatic Stress Network, 2021). Overall, practitioners should further explore the impact of potential race-based and immigration-related trauma on students' acculturation in schools.

CULTURALLY RESPONSIVE ASSESSMENT OF MENTAL HEALTH AND TRAUMATIC STRESS

The process of conducting a culturally responsive assessment of mental health and/or traumatic stress for students includes a series of steps grounded in developmental and ecological models (Bronfenbrenner, 2005; Garcia Coll et al., 1996): (1) engaging in critical reflexivity, (2) developing relationships and earning trust with the student and family, (3) obtaining background information, (4) conducting interviews with caregivers, (5) administering tests and measures, and (6) providing written and oral feedback to the student and caregivers. Further, we describe specific ways that a practitioner can consider trauma and traumatic stress throughout this process.

Evidence-based strategies and considerations should be used to conduct culturally responsive assessment of mental health and traumatic stress. The aim or context of assessment may be different compared with assessments in clinical settings. It may not be necessary for a mental health practitioner to conduct an in-depth psychological evaluation for trauma in the school; a referral to an outside agency may be more appropriate. Indeed, de Arellano and Danielson (2008) suggested conducting a culturally responsive assessment of traumatic stress using the INFORMED approach: "(1) *I*nvestigate the target population, (2) *N*avigate new ways of delivering assessment services based on study of target population, (3) *F*urther assess extended family and other collaterals, (4) *O*rganize background assessment to better accommodate target populations, (5) *M*odify types of trauma-related sequelae assessed, (6) *E*valuate the effectiveness of the modified assessment, and (7) *D*evelop the assessment based on its evaluation" (p. 56). This culturally informed approach focuses on trauma assessment set in clinical settings (e.g., outpatient settings). However, we provide here a process of conducting a school-based culturally responsive assessment with a "trauma lens" to ensure that the student's difficulties are understood in the context and history of trauma (Tishelman et al., 2010, p. 287).

Additionally, this process can be conducted as part of an interdisciplinary team of school professionals, either to develop an intervention plan to support the student's mental health and learning, or to determine whether a student requires additional supports in or outside of school. Importantly, this strengths-based process uses multiple methods and multiple sources, and practitioners should consider the sociocultural factors that contribute to why students may be struggling in schools. Specific recommendations for interventions and counseling are discussed in Chapter 10.

Engaging in Critical Reflexivity

One of the most important steps when conducting culturally responsive assessments is to engage in critical reflexivity prior to and throughout the assessment. As described in Chapter 1, critical reflexivity is the process of intentionally reflecting on and critiquing one's cultural and professional background, knowledge, and skills as a practitioner (Cunliffe, 2016). When a practitioner is working with a student from a culture different from their own, critical reflexivity is a useful tool to ensure that their beliefs, knowledge, and background may not cloud their assessment process. It is not necessarily about being completely "objective" (because, frankly, that is not possible); rather, it is about acknowledging that one's background, biases, and culture can influence their understanding of other's behavior. See Appendix 7A for additional questions.

[Reflexivity Activity]. Here are some questions to consider as you begin a mental health assessment:

- *How does my understanding of mental health differ from those of the students with whom I am working? What is similar?*
- *What are my thoughts and feelings as I am beginning this assessment? What are my areas of discomfort? Why do I feel this discomfort?*
- *How does my understanding of mental health (or thoughts and feelings) impact my assessment with students?*

Establishing Relationships and Trust with Students and Families

During an assessment, it is paramount that the practitioner establish strong relationships and earn the trust of the student and their families with whom they are working. As practitioners, we must *earn* the trust, rather than believe that we automatically have that trust because of our position. In fact, because we are a member of a school, it may be that our positionality must be situated in the sociocultural and historical context of education in the United States. For instance, if schools serve a large population of Indigenous students across a number of tribal nations, the practitioner may need to understand how the school is situated within and representing colonialism, particularly because of the history of the U.S. federal government forcibly removing children from their families and placing them in residential schools (Campbell & Evans-Campbell, 2011). The current public school system may be perceived as simply an extension of this abuse.

One approach to earning this trust is what we call *visiting* (see more detail in Chapter 4). In most societies and cultures, visiting promotes relationship building. We visit each other to build relationships, to develop trust, and to enjoy each other's company. We promote here visiting with the caregivers and their students—whether in school or at home. As an example, using the vignette, Ms. Smith may invite Alejandra's family to the school to learn about their perspectives and experiences. Ideally, this visit would occur in Ms. Smith's office or another comfortable location, rather than a formal conference room. The family and school counselor may sit together for a while and talk about the family's experience and their thoughts about Alejandra's behavior. Visiting also means that for the first few minutes, Ms. Smith may share about her life experiences.

Another important component of relationship building is gathering information about the values and beliefs of the student and family. Taking initiative and deeply learning about the student's cultural identity and linguistic preferences can reflect the practitioners' respect and caring for that student. It may also be important for the practitioner to consult with individuals who are familiar with that population, particularly during a trauma assessment (de Arellano & Danielson, 2008). Cultural liaisons or brokers can be an important link between the school and family, in ensuring that the specific cultural norms and beliefs are respected. For example, in the vignette, Ms. Smith may seek support from a cultural liaison in the community who may be familiar with Alejandra's community and culture.

In addition to gaining cultural knowledge of the student, it is important to create a culturally affirming space where the student feels safe and comfortable prior to beginning the assessment. The physical office should be warm and inviting, with furniture arranged in a way that creates an open space, such as in a half-circle (Cook-Cottone et al., 2014). The practitioner can provide a warm and comfortable physical environment in the office, or perhaps, the student and practitioner will choose to go outdoors and find a private area with trees and in nature. In the office itself, there should also be images that reflect the cultural and linguistic groups of the students and families in the school and community.

Once there is a culturally affirming space, the practitioner can then begin to introduce the student and their family to the process of assessment. A first step is also providing a self-introduction. For example, the practitioner could say,

> *I am so glad you are here. My name is Ms. Smith, and I work at here at Rankin Elementary. My job is to help kids like you. Some kids come to me when they are feeling sad or when they are feeling happy. Some kids come to me when something really bad happened. I'm here to listen and help you. First, I'm going to ask some questions about what happened. Then, I'm going to have you fill out some worksheets and do some activities so we can create a plan to help you in any areas where things might be difficult for you right now. These help me understand how you are feeling. Then, I'm going to write a report that will be shared with your father and a team of other school staff.*

If the practitioner is not from the same cultural background as the student and family, it can also be helpful to provide a self-introduction and reflect on those differences, particularly when interacting with the caregivers. After the initial introduction, Ms. Smith could say,

> *I thought it might be helpful to share a bit about my background, as some parents and caregivers may be curious about who I am. I am a school psychologist and I identify as White and female. You shared that you are Blackfeet. I haven't yet worked with families from your Indigenous community, and I'm honored that I have the opportunity to work with you. There are likely parts of your culture that I am unfamiliar with, and I am here to listen as I work with your child.*

The practitioner should make efforts in providing opportunities for the families to be involved in the assessment process and address any potential barriers. The practitioner should explain the process and purpose of the assessment, including whether it is to inform school-based intervention or as part of special education eligibility or Section 504 process. As part of this explanation, the practitioner should explain the importance of gathering a variety of information, which may include details that are sensitive and personal, and obtain a release of information from the family to gather medical or outside records beyond the educational history.

During this conversation, the practitioner can also ensure that any potential barriers in the assessment process are addressed. For instance, the practitioner may need to consider how to address reducing language barriers. Incorporating interpreters into the assessment process can be challenging, but there are effective ways to broach this (see Chapter 5). Logistical barriers should also be considered, such as making sure that the families and student can access the office with appropriate transportation and flexible scheduling (de Arellano & Danielson, 2008). It may be helpful also to offer additional options to ensure families' participation in the assessment process, such as conducting interviews on a phone call or using a videoconferencing platform such as Zoom. Finally, some families may be hesitant about engaging with the school because of stigma associated with mental health or fear that their immigration status will be affected (e.g., deportation). The practitioner can take steps to alleviate any fears by communicating directly with the family and ensuring confidentiality. These efforts will foster stronger relationships and trust with the family.

Review Records on Medical, Educational, and Psychological History

The next step in conducting a culturally responsive assessment is gathering background information through medical, educational, and psychological records. Obtaining background information through the record review process can be helpful in understanding the factors that may be contributing to the student's traumatic stress or mental health problems (see Chapter 4 for more details about reviewing records), along with determining trends and patterns in academic and attendance history. This process is particularly important if a student had witnessed traumatic event, as de Arellano and Danielson (2008) suggested that an assessment of the students' history is important because research has shown that a student who has experienced one type of trauma is likely to experience another.

When reviewing records, the practitioner can attend to information about the culture and family background. Past medical reports may summarize any initial concerns regarding the student's physical health, as well as provide information for ruling out any physical concerns (e.g., vision issues, reaching developmental milestones). Records may also include information about the family's socioeconomic background and geographic location, which may be helpful in understanding what systems surrounding the family (e.g., access to adequate housing, healthcare) may be barriers to the student's well-being. For example, Ms. Smith may seek information about Alejandra's well-check visits with her pediatrician to make sure to rule out any concerns with her physical health that may be contributing to her anxiety symptoms.

Interviewing Student, Families, and Caregivers

The next step in a culturally responsive assessment is conducting an interview with the student, family, other caregivers, and educators. As we highlighted in Chapter 4, there are a number of components of interviewing that should be considered within a multi-method, multi-source assessment, including (1) establishing relationships and visiting, (2) relational interviewing, (3) integrating cultural components, and (4) completing the interview by bringing everyone together. We focus specifically on conducting relational interviewing and integrating cultural components for assessment of mental health and traumatic stress.

During the interview, the practitioner should consider the power dynamics between themselves and the person they are interviewing. Although we often think of interviews as simply dialogue between two individuals, there are, in fact, dominance and power (Kvale, 2006). The relationships and dynamics between the practitioner and the caregiver, for example, are shaped by the power the practitioner hold as a person within the school as well as what they may represent. When working with Alejandra's parents, Ms. Smith may need to be aware that her position as a school psychologist may be viewed as having more power in the educational decision-making process. Ms. Smith may need to consider the impact of this power on fostering relationships with Alejandra's parents, and she may even need to discuss this when meeting with them. Alejandra's parents may believe that the teacher (such as Ms. Smith) has expertise in that area, while they do not. As a result, they may not be as forthcoming about their perspectives about how to support Alejandra.

RELATIONAL INTERVIEWING WITH THE STUDENT
Within a culturally responsive assessment, there are two purposes for interviewing the student: (1) gathering information to inform intervention, and (2) establishing a strong trusting relationship. Both should occur simultaneously. Importantly, the practitioner should create a relationally safe and culturally affirming space by being open to hearing the student's experience without judgment. Using a "storytelling" tone rather than the typical "singsong" voice that is sometimes used with children can be helpful in providing a safe space for the student (Nader, 2007). Another helpful strategy in culturally responsive assessment is for the student to draw something and share a story about the drawing, as well as have fidget toys to engage in with the practitioner (Nader, 2007).

Once a relationally safe and culturally affirming space is established, the practitioner can engage in *relational interviewing* (see Appendix 7B), which can be done through storytelling (Hydén, 2014) When assessing the student's mental health and traumatic stress, relational interviewing can be helpful in gathering the information about the student's symptoms and surrounding events by fostering a trusting relationship and minimizing judgment. Ms. Smith may begin working with Alejandra with the following statement:

> Alejandra, my name is Ms. Smith and I'm the school psychologist. Here are some paper and markers in case you feel like drawing. I heard from your teachers and your father that they are worried about you. I'm here to support you and learn a bit more about you. First, I'd like to hear a story about you. Share with me a story about a time that you felt proud.

The aim of this interviewing approach is to foster trust between the Ms. Smith and Alejandra. Given that student may feel uncomfortable being asked to leave class and visit with a stranger, this provides the practitioner with a way to initiate a conversation. Throughout the interview, Ms. Smith could state,

> Keep telling me, does this remind you of something you've experienced before? Tell me, is there an image or a picture that expresses what you're talking about?

In order to gather information to inform the intervention, the practitioner could use structured and unstructured interview approaches (see Chapter 4 for a summary). An example of a semi-structured interview includes the Jones Intentional Multicultural Interview Schedule (JIMIS; Jones, 2009), which provides a useful framework and table for interviewing with students and caregivers. There are five domains in the interview: (1) family (e.g., "How do you define family? Who is in your family?"), (2) peers (e.g., "What are some characteristics about you that make you different from people in your group?"), (3) race (e.g. "How does you race impact your relationships with other people?"), (4) ethnicity (e.g., "How do religion and spirituality impact your family every day?"), and (5) personal (e.g., "What situations are the most stressful for you?) (Jones, 2009).

Another semi-structured interview would be the Cultural Formulation Interview (CFI). The CFI was developed because of concerns that clinical interviews and DSM diagnoses had not been adequately addressing the cultural considerations as part of culturally responsive mental health assessment (Lewis-Fernández et al., 2015). The CFI includes four main domains: (1) cultural definition of the problem, (2) cultural perceptions of cause, context, and support, (3) cultural factors affecting self-coping and past help seeking, and finally, (4) cultural factors affecting current help seeking. Although the CFI may be helpful in guiding the process and content of an interview, it is primarily designed for clinical settings (e.g., community outpatient centers), rather than school-based settings. Thus, practitioners may want to consider modifying the interview to align with school-based mental health practices.

Whether a semi-structured or unstructured interview is used, practitioners should consider a number of recommendations when interviewing students for mental health concerns or traumatic stress. For example, Nader (2007) suggested that during the interview practitioners should understand how to interpret the student's body language and thought patterns, particularly as they relate to how the student may show signs of distress. When working with Alejandra, for example, Ms. Smith may ask questions about her experience and observe her body language. Alejandra may avoid discussing witnessing a death, yet she may wring her hands during the interview and complain that she has a stomachache. Another consideration may be the degree to which the student makes eye contact with the practitioner. Although Alejandra may avoid eye contact during the interview, Ms. Smith should also consider that some children across different cultural groups (e.g., Indigenous) may show deference by not making direct eye contact with an elder. Thus, interpreting "lack of eye contact" and other body language must be done in the context of that student's cultural group.

If the student has a history of trauma, it is important to gather information about the incident(s), as well as what occurred prior to and after that incident. The practitioner could ask questions about the student's feelings and thoughts before, during, and after the incident(s), as well as the strategies the student has used that were or were not effective. When asking questions to address the student's trauma, it is important that the questions are asked in behaviorally specific and non-stigmatizing ways. In their INFORMED approach, de Arellano and Danielson (2008) suggested that instead of asking, "Have you ever been physically abused?," the practitioner should ask, "Have you ever been hit so hard that it left bruises?" (p. 55).

When assessing adolescents for traumatic stress, it would also be important to observe and document the student's reactions. Adolescents often want to preserve their self-image, so they may minimize the significance of or suppress emotions related to traumatic event (Habib & Labruna, 2011). Alejandra, for example, may say, "Oh, it really wasn't a big deal. I didn't know the person who died." Further, adolescents may not feel a great deal of trust, and therefore may not be totally accurate in reporting their symptoms (Habib & Labruna, 2011). Alejandra may avoid answering Ms. Smith's questions or stay silent during the interview. Finally, adolescents may be influenced by their peers and tend either to overstress or underreport the severity of the symptoms (Habib & Labruna, 2011). When socializing with her friends, Alejandra may brush off their concerns and simply remark that she can "handle it." Thus, practitioners who are conducting interviews with adolescents may need to exert more effort into fostering a strong rapport and asking questions in different ways to ensure that they are receiving an accurate reporting of symptoms, behaviors, and feelings.

Another consideration when conducting interviews is to determine whether a student has potentially experienced race-based trauma. Bryant-Davis and Ocampo (2006) emphasized that the practitioner should provide a supportive environment where the student can share their experiences of a racist-based incident and discuss the effects of that incident. They recommended asking:

- *"I would also like to ask if you have ever been treated in a disturbing manner because of your race"* or

- *"Have you ever had a bad or upsetting experience because of your race, skin color, facial features, hair texture, cultural, or religious background?"* (Bryant-Davis & Ocampo, 2006, p. 6).

The practitioner should also ask questions about whether the student observed or witnessed a racist-based incident, and how they responded to it.

INTERVIEWING THE FAMILY AND CAREGIVERS

[Reflexivity Activity]. Consider the following questions:

- *Reflect on your interviewing style or approach. From whom did you learn this style or approach? Why were you taught this style or approach?*
- *What aspects of culture influence your interviewing style? Consider your tone, your eye contact, and your nonverbal body language used.*

Like relational interviewing with the student, relational interviewing with the caregiver involves eliciting information through storytelling (Hydén, 2014). Conducting a semi-structured interview with the family and other caregivers in the student's life is helpful in better understanding the student's past and current challenges (de Arellano & Danielson, 2008). A semi-structured approach is helpful for the practitioner, as they can make sure caregivers can express information openly and in multiple ways; however, integrating the storytelling technique in addition to this approach can help facilitate relationship building. The practitioner should begin with a structured approach and then modify it for each student as more information is gathered.

The interview itself should include the primary caregivers (e.g., Alejandra's father), as well as any extended family members or other adults who are important in the student's life. Questions about trauma exposure are sensitive, so it can be helpful for the practitioner to explain the rationale and process for assessment. The practitioner could explain to caregivers that some of the questions they will ask may be sensitive, but they are asked of all students to be sure each student's needs are met. Establishing a strong relationship with the family early can be helpful throughout the assessment, but particularly during the interview.

Further, de Arellano and Danielson (2008) suggested that the caregiver's own trauma history should be assessed, as the caregiver's own experiences of trauma may be affecting their ability to cope and support their child. This component of the assessment may not necessarily be appropriate within some school-based mental health assessments; however, we discuss it here, as it may be important to consider within a broader mental health assessment of a student. Asking questions about the family's coping resources, social support, and additional stressors is particularly important to fully understand the student's experiences and the systems that surround them. For example, a caregiver's culturally related spiritual beliefs may affect how sexual abuse is viewed (de Arellano & Danielson, 2008).

There are a number of culturally specific approaches to conducting interviews. For example, when working with Latinx students and families, Arredondo et al.

(2014) highlighted culturally grounded approaches, including considering *respeto* (respect, deference to authority figures) and *personalismo*, or preference for a personable approach where practitioners must "respond to the tone, emotions, and needs of the client" (p. 148). A *personalismo* approach may include having the practitioner share some minor personal details, such as that they have children or where they are from (importantly, this is based on the practitioner's level of comfort as well). As an example, the authors shared a case of a Latina mother who appeared anxious, watching the clock during the interview, which could be interpreted as a caregiver not valuing the time spent with the practitioner. Yet, later it was revealed that she had been worried about picking up her children and had not wanted to interrupt because it would have been disrespectful (Arredondo et al., 2014). Once the practitioner realizes this, they can empathetically respond by saying, "You are very close to your children and want to make sure they are safe. I want to make sure they are safe too." Overall, relational interviewing of the student and their caregiver provides opportunities to elicit relevant information while fostering trust in a culturally affirming way.

Administer Relevant Tests and Measures

Culturally responsive assessment of mental health and traumatic stress often requires administering relevant tests and measures, such as rating scales. When selecting tools for an assessment, Kisiel et al. (2021) recommended that a multi-informant approach is best, with measures for the student, caregivers, and educators. These measures are given to the student (self-report), caregivers (often called a parent report), and/or educators (teacher report). Multi-source information can allow for validation and convergence of different data. Nonetheless, it is important to be aware that there may be discrepancies between informants on certain measures because there may be differences in how each informant shares information about the child. See Appendix 7A for questions to consider when selecting tests and measures.

Self-report measures are very useful for assessing mental health and trauma symptoms. When selecting the tool, practitioner should consider both age and developmental level, given that self-report tools may less appropriate for students in early childhood settings compared with elementary or high school settings (Kisiel et al., 2021). Ms. Smith could administer a self-report measure (e.g., Behavior Assessment Scale for Children—Third Edition) to Alejandra because she is older and can report the symptoms she is experiencing. Interpretation of results should be done with caution, however, as some students may either underreport or exaggerate behaviors and feelings.

Caregiver and teacher measures are also really helpful. Parents can often observe changes in their children's behavior more accurately, particularly if the child is young or has a developmental disability. There may be differences between parents' responses, however. For example, Alejandra's father may report different symptoms compared with Alejandra's mother, which can have a number

Table 7.1. SELECT MEASURES FOR TRAUMA AND MENTAL HEALTH

Measures for Trauma Symptoms	Brief Description
Trauma Symptom Checklist for Children (Briere, 1996)	Fifty-four-item questionnaire that evaluates acute and chronic posttraumatic symptomatology for children aged 8–18. Screening form with 20 items also available.
Children's PTSD Inventory (Saigh et al., 2000)	Fifty-item structured interview for children aged 6–18.
Multidimensional Anxiety Scale for Children, Second Edition (March et al., 1997)	Multi-rater (parent and self-report) assessing the presence of symptoms related to anxiety disorders in children aged 8–19.
Beck Youth Inventories (Beck, 2005)	Five self-report inventories with 20 items to assess symptoms of depression, anxiety, anger, disruptive behavior, and self-concept in children aged 7–18.
Ages & Stages Questionnaires: Social-Emotional (Squires et al., 2009)	Parent/caregiver measures to screen for self-regulation, compliance, social communication, adaptive functioning, autonomy, affect, and interaction with people for children aged 1–72 months. Languages available: English, Spanish, Arabic, and French.
UCLA Posttraumatic Stress Disorder Reaction Index for DSM-5 (Steinberg et al., 2004)	Multi-rater (caregiver and self-report) that assesses trauma history for children aged 7–18 and children aged 6 and younger.

of explanations. Both parents may observe particular behaviors depending on context, setting, and time of day. Although some scales include a validity scale, practitioners should supplement the measure with individual interviews and follow-up with parents' responses within the measures. Similarly, teachers are also helpful in understanding the student's behavior in the classroom, and whether there have been recent changes in those behaviors. There are a number of different measures, both for free and purchase, that can be helpful in gathering information about symptoms (see Table 7.1).

These multi-informant approaches are helpful within a comprehensive school-based assessment of the student's symptoms that can be examined across a number of domains. Tishelman et al. (2010) suggested a number of domains to focus on when a student is experiencing traumatic stress:

- self-regulation
- physical functioning
- relationships
- academics

For self-regulation, they suggested that assessment should include a focus on the student's abilities (and inabilities) to identify emotions, the degree to which they are hypervigilant to threats or have extreme moods. Thus, interviewing Alejandra's teachers can be helpful in understanding her self-regulation skills (Do Alejandra's moods change across the school day? How does she handle difficult situations?). A second domain is physical functioning, in which there should be a focus on the student's physical symptoms, including the students' boundaries around their peers and perhaps any trauma-related injuries. Alejandra, for example, may exhibit symptoms of traumatic stress through stomachaches or headaches. The third domain is related to relationships, where the assessment should focus on the student's trust and safety, as well as their social skills and competencies. When assessing Alejandra, the practitioner may want to ask questions about her peer relationships as well as her sense of trust with adults. Finally, for academics, Tishelman and colleagues suggested that the focus should be on their executive functioning, processing speed, and language development. Depending on the student, measures of cognitive abilities (e.g., Woodcock–Johnson Tests of Cognitive Abilities) as well as measure of language (e.g., a writing activity) may be helpful in understanding how the traumatic stress has affected their cognitive skills.

Similarly, Cohen et al. (2017) recommended that in addition to assessing symptoms of PTSD, other domains should be assessed. Using the acronym CRAFTS, they suggested that the practitioner consider the following:

- Cognitive problems: These are the patterns of thinking about the self and others, as well as inaccurate thoughts, such as blaming oneself for traumatic events.
- Relationship problems: These types of problems are associated with challenges in getting along with peers and adults, or difficulty with social skills.
- Affective problems: These are internalizing symptoms such as feelings of sadness or fear.
- Family problems: These types of concerns are related to caregiving challenges, such as difficulties with communicating with their children or lack of skills associated with supporting their child.
- Traumatic behavior problems: These are problems associated with avoiding trauma reminders or behaving in ways that are aggressive or unsafe.
- Somatic problems: These types of problems are associated with physiological responses, such as sleep or hypervigilance, or somatic symptoms (e.g., headaches).

BIASES IN TESTS AND MEASURES

Gathering information from tests and measures can be a useful part of a culturally responsive assessment, but there are a number of considerations. First, practitioner bias may be a factor in diagnosing, and misdiagnosing, students. Black youth were rated higher on externalizing behaviors and were rated lower on internalizing behaviors, while White and Latinx youth were rated higher on internalizing behaviors and rated lower on externalizing behaviors (Minsky et al.,

2006). Indeed, racial and gender biases have been seen for many disorders in children and adolescents, including ADHD and conduct disorder (Garb, 2021). Although there are likely systemic and multifactorial reasons why implicit biases occur, practitioner bias is a possibility. That is, practitioners may encounter a student and, based on their race or gender, may subsequently ask questions in an interview that would confirm their hypotheses (Garb, 2021). Students' responses to questions could be perceived in a particular way depending on race, ethnicity, language, or gender. They may emphasize some data more than others depending on the student's social and cultural identities. An important step in conducting culturally responsive assessment is recognizing the potential for this bias. Additional considerations regarding test bias are discussed in Chapter 4.

[Reflexivity Activity]: Consider the following questions:

- *We all have implicit biases. What biases do I have that may influence how I interpret the data gathered during the assessment?*
- *When choosing a test or measure, what sociocultural and ecological factors may be important in this decision?* (van de Vijver & Poortinga, 2020)

ASSESSMENT REPORT AND INTERVENTION PLANNING

Once the culturally responsive assessment is completed, then the practitioner should design an intervention or treatment plan that aligns with the results of the initial assessment. First, an important component of intervention planning is developing a thorough case conceptualization in which all of the assessment information is reviewed and hypotheses are developed to address the underlying concern (Sanchez et al., 2021). Importantly, the entire case conceptualization process should be done with strengths-based and student-centered considerations in mind. Appendix 7C includes a culturally responsive planning tool. Questions to ponder include:

- What has the multi-method, multi-source revealed about the student's strengths? The student's areas of concern?
- What are the primary systems around the student (e.g., from classroom to family to surrounding neighborhood) that have contributed to the student's mental health concerns? What aspects of those systems can be addressed to support that student?
- What scientifically supported interventions are available (in the school or elsewhere) for the student? To what degree have these interventions been tested for that student's cultural and linguistic group? In what ways would these interventions potentially be adapted or redesigned to be culturally responsive?

Depending on the practitioner's role, a formal diagnosis may or may not be made based on the case conceptualization. We argue that diagnoses can be helpful for communication about the student's experiences and symptoms, but it is not necessary for a school-based mental health intervention to be implemented. It is more important that the symptoms, or areas of concern, are the focus of the intervention. That is, the intervention should directly link to the symptoms (e.g., behaviors, emotions) that the student is experiencing. This is done whether the symptoms align with special education categories (i.e., emotional disturbance) or not.

The results of the assessment should also be disseminated to the student and caregivers in both written (e.g., psychological report) and oral (e.g., feedback session) formats. A written report of the results is important so that the process of the assessment is documented, and the results are summarized with practical recommendations offered for home and school. We argue that the written report should be comprehensive, yet succinct (if the report is too long, they are often skimmed or ignored). The report needs to be written in a way that both professionals and caregivers can understand and include (1) the rationale for the assessment, (2) the reasons why particular approaches and instruments are included in the assessment, (3) the sociocultural factors that were considered during the assessment, and (4) the reasons for a particular diagnosis or eligibility for special education. Similarly, when sharing the results orally, each of these steps is explained thoroughly, paying attention to defining concretely any jargon.

The next step is to create intervention goals collaboratively. Given that practitioners will have already begun rapport and relationship building during the assessment process, this stage of intervention planning should be a continuation of that relationship. The student's and family's voice and choice should be integrated regarding what areas of intervention should be prioritized. The practitioner therefore collaborates with the student and their family in considering the primary areas of concern. In their culturally informed model of family-based cognitive-behavioral therapy, Sanchez et al. (2021) suggested that practitioners consider the "family's cultural definition of the problem" and to have the family integrally involved in describing how the problem may be contributing to the student's mental health and well-being. The intervention does not necessarily mean one-on-one counseling for the student but may, in fact, be a classroom-wide intervention, or a schoolwide intervention. If the primary area of concern can be addressed at the systems level, the practitioner should work with administrators and educators to implement an intervention at a larger scale (see Chapter 9).

Further, goals should be developed that are observable and measurable so that both the practitioner and student can monitor their improvement. These intervention goals should consider the contextual variables that may be contributing to the student's concerns as well as what may be causing those behaviors to continue. Additionally, the intervention goals should be based on positive behavioral supports and written in a way that is leading to improved behavior. In a culturally informed approach, Sanchez et al. (2021) suggested that the intervention goal be designed with a hypothesized dependent variable. They suggested for a child with disruptive behavior, for example, writing the goal as, "the child will have three fewer explosive meltdowns per week" (p. 13). Then, the practitioner should also determine how to monitor those behaviors. For example, the practitioner could track from week to week (ideally using some kind of visual means) with "number of explosive meltdowns per week as reported by the student's teacher." The goal and the progress monitoring would help determine whether the intervention was effective in supporting the student's mental health. Overall, throughout the sharing of the assessment results and the development of the intervention goals, the process should be collaborative with both the student and their caregiver.

SUMMARY

The purpose of this chapter was to provide a culturally responsive framework for assessing students who experience difficulties related to mental health and traumatic stress. We highlighted the cultural perspectives of mental health and traumatic stress, such as considering how the construct of mental health or a "life well lived" is shaped by the values of our society. These cultural factors, including expressions of distress and beliefs about help seeking, are critical to consider within a culturally responsive assessment. There are six steps within a culturally responsive assessment: (1) engaging in critical reflexivity, (2) developing relationships and earning trust with the student and family, (3) obtaining background information, (4) conducting interviews with caregivers, (5) administering tests and measures, and (6) providing written and oral feedback to the student and caregivers.

DISCUSSION QUESTIONS

1. Alex is a sixth-grade student referred to you by one of her teachers, Ms. Smith. Alex's home had been burned down in a wildfire, which had destroyed several houses in your community. Alex's family immigrated from Hungary before she was born. They are reluctant to come to the school because their own experience in schools was not positive.
   a. What are some sociocultural and ecological factors that you should consider as you begin an assessment?
   b. What are some advantages and disadvantages to using semi-structured interviews in this case?
2. In what ways can you obtain the caregiver's perspective and beliefs on wellness related to mental health? How will you make sure you have grasped comprehensively what wellness means to the caregivers? How will you make sure you are capturing both the student's and the caregiver's perceptions and beliefs of mental wellness?

APPENDIX 7A
CULTURALLY RESPONSIVE APPROACH TO SELECTING TESTS AND MEASURES: QUESTIONS TO ASK

Purpose

- What information do I want to gather about the student?
- What information about the sociocultural factors and ecological systems may be important for understanding this student?

Norms

- What is the student's primary racial and/or ethnic group?
- Is the student's racial/ethnic group represented in norms in the manual? If so, what percentage of the sample was this racial/ethnic group?

Language

- What is the student's primary language?
- If the student is an English Language Learner, how will this test adequately represent the student's skills?

Administration, Scoring, and Interpretation

- What are some considerations when administering this test or measure?
- If the student's racial/ethnic group is not represented in the norms, how I am going to interpret the scores of this test or measure?

APPENDIX 7B
RELATIONAL INTERVIEWING FOR STUDENT

1. Visiting
Welcome to space, offer snack (if appropriate), provide toys/fidgets/drawings.

Self-introduction and purpose of the assessment
I am so glad you are here. We have not met before, and I'd like to share a bit about myself. As [JOB], my role is to really understand who you are and what kinds of supports you might need. The way I think about my job is that I'm a detective and I'm looking for lots of different clues. No one clue is helpful—I have to look for a lot of clues, from talking with you, talking with your parents and teachers, as well as giving some questionnaires and tests.

I am [SELF-IDENTIFIERS: RACE, GENDER, ETC] and my background may be different from yours, and I acknowledge these differences may shape my perspectives. This is why I want to speak with you. Can I answer any questions about me or this process?

2. Relational Interviewing

Initial Strengths and Concerns
- Share with me a story that makes you proud.
- Tell me about some things that make you worried? When did you begin to worry? When did you notice the changes?
- Share with me some of the things you have done so far that seemed to work. What about things that did not work at all?

Sociocultural Factors
- There are many aspects of our identities that are meaningful to us. Share with me some of your identities.
- I am curious to learn about what aspects of your identity are important to you.
- Spirituality and religion can play an important role in many families' lives. Tell me about your family.
- You mentioned that you recently arrived to this community. Tell me the story about this journey here.
- There are lots of kids who have recently come to the United States from other countries. Has that been your experience?
- Tell me about the important adults in your life? Who are the adults that take care of you?
- Some families have been unhoused or living in shelters. Have you experienced this?

Developmental History
- You might not remember, but tell me what you were like when you were really young.
- In the past, have other adults or professionals (like doctors) told you that they were worried about you?

- Language Skills
  - Tell me what languages you speak at home. How comfortable are you in speaking those languages?

Education History
- Tell me about school.
- Thinking about things you learn in school, how well do you do in reading? Math? Writing?

Medical and Psychological History
- Share with me a time when you needed support or help. What happened and how did you respond?
- What serious medical issues have you experienced? Have you ever been hospitalized? Had any operations? Had any accidents?
- Now I want to learn about your thoughts and feelings.
  - Internalizing symptoms: Tell me about your feelings recently. Have you felt like you had/were. . . [Low Energy, Hopeless, Sad, Helpless]?
    - Self-harm: Cuts, Hits, Kicks, Burns, Self, Bangs Head, Risk Taking
    - Suicidal ideation, attempts
  - Externalizing symptoms: Tell me about your behavior, or action. Have you felt like you had . . . ?
    - Attention issues: Inattention, Distractible, Can't Concentrate
    - Activity level: Over-Active, Hyper-Active, Out of Control, Inactive, Passive
    - Disruptive behaviors/tantrums
    - Cruelty to animals
    - Damaged property
  - Trauma:
    - Some children experience traumatic events. Tell me about any traumatic events in your child's life.
    - Have you been hurt by someone in your life? Have you experienced [Sexual/Physical/Emotional/Verbal Abuse, Accident, Injury]?
    - When you are upset or angry, what are some things that you do to calm down?
- Some parents are comfortable with counseling while other parents are not. Tell me about your thoughts on counseling for your child
- Parents show that they care about and love their children in different ways. Tell me how your parents.

Additional Prompts Throughout:
- I would like to hear a story about your life.
- Keep telling me, does this remind you of something you've experienced before, or is there something more to say about this?
- Is it possible to give me an image, or color or scent, that could express what you're talking about?
- Kids often talk about . . . is this something you think or talk about?

APPENDIX 7C
CULTURALLY RESPONSIVE INTERVENTION PLANNING TOOL

Student Name: _____   DOB: _____

School: _____   Grade: _____

Goal Orientation
Summary of referral and collaborative goals with caregivers

Cultural Dimensions
Sociocultural factors and ecological systems to consider

Baseline Level of Performance
Initial assessment results (e.g., tests and measures, Subjective Units of Distress)
     Measure Used:
     Score:

Procedure
Intervention Approach/Strategies

Arrangement
Location/Frequency/Materials

Progress Monitoring Strategy and Decision-Making Plan
Summary of Formative and Summative Evaluation (including graphs)

Promoting Resilience, Mental Health, and Well-Being of Diverse Students

School-based mental health practitioners aim to support students' mental health or learning. Often, practitioners' work focuses on the students' problems or concerns. In this section, we provide strategies for practitioners to promote students' resilience, mental health and well-being, highlighting strengths-based approaches. We highlight ways to promote safe and positive school climate as well as how to establish culturally responsive multi-tiered systems of support. We also provide specific strategies on how to adapt evidence-based interventions for culturally and linguistically diverse students, as well as implement counseling and psychotherapeutic approaches. Finally, we describe culturally responsive mental health program evaluations as an important tool for practitioners.

Promoting Resilience, Mental Health, and Well-Being of Diverse Students

Developing and Sustaining a Culturally Responsive and Positive School Climate

VIGNETTE

Washington Middle School is located in a large metropolitan school district with a high proportion of Black and Latinx students. The principal of Washington Middle, Ms. Campbell, is interested in understanding the students' and educators' perceptions of school climate, particularly after several incidents in the past two years in which there has been increased vandalism, harassment via social media, and teacher burnout. Ms. Campbell has noticed strengths among student–teacher relationships and believes the overall school climate could be more positive.

QUESTIONS

- *How would Ms. Campbell proceed in gathering perceptions from students and educators about the climate at her school?*
- *How would Ms. Campbell use this information to promote a more positive school climate?*

School professionals, like Ms. Campbell, want their schools to provide a positive and safe learning environment for all their students. Indeed, research has shown that schools that have positive school climates have higher student academic achievement (Daily et al., 2019). Yet, developing and sustaining a positive school climate can be challenging for school professionals because it requires them to gather information on students', teachers', and staff's perceptions of school life, which can be difficult to measure, and to choose and implement effective programs to address those perceptions. Further, some students may believe the school environment as positive, while others may perceive it as not. Some of the reasons why schools may not have a positive climate may be due to systemic or ecological issues that often mitigate efforts to promote inclusion, diversity, and equity, especially those who have been marginalized or culturally and linguistically diverse (CLD) students.

The purpose of this chapter is to provide school professionals with strategies to develop and sustain a culturally responsive and positive school climate. First, we describe school climate, its various dimensions, and its association with positive student outcomes. Then, using one particular framework, the cultural-ecological model of school climate (CEMSC; La Salle et al., 2015), we describe the steps for individuals to engage in reflexivity, develop objectives, gather data, and implement programs that support a positive school climate for all students, particularly those who are from CLD backgrounds.

SCHOOL CLIMATE

School climate encapsulates a broad pattern of people's experiences of school life and reflects the goals, values, interpersonal relationships, teaching and learning practices, and organizational structures of schools (Cohen et al., 2009; National School Climate Center [NSCC], 2021b). Although many definitions exist, we define school climate as the individual and collective experiences, attitudes, and feelings that students, teachers, and staff have about the school. Therefore, a positive school climate is a product of the perceived interpersonal experiences of those individuals to form an atmosphere of support, safety, and belonging. A positive school climate promotes student learning and well-being, where

> students, families and educators work together to develop, live, and contribute to a shared school vision. Educators model and nurture an attitude that emphasizes the benefits of, and satisfaction from, learning. Each person contributes to the operations of the school as well as the care of the physical environment. (NSCC, 2021b)

Although related, school climate is different from *school culture*, which is "the school's ethos and social environment (traditions, beliefs)" and represents the broader organizational or institutional culture and professional relationships (Avalos, 2011, p. 12). That is, school culture may reflect underlying norms, shared values, belief patterns, practices, rituals, and interactions that are built up over time, which results in deeply ingrained expectations. These expectations are unwritten rules to which each person in the school conforms in order to remain in good standing with peers or colleagues. The school therefore develops a common culture that passes on these expectations to the next generation. As an example of school culture, perhaps all classroom teachers at an elementary school offer Pizza Day at the end of the week to celebrate student effort or achievements. This weekly routine may result in students and teachers perceiving the school climate as positive and supportive. In this case, the school culture seems to drive school climate. On the flip side, if students and teachers do not feel supported and perceive a negative school climate, they may be less likely to hold Pizza Day events each week, and this event would not be part of the school culture. Thus, school climate can be thought of as "how people feel about the school," whereas school culture can be described as "how things are done at the school."

We specifically focus on school climate because perceptions and attitudes are more malleable than deeply rooted practices of school culture. Certainly, changes in climate can influence culture. A sustained and positive school climate has been linked to positive student learning, academic achievement, effective risk prevention and health promotion, high graduation rates, low dropout rates, and teacher retention (Thapa et al., 2013). Positive perceptions of school climate can lead to increases in positive mental health and life satisfaction, and also decreases in internalizing and externalizing behaviors (Suldo et al., 2012). Further, school climate has been associated with positive social-emotional competence (Kwong & Davis, 2015). Importantly, school climate has also been found to be associated with increased academic achievement (Demirtas-Zorbaz et al., 2021). For example, high school students who feel supported and encouraged to succeed academically (by their peers, teachers, and their parents) are more likely to perform better on standardized test scores on math and reading (Kwong & Davis, 2015). Overall, positive school climate has important implications on students' social, emotional, behavioral, and academic skills.

DIMENSIONS OF SCHOOL CLIMATE

Scholars have conceptualized school climate as being composed of various interrelated dimensions. Although some scholars have proposed a number of dimensions, we outline six dimensions of school climate that may be helpful for practitioners to consider: (a) safety, (b) relationships, (c) teaching and learning, (d) institutional environment, (e) school improvement process, and (f) social media (Thapa et al., 2013). Sub-dimensions have been proposed by the National School Climate Center (Cohen et al., 2009), which can be found in Table 8.1.

Safety

In the first dimension, safety refers to students' feelings of safety, whether physically, emotionally, or socially (Thapa et al., 2013). Safety is a foundational and basic need for students. Before students can learn, they must feel safe; thus, school climate should be assessed with regard to students' physical safety and social-emotional security. *Physical safety* refers to the protection of individuals from violence, physical aggression, and bodily harm (Darling-Hammond & Cook-Harvey, 2018). *Social-emotional security*, on the other hand, refers to feelings of safety where individuals demonstrate the confidence to express emotions, thoughts, and

Table 8.1. DIMENSIONS AND SUB-DIMENSIONS OF SCHOOL SAFETY ADAPTED
FROM NATIONAL SCHOOL CLIMATE CENTER

Dimensions and Sub-Dimensions	Examples
Safety	
• Rules and Safety	Clearly outlining school/classroom rules, expectations, and responses to violation of rules
• Sense of Physical Security	Feeling safe from physical or bodily harm
• Sense of Social-Emotional Security	Feeling safe about identity and feeling included
Relationships	
• Social Support - Adults/Teachers	Developing positive and responsive relationships between educators, school staff, and students
• Social Support - Students/Peers	Developing positive peer relationships and friendships
Teaching and Learning	
• Support for Learning	Providing challenging academic material, while also giving positive and constructive feedback to improve
• Social and Civil Learning	Promoting learning of skills related to self-regulation, conflict resolution, and empathy
Institutional Environment	
• School Connectedness and Engagement	Promoting sense of belonging and participating in school-related activities
• Physical Surroundings	Setting up physical environments and classroom layouts that are conducive to effective learning
School Improvement Process	
• Leadership	Displaying clear mission and vision of the school related to safety
• Professional Relationships	Promoting positive relationships between staff, administration, and families
Social Media	
• Social Media	Use of social media productively and ensuring safety from technological misuse (e.g., cyberbullying prevention)

NOTE: Adapted from *ED School Climate Surveys (EDSCLS)*, by the National Center on Safe Supportive Learning Environments, 2021 (retrieved December 17, 2021, from https://safesupportivelearning.ed.gov/edscls).

ideas or take risks to try something new without verbal abuse, teasing, and exclusion (Darling-Hammond & Cook-Harvey, 2018). Safety occurs when rules and regulations are clear, consistent, and fair. Rules should be developed collaboratively by representatives of the total school community and consistently enforced.

Students' perceptions of safety have been found to be associated with school suspensions and dropouts. For example, students' attitudes related to aggressive behavior and rule breaking were associated with high school dropout rates (Lee et al., 2011). There are differences, however, among racial minoritized groups. When comparing Black and White students, students' aggressive attitudes and beliefs in school rules were not associated with dropout rates of Black students; the school suspension rate, however, was associated with dropout rates for this group (Lee et al., 2011).

Cultural differences exist related to school security and perceived student connectedness among students from White and minoritized groups, as well as across grade levels. In one study, Black students reported lower perceptions of school climate compared with students identified as Hispanic/Latinx, White, Asian or Other (Parris et al., 2018). In another study, minoritized fifth-grade students were more likely to report less connectedness to adults at school (e.g., teachers) compared with their White peers, even when taking into consideration gender and grade (Anyon et al., 2016). Minoritized fifth-grade students perceived the environment as less safe and reported lower levels of achievement motivation even after controlling for classroom- and school-level factors (Koth et al., 2008). When students perceive racial inequity and disproportional discipline by adults, *all* students feel less connected to adults at school (Anyon et al., 2016).

Gaps in school connectedness particularly exist in middle schools when there are both Black and White students. Black students reported lower levels of safety and perceived connectedness in schools that had larger numbers of both Black and White students; similarly, when there were larger numbers of Hispanic and White students, Hispanic students reported lower levels of safety and perceived connectedness (Voight et al., 2015). Importantly, these racial climate gaps were also associated with racial achievement gaps. Students' perceptions of safety in school, therefore, may differ depending on their personal racialized experiences, their cultural or ethnic identity development, teacher–student relationships, and the context of the school, such as the neighborhood and access to public school funding.

Relationships

In the second dimension, relationships refer to how people are connected to each other within the school context (Thapa et al., 2013). These may be student-to-student, student-to-teacher, or teacher-to-teacher relationships. All these relationships are key in supporting a positive school climate. Darling-Hammond and Cook-Harvey (2018) emphasized that "human relationships are the essential ingredient that catalyzes healthy development and learning" (p. 5).

Interestingly, although school climate factors were important for student academic achievement, longitudinal research has shown that student–teacher relationships had strongest effects overall (Daily et al., 2020). Students who have positive relationships with teachers and other adults are less likely to have behavioral challenges in schools (Gregory et al., 2010). In another study, sixth-grade students who have positive perceptions of school climate and positive student–teacher relationships demonstrate more positive behavior (Wang et al., 2010).

Further, positive teacher–student relationships serve as an important protective factor in secondary school for CLD students (Sabol & Pianta, 2012). Thus, relationships, particularly student–teacher relationships, are key in fostering a positive school climate.

Teaching and Learning

The third dimension of school climate is characterized by teachers' and administrators' ability to establish a positive learning and teaching environment by promoting respect, positive values, and cooperative learning (Thapa et al., 2013). Specifically, this dimension includes (a) social, emotional, civic and ethical education, which can also integrate social-emotional learning (Durlak et al., 2011), (b) service learning through hands-on, real-life projects, and (c) teachers' and students' views of school climate. Teachers deliver culturally responsive pedagogy and challenging academic material while also ensuring students receive constructive feedback to improve. There are several ways for educators to provide constructive feedback that supports a positive school climate:

- *Provide specific feedback.* Indicate what the student did well and areas that could use improvement (e.g., stating, "Your ideas in this essay were very imaginative, although I noticed that some of the punctuation is missing . . . ").
- *Provide timely or immediate feedback.* Timely verbal, nonverbal, and written feedback can aid students in remembering the experience and associating the feedback with the skill for future application (e.g., providing a "thumbs-up" immediately after a student raises their hand to ask a question).
- *Connect the feedback with the short-term or long-term goal.* Students may be more motivated to improve if they learn the goal for the assignment so that it is meaningful (e.g., teaching "greetings" to help a student develop a friendship with a classmate).
- *Provide a model.* Students often learn better if they see model behavior or an assignment to clarify expectations and avoid miscommunication (e.g., demonstrating steps to complete a math problem on the board).

Institutional Environment

The fourth dimension of school climate is the institutional environment, which Thapa et al. (2013) characterized as (a) school connectedness and engagement, and (b) physical layout and structural organization of the school. School connectedness and engagement refer to the degree to which students perceive that teachers and fellow students care about them as individuals and care about their learning (Centers for Disease Control and Prevention, 2009). Students need to feel connected to their teachers and peers and to believe that that teachers care about them. School connectedness has been found to have a mediating role between school climate and peer victimization (Eugene et al., 2021) as well as lower school violence (Skiba et al., 2004).

The institutional environment also includes the physical layout and structural organization of the school. For example, it can include the school's heating, lighting, or cleanliness, as well as structural organization, such as the class size (Wang & Degol, 2016). The size of the institutional environment can be an important factor, as research has shown that smaller schools or low teacher–student ratios are associated with positive school climate (McNeely et al., 2002). When schools do not have adequate facilities, there is less focus on academic achievement, and students and teachers perceive the learning environment as less serious (Uline & Tschannen-Moran, 2008). Thus, in addition to other dimensions of school climate, the institutional environment is important for fostering positive school climate.

School Improvement Process

Finally, the fifth dimension of school climate is the school improvement process, which is characterized by how the school effectively implements programs to promote school improvement (Thapa et al., 2013). School leaders, educators, special educators, school psychologists, counselors, and other professionals play critical roles in school improvement plans, ensuring that expertise is available and shared with collaborative partners to develop culturally responsive programs and improve school climate based on data gathered from students and adults. An important foundation for school improvement efforts is meaningful involvement of community members and families, which allows for a shared vision, goals, and core values (NSCC, 2021b).

The measurement of school climate also provides school professionals with the necessary data to identify school needs, set goals, and track progress toward improvement. Many school climate data are based on surveys collected at the school-, district-, or state level. Instead of using external models that proved effective in other schools, Berkowitz et al. (2017) recommended that schools design their own climate improvement programs, tailored to their organizational characteristics and needs. We highlight some of these strategies in the next section.

Social Media

Social media has become ubiquitous in our professional work, social lives, and dissemination of news and events to students. Many organizations, including schools, have developed policies that ensure safety and productive use of social media, which includes Internet use, and regulation of cell phones and other electronic mobile devices for learning, networking, or communication (Pham, 2014;

Segool et al., 2016) to prevent cyberbullying. *Cyberbullying*, a form of bullying or harassment using online or digital technologies, can be difficult to define since this type of bullying can be based on a single act of aggression or repeated acts of harassment (Selkie et al., 2016). Studies have indicated that cyberbullying incidents are more prevalent during adolescence (median prevalence of 23%; Hamm et al., 2015). Various forms of cyberbullying may include: (a) harassment via computer, telephone, cell, or text messaging device, (b) sending or threatening to share verbal, textual, or graphic material that would cause intimidation, humiliation, or embarrassment to another person, such as nonconsensual pornography (Eaton & McGlynn, 2020), and (c) posting inflammatory, hateful, or malicious speech or comments with the intent to harm a person. Schools must create physical and digital environments that protect students from physical harm, verbal abuse/teasing, gossip, and exclusion when using online or electronic devices, including Facebook, Snapchat, TikTok, Twitter, and other social media platforms, by an email, text messaging, posting a photo/video, etc. Student responses to cyberbullying are most often passive, with a lack of awareness or assurance that anything can be done. One study found that students who reported being bullied at school and online were likely to report suicidal ideation and attempts (Hinduja & Patchin, 2019), with minoritized groups demonstrating higher risk (e.g., sexual-minority and gender-expansive youth; Abreu & Kenny, 2018). Several strategies to prevent cyberbullying include (a) implementing cybersecurity software to monitor student computer use, (b) providing staff training and psychoeducation to students and families on reporting instances of cyberbullying with focus on recipients and bystanders, and (c) implementing evidence-based bullying prevention programs that specifically discuss issues related to cyberbullying, productive use of social media, and social-emotional learning (Tanrikulu, 2018).

SCHOOL CLIMATE AMONG CULTURALLY AND LINGUISTICALLY DIVERSE STUDENTS

Given the differential impact of school climate on racially, culturally, and linguistically diverse students, there has been more attention on how to promote a positive school climate that is also culturally responsive. Racial school climate is characterized as the norms and values within the school related to race and racial diversity, and it is related to interracial interactions, stereotypes, equitable treatment of minoritized students, and institutional support for a positive racial school climate (Byrd, 2015; Byrd & Chavous, 2011). Like the larger society, oppression and marginalization are embedded in the classroom and school. Thus, practitioners and schools should consider the differential experiences of students' perceptions of school climate, which go beyond student outcome data.

For example, data from the National Center for Education Statistics (Seldin & Yanez, 2019) indicated that Asian American adolescents reported lower rates of bullying (7.3%) compared with White (22.8%), Black/African American (22.9%), and Latinx (15.7%) adolescents. However, Asian Americans reported increasing levels of negative stereotyping and peer discrimination, with males being more at risk than females (Huang & Vidourek, 2019). High rates of school victimization among Asian Americans, for example, have been associated with poor academic and psychosocial outcomes, including depression, low self-esteem, substance use, and suicidal ideation in middle and high school (Huang & Vidourek, 2019; Stone & Carlisle, 2017). During the COVID-19 pandemic, there was an increased number of reports of microaggressions, discrimination, and racism against Asian Americans (National Association of School Psychologists, 2021). From an ecological perspective, current events, court cases, and societal forces can shape the climate within a school.

There has been an increasing focus on understanding how students' cultures can be infused in the schooling experience in order to increase their engagement and belonging in school. Mattison and Aber (2007) found that students who had positive perceptions of the school racial climate had higher academic achievement and fewer office discipline referrals, such as detentions and suspensions. There was variability, however, across racially minoritized students. Black students perceived the racial school climate more negatively compared with White students (Mattison & Aber, 2007). Further, there may be a disconnect, or *cultural incongruity*, between home and school cultures. *Cultural incongruity* refers to perceived mismatches in cultural values and expectations between the students' heritage culture and the academic environment (Chun et al., 2016). Schneider and Duran (2010) found that middle school students of color suggested that "the greater the difference between home and school culture, the stronger the need for students to 'disconnect' from home practices and thus the more difficult it becomes for students to focus on academic issues" (p. 35). Findings from a systematic review of the literature also indicate that classrooms characterized by positive school climates can level the playing field for students from low-income and economically marginalized (LIEM) groups (Berkowitz et al., 2017). Positive school climates have potential to reduce opportunity gaps among students of different LIEM backgrounds.

One approach to developing a positive racial climate is *cultural pluralism*, which is described as "a value based on an appreciation for and encouragement of cultural diversity through simultaneously acknowledging cultural distinctions, promoting cross-cultural relationships, and encouraging the maintenance of the unique cultural identities of subgroups" (Smith et al., 2020, p. 52). This requires intentionally learning, accepting, and incorporating students' culture into the school environment or instruction. Cultural pluralism has been associated with better student adjustment. For example, racially minoritized students who rated school as having support for cultural pluralism also reported higher levels of adjustment (Brand et al., 2003). Similarly, schools that support cultural pluralism and value inclusion are associated with positive outcomes for Black youth, including improved student–teacher relationships, more positive peer interactions, and a stronger sense of school belonging (Smith et al., 2020). Thus, schools that supportive inclusion and diversity may be a protective factor for Black youth.

In addition, culturally responsive pedagogy has been a critical approach to promoting positive racial climate. Culturally responsive, or culturally relevant pedagogy, as further discussed in Chapter 9, integrates the students' culture, racial and ethnic heritage, and the contemporary and historical experiences of oppression into teaching and learning (Gay, 2018; Ladson-Billings & Tate, 1995). This work has extended to *culturally sustaining pedagogy* to move away from simply integrating books or curriculum highlighting cultural diversity and instead focusing on pedagogical theory and practice that addresses the underlying power and oppression that differentially affects minoritized students (Ladson-Billings, 2014). McCarty and Lee (2014) similarly extended this idea to both sustaining and revitalizing pedagogy for Indigenous students. That is, teaching and learning should move beyond performative activities and be a force in addressing oppression and marginalization. In sum, as Blitz et al. (2016) aptly described, "Racial school climate matters for all students as it informs how children experience their school and where they are likely to be positioned in relation to social constructions of middle-class Whiteness" (pp. 97–98).

CULTURAL-ECOLOGICAL MODEL OF SCHOOL CLIMATE

One framework that schools could use to develop and sustain a culturally responsive and positive school climate is the CEMSC (La Salle et al., 2015). This framework uses an ecological approach (Bronfenbrenner, 2005) to focus on the individual, family, school, and community characteristics and how these may influence the student's perceptions of school climate. This framework emphasizes three main tenets:

(a) Students are active participants in the construction of social settings and are capable of utilizing personal, cultural, and environmental influences to adapt to their environment;

(b) the proximal contexts of the individual (i.e., family, community, school) transmit cultural norms, values, behaviors, and expectations; and

(c) perceptions of school climate are influenced by bidirectional influences across personal, cultural, and contextual variables. (La Salle et al., 2015, p. 160)

As part of the CEMSC framework, students' personal characteristics, such as race, ethnicity, gender, and intersectional identities may influence how others respond to them, and reciprocally, how the student may respond to others. Further, characteristics associated with privilege may also have a reciprocal influence. La Salle and colleagues (2015) provided the example of how perceptions of boys' higher aptitude for math compared with girls may shape how teachers may call on boys more than girls. School-level characteristics that include provision of resources and basic needs, such as healthcare, food are important considerations in how students perceive the school climate.

Table 8.2. FACTORS TO CONSIDER WITHIN THE CULTURAL-ECOLOGICAL MODEL

Family	School and Classroom	Community
• Family composition	• Structural aspects of school (e.g., school size)	• Geographic location
• Occupational stability		• Community type (e.g., rural, urban)
• Parent education	• Physical features (e.g., quality of building)	
• Childrearing practices		• Resources (e.g., library, hospitals, economic resources)
• Beliefs about education	• School resources (e.g., per pupil expenditure, curriculum)	
• SES		• Neighborhood demographics (e.g., crime rates, residential transiency)
• Parent educational experiences	• Composition variables (mean student achievement, ethnicity, SES)	
• Financial resources		
• Religious beliefs		• Community extracurricular programs
• Family expectations	• Student mobility	
• Structure of the family	• Behavior disruptions	
• Social stigma	• Class composition	
	• Teacher characteristics (e.g., highest level of education, management strategies)	
	• Student–teacher ratio	

NOTE: Summarized from "A cultural-ecological model of school climate," by T. P. La Salle, J. Meyers, K. Varjas, & A. Roach, 2015, *International Journal of School & Educational Psychology, 3*(3), 157–166 (https://doi.org/10.1080/21683603.2015.1047550).

In their framework, context and culture are also important in student's perceptions of school climate. They suggested that the contexts (e.g., microsystems, macrosystems) influence the individuals' development and educational experience. The norms and beliefs of these systems influence each other. For example, one of the microsystems may be the student's home life, which may shape the student's educational experience. If the student is being raised by a single caregiver who works multiple jobs, the student may be required to take care of their siblings and thus may be unable to complete their homework. This subsequently affects their ability to obtain grades for homework completion at school. Specific family, school and classroom, and community variables to consider are included in Table 8.2.

DEVELOPING AND SUSTAINING POSITIVE SCHOOL CLIMATE

The purpose of the CEMSC (La Salle et al., 2015) is to foster and sustain a positive school climate within a multi-tiered system of support (MTSS) by implementing specific approaches using a culturally responsive assessment of school climate.

We suggest using the following steps: (1) Engage in critical reflexivity about the practitioner's role and the rationale for developing and sustaining a positive school climate, (2) establish trusting relationships with stakeholders to develop a team, (3) develop objectives that are relevant to stakeholders, (4) select multimethod and multisource data collection and interpret data with a culturally responsive lens, (5) implement the program, (6) evaluate the program, and (7) disseminate results back to the school and community (see Figure 8.1). Practitioners should also take a close look in Chapter 11, as we specifically discuss the *school-based*

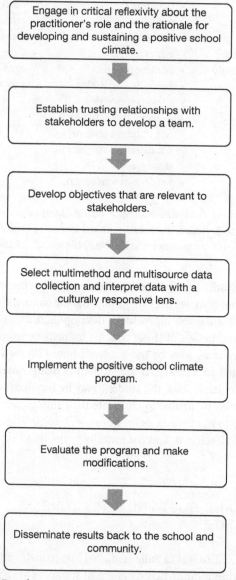

Figure 8.1. Steps in Developing and Sustaining a Culturally Responsive Positive School Climate.

culturally responsive program evaluation model, which practitioners may find helpful as a foundation for evaluating school-based programs.

Engage in Critical Reflexivity and Establish a Team

In the first step, the practitioner should engage in critical reflexivity and establish a collaborative team. As highlighted in Chapter 1, practitioners must reflect on their culture, norms, and beliefs as they relate to their own perceptions and contribution to the current school climate. Throughout the process of developing and sustaining a safe and positive school climate, schools should be intentional about how culture, norms, and beliefs may be influence decision-making. Pausing and reflecting on one's own values and behaviors can allow practitioners to ensure that none of their biases or stereotypes about students or families inadvertently affect students disproportionately.

Importantly, the practitioner should consider their positionality within the school context as they engage with their colleagues (e.g., teachers, administrators) to address school climate. For instance, if the practitioner is a non-Hispanic White person in a school that is predominantly Latinx, they should consider how their race and privilege may shape their worldview and how stakeholders (e.g., parents, community members) may perceive the practitioner. Depending on the cultural values, caregivers may rely on teachers and practitioners in making education-related decisions because they believe they are experts in the area. Other caregivers, however, may believe they should play an integral role because they are experts in their children's lives. Most importantly, caregivers' and community members' voices should be a part of decision-making as part of culturally responsive practice.

[Reflexivity Activity]. Consider the following questions:

- *Reflect on your culture, norms, and values. To what degree do they align with the community in which you work? How do you work to close the gap?*
- *School climate is a complex construct. What aspects of school climate feel the most comfortable for you to discuss? Which aspects feel the least comfortable?*
- *Change can be difficult. What if a caregiver suggests that the process is not culturally sensitive? How will you respond? What if your colleagues respond defensively? How will you support dialogue across different stakeholders?*

After initially engaging in critical reflexivity, the next step is establishing a school-based team to develop a school improvement plan that includes collection and review of school climate data. The team members should include representatives from both the school and the community who have knowledge of the cultural context and who are most directly impacted by the program. Further, practitioners should be sure to include voices that have been marginalized or neglected in that school and community. Successful program development and implementation will likely be much more successful with strong and trusting partnerships (Askew et al., 2012).

Throughout this process, the team members must also have enough trust to be able to have difficult conversations surrounding both positive and negative perceptions of the school climate, teacher–student interactions, or current expectations of student performance. In their guidelines for rooting out racial disparities in disciplinary practices, the National Center on Safe Supportive Learning Environments emphasized the importance of being able to "tackle the tough conversations" (Osher et al., 2015, p. 3). To have these types of conversations, school professionals need to create safe spaces with people who are willing to be open and take risks to talk about these important subjects. Productive discourse that explicitly addresses difficult issues is often called "courageous conversation," which facilitates open dialogue about emotionally charged or sensitive topics through strength-based approaches. As the principal of the middle school, for example, Ms. Campbell, and the school counselor, can facilitate a town hall or a small group meeting to initiate these tough conversations. They could also receive feedback from an anonymous survey completed by stakeholders, including collection of any preliminary school climate data, which can be gathered before these meetings to help guide the discussion by revealing any common patterns or themes in their questions or concerns. Overall, the aim of these tough conversations is to ensure that multiple voices and perspectives are being heard.

Develop Objectives

The next step in developing a positive school climate is to generate objectives for the school improvement plan. There should be four to five primary objectives of the program, which then link with the data that would be gathered to meet those objectives (Spaulding, 2013). These four or five objectives should be directly relevant to the students and community and can be developed using collaborative brainstorming, focus groups, individual interviews, or anonymous surveys.

The National Center on Safe Supportive Learning Environments (NCSSLE) developed a guide (see Osher et al., 2015) for educational professionals on gathering information about disparities in school disciplinary practices. They suggested three stages: (1) digging into the data (asking, "Do disparities in school discipline exist in our school or district?"), (2) getting at the roots of disparities (asking, "What are the root causes of our disparities in school discipline?," and (3) creating an action plan (asking, "How will root causes of disparities in school discipline be addressed?"). When digging into the data (Stage 1), the team should gather and examine school discipline data by:

  (a) determining data needs
  (b) designating data gatherers

(c) identifying the data that is already being collected

(d) determining additional data needs

(e) ensuring data privacy and quality, and

(f) disaggregating data to determine differences.

Ms. Campbell and her team should first understand what information already exists and what other information needs to be gathered, designate certain team members to facilitate the data gathering, and ensure that all of the information that is gathered is private. Osher et al. (2015) suggested a number of questions to guide this stage, such as:

- How many students are suspended (in school and out of school), expelled, or subjected to corporal punishment annually?
- Which student demographic groups are at the greatest risk for disciplinary action? In terms of the total number of disciplinary actions taken by your school or district, which student demographic groups are being disciplined at higher rates than others (or have a higher percentage of disciplinary actions relative to their peers)?

Gather and Interpret Information with a Culturally Responsive Lens

Once the objectives are generated, then the next step is to gather information using multiple methods and multiple sources. Since school climate comprises multiple dimensions, it is important to examine how these dimensions apply to students, teachers, administrators, and even caregivers. Additionally, information should be gathered both formatively (during the program implementation) and summatively (at the completion of the program; Spaulding, 2013). School teams should use ongoing assessments with items or questions that are attuned to children's developmental and grade level. Given that standard approaches to gathering data (e.g., surveys) may be considered Western, Eurocentric approaches, it may be important to consider other approaches, such as storytelling through individual meetings or focus groups because they align with how most people typically communicate (Chilisa, 2020).

The NCSSLE provides a compendium of sample school climate surveys, which can be completed by K–12 staff, parents, and students as young as in Grades 2 or 3 depending on the reading level of the items. Responses can be in the form of Agree/Disagree or Undecided for the student survey items such as "My teachers are interested in how I do in the future" or "My school counselor helps me with school and personal problems." Items related to diversity, equity, and inclusion should also be developed, such as those administered by the Iowa City Community School District (2021), which are given to students from Grades 5 to 12:

- There are opportunities in my class to talk about race.
- I see myself as a valuable member in my classroom.

- My teachers present positive images of people from a variety of races, cultures, and backgrounds.
- I feel unable to share my views in class because of my gender identity.

There are a number of additional assessment tools that schools can use, such as the Delaware School Climate Survey (Bear et al., 2011), the Georgia School Climate Survey (La Salle et al., 2021), or the Comprehensive School Climate Inventory (National School Climate Center, 2021a). The U.S. Department of Education also provides adaptable ED School Climate Surveys (National Center on Safe Supportive Learning Environments, 2021). Ms. Campbell and her team may want to review each of these assessment tools, including closely looking at individual items to be sure that they accurately reflect the culture, norms, and values of the school and surrounding community.

After information is gathered, it is also important to consider that all information is grounded in the culture and context of that school and community. Whether the information includes averages and standard deviations or themes derived from personal narratives, the information should be interpreted within that particular culture. Thus, the school team that is interpreting the data should continue to engage in critical reflexivity, intentionally considering how their worldview and biases may affect the way they interpret the information. Triangulation of data (e.g., gathering information from multiple sources through multiple methods) and member checking (e.g., going back to the original sources) can help contextualize data and ensure that those interpreting the information are doing so in culturally responsive ways (Birt et al., 2016).

Analyzing the data using a culturally informed lens also means understanding the systemic issues and barriers that may be contributing to disparities. These factors refer to a school's leadership, organizational structure, and procedures, as well as staff and student competencies. In their guidelines for addressing disparities in school disciplinary practices, the NCSSLE recommended conducting a "root cause analysis" in which the underlying reasons for disparities are examined closely with the existing data (Osher et al., 2015, p. 52). In this analysis, the first level is focusing on the "red flag issue," which is identified through the initial data analysis. In their example, a red flag issue was identified in which a rural school noticed that students were arriving late, leading to referrals for tardiness. Specifically, data showed that more girls than boys were arriving late, and more Indigenous students than other minoritized students (Osher et al., 2015). The root cause analysis would lead to additional data gathering to reveal systemic issues contributing to this disparity, including that buses did not arrive on time in areas that were far away from school or that some students were taking their sibling(s) to school prior to their own arrival at the school. By understanding these systemic barriers, the corrective actions would not be simply disciplining students more; rather, it is about adjusting school bus schedules or changing the school day to start later (Osher et al., 2015).

Implement the School Climate Program

Once information is gathered using culturally responsive approaches and the specific needs of the school are determined, then the school team can implement the program to improve school climate. The team should use the initial data gathering to inform the action plan, which should include both short- and long-term strategies (Osher et al., 2015). School teams should work to include practices that are implemented schoolwide to address students' social, emotional, behavioral, and academic skills. It is important that school teams choose programs that are supported by research. There are often resources that include lists of research-based programs, such as:

- What Works Clearinghouse from the Institute of Education Sciences (http://ies.ed.gov/ncee/wwc),
- National Registry of Evidence-Based Programs and Practices from the Substance Abuse and Mental Health Services Administration (http://www.samhsa.gov/nrepp)
- Model Programs Guide from the Office of Juvenile Justice and Delinquency Prevention (http://www.ojjdp.gov/mp).

Through these resources, and others, there are a number of specific programs available to improve school climate. For example, these schoolwide programs include:

- Child Development Project (Battistich et al., 2000)
- Olweus Bullying Prevention Program (Olweus & Limber, 2010)
- Project Achieve (Knoff, 2000).

In addition to making decisions about which program aligns with their strategic goals, the school team may also want to consider other methods that may supplement the program to improve equity for students who have been historically marginalized. A number of approaches exist to address equity, but we highlight two key evidence-based practices: (1) respectful and culturally responsive school and community, and (2) consistent and clear expectations and instruction.

RESPECTFUL AND CULTURALLY RESPONSIVE SCHOOL AND COMMUNITY
Overall, a school with a positive school climate should include a community where students are cared for, respected, and supported, with both social, emotional, and physical safety (Darling-Hammond & Cook-Harvey, 2018). In a report on promoting equity in schools, the National School Climate Center emphasized that schools should (1) encourage reflective practice and build cultural awareness in students and adults, (2) increase understanding of diverse cultures, (3) keep diverse schools physically and emotionally safe, (4) make high expectations

culturally responsive, (5) design multiple pathways to meaningful participation, (6) demonstrate caring by knowing students' unique emotional needs (Ross, 2013).

Schools should include messages of respectful behavior that should be clearly conveyed and posted in classrooms and hallways, where displays of such behaviors are recognized and rewarded. Students should have knowledge of student support resources, including location of the school counselor, school psychologist, or social worker. In addition to having a culturally responsive community, there should be deep trust and respect between and among educators, staff, students, and caregivers (Darling-Hammond & Cook-Harvey, 2018). As mentioned in Chapter 3, this relational trust between school and home is essential in supporting children's well-being and learning. This trust is foundational in fostering a positive school climate, as well as home–school relationships.

CONSISTENT AND CLEAR EXPECTATIONS AND INSTRUCTION

Another important component of a positive, culturally responsive school climate is having "continuity in relationships, consistency in practices, and predictability in routines that reduce cognitive load and anxiety and support engaged learning" (Darling-Hammond & Cook-Harvey, 2018). That is, there should be consistent and predictable expectations for behaviors and routines for all students. They should have connections with their teachers and have a clear understanding of what is expected in terms of their positive behaviors. These expectations should be clear so that students understand what steps they need to do to well in school.

Further, educators should use evidence-based practices in their instruction to engage their students and meet their needs. Darling-Hammond and Cook-Harvey (2018) recommended that teachers use "inquiry and discovery as major learning strategies, thoughtfully interwoven with explicit instruction and opportunities to practice and apply learning" as well as "opportunities to receive timely and helpful feedback, develop and exhibit competence, and revise work to improve" (p. 9).

Evaluate and Disseminate Results to School and Community

After implementing the program, it is critical that information is gathered to evaluate the effectiveness of the program (see Chapter 11). Gathering information during and after the program completion will help the school team determine whether the program successfully met the objectives and what additional changes or modifications are necessary.

Then, the team should disseminate the results back to the stakeholders. This information should be shared during the implementation of the program through either brief summaries at meetings or written reports (Spaulding, 2013). The NCSSLE recommends disseminating information *before* the action plan is implemented. They suggested that the team provide (a) a short summary of the process, (b) critical issues explored by the team, (c) data issues such reliability and validity and how any challenges were addressed, (d) key findings (as transparently as possible while respecting privacy rights), (e) strategies being considered, and (f) what happens next, including when a draft plan will be made available for review and how people can provide input (Osher et al., 2015, p. 58). Overall, disseminating results back to the school and community, or posting results online publicly, is essential in ensuring that families and communities recognize that their perspectives are heard and integrated into decision-making to develop and sustain a positive school climate.

SUMMARY

In this chapter, we provided an overview of school climate, which is defined broadly as the students', teachers', and staff's feelings, attitudes, and experiences of their school life. Further, there are a number of dimensions of school climate, including safety, relationships (student–student as well as student–teacher), teaching and learning, institutional environment, school improvement, and social media. We then introduced one specific framework, the cultural-ecological model of school climate (CEMSC; La Salle et al., 2015), that can be helpful in developing and sustaining a safe and positive school climate. School climate is multidimensional and is related not only to student academic success and emotional well-being, but also to teacher morale and support. Ultimately, social contexts and relationships influence student and staff perceptions of what constitutes a safe and supportive school climate. Thus, student and staff input are instrumental when reviewing school climate data and implementing school improvement plans. Mental health professionals should take the lead in developing, adapting, and delivering effective violence prevention and intervention programs based on data to ensure that they make a difference in developing a positive school climate and promoting safety. School climate data can also contribute to the development of refined policies to ensure that procedures, processes, and positive outcomes are sustained.

DISCUSSION QUESTIONS

1. Consider the school in which you work. What potential systemic issues may exist that contribute to disparities in the school? How would these systemic issues potentially contribute to the school climate?
2. In what ways can school climate data be used in conjunction with school-based prevention and intervention programs?
3. The principal of a high school seeks to understand students' perceptions of the classroom and school climate after several students share with him privately that they do not feel safe or connected to their teachers.
   a. What steps should the principal take to gather systematic data about the middle school climate?
   b. In gathering school climate data, what systemic issues should he consider? Which school professionals should be involved in gathering this information?

Culturally Responsive Multi-Tiered Systems of Support and Evidence-Based Interventions

VIGNETTE

David, a third-grade boy who immigrated with his family from Mexico, has been enrolled in a new school for the past year. He has been receiving daily support from a reading specialist, Mr. Rappaport, to improve his phonics and reading comprehension. However, Mr. Rappaport indicated that David has been noncompliant, refusing to participate in the small-group reading intervention with his peers for the past 2 weeks. David expressed little interest in reading the books given to him and would run around the room, requesting to be on the computer. Frustrated, Mr. Rappaport is thinking about giving David a discipline referral if he continues to be disruptive and avoid work in the classroom.
Consider the following questions:

- *In what ways does Mr. Rappaport or the school address David's behavior?*
- *What are some issues to consider when delivering interventions for David who demonstrate both academic and behavioral difficulties?*

Culture influences the way in which teachers and practitioners see themselves, their students, and their environment. When teachers evaluate how their own cultural values and beliefs shape their instruction in the classroom, they are more likely to seek ways to minimize negative perceptions or bias when addressing student behavior and to be more inclusive in their practices. Although efforts for supporting student learning and positive behavior may fall under the responsibility of the teacher, it is ultimately the responsibility of all school professionals to ensure their success by fostering an inclusive and supportive environment. For classroom instruction to be effective for students like David, practitioners should consider sociocultural and ecological factors before implementing an intervention plan.

Instruction or behavioral interventions that do not take into account the cultural context of the student may impede the student's ability to succeed in the classroom. Before designing interventions for David, teachers should determine the function or reasons for his behavior. David may still be adjusting to his new school environment. He may feel intimidated, uncomfortable, or anxious if reading with peers in the classroom. He also may feel disconnected from some of the reading material if it is not culturally relevant to him. David may still be learning about the academic and behavioral expectations of his school and classroom. Taking time to analyze his behavior can help determine the best supports for him to succeed without quickly resorting to disciplinary action.

These issues warrant open discussion with practitioners given the long history of minoritized students being excluded from instruction through exclusionary discipline compared with White students (Girvan et al., 2019; Fadus et al., 2021). For example, the Office for Civil Rights (OCR) reported significant disproportionality in the use of disciplinary practice, particularly with an overrepresentation of culturally and linguistically diverse (CLD) students and students with disabilities, after accounting for the effects of socioeconomic status (Losen et al., 2015). One reason for this disproportionality may stem from educators' low expectations and implicit racial biases of students. In their examination of school experiences, Irvin and colleagues (2016) found that teachers' expectations were highest for White students and lowest for Indigenous, Latinx, and Black students. To mitigate disproportionality in student outcomes, schools need to incorporate a culturally responsive system of practices (e.g., screening, prevention, intervention) guided by the use of data that inform student academic and behavioral progress and educational decision-making.

The purpose of this chapter is to inform practitioners about the provision of instructional and behavioral supports for students from CLD backgrounds. We describe a culturally responsive approach to multi-tiered systems of support (MTSS), frameworks for providing learners with individualized supports needed to succeed academically and behaviorally. We discuss how to deliver evidence-based interventions (EBI) for CLD students, support professional educator and staff behavior, and implement culturally valid data-based decision-making, with the goal of equitable academic, social, and behavioral outcomes. Then, we discuss culturally adapted interventions for those students who may require additional individualized support.

MULTI-TIERED SYSTEMS OF SUPPORT

Stemming from public health models, the MTSS is a tiered framework that provides a continuum of services to improve students' academic and/or behavioral outcomes (Sugai & Horner, 2009). Educational policies have recommended the need for models that promote early identification and intervention, monitor progress, and analyze data to inform student progress (e.g., Individuals with Disabilities Education Improvement Act, 2004). These prevention models often include three or more tiers (see Figure 9.1). In Tier 1 (universal), all students receive the same curriculum or classroom instruction. In Tier 2 (targeted), selected students receive additional supports. Finally, in Tier 3 (intensive), a much smaller group of students or a student is given more individualized supports (Sugai & Horner, 2009). These initiatives have led to emergence of schoolwide problem-solving MTSS frameworks, such as Response to Intervention (RTI) and Schoolwide Positive Behavioral Interventions and Supports (SWPBIS). Since academic and behavioral difficulties are often intertwined (Nelson et al., 2004), a

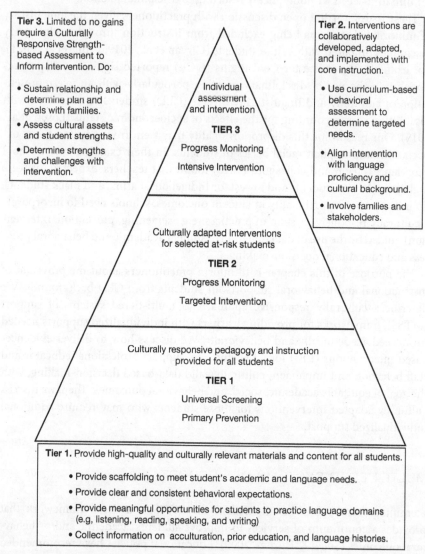

Tier 3. Limited to no gains require a Culturally Responsive Strength-based Assessment to Inform Intervention. Do:

- Sustain relationship and determine plan and goals with families.
- Assess cultural assets and student strengths.
- Determine strengths and challenges with intervention.

Tier 2. Interventions are collaboratively developed, adapted, and implemented with core instruction.

- Use curriculum-based behavioral assessment to determine targeted needs.
- Align intervention with language proficiency and cultural background.
- Involve families and stakeholders.

Individual assessment and intervention

TIER 3

Progress Monitoring

Intensive Intervention

Culturally adapted interventions for selected at-risk students

TIER 2

Progress Monitoring

Targeted Intervention

Culturally responsive pedagogy and instruction provided for all students

TIER 1

Universal Screening

Primary Prevention

Tier 1. Provide high-quality and culturally relevant materials and content for all students.

- Provide scaffolding to meet student's academic and language needs.
- Provide clear and consistent behavioral expectations.
- Provide meaningful opportunities for students to practice language domains (e.g, listening, reading, speaking, and writing)
- Collect information on acculturation, prior education, and language histories.

Figure 9.1. Culturally Responsive Multi-Tiered Systems of Support.

schoolwide MTSS framework serves as a contemporary approach for effective instruction by integrating RTI and SWPBIS to meet the student's learning needs (Hoover & Patton, 2017).

In general, schools that use MTSS provide layered educational supports when general classroom strategies indicate that the student has not made improvement over time (Sugai & Horner, 2009). Schools implementing a comprehensive framework of MTSS include essential and intersecting components that address academic, behavior, and mental health areas (OSEP Technical Assistance Center on Positive Behavioral Interventions and Supports, 2015):

1. Outcomes: What student results are targeted based on data?
2. Data: What information is collected to answer what questions?
3. Practices: What interventions are selected based on data and outcomes?
4. Systems: How prepared are the staff in implementing practices?

Some schools using MTSS have a narrowly conceived model that is conceptualized as "culturally neutral" or as a "one size fits all approach" for how to support students, yet there has been little focus on how to address the sociocultural factors in these frameworks (e.g., Bal, 2015; Orosco & Klingner, 2010). Moreover, some school districts may lack the expertise to develop programs that meet their specific needs. Yet there is a large need to ensure that the MTSS is implemented not only with fidelity but also to ensure equitable outcomes.

Educational disparities between CLD students and White students are largely the result of inequitable systems that have been in place for many years, from school discipline to opportunity gaps (Sullivan & Bal, 2013). Studies have found, however, that race remains a strong factor when it comes to referrals (Bradshaw et al., 2010). There have been promising results of using a schoolwide framework for CLD students, showing decreased rates of office discipline referrals (ODRs; McIntosh et al., 2021). However, more research is needed to evaluate effectiveness of MTSS practices with students with disabilities and English language learners (ELLs; Hernandez Finch, 2012), as some studies have shown mixed results (Vincent, Swain-Bradway, et al., 2011). Such data, including ODRs, underscore the need to consider issues related to culture, language, power, and privilege in ways that value diversity in schools and require systems-level change (Pham et al., 2021).

Culturally Responsive Multi-Tiered Systems of Support

To address these issues, schools started implementing culturally responsive MTSS as an overarching goal for systemic change. When guided by inclusive practices and data, MTSS should lead to more equitable academic and behavioral outcomes for CLD students. We also emphasize *ecological decision-making*, which is the interaction among various ecological factors (i.e., learner, classroom, home/community) when making decisions regarding educational planning, referral,

Table 9.1. COMPARISON OF STANDARD MULTI-TIERED SYSTEMS OF SUPPORT
WITH CULTURALLY RESPONSIVE MULTI-TIERED SYSTEMS OF SUPPORT

Components	Standard Implementation of MTSS	Culturally Responsive MTSS
Mission and Commitment	• Improve academic and behavioral outcomes.	• Address racial/ethnic disparities. • Improve academic and behavioral outcomes.
Team	• Form representative team of administrators, teachers, practitioners.	• Form team that is diverse (e.g., racial/ethnicity, SES) and representative of the school and community.
Schoolwide Expectations	• Define schoolwide behavior expectations. • Align curriculum with state-level expectations.	• Engage in culturally responsive pedagogy. • Examine intersection of culture and behavior.
Establish Systems of Gathering Data	• Develop process and procedures for universal screening, referrals, and educational decision-making.	• Evaluate existing systems and procedures to ensure equity in referrals and ecological decision-making. • Disaggregate outcome data • Focus less on individual pathology
Build Capacity, Training, and Support	• Pursue professional development and training in assessment, intervention, and systems-level change.	• Pursue professional development related to cultural issues (e.g., implicit bias) in assessment, intervention, and systems-level change.

interpretation of assessment results, and developing interventions. Table 9.1 displays differences between standard implementation of MTSS and our view of culturally responsive MTSS.

There are a number of guidelines and considerations for implementing culturally responsive MTSSs, although most of the work applies to SWPBIS, and emerging frameworks are developing for ELLs (Hoover & Soltero-González, 2018). Vincent and colleagues (2011) described four elements as key to implementing culturally responsive MTSSs: (1) culturally responsive EBIs for student learning and behavior, (2) professional educator and staff behavior, (3) culturally valid data-based decision-making, and (4) equitable academic, social, and behavioral outcomes. These elements also expand on and seek to improve the components of MTSS (e.g., outcomes, data, practices, and systems).

ELEMENT 1: CULTURALLY RESPONSIVE EVIDENCE-BASED INTERVENTIONS FOR STUDENT LEARNING AND BEHAVIOR

The first element of culturally responsive MTSS is applying relevance of culture to evidence-based practices (EBPs) and interventions. Schools often struggle with how to integrate the student's cultural practices and worldview into the classroom while implementing EBPs that are primarily designed to be implemented in a standardized manner for all students. Much research on CLD students' school performance focuses on examining how students develop awareness of their own and others' racial-ethnic identities and how teachers' language and verbal behavior patterns affect students' behavior (Rivas-Drake et al., 2014). A strong sense of racial-ethnic identity was related to fewer behavioral problems and greater academic achievement (Smith et al., 2009).

Within culturally responsive MTSS, academic and social skills instruction or intervention requires teachers and practitioners to validate and acknowledge students' cultures, increase cultural relevance by incorporating instructional materials that match students' cultural or linguistic backgrounds, and encourage parents and teachers to reinforce the desired behaviors at school or at home (Vincent, Randall, et al., 2011). Supports may include adapting interventions or tailoring them to meet the student's individual needs. However, if a student does not respond to an intensive intervention, does this automatically mean that the student has a deficit? Often educators need to reframe these issues and questions by asking, "Was the intervention that was implemented or adapted meeting the child's needs?" If not, then practitioners should consider changing the level of supports or gathering more data to address the student's current progress. This often requires professional and staff training to challenge previous ways of thinking.

Element 2: Professional Educator and Staff Behavior

The second element of culturally responsive MTSS is supporting professional educator and staff behavior. Training in culturally responsive practices is a lengthy process and requires a plan to support knowledge and skills in professional development. To support educators' use of culturally relevant and validating behavior support practices and ecological decision-making, school administrators must support these trainings and collaborate with consultants to troubleshoot any issues that may arise (Blanco-Vega et al., 2007).

Equity task forces can be one approach to supporting educators and staff. Equity task forces are intended to promote teachers' and staff's cultural responsiveness by addressing issues related to cultural awareness, fidelity in MTSS implementation, and sustainable use of EBPs and data for decision-making (Sugai et al., 2012). Schools should develop an equity task force that is made up of members who represent the cultural, racial, ethnic, and linguistic diversity of the school and community as well as have members with various experiences and expertise. At the high school level, selected students should be representative of the diversity in the building (e.g., ethnicity, disability status, gender, gender identity, sexual orientation, religion) and nominated by the equity task force.

The equity task force could then provide recommendations for specific topics for professional trainings. We recommend that practitioners review Chapter 2 as the basis for engaging in discussions about race, racism, and discrimination.

Other topics include addressing snap judgments, which refer to quick or automatic decisions, without reflection or discussion, that are often made from implicit bias (e.g., sending student to the principal's office based on the impression or judgment that student is "lazy") or due to emotional distress. These reactions are also common in situations in which discipline decisions are likely to be made, also known as vulnerable decision points (VDPs; Smolkowski et al., 2016). To illustrate, if a teacher feels stressed, hungry, or simply worn out, then they may be more likely to overreact to the student who did not turn in his homework after lunchtime. Because Mr. Rappaport may be exhibiting high levels of frustration, David may be scolded for running in the classroom, be sent to the office for noncompliance, or receive a low grade for not completing a reading assignment (see Figure 9.2). David subsequently may refuse to come back into the classroom. Mr. Rappaport could have made a snap decision, which could have been resolved through an alternative response. Identifying specific VDPs can help the equity task force go beyond documenting disparities to pinpointing their root causes and responding to student behavior without intensifying the situation (McIntosh et al., 2018).

When VDPs are identified, schools can then develop strategies, or neutralizing routines, for learning how to de-escalate conflicts when they arise (McIntosh et al., 2014). *Neutralizing routines* are replacement behaviors that allow individuals to maintain self-control during power struggles. Although strategies and responses may vary, neutralizing routines are intended to slow down the decision-making process to allow conscious thought and regain "emotional balance," which is similar to what we teach students to do when they experience peer conflict. Several examples may include promoting self-care (e.g., taking deep breaths, demonstrating classroom calm-down strategy), delaying the decision (e.g., having the student see teacher after class, asking student to reflect on behavior), and reframing the situation (e.g., telling the student that you respect them, but their behavior is not okay). McIntosh and colleagues (2021)

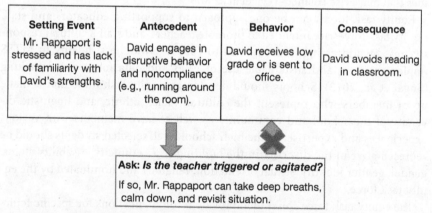

Setting Event	Antecedent	Behavior	Consequence
Mr. Rappaport is stressed and has lack of familiarity with David's strengths.	David engages in disruptive behavior and noncompliance (e.g., running around the room).	David receives low grade or is sent to office.	David avoids reading in classroom.

Ask: *Is the teacher triggered or agitated?*
If so, Mr. Rappaport can take deep breaths, calm down, and revisit situation.

Figure 9.2 Responding to Behaviors with Neutralizing Routines.

implemented an equity-focused SWPBIS, which included a neutralizing routine called TRY that involves: (a) *taking a deep breath*, (b) *reflecting on your emotions*, and (c) *responding to the youth's best interest*. Similarly, school teams can adopt similar strategies from social-emotional learning programs as part of their MTSS framework.

[Reflexivity Activity]. Reflect on the school(s) in which you work. Provide three to four examples of neutralizing routines that you may consider using in your classroom or school. Propose a schoolwide neutralizing routine that you would want all educators, practitioners, administrators, staff, and students to use.

ELEMENT 3: CULTURALLY VALID DATA-BASED DECISION-MAKING

The third element of culturally responsive MTSS is supporting culturally valid data-based decision-making. Culturally valid data-based decision-making is characterized as a process by which decisions are made considering the cultural factors and sociocultural context when gathering, analyzing, or evaluating student data with the goal of minimizing educator or practitioner bias (Vincent et al., 2011). Data-based decision making is a critical aspect of MTSS to promote equitable decisions for all students. When it comes to making equitable decisions about students' placement or support, school teams should collect and review data on a frequent basis (Sugai et al., 2012). It can be very difficult, however, to describe a (mis)behavior without being subjective or personal. Further, caregivers and educators may have different perspectives and expectations that can, inadvertently, become part of a description. Thus, to arrive at defensible decisions, school teams should discuss how observable behaviors and outcomes are defined, to minimize ambiguity.

For example, using the vignette, a teacher might describe David's behavior in this way: "He should have known how to sit down and read with his group but instead chose to run around the room." This statement assumes that David learned and generalized Mr. Rappaport's classroom rule and that he made an active choice to "misbehave." While this description may be accurate, it may also be incorrect. David might not have understood what was expected or might start running without intending to misbehave. He also could have felt insecure with his peer group or anxious when asked to read in front of them. Consequently, to reduce the likelihood of cultural bias, school teams should involve and discuss with families from CLD backgrounds when defining inappropriate behaviors. Caregivers and community members can help develop schoolwide behavioral expectations and reinforcements for students, thus motivating them toward the same goal and decreasing the likelihood of inequitable decision-making (Sugai & Horner, 2009).

Another approach to promoting culturally valid decision-making is to assess the presence of potential bias in the classroom. School teams can disaggregate data by student groups (e.g., race, ethnicity, language, gender, disability) to identify where some groups may be receiving inequitable discipline or outcomes. The team can further analyze VDPs to determine when, where, and why disproportionate services or outcomes are more likely to occur. For example, a school team may review disaggregated data and find that Black middle school students are more likely to receive discipline for defiance in the morning just after going into the classroom, or a school team may find that there is higher percentage of referrals for Tier 2 services among immigrant students.

For interventions, culturally valid data-based decision-making entails gathering data on their implementation fidelity and social validity. *Implementation fidelity* refers to the degree to which the service is implemented as intended (Carroll et al., 2007), and it is a contributing factor in the success of the intervention. Fidelity is often measured using observation tools, checklists, and self-reports. Examples of implementation fidelity scales include the *Schoolwide Evaluation Tool* (SET; Horner et al., 2004) and the *Self-Assessment Survey* (SAS; Sugai et al., 2009).

Additionally, *social validity* helps to identify whether the goals, outcomes, or procedures are socially acceptable to families or students and to address concerns. School teams often gather social validity data formally using brief interviews, focus groups, or formal rating scales. One example of a social validity scale used for MTSSs is the Primary Intervention Rating Scale (PIRS; Lane et al., 2009). Data gathered from these tools can be used to develop or refine practices further while meeting student and family needs.

ELEMENT 4: EQUITABLE ACADEMIC, SOCIAL, AND BEHAVIORAL OUTCOMES

Within a culturally responsive framework, students' academic, social, and behavioral outcomes endorsed by the school team drive implementation of practices, systems, and how the team makes decision when analyzing the data (Sugai et al., 2012). Schools have a primary goal of fostering social, behavioral, and academic competencies for all students. It is essential for the school team to review disaggregated data to ensure that practices are implemented equitably across all student backgrounds. When supporting ELLs, for example, the school team may discuss issues related to how students, both ELLs and non-ELLs, perform during reading assessments, referral processes related to MTSS, teacher expectations, and prior student experiences (Hoover & Soltero-Gonzalez, 2018). This element depends on successful development and implementation of the first three elements.

Culturally equitable student outcomes can be difficult to define. Is it that all students achieve the same academic outcomes? Is it that the school wants to see a decrease in disciplinary rates for specific groups of students? Does it entail meeting a specific criterion? Although changes in student outcomes may take time, implementing a systems-level change requires ongoing professional development and training. Staff turnover is common in schools and even more so in schools serving CLD students (Carter-Thomas & Darling-Hammond, 2017), and thus new staff will need to be informed of MTSS procedures at least three times a year or on a monthly basis. Table 9.2 provides examples of guidelines and methods school teams can use to build culturally responsive MTSS in each tier.

Table 9.2. Culturally Responsive MTSS Elements and Examples

Element	Tier 1	Tier 2	Tier 3
Equitable Academic, Social, and Behavioral Outcomes	Emphasize teaching clear classroom expectations of all students.	Determine academic and behavioral needs and goals of students.	Continue support of developing academic or behavioral skills in diverse contexts.
Professional Educator and Staff Behavior	Participate in training on implicit bias and self-awareness with all school personnel.	Assess cultural factors, strengths of students that contribute to improving learning and behavioral goals.	Reflect on any biases about student and refrain from having preconceived judgments when reviewing referrals.
Culturally Responsive Evidence-Based Interventions for Student Behavior	Implement primary prevention and practices promoting inclusive school climate.	Use culturally relevant or adapted interventions for teaching appropriate skills and behavior.	Evaluate effectiveness of culturally relevant or adapted interventions.
Culturally Valid Data-Based Decision-Making	Review universal screening data, and disaggregate by student race and ethnicity to assess presence of bias.	Monitor progress and use intervention fidelity checks; assess social validity; involve stakeholders.	Analyze test data collection instruments regarding validity with diverse populations.

NOTE: Adapted from "Toward a conceptual integration of cultural responsiveness and schoolwide positive behavior support," by C. G. Vincent, C. Randall, G. Cartledge, T. J. Tobin, & J. Swain-Bradway, 2011, *Journal of Positive Behavior Interventions*, 13(4), 219–229 (https://doi.org/10.1177/1098300711399765).

CULTURALLY RESPONSIVE PEDAGOGY (TIER 1)

At Tier 1, classrooms focus on high-quality instruction to meet the learning needs of the entire student population with an emphasis on grade-level standards and schoolwide behavioral expectations. Students from CLD backgrounds may come to the classroom with vastly different life and school experiences and understanding of cultural references. Inequitable outcomes can therefore occur at the classroom level if instructional practices are not adapted in some way for CLD students, and if referral practices and disciplinary actions (e.g., office discipline referrals) unfairly target those students.

Culturally responsive pedagogy can be one method to reduce inequitable outcomes in the classroom (Gay, 2002). Given the link between academic, social-emotional, and behavioral success (Algozzine & Algozzine, 2009), *culturally responsive pedagogy* is the use of students' cultural knowledge, prior experiences, and frames of reference to make learning more relevant and effective for them. Integrating academic content using student experiences to scaffold instruction promotes students' understanding of key concepts and fosters a positive, inclusive learning environment for CLD students (Klinger & Gonzalez, 2009). Culturally responsive educators teach content through a cultural lens, such as using vignettes, scenarios, and examples, to enhance students' understanding of content and help them generalize those ideas outside the classroom. Practitioners and educators must have critical awareness of their roles as agents of change, maintain high expectations for all students, use student-centered and content-driven curricula, and build positive relationships with students, staff, families, and communities (Farinde-Wu et al., 2017).

Validation, Affirmation, Building, and Bridging

Society, and in particular school systems, often has made minoritized students' culture and language illegitimate (Hollie, 2019). Thus, to validate and affirm means appreciating, building, and integrating student's cultural background and language into instruction, so that learning continues to be meaningful to them (Hollie, 2019). Culturally responsive practitioners, therefore, foster a supportive and inclusive learning environment through understanding, sensitivity, and empathy rather than through negativity, indifference, or apathy. Disruptive student behaviors (e.g., aggression, bullying, disrespect) are never appropriate in a school setting and thus should be addressed to ensure that all students are learning in a safe and supportive environment.

One approach, Validation, Affirmation, Building, and Bridging ([VABB]; Hollie, 2011) is a set of strategies that promote culturally responsive practice in schools and facilitate learning about students and expectations. According to Hollie (2011), culturally responsive practice is the validation and affirmation of cultural and linguistic behaviors of all students, as well as the building and bridging of those behaviors to success in the context of school culture.

VALIDATION

Validation refers to accepting the cultural values of students who have been historically marginalized by society or majority culture. Practitioners validate by supporting students' cultural knowledge, identities, language, traditions, and experiences that play a prominent role in students' and families' lives. Importantly, validation also means recognizing and appreciating these social identities, rather than taking a "colorblind" or "culturally neutral" approach. That is, schools recognize, value, and demonstrate understanding of different cultural identities and their intersectionality (MacPherson, 2010).

The broader U.S. culture and educational system values individuality and assertiveness to be successful academically. In some communities within the United States, however, such as Indigenous populations, perceived social support, mentorship, strong connections to the community, and establishing trusting relationships with educators are valued in promoting student's academic persistence and achievement (Fryberg et al., 2013). Schools that encourage cultural matching (Stephens et al., 2012) can help foster students' sense of belonging and feelings of being successful. *Cultural matching* occurs when the norms and values promoted by the school are similar to those of the student. However, understanding the relation among students' cultural identities, school cultural values, and student outcomes is not a matter of differentiating whether the school reinforces a majority or minority culture, but of how the school interacts with the student's cultural identity.

One approach that educators can take to validate student's cultural identities is integrating content, texts, and other learning materials that reflect diverse cultural backgrounds, or *cultural relevance*. For instance, Mr. Rappaport can validate David's lived experiences by providing books that highlight themes related to David's experiences or cultural identity. Mr. Rappaport could choose books that reflect David's Mexican heritage and choose books that reflect children who are navigating acculturation, making new friends, or learning new languages in school.

Another example of validation is having educators highlight positive aspects of students' interests outside of the classroom, which could be a productive or effective form of student engagement. For instance, rap or hip-hop music (which has been perceived as a negative connotation due to explicit language or themes) could be used as a creative form of communication and learning. Practitioners can demonstrate validation by displaying aspects of students' culture or language in the classroom and around the school, asking students to share their experiences, and actively listening to students without judgment.

AFFIRMATION

A second culturally responsive practice to facilitate student learning is communicating with students empathetically through affirmation. *Affirmations* are used to acknowledge explicitly the positive aspects of student's behavioral intentions (Hollie, 2019). Teachers and practitioners can demonstrate affirmation by holding high expectations for students, stating the positive intent of students' behaviors, and informing them about situational appropriateness. *Situational appropriateness* refers to changing student behaviors when settings, contexts, or

Instead of:

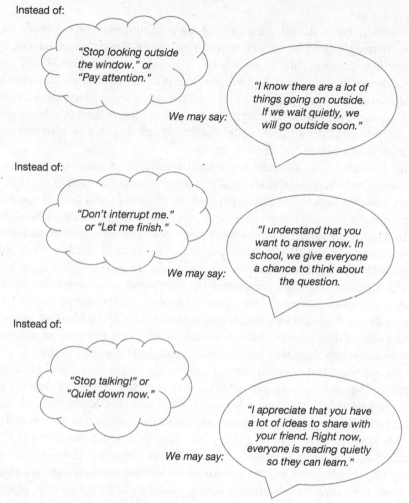

Figure 9.3. Affirmation Statements.

circumstances change. Generally, students learn behaviors when they are provided with direct and positive feedback with opportunities to improve and practice in different environments. Figure 9.3 provides examples of an educator's initial thoughts (in bubbles) to a student engaging in a behavior (e.g., *"Stop looking outside the window"*). Educators can express statements of validation and affirmation shown as the first sentence in the bubble (*"I know there are a lot of things going on outside."*) with the second sentence describing situational appropriateness (*"If we wait quietly, we will go outside soon."*). These *affirmations* serve to inform the student about why behaviors may not be suitable at this point in time or outline conditions for when these behaviors may be appropriate.

In the case of David, Mr. Rappaport can affirm that David may be feeling nervous when reading aloud by himself, so the teacher or other students can read aloud or together first. Subsequently, Mr. Rappaport can provide positive reinforcement for David's successful attempts in reading aloud. Other behaviors

Table 9.3. EXAMPLE OF A PERSONAL MATRIX

Expectation	What does it look like at school?	What does it look like at home?	What does it look like at recess?
Be Respectful	Raise hand for assistance		
Be Responsible	Follow directions		
Be Safe	Hands to self		

NOTE. Adapted from *PBIS Cultural Responsiveness Field Guide: Resources for Trainers and Coaches,*

by M. Leverson, K. Smith, K. McIntosh, J. Rose, & S. Pinkelman, 2021, Center on Positive Behavioral Interventions and Supports, University of Oregon (https://www.pbis.org/resource/pbis-cultural-responsiveness-field-guide-resources-for-trainers-and-coaches).

determined to be unacceptable in the school setting must be grounded in a clear purpose (e.g., to keep students safe). If peers have been teasing or bullying David, then Mr. Rappaport should provide explicit instruction and rules for addressing inappropriate behaviors and reward prosocial behavior in the classroom.

Practitioners who seek to validate and affirm students should refrain from making assumptions about student behavior and, instead, seek to understand it. Mr. Rappaport can ask all of his students, including David, to identify what their expectations are at home. Importantly, the home expectations should be viewed in context of the purpose or goal. To build connections and communication, Mr. Rappaport may discuss how his students' home expectations are similar or different from his classroom expectations and then determine whether he should revise one or two classroom expectations or provide additional support to students (see Table 9.3). Mr. Rappaport could welcome and incorporate home language in instruction by asking David to create stories or write reflections in David's heritage language to share with other students. In that way, David's learning history is valued, and he might be more willing to engage in reading tasks in the classroom. Other students should also understand their peers' histories rather than just those within the host culture.

BUILDING

A third approach to culturally responsive practice is building. *Building* is characterized as providing specific instruction on learning desirable behaviors in the school setting, while connecting with the student's culture or language. This approach may include teaching students the expectations across settings, rather than assuming students should inherently know or understand those expectations. Similarly, it is about teaching the student that disruptive or aggressive behaviors are unwanted behaviors or "not for school," as opposed to describing them as wrong or "bad" behaviors (Hollie, 2019).

As an example of building, Mr. Rappaport could meet with David several minutes before entering the classroom, and if he feels anxious, David could learn and use relaxation techniques to help him calm down before reading, or even say "Pass" if he prefers to read at a later point in time to the group. Mr. Rappaport could also prepare and prompt David when he would be asked to read aloud (e.g., 10 minutes after entering the classroom) to allow the student time to prepare. David can decide on what mode of communication (e.g., verbal or nonverbal) to inform Mr. Rappaport when he is ready.

BRIDGING

Lastly, *bridging* also allows students opportunities to practice and build fluency in school behaviors with performance feedback (Hollie, 2019). Practitioners or educators can use a number of strategies for bridging, include developing lessons for active practice for engaging in productive behaviors, acknowledging students regularly for following expectations, providing reinforcement, and including nonjudgmental feedback when needed. For example, David may initially prefer to read alone or one-on-one with an adult, which Mr. Rappaport should praise and acknowledge but eventually reward when the student successfully transitions to reading in small groups with supportive peers.

Bridging is a proactive teaching approach. Proactive teaching has been shown to reduce the use of school discipline and to keep students engaged in learning (Nese et al., 2016). Thus, by stating school and classroom expectations clearly and positively, students can easily learn what they are expected to do, rather than what they are not to do. Teachers and practitioners can use proactive approaches to respond to students and to improve student compliance and academic productivity. These may include improving student–teacher relationships (e.g., positive greetings at the door), teaching prosocial behaviors (e.g., helping, sharing with peers), and responding to unwanted behaviors (e.g., ignoring jokes and teasing). One strategy is using a Personal Matrix (see Table 9.1; Leverson et al., 2021), an activity that helps bridge expectations between school and home that has been shown to increase equity (Muldrew & Miller, 2021). These strategies align with the MTSS approach and principles of culturally responsive practice by documenting cultural gaps and students' perceptions of expectations across settings.

In sum, culturally responsive pedagogy encourages high expectations and contextual learning to maximize student strengths. It provides an opportunity for schools to examine and reflect on their routines and procedures and to identify areas where aspects of the students' prior cultural experience can be beneficial to include within classrooms. It can also serve as a foundation when implementing school-level supports from which to address students who may continue to struggle academically and behaviorally, while ensuring equitable outcomes. The following section discusses culturally adapting EBIs for students who may require additional support.

CULTURAL ADAPTATION OF EVIDENCE-BASED INTERVENTIONS (TIERS 2 AND 3)

Culturally responsive pedagogy is a useful strategy to support all students, particularly those from CLD backgrounds. Some students would benefit from more targeted EBIs within MTSS. Federal law through the Individual with Disabilities Education Act (IDEA) of 2004 stipulates that schools use practices that are based on peer-reviewed research to the extent that such practices are practical. Despite the progress made on the development of EBIs in school settings, these interventions were seen as culture free, culturally neutral, or universally appropriate for "treating" or "fixing" student behaviors. That is, historically, these interventions have been developed and tested with mainly middle-class White Americans, often with the assumption that they would also be effective for CLD students (Bernal et al., 2009; Castro-Olivo & Merrill, 2012). Achieving a balance between culturally responsive practice and selection of interventions that are scientifically rigorous is especially challenging when implementing interventions in schools due to issues related to adherence to the intervention (i.e., fidelity), cultural relevance, or fit (Castro et al., 2004).

It is unclear whether current EBIs work with all students. Some researchers highlighted the importance of cultural adaptation of EBIs for improved outcomes and acceptability among CLD populations (Castro et al., 2004). *Cultural adaptation* is a systematic modification of an intervention protocol to consider language, culture, and context in such a way that is compatible with the students' cultural patterns, meaning, and values (Bernal et al., 2009). Although a number of models exist to facilitate cultural adaptation (e.g., Hwang, 2009; Nicolas et al., 2009), progress toward the development of a comprehensive set of adapted interventions is still emerging. Research has shown improvement in student outcomes of culturally adapted interventions in school settings (Castro-Olivo & Merrill, 2012), in low-and-middle-income communities (Murray et al., 2013), across countries (Kumpfer et al., 2017), and that require technology (Sit et al., 2020). Incorporating cultural elements, such as language translation and spiritual beliefs, and taking account of the school context and needs of the target population, can improve family attitudes toward the intervention (Zubieta et al., 2020).

Cultural adaptations of interventions can be a labor-intensive process. It requires practitioners to understand the components of the intervention, the needs of the students and families who will participating in the intervention, and the procedures for determining which aspects of the intervention to adapt, while also maintaining the integrity of the intervention. A commonly used method involves gathering data from focus groups, families, or cultural liaisons and consultants to guide the fit or match to the target group (Resnicow et al., 2000).

Focus groups are potentially valuable for developing culturally responsive messaging and understanding cultural nuances or variations when implementing the intervention with a diverse group of students. Several frameworks applied for cultural adaptation include the ecological validity model (Bernal et al., 1995) and the heuristic framework of cultural adaptation of interventions (Barrera & Castro, 2006) for EBIs with children. We will discuss these briefly, although more emphasis is placed on the heuristic framework as a guiding framework for cultural adaptation in schools.

The ecological validity model (Bernal et al., 1995) includes eight interrelated domains (i.e., language, persons, metaphors, content, concepts, goals, methods, context) and is described in Table 9.4. It is one of the first frameworks in the development and implementation of culturally sensitive interventions, particularly

Table 9.4. ECOLOGICAL VALIDITY MODEL DOMAINS

Domain	Sample Question	Example
Language	Are intervention manuals and materials translated and culturally appropriate?	Translating and back-translating intervention materials
Persons	How are ethnic/racial similarities and differences between practitioner and student considered in the development of the intervention?	Providing additional time for communication and learning
Metaphors	How are sayings, expressions, and visual symbols incorporated in the intervention?	Using and discussing symbols of cultural significance in intervention materials
Content	How are cultural knowledge, values, and traditions integrated in the intervention?	Incorporating caregiver's or student's viewpoints on mental health
Concepts	Are intervention concepts conveyed in a culturally relevant manner?	Simplifying language, or using terms in student's developmental level
Goals	Do the intervention goals meet student needs?	Increasing student autonomy or improving peer relationships
Methods	How are considerations made in facilitating delivery of the intervention within the student's cultural context?	Providing support if delivering using technology
Context	Does the intervention address the changing developmental, social, political, and/or economic contexts of the student?	Mitigating concerns related to social stigma or deportation

NOTE: Adapted from "Ecological validity and cultural sensitivity for outcome research: Issues for the cultural adaptation and development of psychosocial treatments with Hispanics," G. Bernal, J. Bonilla, & C. Bellido, 1995, in *Journal of Abnormal Child Psychology, 23*(1), 67–82 (https://doi.org/10.1007/BF01447045).

with Latinx populations. Bernal and colleagues (1995) indicated that when culturally sensitive elements are incorporated into an intervention, then the *ecological validity*, or the degree to which elements of the intervention match with the environment as experienced by the individual, is likely to improve. Since culture determines meaning, the cultural context would be a starting point for designing the intervention (Bernal et al. 1995). Thus, the development and adaptation of interventions would come from a cultural context. While cultural adaptations of interventions are likely to increase the ecological validity of an intervention, they do not always guarantee desired outcomes.

Heuristic Framework for Cultural Adaptation of Interventions

When deciding whether to adapt interventions, practitioners often make initial comparisons between student groups to determine whether an existing intervention is effective for one group, and whether this can be adapted to another group. Barrera and Castro (2006) suggested examining differences in both *engagement* (e.g., participation in the intervention), *action theory* (e.g., protective or risk factors of target group as mediators), and *conceptual theory* (e.g., addressing relationship between mediators and outcomes). Lau (2006) argued that cultural adaptations should be considered when evidence of unique protective and risk factors exist that underlie the intervention's theoretical framework.

Engagement in the intervention involves participation in and acceptability of the intervention, or the students' "buy-in". It can also depend on the participant sample in which the intervention was tested, and whether characteristics of the sample are similar to the targeted group in the community (Barrera & Castro, 2006) or to a sample that is unrepresentative with respect to important characteristics such as acculturation, education, or language use.

Engagement may include making structural changes at a surface level (e.g., use of culture-congruent images) or a deeper level (e.g., content of messages) to the intervention materials (Castro et al., 2004). *Surface structural levels* refers to matching intervention materials and messages to tangible or observable characteristics of a target population. This may include conveying images of people, places, language, product brands, music, and food familiar to, and preferred by, the target audience. *Deep structural levels* refer to incorporating cultural, social, and historical elements that influence core values, attitudes, beliefs, feelings, and behavior in the proposed target population. For example, Vietnamese families emphasize interpersonal and interdependent relationships and view them as important to sustaining cultural norms compared with individualistic or independent orientations. Reviewing these structures is necessary for welcoming CLD students and families into classrooms that are sensitive to their needs, in an experience that they perceive is designed for them.

There are also certain mechanisms or mediators through which interventions can be modified to achieve desired outcomes (Barrera & Castro, 2006). Some examples of mediators include risk and protective factors that pertain to specific cultural groups. If there should be differences in groups based on these mediators, then elements of the intervention would need to be adapted to strengthen their effects or be included in the intervention to address unique mediators (Lau, 2006). In David's case, he may likely be experiencing acculturative stress or language barriers. Cultural adaptations within a social-emotional intervention, for example, can address these specific mediators to improve David's engagement and outcomes.

When considering cultural adaptation of EBIs, it is important to consider the core elements and the elements that could be modified. Kelly et al. (2000) provide an analogy for specifying the core elements using the process of making chocolate-chip cookies:

> The core elements in a recipe, such as flour, sugar, and chocolate chips, are essential to the identity and successful production of chocolate-chip cookies. If any ingredients are omitted, substituted, and measured inaccurately, the product would not be recognizable as a chocolate-chip cookie. On the other hand, the cookie preparation, or key characteristics, can be adapted to the kitchen and the cook. Using a mixer or a spoon, baking in a gas or an electric oven, and shaping the dough into bite-sized or plate-sized pieces would still produce the recognizable chocolate-chip cookie. (p. 90)

By recognizing the key components of the "recipe," the other methods or ingredients can be modified without compromising the product. Practitioners need to know what aspects of the intervention can be adapted so that the integrity of the intervention is not diminished. Rather, appropriate and careful modifications would likely increase the effectiveness of the intervention for the students.

Steps to Cultural Adaptation of Evidence-Based Interventions

There is a growing consensus about the steps practitioners should take to design adaptations to both engagement and intervention procedures. Using the heuristic framework (Barrera and Castro, 2006), practitioners can take specific steps to adapt EBIs culturally (see Figure 9.4).

DEVELOP A CULTURAL ADAPTATION TEAM TO ESTABLISH RATIONALE AND GOALS

The first step in making an EBI culturally responsive is to recruit members for the *cultural adaptation team*, which includes major stakeholders such as program developers, parents, staff, and cultural consultants. Investing in cultural knowledge is not simply observing the community; rather, cultural knowledge should include working with the community in all aspects of the design and implementation (Barrera & Castro, 2006). The cultural adaptation team provides a unique opportunity for community leaders and program implementation

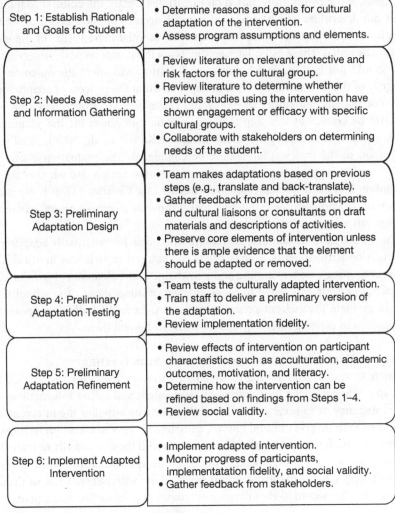

Figure 9.4. Steps for Cultural Adaptation of Interventions.
SOURCE: M. Barrera & F. G. Castro (2006). A heuristic framework for the cultural adaptation of interventions. *Clinical Psychology: Science and Practice, 13*(4), 311–316. https://doi.org/10.1111/j.1468-2850.2006.00043.x

experts to work together to understand the culture of the community. Some questions to consider include:

- Which members should be involved from the school and community?
- What aspects of the culture should be addressed?
- What are the program goals and the level of resources that are available?

The team should determine the rationale for potential adaptations to an intervention. They can create a strategic plan, which involves the goals of the EBI and the needs of the community. Based on this strategic plan, the cultural adaptation team can determine which aspects of the EBI need to be modified. During this step, it is critical that key components or "the essential ingredients" of the intervention be noted. These essential ingredients are those aspects of the intervention that should not be modified because modification will affect the outcome and integrity of the intervention. It is also important that the process of adaptation is fully documented for future reference and evaluation. An implementation plan can also be created at this step that can include milestones for the adaptation, implementation, and progress monitoring (McKleroy et al., 2006). Finally, an evaluation of the intervention should be completed. The evaluation allows the team members to examine the outcomes of the intervention and whether the intervention had been implemented with fidelity (see Chapter 11). It is especially important to compare these outcomes with those of a control group, where the adaptations were not put into place.

The school team should discuss reasons and goals for potentially adapting an intervention with students' unique needs and cultural experiences in mind. This requires thorough understanding and knowledge of the elements of current EBIs and school resources needed to make changes or adaptations. The school team should evaluate the current progress of the student and whether any potential adaptations to existing interventions would likely benefit them.

Conduct Needs Assessment and Information Gathering

In order to choose and subsequently adapt an intervention for the school, the next step is to conduct a thorough needs assessment and gather information. An initial step may be to review the research literature on whether the interventions were used with diverse cultural groups, complete surveys to assess preferences of parents and students, and conduct focus groups with the community or interview with experts who are experienced in working with specific cultural groups. These data will help schools identify cultural needs, along with relevant risk or protective factors, that would likely influence outcomes of prospective participants.

Develop a Preliminary Adaptation Design

The practitioner and the cultural adaptation team can use the ideas gathered from the previous step to develop a plan for intervention adaptation. For example, translation and back translation of content and instructions may be needed to ensure accuracy in program delivery. Information gathered from the literature review and qualitative research can inform content adaptations in both surface and deep structural levels. For example, discussion of cultural values and spiritual beliefs can be incorporated in a parent-training intervention program for caregivers to discuss similarities and differences in how they perceive behavioral management or positive reinforcement.

Preliminary Adaptation Tests

School teams can conduct a preliminary test of the adapted intervention with individual students or small groups. Information gathered from interviews or surveys should be analyzed to determine if the desired goals of adaptation were achieved. Team members can then identify and discuss issues related to (a) cultural relevance of the program; (b) implementation difficulties; (c) challenges with understanding of program content or activities; (d) satisfaction with treatment elements, including cultural features; and (e) suggestions for improvements (Barrera & Castro, 2006). Exit interviews may be used with participants and staff to determine ways of improving and modifying the intervention.

ADAPTATION REFINEMENT

The school team can revise or modify intervention adaptation procedures, content, and activities after analyzing qualitative or quantitative data from the interviews or surveys. When evaluating the interventions for effectiveness, the school team should continue to review Steps 1–4 for any differences that may occur in engagement and outcomes between subgroups or between students. For example, if intervention data showed limited growth in a student's social-emotional learning after 3 months, the school team should review the components implemented for the participants (e.g., students, caregivers) to determine if there were difficulties or issues with clarity of instructions, activities/tasks, delivery of feedback to participants, or follow-up, which can also affect implementation fidelity.

Addressing Challenges with Implementation Fidelity and Replication

Although these steps outline approaches to adapting interventions for diverse students, implementation fidelity and replication of the intervention across classrooms, schools, and other settings are core issues for determining effectiveness. To be considered evidence based, researchers must develop and test these interventions under the same conditions and contents for all of the participants assigned to an intervention condition (Kratochwill, 2007). However, we do not necessarily view this approach as sensitive to within-group variations in cultural needs and preferences, as cultural responsiveness relies on differentiation and addressing unique needs of students. One way to address this issue lies with the intervention procedures, which should involve standardized decision rules for varying the content and "dosage" of the intervention, depending on the characteristics of the participants, presenting problem, problem severity, and family resources (Castro & Yasui, 2017). In many ways, a prescriptive approach emulates practice in schools because the intervention would provide explicit guidelines for the delivery of different dosages of intervention components depending on the individual needs of students. Providing standardized decision rules would also allow fidelity and replication of interventions in practice and research and holds promise for individuals with intersecting identities and diverse student groups (Piña et al., 2019).

RECOMMENDATIONS FOR SETTING UP SCHOOLWIDE CULTURALLY RESPONSIVE PRACTICES

Establishing and maintaining school-wide culturally responsive practices requires systems-level change and long-term commitment in learning and advocacy. The following recommendations represent features that ground educator preparation in the development and implementation of a culturally responsive MTSS and EBIs. These include: (a) establishing university–school–family collaborative partnerships, (b) developing an integrated model of the MTSS that integrates cultural and linguistic features, (c) establishing a strong leadership and equity task force, (d) delivering professional development, and (e) establishing sustainability as a goal.

Form University–School–Family Partnerships

Systems-level change and transformational learning most frequently occur when schools are prepared to develop, enhance, and maintain partnerships between universities, families, and communities (Hoover & Soltero-González, 2018). These partnerships also allow for educator preparation programs to prepare current and future teachers best, and to inform and support school districts in using current EBPs and EBIs that are culturally responsive to students and families of various cultures. Partnerships can define goals that emphasize the importance of sustaining culturally responsive practices (i.e., improved ecological decision-making, appropriate referrals, culturally adapting interventions) and attaining the identified outcomes for families and students (i.e., improved student achievement, reducing disproportionality in student discipline).

Develop an Integrated Model of the MTSS

Schools should develop an integrated model of the MTSS that incorporates culture, achievement, behavior, and mental health, which can be used as an assessment and training tool. School teams should also complete a needs assessment of current MTSS models being used that can be modified to ensure culturally responsive practice. Criteria should be established to determine whether decision-making is done responsibly in each tier. Team members should also outline particular roles in each tier to ensure accountability. These modifications can be used for training, follow-up support or coaching, and sustainability efforts (Hoover & Soltero-González, 2018).

Form a Strong Leadership and Equity Task Force

As mentioned earlier, an equity task force that encourages discussion of these critical issues helps to identify and eliminate barriers that CLD students face at school. In addition, strong leadership is an important aspect of this work. MTSS teams that include administrators, school psychologists, counselors, teachers, parents, staff, and other stakeholders from CLD or racial/ethnic backgrounds can change the processes and procedures that result in educational inequities and hinder student learning. However, MTSS teams must be committed to producing equitable outcomes and implementing MTSS with fidelity.

Organize Professional Development and Learning

Professional development that focuses on critical reflexivity (see Chapter 2) and implicit bias enables educators and professionals to implement and sustain culturally responsive pedagogy and practices (Pham et al., 2021). Becoming a culturally responsive professional requires personal and professional reflection while learning and building new skills. Within the MTSS framework and when developing adaptations for existing EBIs, ongoing professional development is a key element for ensuring facilitation and integrity (Hoover & Soltero-González, 2018). Resources from nearby colleges or universities and from professional organizations help sustain these efforts with the goal of eliminating systemic and linguistic barriers to learning for all students.

Establish Sustainability as an Outcome

School teams should establish goals to ensure that culturally responsive practices are sustained and that equity is an ongoing commitment (Vincent, Randall, et al., 2011). School resource supports are often not readily available in many schools, creating instructional delivery challenges. For example, schools may be concerned with securing and retaining professionals with training in MTSS or allocating financial resources necessary to support trainings. Sustaining this type of model or program requires continuation of successes achieved through implementation during capacity-building efforts. For example, school staff can provide input in and goals for how they plan to sustain various elements of MTSS, which can be reviewed by an equity task force. School teams can develop a checklist from these goals, which can be used as a tool to complete follow-up observations and interviews and to evaluate sustainability of MTSS. Sustainable results may be best achieved when expectations for sustainability are expressed early and periodically throughout model development and implementation. Partnerships with scholars from colleges and universities can provide guidance, preparation, and professional development to ensure that school teams are equipped with skill sets necessary to guide sustainable efforts.

SUMMARY

Integrating culturally responsive approaches in the provision of academic and behavior supports provides an opportunity for schools to increase student belonging and improve teacher–student relationships. By infusing cultural awareness, knowledge, and skills in each tier of support, schools create an inclusive environment where students are able to cultivate their learning strengths, positive behavior, cultural and linguistic histories, and sociopolitical background. Through intentional efforts in culturally responsive pedagogy, implementation of MTSS, and adaptation of EBIs, schools would be better equipped to address the unique and diverse needs of students where they feel safe, heard, and valued.

DISCUSSION QUESTIONS

1. In what ways do you build relationships with students in the classroom or school? How do you teach students the behavioral expectations in the classroom?
2. Describe the rationale for culturally responsive pedagogy. What are some specific strategies you have observed in your schools that draw on students' cultural backgrounds and experiences to connect them with content in the classroom?
3. What are the advantages and disadvantages of culturally adapting EBIs?
4. Discuss the interrelatedness of the four elements of culturally responsive MTSS as described. In other words, if one element were "left out," how would the other three elements be affected?

Counseling and Psychotherapy to Support Diverse Students

VIGNETTE

Aisha is a Syrian American eighth-grade cisgender female who was referred for counseling with Mr. Smith, the school counselor. Aisha's teacher noticed that she has recently become withdrawn, avoiding interacting with her peers, and after checking in with her, she explained, "I just feel jittery all the time." Aisha appeared interested in receiving some counseling in the school but was worried about what her parents would think. Aisha's parents are recent immigrants from Syria and consider themselves religious as Sunni Muslims.

- *In what ways might Mr. Smith engage in critical reflexivity in conducting an initial assessment and treatment plan?*
- *How might she develop an authentic partnership with Aisha's parents before, during, and after counseling?*

The meaningful and deep connections practitioners have with students during counseling or psychotherapy can have a significant impact on their learning and well-being. Through these connections, practitioners can then aid students in navigating the complexities of school and life successfully. Teaching these skills is particularly important because nearly 1 in 6 students experiences emotional or behavioral difficulties that are significant enough to meet criteria for mental health disorders (Danielson et al., 2021). Further, children and adolescents who are from minoritized groups are likely to have higher rates of mental health challenges and are less likely to access and receive mental health care than their White peers (American Psychological Association, 2017; Liang et al., 2016). Historically, education and mental health systems have created disparities for many of these children. They may experience more stress due to poverty, neighborhood violence, parental instability, or maltreatment (Alegria et al., 2015). Additionally, a report on mental health disparities showed that among those youth who need mental health services, less than 40% are likely to receive them (American Psychological Association [APA], 2017).

Meaningful and deep connections through individual or group counseling can be critical in supporting these students. The counseling techniques that practitioners use and the skills that they teach, however, should be responsive to the students' strengths, needs, and culture. Although there are many evidence-based practices for addressing students' mental health, practitioners must also consider the degree to which these practices are responsive to individual students. As discussed in Chapter 9, there is tension between implementing evidence-based interventions that have been scientifically supported yet may need to be adapted to individual students' needs.

We use the terms *counseling* and *psychotherapy* interchangeably in this chapter. *Counseling* or *psychotherapy* refers to any intervention that is targeted to support a student's well-being through a meaningful connection with a trained mental health professional. There are many different types of approaches to counseling, such as cognitive-behavioral therapy, dialectical behavioral therapy, or solutions-focused counseling. Counseling can occur in any physical space (e.g., outpatient clinic, hospital) or via telepractice, and we advocate for counseling to occur in schools because of the accessibility for many students. Further, a great deal of research has shown that counseling is feasible and effective for minoritized children and adolescents with a number of psychosocial issues, including anxiety-related problems, attention issues, depression, and trauma-related syndromes (Huey & Polo, 2008).

In this chapter, we discuss culturally responsive approaches to providing counseling and psychotherapy to culturally and linguistically diverse (CLD) students, since these services are routinely delivered by school counselors, school psychologists, and social workers. First, we discuss the ecological perspectives of mental health and well-being. Second, we summarize specific culturally responsive techniques that may be useful when providing counseling and psychotherapy in schools. Finally, we highlight some key professional, ethical, and legal considerations for providing counseling to CLD students.

ECOLOGICAL PERSPECTIVES ON MENTAL HEALTH AND WELL-BEING

In order to provide counseling and psychotherapy to CLD students, practitioners should first consider ecological factors and systems that shape the student's development, including learning and mental health (see Table 10.1). Practitioners must be able to examine the multiple layers, systems, and factors that may impact their well-being and learning. By doing so, practitioners are focusing on the systems that are negatively affecting the student's mental health. That is, rather than focusing on the deficits (*What is wrong with this student?*), the ecological model promotes a focus on systems and resilience (*What factors exist that contribute to the student's well-being?*).

Table 10.1. SOCIOCULTURAL FACTORS AND CULTURAL DIMENSIONS

Factors	Dimensions
Identity	Racial and ethnic identity development
	Ethnic pride
	Experiences of prejudice, racism, or microaggressions
	Immigration journey
	Ability/disability
	Sexual identities (romantic and sexual attraction)
	Gender expression
	Gender role socialization
Culture and Values	Cultural values
	Spirituality and religiosity
	Culture-based strengths
	System-based strengths
Acculturation	Levels of acculturation
	Navigating degree to which the student adheres to their heritage and host cultures
	Caregiver–child acculturation differences
Language	Primary and secondary language development
	Basic interpersonal communicative skills (BIP)
	Cognitive academic language proficiency (CALP)
	Use of metaphors and storytelling
	Caregiver's primary language
Family Factors	Definition of family and caregiving
	Extended networks/kinship networks
	Communication style
	Problem-solving preferences
	Values, rituals, roles
	Parenting style
	Income level and employment
	Language
	Education
	Immigration journey and migration status (voluntary vs. involuntary)
Geography and Physical Space	Rural to urban
	Access to healthcare
	Environmental and climate impacts
	Neighborhood safety and resources
Help Seeking	Perceptions of mental health and stigma
	Access to healthcare

In the ecological systems model (Bronfenbrenner, 2005), multiple systems surround and interact with the student. The student is within a larger *microsystem* that includes the student's family, school, religious community, etc. The *mesosystem* comprises the connections between these microsystems (e.g., how families and schools interact). The *exosystem* comprises the indirect environments (e.g., economic systems, governments) that surround a student. Encompassing all of these systems is the *macrosystem*, the norms and values of the culture that influence and interact with all of these systems.

To supplement this model, practitioners also must understand the various factors and competencies that contribute to the well-being and development of students from culturally, racially, ethnically, and linguistically minoritized groups. Within all of these systems are factors that impact these students more than White students because of the history of oppression and racism that particularly affects their lived experiences. These factors include: (a) the student's social position (e.g., social class, gender), (b) their experiences of racism, prejudice, and discrimination, (c) the student's environments (e.g., school, healthcare) that promote or inhibit their well-being, (d) family (e.g., structure, values), and (e) their adaptive culture (e.g., cultural legacies, acculturation; Garcia Coll et al., 1996). By recognizing the interplay of these factors, practitioners can understand the issues that impact a student's well-being and subsequently develop and deliver culturally responsive counseling that specifically meets the student's culture and needs.

The *ecological model of counseling* is an approach to ensure that sociocultural variables and ecological factors are considered in addressing student well-being. McMahon et al. (2014) explained that practitioners who engage in ecological model of counseling (1) seek to understand their students within their multiple and unique contexts, (2) participate in an ongoing cycle of multilevel assessment and multilevel interventions, (3) work directly with students from an ecological perspective, and (4) use leadership, advocacy, and collaboration to help create and sustain a healthy school-as-system that promotes success for all students. Practitioners who engage in this model understand that the students are not living on an isolated island; rather, the student's development, learning, and well-being are being affected by and embedded within multiple systems. In sum, using this ecological model can help practitioners look beyond within-student deficits and instead examine the various systems that contribute to the student's experiences, with the goal of making changes within the environment or teaching strategies to support the student in adapting to that environment.

Implementing culturally responsive counseling requires recognition that much of psychotherapy and counseling is based on Western notions and worldviews. Some scholars have argued that counseling is based on individualism, or the idea that counseling focuses on "the self as individualistic, rationalistic, monological, univocal, and egocentric" (Wendt & Gone, 2011, p. 211). That is, counseling is primarily based on Western worldviews of individualism. For example, the theoretical assumptions of cognitive-behavioral therapy suggest a focus on the individual, rather than on the collective. Culturally responsive counseling, therefore, should be more than simply having the practitioner develop cultural competence; rather, it is also about changing the perspective that the *counseling approach itself is Western based* (Wendt & Gone, 2011).

[Reflexivity Activity]: Reflect on your training in counseling. What components are specifically Western based? What components may be derived from other cultural traditions?

To address this issue effectively, Pedersen (2009) highlighted *inclusive cultural empathy*, which "recognizes that the same behaviours may have different meanings and different behaviours may have the same meaning" (p. 151). That is, practitioners should consider how the behaviors they may see from their students may not necessarily align with their own culture, and vice versa, that some of the student's behaviors may appear different but have the same underlying meaning. Ultimately, practitioners must critically reflect on their assumptions behind students' behaviors.

CULTURALLY RESPONSIVE COUNSELING APPROACHES

Although there are various techniques and strategies when providing counseling to CLD students, it can be difficult to determine the best approach for each student. This is particularly the case because, as discussed in earlier chapters, practitioners must balance their cultural knowledge of a group of people while recognizing the heterogeneity of each group. Thus, we provide a framework that practitioners can use to provide effective and culturally responsive counseling to students (see Box 10.1). Based on Liu and Clay's (2002) decision-making framework, we outline several steps that a practitioner can take when providing counseling to CLD students in schools: (1) Engage in critical reflexivity of the practitioner's knowledge and skills to determine whether the practitioner should provide counseling or refer to someone else, (2) build relationships, develop goals, and create a culturally affirming space, (3) consider the salient sociocultural factors and cultural dimensions that may be relevant in the case, (4) examine how to incorporate sociocultural factors or cultural dimensions into the counseling, (5) review the potential counseling approaches and understand the cultural assumptions of each, (6) implement the treatment using cultural strengths, and (7) evaluate the effectiveness of the counseling.

Box 10.1.

STEPS IN CULTURALLY RESPONSIVE COUNSELING

Step 1	Engage in critical reflexivity of the practitioner's knowledge and skills to determine whether the practitioner should provide counseling or refer to someone else.
Step 2	Build relationships, develop goals, and create a culturally affirming space.
Step 3	Consider the salient sociocultural factors and cultural dimensions that maybe relevant in the case.
Step 4	Examine how to incorporate sociocultural factors or cultural dimensions into the counseling.
Step 5	Review the potential counseling approaches and understand the cultural assumptions of each.
Step 6	Implement the treatment using cultural strengths.
Step 7	Evaluate the effectiveness of the counseling.

Engaging in Reflexivity and Cultural Humility

Our connection and relationship with a student and their family must be founded on a sense of trust, as well as the intentional process of critical reflexivity. As described in Chapter 1, critical reflexivity is a process in which practitioners give time and space to reflect and self-critique their knowledge and skills as they relate to working with CLD students (Cunliffe, 2016). It is intentionally allowing ourselves to be vulnerable—and maybe even uncomfortable—in order to improve our counseling skills.

Certainly, as the practitioner begins the counseling relationship with a student, it is important that the practitioner engage in cultural humility so that the practitioner and student (and the student's family) can have a strong therapeutic alliance. The therapeutic relationship is essential for change (Norcross & Wampold, 2011), and engaging in cultural humility while establishing the therapeutic relationship is particularly important (Hook et al., 2017). The practitioner needs to honor and respect the student's cultural values, as well as being emotionally engaged with the student, in order to form a strong therapeutic alliance.

Further, engaging in critical reflexivity and cultural humility provides opportunities for the practitioner to understand their feelings of discomfort, and, importantly, *from where* those feelings are derived. When working with Aisha, for example, Mr. Smith may feel some discomfort in working with a female Muslim student because he had heard that there were different gender expectations among some Muslim families. He felt worried that Aisha's family would not want him to work with her, and he was avoiding speaking with her family about these concerns. Not only is it important that Mr. Smith reflect on ways to provide culturally responsive counseling to Aisha, but he is also engaging in reflexivity about *why* he is feeling that way.

Having difficult conversations with students and their families can lead to feelings of anxiety or fear, to the point where some practitioners avoid having these conversations completely. Hook et al. (2017) suggested that practitioners reflect on their cultural security (e.g., when the practitioner feels secure or grounded) and their cultural anxiety (e.g., fear of a cultural mistake). These feelings are natural, yet practitioners must challenge that discomfort to support the student. In Mr. Smith's case, he can reflect on his feelings of cultural anxiety related to gender roles and consult with a colleague. Through these reflections and the consultation, Mr. Smith may then visit the family in their home and ask their thoughts about the best way to support Aisha. Reflecting on those situations or feelings can be helpful in pushing through the discomfort.

In addition to engaging in reflexivity, practitioners should also recognize their thoughts, feelings, and behaviors related to broaching the student's racial, ethnic, and cultural identity. *Broaching behavior* refers to the degree to which a counselor is comfortable discussing race, ethnicity, and culture within the counseling relationship (Day-Vines et al., 2007). The multidimensional model of broaching behavior (Day-Vines et al., 2020) is a model of how counselors can approach a student's race, ethnicity, and culture (REC) to facilitate a stronger therapeutic alliance and to reduce distress. There is a continuum of broaching behavior from *avoidant* to *infusing* (Day-Vines et al., 2007; see Table 10.2). *Avoidant counselors*, for example, may actively ignore issues of REC and perhaps even deflect when the client brings up the topic. *Isolating counselors* bring up these topics at a minimum

Table 10.2. BROACHING RACE, ETHNICITY, AND CULTURE IN COUNSELING: TYPES OF PRACTITIONERS

Type	Description	Example
Avoidant	Practitioner may actively ignore issues of race, ethnicity, or culture (REC). They may try to change the topic when the student or caregiver brings it up.	During counseling, a Black student states, "I was in history class, and when they started talking about slavery, Mr. Johnson and the rest of the class looked at me." The practitioner then changes the topic.
Isolating	The practitioner is able to bring up the topic of REC, but only at a minimum level and perhaps only because the practitioner feels obligated to.	After the student comments on their experience in history class, the practitioner states, "Oh that sounds difficult. I'm sure they didn't mean it."
Continuing/ Incongruent	The practitioner may bring up the discussion more awkwardly, with little skill.	After the student comments on their experience in history class, the practitioner states, "Ah, let's explore that. What was difficult about that experience?"
Integrated/ Congruent	The practitioner can effectively discuss issues of REC more effectively. They are also able to support the student and connect their experiences and concerns with these topics.	The practitioner, in response to the Black student's experience in history class states, "Tell me about how you felt when everyone was looking at you." They may also follow up, saying, "As the only Black student in that class, it's unfair that everyone believed that you should speak to the Black experience. This is called a microaggression. Have you heard this term before?"
Infusing	The practitioner takes on counseling with a lens of social justice. They have a solid understanding of the systemic barriers to the student's well-being.	The practitioner understands that there is systemic racism in school and that educators and students' reactions to race affect the academic experience of this Black student.

NOTE: Based on "The multidimensional model of broaching behavior," by N. L. Day-Vines, F. Cluxton-Keller, C. Agorsor, S. Gubara, & N. A. A. Otabil, *Journal of Counseling & Development*, 2020, *98*(1), 107–118 (https://doi.org/10.1002/jcad.12304).

level and perhaps with some obligation. *Continuing/incongruent counselors* may bring up the discussion more awkwardly, with little skill. *Integrated/congruent counselors* discuss issues of REC more effectively and are able to help clients connect their concerns with these issues. *Infusing counselors* have more of a social justice focus, where they understand and address barriers to their well-being with a social justice lens.

[*Reflexivity Activity*] *Based on the broaching behaviors, what category of counselor are you? Reflect on the feelings that you may be having when considering this category.*

In addition to the different types of counselors, there are also four dimensions of broaching issues of REC: intracounseling, intraindividual, intra-REC, and inter-REC (Day-Vines et al., 2020). *Intracounseling* refers to the practitioner's ability to work within the counseling relationship on topics related to REC, and to engage in cultural humility (Hook et al., 2017). When working with students, these practitioners may emphasize that these discussions are allowed within the counseling space, but they also may not be completely aware of how or if these issues may be relevant to the student. For example, if a White school counselor was providing solutions-focused counseling to a Black student, she may be engaging in intracounseling when they open up the conversation: "I know I am a White woman. I will never completely understand or know your experience as a Black student. This is a space to talk about race, and I am here to listen and support you the best I can."

The second dimension is *intraindividual*, where the practitioner broaches the discussion on REC with the student to explore the student's overlapping and complex identities (Day-Vines et al., 2020). When providing counseling, the practitioner's recognition of intersectional identities (Crenshaw, 1989) may be important for that student. For example, a Latina school social worker may open the conversation during a counseling session with a Latino student by saying, "There are many aspects of our identities. Tell me about your different identities."

The third dimension is *intra-REC*, where the practitioner may address cultural issues with the student that are relevant to themselves and that are relevant to their family or community. This dimension addressed acculturation, and particularly navigating the student's heritage and host cultures (Berry, 2005). That is, in this dimension, the practitioner may broach topics that highlight how the student's cultural values, beliefs, and norms may differ from those with whom they live. For example, a Sri Lankan student may be navigating their parent's strong maintenance of their heritage culture (Sri Lankan) and their upholding of their American culture. The counselor may provide space for the student to reflect on this dimension.

Finally, the fourth dimension is *inter-REC*, where the practitioner generates discussions about how the student may encounter forms of racism, microaggressions, and discrimination, and structural inequality. For example, a Black school psychologist may provide space for a Black student seeking counseling to reflect on their experiences of a microaggression in the classroom. This dimension is helpful in allowing time and space to process their experiences as a minoritized student in the school.

[Reflexivity Activity]: Think about a recent time when you worked with a student in which there was a discussion about race, ethnicity, culture, or identity(ies). From what dimension did you work?

Overall, the first step in providing culturally responsive counseling is to engage in critical reflexivity and cultural humility. Practitioners should think deeply about their thoughts and feelings about discussing REC and consider their feelings of discomfort before, during, and after providing counseling to minoritized students.

Relationship Building and Goal Orientation

BUILDING RELATIONSHIPS WITH STUDENT AND FAMILY

In the next step in the model, practitioners develop strong relationships with the student and their family, which will facilitate effective goal orientation. An important aspect of culturally responsive counseling is building meaningful relationships, engaging in reciprocity, and earning trust with both the student and their family. Building relationships with families is one of the most important steps in providing counseling and psychotherapy to students, particularly when gaining consent. Authentic and meaningful relationships between the school, family, and community are the bedrock of culturally responsive practice (see Chapter 3). Ibrahim and Heuer (2016) recommend that the practitioner establish a mutual relationship that is co-constructed. That is, they recommend that the practitioner recognize that in order for there to be effective counseling, there should be an equal distribution of power. Establishing relationships requires an intentional process where trust is earned. These values are similarly held in Arab, Middle Eastern, and North African (AMENA) cultures, where the parents have authority and respect from their children (Melhem & Chemali, 2014).

Building relationships with families is particularly important for promoting family engagement in services. Trauma-informed services are important to address for many minoritized students, yet engagement in services can be challenging for some families. Thus, it is not only about adapting counseling approaches, but also about considering the barriers that impede the ability for minoritized students to receive services in the first place. Among Latinx families, for example, practitioners must consider the logistic, cultural, and social barriers that may impact their ability to seek services, such as societal barriers (e.g., stigma of trauma and mental health), family mistrust of the system (e.g., experience with services), or interpersonal barriers (e.g., presence of intergenerational trauma; Meléndez Guevara et al., 2021).

If a student like Aisha was referred for counseling because of symptoms of anxiety, one of the first tasks would be to establish relationships with her family and to increase buy-in about the need for mental health support at school. Practitioners may work with families who may be hesitant to have their child participate in

services at school; however, practitioners can use a number of strategies to increase buy-in. Practitioners who work with Latinx families have noted that
building relationships with families is paramount to providing successful mental
health services by actively listening and "giving them voice" to engage with the
services (Meléndez Guevara et al., 2021, p. 333).

Additionally, there are a number of strategies to use to engage in reciprocity and
earn trust. Hays (2008) suggested that self-disclosure can be a helpful way to develop rapport. Many counselors are trained to avoid self-disclosure because of the
assumptions that it promotes transference; however, these theories are based on
Eurocentric approaches that may not be relevant for some families (Hays, 2008).
Self-disclosure can be a very helpful tool, as it aligns with the values of reciprocity,
where stories are shared between people. Indeed, counseling, as it has been historically designed, has focused on one-sided storytelling. Some self-disclosure can
be helpful in promoting reciprocity (*I will share something, then you share something*). When working with caregivers, for example, some self-disclosure about the
difficulties of parenting a teen can show both empathy and understanding (e.g., "I
hear you, parenting can be challenging. I work hard to parent my 13-year-old").

Building relationships with families also may require practitioners to be
thoughtful about the words and terms they use and hear. When working with
Aisha, Mr. Smith may want to provide some psychoeducation with her parents,
such as ways to describe what anxiety looks like and how Aisha experiences that
anxiety. Instead of using "cognitive distortions" for example, Mr. Smith want to
consider using "inaccurate thoughts." Similarly, it is helpful to ask families themselves what they mean by certain terms. For example, if they state, "My family
is dysfunctional," it would be important to clarify what they mean by the term
"dysfunctional" because it has underlying assumptions about how families are
designed and characterized (Hays, 2008).

Co-Creating Goals for Counseling

Once the relationships are developed and fostered, then the practitioner can begin
co-creating goals with the student and their family. As described in Chapter 4,
changing the question from *What is the problem?* to *What are the student's and
family's goals?* allows practitioners to move away from the deficit-focused to
strengths-based approaches. It is not that the practitioner ignores that a problem
exists. Indeed, support or help would not be sought if there were no concerns
from teachers, caregivers, or the student themselves. However, when changing the
view from *problem* to *goal*, the focus of the counseling is not to solve a problem,
but instead to reach a mutual goal that is co-created with the student and family.

Additionally, goal orientation allows for deeper case conceptualization. As
discussed in Chapter 4, developing treatment goals and conceptualizing the reasons
for specific mental health concerns beyond the student allow for practitioners to
recognize that there are multiple systems that influence the student's well-being.
For example, when considering how to support Aisha, the practitioner reframes
the traditional *What is the problem?* to *What are Aisha's goals?* Aisha's teachers

may be concerned that she has anxiety, because they have observed her standing away from her peers and not participating in the class discussion. Aisha's teacher reached out to Mr. Smith because she hoped that Aisha would be participating more in class and wanted her to be successful at school. Mr. Smith, however, must consider the systems that surround Aisha and reframe his question to *What are Aisha's goals? What are her family's goals?* This question then leads to a different process of answering it. It may be that Aisha is content to be quieter in class and is doing fine academically. The culture and norms of the classroom in the United States suggest that classroom engagement (e.g., verbally answering a question, raising the hand) is not only appropriate but encouraged. This norm, however, may not align with Aisha's experience in the classroom in Jordan. Thus, Aisha's level of acculturation should be considered.

Consider the Sociocultural Factors and Cultural Dimensions

When providing counseling, the practitioner should consider the various sociocultural factors and cultural dimensions that may be relevant for that student and their family. Practitioners may underestimate the importance of this process. To understand fully how to provide culturally responsive counseling, there must be a clear assessment of the concerns that caregivers and teachers may have, as well as the strengths the student carries to the counseling relationship. These sociocultural factors can be gathered during the intake and assessment component of the process (see Chapters 4 and 7). We recognize that a formal intake may not necessarily occur during school-based counseling, particularly when the practitioner is providing the services under the student's individualized education program (IEP) or 504 plan. A brief assessment through administration of screening measures or a review of previous psychological evaluations may provide sufficient information about the sociocultural factors and cultural dimensions. By understanding the sociocultural dimensions that surround the student, the practitioner can understand the factors that may be contributing to those concerns, as well as focus the counseling on building upon the student's existing strengths.

One of the most important sociocultural factors to consider is the student's worldview. When conducting culturally responsive and social justice counseling, Ibrahim and Heuer (2016) recommend that a cultural assessment be conducted that includes a particular focus on the student's worldview. A student's *worldview* is the "beliefs, values, and assumptions that are derived from a cultural context" (Ibrahim & Heuer, 2016, p. 55). That is, the student's worldview is shaped by their family's and their society's values and norms, including the sociocultural factors and cultural dimensions, shown in Table 10.1. Practitioners use multiple ways to gather this information from record reviews, school and classroom observations, relational interviewing with the student and caregiver, and tests and measures (see Chapter 7 for detail on how to conduct culturally responsive assessment for mental health and traumatic stress).

Review Counseling Approaches and Cultural Assumptions

There is much debate about the evidence, feasibility, and sustainability of counseling and psychotherapeutic approaches with culturally and linguistically diverse students. As we highlighted in Chapter 9, there is a tension between using scientifically supported (i.e., efficacious) treatments and interventions as designed, and adapting those interventions to be culturally responsive with the target population. Counseling and therapy that use evidence-based practices are critical to ensure that they are improving mental health outcomes for the student.

Various counseling and therapeutic approaches have been shown to be effective with minoritized children and adolescents (Kataoka et al., 2010). For example, to address symptoms of depression, interpersonal therapy for adolescents (IPT-A) has been found to be effective for Puerto Rican adolescents, where cultural aspects of *familismo* and *respeto* were integrated into the IPT (Rosselló et al., 2008). Attachment-based family therapy was also found to be effective for African American females experiencing trauma and loss (Diamond et al., 2002). To address symptoms of anxiety, cognitive-behavioral therapy (CBT) has also been found to be effective with Latino youth (Silverman et al., 1999) and African American adolescents (Ginsburg & Drake, 2002). Further, to address post-traumatic stress disorder, cognitive behavioral intervention for trauma in schools (CBITS) has been shown to be highly effective with multiple ethnic minoritized groups, including Latin middle school students (Allison & Ferreira, 2017). Thus, there are clearly effective interventions to improve minoritized student's well-being.

Yet, there is continual debate in the field of psychotherapy about whether the actual counseling approach is based in Eurocentric theories and assumptions and therefore is inherently ineffective for certain populations. Some scholars have argued that the profession needs to reimagine or reconceptualize counseling (Wendt & Gone, 2011). Scholars have emphasized that counseling theories focus on individualistic value systems and do not align with the cultures and values of minoritized groups (Nagayama Hall, 2001), and thus providing culturally responsive counseling and interventions is important in ensuring that student's culture, ethnicity, and race are considered.

Instead, it may be helpful to implement counseling approaches that are personally relevant for each student, particularly for students of color. Personal relevance integrates existing evidence-based intervention with culturally specific approaches (Nagayama Hall et al., 2021) and considers the student's individual, group, and universal contexts. A practitioner, therefore, would consider how to make the counseling more personally relevant to the student. At the universal level, the student's social context would be considered, as well as the existing evidence-based interventions that have been shown to be effective for their age and developmental level. Mr. Smith may consider the aspects of the broader cultural group that may be meaningful. For instance, for Aisha, the more collectivist culture of Syria may be considered. At the group level, the practitioner could take into consideration the student's cultural context as well as the culturally adapted interventions. For example, Mr. Smith may want to consider Aisha's level of accul-turation, whether she speaks Arabic at home, and how Islam shapes her family's beliefs. At the individual level, the student's personal context, as well as the implementation and effectiveness of the intervention, would also be considered. Mr. Smith, for example, may want to consider her intersectional identities (Muslim, Syrian, female) in order to integrate culturally responsive approaches. In other words, it is about considering "delivering the right treatment to the right person at the right time" (Nagayama Hall et al., 2021, p. 95).

There has also been increased attention in viewing culture as treatment. That is, interventions have been developed that move away from adapting the intervention to certain cultural groups and consider that culture itself should be the focus of intervention. For example, in the Teen Health Resiliency Intervention for Violence Exposure (THRIVE) study, researchers developed a school-based intervention that supplemented CBITS called *Our Life*, a 6-month intervention developed to build resiliency and well-being among Native American adolescents (Goodkind et al., 2010). In this intervention, both deep-structure and surface-structure adaptations were made, including removing Eurocentric examples of cognitive restructuring that were offensive, as well as integrating stories and examples based on the student's cultural beliefs. In this example, CBITS was chosen as an evidence-based intervention that was modified to meet the needs of the students across multiple tribal nations.

When working with undocumented refugee minors, for example, practitioners can put effort into earning trust with the student's family, reinforcing the idea of confidentiality within the counseling context. Further, practitioners can learn about the student's beliefs, norms, and culture when implementing culturally responsive interventions in the schools (Franco, 2018). Practitioners could integrate culturally relevant factors within evidence-based approaches, including trauma-focused cognitive behavioral therapy ([TF-CBT]; Cohen et al., 2000). For instance, Franco (2018) presented a case "Yaretzi," a high school girl originally from El Salvador who was referred to a school social worker because teachers noticed she had been losing weight, missing school, and falling asleep in class. The school social worker created a group with five other girls from Central America and utilized TF-CBT principles, including psychoeducation. Culturally relevant approaches enable Yarezti and the other girls to identify sources of safety that included their faith leaders (priests) and other practitioners of traditional medicine (*Curanderas*) within the broader intervention (Franco, 2018).

Implement Culturally Responsive Counseling

Once a counseling approach is chosen and the practitioner adapts aspects of the intervention, the practitioner can (1) integrate the student's personal and cultural strengths throughout the counseling, (2) plan the communication and connection, and (3) incorporate cultural expressions, metaphors, and storytelling.

For personal or character strengths, the practitioner collects information from multiple sources to determine the student's positive character traits that will contribute to optimal development and resilience (Park & Peterson, 2008). These trait categories are associated with asset-based approaches to positive well-being, including (a) wisdom and knowledge (strengths related to creativity, open-mindedness, and curiosity), (b) courage (strengths related to persistence and honesty), (c) humanity (strengths related to helping others), (d) justice (strengths related to leadership and teamwork), (e) temperance (strengths related to self-regulation), and (f) transcendence (strengths related to hope, religiosity, or spirituality). Ibrahim and Heuer similarly recommended that the practitioner identify and affirm the individual's strengths. From this affirmation, students can also acknowledge and build on these sources of strengths as a way for them to develop resilience and a positive outlook.

For cultural strengths, the provision of counseling services should continue to build on and respect the student's culture. For example, Arredondo et al. (2014) noted that when working with Latinx families, counseling should focus on their cultural strengths, such as social relatedness (*personalismo*), gratitude, and trust. Similarly, Woods-Jaeger et al. (2021) emphasized that cultural assets should be integrated into intervention and treatment when working with Black youth. For example, they suggested that Black parents can teach their children the cultural knowledge to function in society, an important aspect of racial socialization and one that was found to be protective from the effects of racism. Further, they suggested that coping skills for Black youth could be grounded in African-centered perspectives, such as focusing on communal rather than individualistic approaches and integrating spirituality and faith (Woods-Jaeger et al., 2021).

COMMUNICATION AND CONNECTION

Intentional communication through multiple methods can foster effective counseling for culturally and linguistically diverse students and their families. Communication, or expressiveness, can be done through verbal, emotional, and behavioral means. Sue and Sue (2013) highlighted that many practitioners believe that students must be able to articulate their thoughts and feelings using Standard English during counseling sessions. That is, there is an underlying value of emotional and behavioral expressiveness. They argue, though, that these values put students in minoritized groups at a disadvantage.

Additionally, practitioners should be observant during counseling when it comes to patterns of communication, including both verbal and nonverbal means. Cross-cultural counseling requires the practitioner to understand both the cognitive (thoughts) and affective (feelings), and that empathy is expressed through either verbal and nonverbal cues (Lorié et al., 2017). Sue and Sue (2013) highlighted several types of communication to consider within the counseling relationship, including proxemics, kinesics, and paralanguage. *Proxemics* refers to interpersonal space, where there are cultural norms associated with space during interpersonal interactions. The physical distance between two people is based on social norms, as well as the status, privilege, and power of each person

(Sue & Sue, 2013). For example, in the predominant culture in the United States, someone with status (e.g., a professor) has more flexibility in how close they can be to someone of lower status (e.g., a graduate student). Latinx families may be more comfortable with physical touch, such as hugging (Arredondo et al., 2014).

Kinesics and *paralanguage* are also important to observe during counseling. Kinesics is associated with facial expression, bodily movements, gestures, and eye contact, while paralanguage refers to the vocal cues, such as tone of voice, volume, groans, and pitch, that modify meaning or convey emotion. There are often rules associated about when or where to use certain vocal cues and are culture specific (Sue & Sue, 2013). Expressiveness is often based on cultural norms and expectations. As Lim (2017) described Arab expressiveness and emotion, "While most cultures view language as a means of transferring meanings, Arabs see the role of their language as an art form and religious phenomenon, and tool of expressing their identity" (p. 191). Practitioners use facial expressions to interpret a student's thoughts and feelings, yet facial expressions are also culturally bound. For example, the degree to which a child makes eye contact with an adult may depend on the cultural norms. Some children are expected to look slightly away from the adult's eyes to reflect deference and respect. There are cross-cultural differences in silence, as well. In a Western-based society like the United States, two people sitting next to each other in silence for long periods of time may experience discomfort, yet in other cultural groups, such as Japan, long silences between acquaintances may suggest a close relationship (Lim, 2017).

Practitioners may be required to use interpreters when providing counseling to linguistically diverse students. Logistically, the interpreter should also position themselves directly next to the counselor, sitting slighting behind so that the student or parent is facing both (Paone & Malott, 2008). The practitioner should also speak slowly and pause more often so that the interpreter is able to communicate accurately. Paone and Malott (2008) recommend that the practitioner and interpreter meet prior to (pre-session) and after (post-session) to ensure that there is ongoing communication. During the pre-session briefing, the practitioner and interpreter can establish clear expectations and discuss confidentiality. After the session is completed, it may also be helpful to debrief with the interpreter, particularly to follow up about any culturally relevant statements or behaviors.

During the session, the practitioner should also make sure to maintain rapport with the student, rather than focusing on the interpreter. That is, the practitioner should maintain eye contact with or position their body toward the student, even when the interpreter is speaking. They can also explain to the student or parent the role of the interpreter and clarify that they are maintaining confidentiality.

CULTURAL EXPRESSIONS, METAPHORS, AND STORYTELLING

Storytelling is widespread across many cultures and can be a useful tool during counseling. In most societies and cultures, stories—whether as oral histories through our elders or TV comedies—are how we pass on knowledge, provide guidance, and connect with others. Indeed, the use of therapeutic metaphors is common and can be effective, particularly with children and adolescents because it provides opportunities for children to understand difficult concepts at their developmental level (Killick et al., 2016). For example, Killick et al. (2016) highlighted a number of useful metaphors (e.g. "seeds of change") and particularly the metaphor of "traffic lights" as helpful for children in considering different cognitive strategies (e.g., unhelpful thoughts are red thoughts).

For students who are religious or spiritual, metaphors can be a useful tool within counseling. Muslim students, for example, may be able to understand metaphors based on the Quran, because of the deep symbolism and meaning of their faith and healing. For instance, in describing metaphors in counseling, Ahammed (2010) suggested one metaphor:

> "the moon in its stages of waxing and waning in reflecting the sun's light" (likened to light from a lamp) (Surah Nuh: 16) is meaningful for counseling. Among the many problems the moon metaphor might relate to is a person's responses to particular challenges and accomplishments; the reassurance of a grieving person in things returning to greater normalcy; or the insight needed for a person seeking spiritual growth. (p. 252)

In addition to metaphors and storytelling, Jones (2015) suggested that during culturally responsive interpersonal psychotherapy, the practitioner should "listen for culturally laden cues" that highlight some culturally relevant aspects of the student's life (p. 73). Specifically, Jones (2015) recommended looking for statements such as "people like me," which highlight that the student may be seeing themselves as different from others and perhaps also convey that they are experiencing racism or microaggressions. Another statement, "I have no idea who I am or who I am supposed to be," may imply questions surrounding the student's racial or ethnic identity. Finally, Jones suggested that statements such as "my world collided today" may highlight the student's experiences navigating cultures or feeling acculturative stress.

Evaluate the Counseling Effectiveness

A final component is evaluating the effectiveness of the counseling approach. We strongly emphasize monitoring student progress along with collecting and analyzing data regularly to ensure that the counseling or psychotherapeutic approach is culturally responsive. When adapting an intervention, culturally relevant themes or modifying aspects of an evidence-based practice should lead to change. Guessing, or what we call "feelings-based decisions," is not sufficient. Gathering data frequently is important in order to ensure that the counseling is effective for that specific student.

Progress monitoring, or sometimes called *routine outcome monitoring*, is the process of collecting data to inform whether the counseling or psychotherapy is effective (Overington & Ionita, 2012). Importantly, the tools used to gather information should be specific to address the goal of the counseling. For Aisha, the goals were to decrease symptoms of anxiety and increase engagement with her peers. The practitioner should work with the teacher, families, and the student so they can recognize and monitor (or self-monitor) behaviors related to approaching peers or adults. The tools for progress monitoring should therefore directly link the goal with the measure.

There are formal progress monitoring tools that can be used for students, such as the *Ages and Stages Questionnaire: Social Emotional* (ASQ: SE; Squires et al., 2002) or *BASC-3 Behavioral and Emotional Screening System* (BESS; Kamphaus & Reynolds, 2007). Depending on the focus of the counseling, the *Strengths and Difficulties Questionnaire* (SDQ; Goodman, 2001) as well as domain-specific measures, such as the *Beck Anxiety Inventory* (BAI; Beck et al., 1988), can also be useful in gathering specific data. Overall, these formal measures can be helpful in gathering baseline data (progress prior to counseling) as well as formative data (progress during counseling). Mr. Smith may choose to administer one or more measure as part of the initial assessment of Aisha and then use the same as the progress-monitoring tool. Some practitioners may choose to administer them weekly or biweekly. Depending on the behavior or the length of the measure, biweekly administration may be sufficient.

There are other tools for progress monitoring, including observations or a Subjective Units of Distress Scale (SUDS; e.g., "feelings thermometer"). One of the advantages of school-based mental health services is that practitioners can conduct observations of the students in the classroom or recess to determine whether the counseling is effective (see Chapter 4 on types of observations). If a student demonstrates difficulties sustaining attention and counseling focuses on improving executive functioning skills, the practitioner can observe the student in the classroom, such as off-task behavior or generalizing the specific skills learned in counseling. The disadvantage of observations is that it does take some time, compared with a quick screening tool. Mr. Smith may conduct an observation of Aisha in the cafeteria to see whether she is socializing with her peers (perhaps operationalizing by initiating conversation).

SUDSs are also very helpful in progress monitoring. Practitioners can use a feelings thermometer to gauge the student's feelings of distress. It can be individualized, designed with anchors. For Aisha, the anchors could be 1 = *very relaxed (body is loose, like a noodle)* to 5 = *very anxious (my body is very tight, like a robot)*. These ratings can then be gathered quickly each week and charted on a graph. Not only is this helpful for Mr. Smith to determine whether the counseling is effective for Aisha, but it is also helpful for Aisha to monitor her own improvement. No matter what kind of tool is used for progress monitoring, information must be gathered to determine improvement in student behavior and adjustment.

PROFESSIONAL, ETHICAL, AND LEGAL CONSIDERATIONS

There are a number of professional, ethical, and legal issues that a school-based mental health professional should consider when providing psychotherapy or counseling to CLD students. For this chapter, we focus on those issues that are relevant to culturally responsive practices, as each profession has its own terminology and expectations; thus, it is important that each practitioner carefully read their professional association's ethical codes (e.g., American Psychological Association, 2017; National Association of Social Workers, 2021a) and state-specific legal requirements as they pertain to counseling.

The Ethical Imperative of Cultural Competence

Importantly, the underlying idea of ethics is cultural. Practitioners in schools should recognize that providing culturally responsive counseling is an ethical responsibility. In fact, the Society of Indian Psychologists (SIP) completed a commentary of the American Psychological Association's code of ethics and stated, "It is not possible to understand ethics separate from culture. The abuse of power, whether intentional or unintentional, plays a major role in the harm experienced by Indigenous people as well as other marginalized and stigmatized people" (García, 2014).

Each practitioner should consider their background, training, and experience when considering whether to provide culturally responsive counseling. Indeed, the SIP specifically noted in their commentary that it is not possible to be competent as a practitioner without being multiculturally competent (García, 2014). Some of the professional ethics (e.g., National Association of Social Workers, 2021b) emphasized that cultural competence is an ethical responsibility, whereby they "should demonstrate awareness and cultural humility by engaging in critical self-reflection (understanding their own bias and engaging in self-correction), recognizing clients as experts of their own culture, committing to lifelong learning, and holding institutions accountable for advancing cultural humility." Thus, it is imperative that practitioners consider it their ethical responsibility to ensure that the counseling is meeting the students' needs and addressing their well-being.

Practitioners should engage in critical reflexivity about their knowledge and skills prior to working with CLD students. If, through that process, they recognize that they have not yet attained these competencies, then they should refer the student to another practitioner. In schools, this can be challenging because the service provider may already have been selected during an IEP meeting (e.g., a school psychologist may have been indicated to provide counseling within the IEP plan). If the practitioner does not have the training to support the student, it may be worthwhile to meet as an IEP team to change the listed provider to someone who is a better fit. Of course, this may not be an option in some schools with few resources or a limited number of personnel; thus, it would be critical that the practitioner seek a consultant or supervisor with those competencies to provide additional support. Further, given that practitioners should work from a place of cultural humility, it can be difficult to determine whether they are sufficiently prepared to deliver culturally responsive counseling to that student. Some questions that the practitioner could consider are:

- How long have I been exploring issues related to culturally responsive practice? What are my current skills, knowledge, and awareness?
- How ready am I to provide culturally responsive services to this student? Am I feeling nervous? If so, what are some of the reasons why I might feel nervous?
- I may be the only practitioner in this school who can provide this service given the resources and personnel. How am I going to ensure that I'm engaging in critical reflexivity? What support should I obtain?

Privacy and Confidentiality

Privacy and confidentiality for the student are of the utmost importance. Practitioners should ensure that each student's privacy is maintained, and that the information that they share is kept confidential, with some limits (to be discussed next). Across ethical codes, students have a right to privacy, to ensure that they can share information with the practitioner during counseling. This right to privacy and confidentiality should be discussed with the student and caregivers at the beginning of counseling, as well as reviewed throughout the sessions.

The right to privacy and confidentiality, however, also has limits, particularly when it relates to the student being a minor. What is particularly challenging in counseling students is that parents have a right to access information that occurs during counseling. It can be difficult "to balance parents' right to know with students' right to confidentiality" (Brennan, 2013, p. 309). Sori and Hecker (2015) outlined several different approaches to managing confidentiality with minors. A practitioner could promise the student *complete confidentiality*, except as mandated by law, *limited confidentiality* (in which the student waives their right to know what was shared with their parent), *informed forced consent* (in which the student does not have any power in what is disclosed but is informed if disclosure it made), *no guarantee of confidentiality* (in which all information could be shared with the parent), or *mutual agreement regarding confidentiality* (in which an agreement with the practitioner, student, and parent is made about what will or will not be disclosed to the parents; Sori & Hecker, 2015).

Balancing the student's confidentiality with the caregivers' right to know is challenging, so practitioners should review the values, beliefs, and culture when questioning whether to maintain or break confidentiality and when providing informed consent. When working with Arab Americans, for example, informed consent may require not just obtaining consent from a student's individual parents; rather, it may include discussions of limits of confidentiality with a number of family members (Cho, 2018). Further, there may be concern that information disclosed by the student may be shared with others in the community, and thus conversations with the student and caregiver should clarify the scope and limits of confidentiality in the counseling relationship (Cho, 2018).

Relevant Legal Issues

There are also some legal considerations for providing culturally responsive counseling. Practitioners must be knowledgeable about the Family Education and Rights Privacy Act (FERPA, 1974), which protects the privacy of the student's records. Practitioners should be careful not to share any of the student's records with anyone outside of the school setting without explicit written consent from the student's caregivers. Further, if there are components of the counseling that the practitioner wants to keep confidential, they should separate those records (e.g., progress notes from the counseling session) from the student's other educational records (Brennan, 2013).

Providing counseling to students who may be undocumented in the United States may also present particular legal issues. When providing counseling to students in groups, Chen et al. (2010) recommended a number of strategies for supporting rights of undocumented immigrant students. First, they suggest that practitioners become knowledgeable of existing laws because they vary across states and may depend on the geographical and sociopolitical context (states on the U.S. border versus other states). Second, they suggested that professional development on these topics should be regularly delivered to school staff and educators to promote awareness of challenges, strengths, and circumstances that apply to undocumented immigrant students and to support them better in the schools. Third, when recruiting undocumented students for group counseling, practitioners should be aware that students may feel hesitant about coming forward. Thus, reaching out to parents, community members, and teachers may be useful as well as using terms such as "educational" groups, rather than "counseling" (Chen et al., 2010).

SUMMARY

In this chapter, we provided an overview of the culturally responsive approaches to providing counseling and psychotherapy to CLD students. Practitioners should consider the ecological perspectives of mental health and well-being, particularly in ensuring that the counseling is from a strengths-based, and not deficit-based, perspective. Adapting evidence-based practices may be needed to value and foster cultural and individual assets and promote resilience. Practitioners should (1) engage in critical reflexivity of the practitioner's knowledge and skills to determine whether the practitioner should provide counseling or refer to someone else, (2) build relationships, develop goals, and create a culturally affirming space, (3) consider the salient sociocultural factors and cultural dimensions that may be relevant in the case, (4) examine how to incorporate sociocultural factors or cultural dimensions into the counseling, (5) review the potential counseling approaches and understand the cultural assumptions of each, and (6) implement the treatment using cultural strengths. Finally, we highlighted some key professional, ethical, and legal considerations for providing counseling to CLD students.

DISCUSSION QUESTIONS

1. Describe the steps in culturally responsive counseling. What steps do you feel the least prepared for? The most prepared for?
2. Eduardo is a 15-year-old male who was referred to you for counseling by his parents because they noticed that he is becoming increasingly withdrawn. They feel more comfortable having him receiving counseling services in school because they fear that their friends and community may judge them as parents.
   a. What are the steps you would take to provide culturally responsive counseling for Eduardo?
   b. What are some potential ethical and legal considerations?

Evaluating School-Based Programs for Diverse Students

VIGNETTE

Mariposa High School is located in a rural area with a high immigrant and refugee population. School staff introduced a suicide prevention program, "Be Well," due to the increasing rates of emotional concerns among the students. This program engages the students, teachers, and parents and includes three domains: (1) behavioral screenings, (2) skills training that focuses on social skills, communication, problem-solving, and coping, and (3) collaboration with families and school personnel. The "Be Well" program" aims to (1) identify individuals who are at risk and may need more specialized support, (2) enhance protective factors by helping the students acquire new coping skills, (3) provide education on identifying early warning signs (e.g., depressive symptoms) that elevate the risk of potential suicide, and (4) teach students and other community members who they can turn to at school for help, if they need it. To evaluate whether the program meets the goals, the evaluation team asked the students to complete multiple-choice surveys and the parents to complete a short questionnaire. All measures were written in English. The team collected and analyzed the results and shared the report with the school principal.

- *How might the program evaluation team consider the unique context of Mariposa High?*
- *What strengths might a team leverage? What challenges might they encounter?*

Culturally responsive program evaluation is a decision-making process that involves critical reflexivity and collaboration with various caregivers, community members, educators, and administrators in order to assess strengths and needs of students. Program evaluation, like all other aspects of mental health service delivery, is bound by culture and cultural context. Generally, *program evaluation* is defined as a process of decision-making to determine the effectiveness of a particular program (Spaulding, 2013). *Culturally responsive program evaluation*, however, is not just about finding out whether a particular practice works or not; rather, it is about engaging collaboratively with people to think critically about whether a particular program aligns with the context in which it is being implemented (Schwandt, 2005). It fosters inclusion of the voices and perspectives of historically marginalized individuals to ensure that the program is responsive to the strengths and diverse needs of the students in that school. As Kirkhart (2005) describes, "The influence of evaluation theory and culture is bidirectional; culture both impacts and is impacted by evaluation theory" (p. 25). That is, the professional choice in how to evaluate the effectiveness of a school-based program is shaped by the school's (and community's) culture, and, reciprocally, the culture shapes the program evaluation process.

In the vignette, the school-based evaluation team's role is not only to figure out whether this schoolwide suicide prevention program was effective, but also to explore how the community perceives the program, the culture, and context of that high school, and to determine whether the program meets the needs of all students. There are several questions that this team should ask: *In what ways was the program strengths based and grounded in the culture of the students and their community? In what ways were historical context, race, privilege, and power considered in the program development and delivery? How did the program align with the objectives that are meaningful and relevant to the lived experiences of students?*

In this chapter, we introduce the *school-based culturally responsive program evaluation model*, which uses critical reflexivity throughout the program development, delivery, and evaluation and is grounded in the context and culture of the students' school and community. First, we will discuss culturally responsive program evaluation broadly and ways that program evaluators can consider culture and context in program development and evaluation. We then describe the school-based culturally responsive program evaluation model's six steps to guide practitioners through the process: (1) critically reflect on their role in the school and community, (2) establish trusting relationships with community members to develop an evaluation team, (3) develop objectives that are relevant to community members, (4) select multimethod and multisource data collection, (5) interpret data with a culturally responsive lens, and (6) disseminate results back to the school and community. Finally, we discuss ethical and social justice considerations as practitioners undergo culturally responsive evaluation (CRE).

CULTURALLY RESPONSIVE EVALUATION

CRE is an approach to evaluation that honors and legitimizes the lived experiences and the cultural background of the community members starting from the initial stages of program development to collection of program outcome data (Thomas & Parsons, 2017). CRE acknowledges that the underlying systems in education and mental health may not be aligned with values or perspectives of some minoritized groups, and that evaluators need to shift their views fundamentally from expert to collaborator.

CRE includes three tenets: (1) a strengths-based approach, (2) promotion of social justice, and (3) a holistic way of thinking (Thomas & Parsons, 2017). First, CRE takes a strengths-based approach in which the focus is on *opportunities* instead of problems (Thomas & Parsons, 2017). Members of the evaluation team cultivate the existing strengths within that community and recognize opportunities for growth, instead of the issues and problem-solving that often lead to deficit thinking. To do so effectively and using cultural humility, practitioners will need to collaborate closely with community members to assess the cultural strengths from which to build the program. For example, instead of targeting problems that students may be experiencing associated with bullying in school, the evaluation team may instead focus on opportunities that students have in engaging with their peers in healthy and meaningful ways (e.g., promoting leadership skills). CRE, compared to traditional program evaluation, is shifting the focus from problems to opportunities (see Table 11.1).

Moreover, engaging in CRE means using collaborative and participatory action approaches, in which the community is actively involved in all stages of the evaluation process (Askew et al., 2012). CRE requires connections, and collaboration with evaluation team members, which can include students, parents, educators, university partners, community members, and spiritual leaders. Establishing and sustaining these relationships from the initial program development stage to the evaluation stage ensures that the program is culturally grounded and is monitoring outcomes. These community members bring their values and culture to the evaluation team. Practitioners would discuss goals and their short-term (proximal) and long-term (distal) impact, based on the needs and relevance within the school and community. Additionally, collaboration within CRE increases the likelihood

Table 11.1. COMPARISON BETWEEN TRADITIONAL PROGRAM EVALUATION AND CULTURALLY RESPONSIVE EVALUATION

Traditional Program Evaluation	Culturally Responsive Program Evaluation
Identification of problems or weaknesses	Strengths-based focus
Perpetuation of existing systems that may cause harm, particularly to culturally, racially, or ethnically minoritized students and families	Promotion of social justice
Analytic thinking	Holistic thinking
Expert approach to data collection	Collaborative data collection with different community members
Dissemination only to other experts or individuals directly involved, often in written format	Dissemination of results back to school and community using different methods (e.g., through stories)

that community members see value in the program and thus will have a shared responsibility in its implementation and, hopefully, success (Askew et al., 2012).

The second tenet of CRE is that evaluations should include active promotion of social justice. Power and privilege are often underscored through program evaluation, and CRE emphasizes that there should be active focus on advocacy and support of marginalized groups. In particular, culturally responsive program evaluation provides opportunities to include variables that may have been ignored in the past (Thomas & Parsons, 2017). That is, the evaluation allows for critical reflexivity by all members of the program evaluation team to review and discuss historical contexts, race, privilege, and power that directly or indirectly affect students within those groups. As Thomas and colleagues stated (2018),

> Evaluation is not an examination into the inert, static, and external realities of programs but, instead, into the fluid subjective world of people's lives as experienced, interpreted, recalled, and mediated by them and the, oftentimes, racialized contexts of the systems that programs, communities, and individuals are embedded. (p. 516)

Programs are bound within contexts, including historical contexts that have been molded from racism and oppression. Thus, in order to use CRE, practitioners must have awareness of the historical and current cultural context of the program and how this context may influence the students, families, or community involved in the program. Importantly, it also includes acknowledging those *not* being served by the program, or whom it neglects. Promoting social justice requires acknowledging who has power—and who does not.

Finally, the third tenet is using a holistic way of thinking throughout the program evaluation (Thomas & Parsons, 2017). The team must demonstrate awareness of the norms, values, beliefs, and relationships within and outside the school in which the program is being evaluated. Culture and context mediate anything we learn, because how we learn is shaped by our previous learning and culture. Indigenous knowledge, for example, is based on a sense of place and how living and spiritual things are interrelated, and these influence the understanding of knowledge or truth (LaFrance et al., 2012). Overall, CRE allows for development of relationships of those who were historically marginalized, and it promotes discourse and building of community, with the goal of attaining equitable student outcomes and improving program acceptability within families and the community.

SCHOOL-BASED CULTURALLY RESPONSIVE PROGRAM EVALUATION MODEL

CRE in schools focuses on opportunities for growth and is grounded in the culture and context of that school and community. In this section, we provide a step-by-step guide in conducting a school-based CRE (see Figure 11.1).

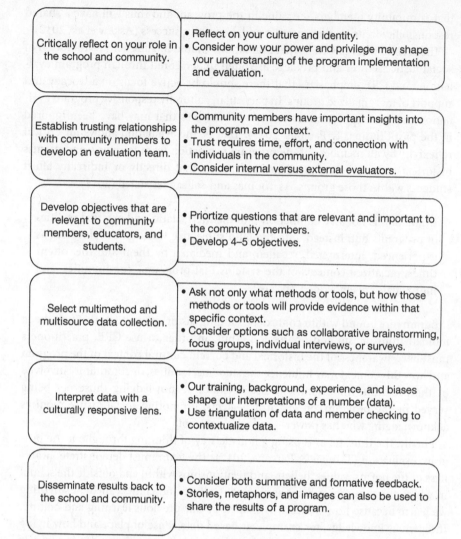

Critically reflect on your role in the school and community.	• Reflect on your culture and identity. • Consider how your power and privilege may shape your understanding of the program implementation and evaluation.
Establish trusting relationships with community members to develop an evaluation team.	• Community members have important insights into the program and context. • Trust requires time, effort, and connection with individuals in the community. • Consider internal versus external evaluators.
Develop objectives that are relevant to community members, educators, and students.	• Priortize questions that are relevant and important to the community members. • Develop 4–5 objectives.
Select multimethod and multisource data collection.	• Ask not only what methods or tools, but how those methods or tools will provide evidence within that specific context. • Consider options such as collaborative brainstorming, focus groups, individual interviews, or surveys.
Interpret data with a culturally responsive lens.	• Our training, background, experience, and biases shape our interpretations of a number (data). • Use triangulation of data and member checking to contextualize data.
Disseminate results back to the school and community.	• Consider both summative and formative feedback. • Stories, metaphors, and images can also be used to share the results of a program.

Figure 11.1. Steps in School-Based Culturally Responsive Program Evaluation.

Engage in Critical Reflexivity

In the first step of displaying culturally responsive program evaluation in schools, practitioners need to use critical reflexivity to examine deeply and intentionally their own culture, values, and personal views on the students that the program targets (Cunliffe, 2016; Thomas et al., 2018). It is important that the practitioner be intentional and thoughtful about the process. Practitioners should consider their own power and privilege, their own assumptions, and their relationship to the individuals within the school and community. We recommend reviewing topics in Chapter 2, for examples, to consider the sociocultural and historical contexts that have shaped the community, and how they fit within that context.

Additionally, practitioners need to critically reflect on *why* they want to develop or implement the program, as well as the purpose of the program. Program development and evaluation often focus on a *problem*, which inherently pathologizes the target population (Thomas et al., 2018). Members of the school-based evaluation team should examine how their potential biases, assumptions, and stereotypes may affect their work with students, families, or community when providing any service delivery.

[Reflexivity Activity]. Reflect on the following questions:

- *In what ways might your social and cultural identities influence your ability to conduct a program evaluation?*
- *What institutional, historical, and systemic contexts have limited or strengthened opportunity for some groups in your schools, and not others? How might this affect your and your team's ability to conduct a program evaluation?*

Establish Trusting Relationships when Developing an Evaluation Team

The second step is to work intentionally to earn the trust of, and foster relationships with, the evaluation team members, which include students, parents, community members, educators, and administrators, whose values and roles are integral for its success (Hood et al., 2015). Although particular members may be invested in the program or evaluation, there may be differences in the type or level of investment (e.g., personal resources, time, or effort needed). For example, in the vignette, some immigrant parents may demonstrate high investment in the program because the program directly affects their children's socialization and access to peer support, and thus, the success of acculturation. Others may view the process by analyzing the economic costs, along with the short-term and long-term benefits of the program related to academic outcomes or school climate.

Schools develop partnerships and collaborations with the community throughout the evaluation process. One particular method is *collaboration evaluation*, which is an intentional approach whereby all members are perceived as partners and have shared responsibilities within the program evaluation that empowers them to be engaged throughout the evaluation process (Askew et al., 2012). Evaluation team members have important insights into the program and the context; they can provide critical information about the history and background of the program that can assist in determining the best way to evaluate program-level and student-level outcomes. Further, these partnerships can lead to more successful program utilization (Askew et al., 2012). Programs are more likely to be implemented and be successful if the evaluation team is willing to put in time, effort, and resources into them.

To develop this partnership and collaboration, however, practitioners must earn their trust. We emphasize in Chapter 1 that that the practitioner needs to *earn* the trust; it is not automatically given to them because they are an expert or have established professional credentials. There is a troubled history of program evaluation research with Indigenous communities where scholars were viewed as opportunistic, exploiting the people of these communities to further their professional careers (Sobeck et al., 2003). Some researchers enter these communities, gather sensitive information from the people, and subsequently use this information to manipulate or control them. Whether as practitioner or researcher, they may still represent the institutions that have caused harm. Thus, they must earn trust, as well as be intentional and respectful—and this takes time and great effort.

To earn this trust and respect, the practitioner must listen to their stories and understand who is telling them (Hood et al., 2015). Visiting with community members and spending quality time with them will foster those relationships. The practitioner can ask themselves, *What is at the center of these stories and why are they sharing them? Who has the power within this community and what are the relationships that are valued? What are the community's perception of others?* (Hood et al., 2015). Further, cultural protocols should be considered within the context of a program evaluation. For instance, there are often situations in which prior to speaking with specific individuals and collecting data, time should be dedicated to establishing those trusting relationships (Hood et al., 2015).

Once trust is earned and relationships are fostered, the practitioner can then begin to develop a program evaluation team collaboratively and intentionally. The number of team members (perhaps 5 to 7) may be important, as there needs to be representation from the school and the community. Within a culturally responsive program evaluation model, members of the team should be those who have an understanding of the cultural context, who demonstrate commitment, and who are most impacted by the program. To ensure equity, the team should include voices that have been historically marginalized or neglected. For example, in the vignette, refugee families in the school and community should be invited to be part of the team. Having too few members may appear as not being inclusive, while having too many members can prove difficult and may increase the likelihood that the voices or perspectives among those historically marginalized may be overridden or ignored.

It is also important to consider members of the team who are *internal evaluators* and those who are *external evaluators*. Internal evaluators are individuals within the school and community who understand the culture and values of that school and community (Holden & Zimmerman, 2009). These internal evaluators may include administrators, staff, teachers, or parents. The advantage of having an internal evaluator is that they may represent a team member who is already "bought-in" within that context. They may already know the key members of that school or community, may have a sense of the school culture and relationships within that context, and can therefore navigate challenging situations more smoothly. The disadvantage of an internal evaluator is that other members of the team such as students, families, or teachers may not feel comfortable sharing information openly with someone they view as a member of that school or community. For instance, if members of the community know the evaluator, they may be concerned that the evaluator will know more deeply personal information and be unwilling to disclose necessary information.

In contrast, external evaluators are individuals who are invited from outside of that school and community (Holden & Zimmerman, 2009). These external evaluators are sometimes hired by the school district or may be part of a university team. They may be the sponsor of the evaluation (i.e., from the agency funding the program) or university researchers. The advantage of having an external evaluator is that the person has no relationships with the school or community, so they are able to gather information with less bias from students, families, or teachers. On the other hand, if the evaluator is viewed as an outsider, members may be wary of sharing information with them. Further, an external evaluator will need to allocate time to learn about the norms, beliefs, and values of the school or community and may make more errors when gathering required information in the evaluation process. Nonetheless, external evaluators are advantageous in providing additional or objective perspectives given their experiences in working with other schools or communities.

Develop Objectives That Are Relevant to the School Community

When designing and determining how a program should be evaluated, the most important task is to choose and prioritize questions that are important to the *school community*. Sometimes, those with power (e.g., school administrators, the school board, the practitioner) may make decisions about the program content and program evaluation process that are not relevant to the individuals who are supposedly the target of the program or intervention. If a program is to be developed, then voices and perspectives from those individuals who are most directly impacted by the program should be included in that discussion. Part of that discussion should also be how those individuals conceptualize "success" or "effectiveness" of the program. There should be frequent and continuous conversations about what is important to them.

Generally, the team should develop four to five primary short-term and long-term objectives of the program and determine what data are needed to meet those objectives (Spaulding, 2013). The objectives that are most directly relevant and meaningful to the evaluation team should be prioritized. Although these objectives may be carefully developed initially, objectives can evolve over time, depending on evaluator feedback or preliminary assessment data—some that were relevant initially may become less relevant later on.

There are a number of approaches to develop these objectives, such as collaborative brainstorming, focus groups, individual interviews, or surveys (see Step 4 of the model). We also suggest using the appreciative inquiry method (AIM), which emphasizes a strengths-based approach whereby the evaluator steps away from the role of an expert to give voice to others who have perspectives to share (Boyd & Bright, 2007). AIM reconceptualizes the program evaluation as an opportunity for growth and affirming the topics and concerns that the community wants to address.

There are four phases in AIM: (1) Discovery, (2) Dreaming, (3) Design, and (4) Destiny (Boyd & Bright, 2007). First, in *Discovery*, the evaluation team uses stories and images to reflect critically on the current context, as well as the capacity or potential for the school (with respect to the topic). There is typically an opening activity to encourage members to discuss what is currently in place as well as the potential that a program may have to improve on student outcomes. From the vignette, the evaluation team may invite and ask families to share their experience in the school community and their countries of origin. This may open the dialogue about their perceptions of how to cope with emotions based on past experiences and cultural values. In *Dreaming*, the team members imagine the ideal school or community. It also encourages them to think about the existing strengths in the students and school and to leverage those strengths toward a goal. Often, during this stage, art, poetry, or other activities can foster those ideas (these can be gathered from school or home). From the vignette, the team may invite students, teachers, and families to brainstorm the ideal community for the school. This could include conversation, drawing, and other creative ways to generate ideas.

In *Design*, the teams consider what the actionable steps or ideas are, and in what ways they would be implemented. This is a transition from critical reflection to action. From the vignette, the team may decide to focus on one or two aspects of the ideal community they articulated in the previous step and consider ways to make the dream a reality. This may include developing a plan outlining the timeline and resources that would be required. Finally, in *Destiny*, the team considers what they may actually do to bring the change they first dreamed of, and what ways they can track and encourage progress toward that dream. For the team at Mariposa High School, administrators and teachers may be able to provide context for realistic steps to begin making progress toward the goals that are selected as the first priority.

Select Multimethod and Multisource Data Collection

The next step is for the evaluation team to choose methods and sources of information (i.e., data) collaboratively and intentionally that would help the team determine whether the program is aligned with the objectives. In this step, it is important not to think about the methods first, but to consider which methodology will provide the most meaningful data for which individuals and under what context (LaFrance et al., 2012). That is, it is about identifying not only what methods or tools the practitioner may have as a program evaluator, but also how those methods or tools will provide evidence within that specific context. The context includes the sociopolitical structures, values, beliefs, and history of that school and community where the program will take place. In this approach, the *context* comes first—the culture of the community, the ethnic, racial, or socioeconomic characteristics of students, and the individuals who hold power in the community and the school.

In this stage, it is important to ask and select the methods that will be used to gather information that aligns with the prioritized objectives in the previous step, and whether this information will be used in a formative or summative manner. In other words, the team must determine the purpose of gathering that information and how it will be useful in evaluating whether the program was successful, as defined by that school and community. Formative evaluation is a process of analyzing and evaluating data during the implementation of the program for the purpose of decision-making, while summative evaluation is a process of analyzing and evaluating data used at the completion of the program (Spaulding, 2013). As an evaluation team member, the practitioner must decide whether they need information during the implementation of the program, after the implementation, or both.

A useful process is to work collaboratively with the team in completing the evaluation matrix (see Appendix 11A as an example). By completing the evaluation matrix, members can discuss the advantages and disadvantages of each tool, for which the community would provide the information needed, and when the information would be collected. Disagreements may arise during this discussion, and this is an excellent opportunity to talk through those disagreements prior to the data collection phase.

There are a number of ways to gather information, either through formative or summative evaluation, or other methods such as (1) interviews, (2) structured focus groups, (3) questionnaires/measures, and (4) community forums (see Table 11.2). Interviews are a helpful method not only for collecting information for the program evaluation, but also to foster relationships with various community members. There are three types of interviews: (1) unstructured or nonstandardized interviews (completely open ended without questions), (2) semi-structured interviews (some questions), and (3) structured or standardized interviews (a set of questions). These Western, Eurocentric approaches are commonly used to gather information efficiently toward a set of objectives.

Although these Western interview approaches are useful, listening to someone's lived experience is incredibly powerful, and there is a great deal of connection that can occur during this exchange. Through a decolonizing lens, interviews can be a method of reinforcing a relational way of knowing. The construction of knowledge (i.e., what we call "data") is collectively created through relationships, personal connections, and respect (Chilisa, 2020). Alternatively, knowledge can be co-created through storytelling between the interviewer and the interviewee. This method, called the relational interview method, shifts the focus of interviewing to fostering relationships and recognizing that knowledge is created (there is no absolute knowledge; Chilisa, 2020). The stories that can be elicited through an interview can really be a web of connections between people and their culture, context, and environment. Thus, the practitioner may want to consider moving away from standard Western approaches and consider how interviews can facilitate storytelling with members of marginalized groups whose voices may have been neglected.

Table 11.2. TYPES OF MULTIMETHOD AND MULTISOURCE DATA FOR CULTURALLY
RESPONSIVE PROGRAM EVALUATION

Types of Methods	Types of Sources
Interviews	• Parents of students
• Unstructured or nonstandardized interviews (completely open ended without questions)	• Students within the school district
• Semi-structured interviews (some questions)	• Elders or community leaders
• Structured or standardized interviews (a set of questions).	• Faith leaders
Focus Groups	• School administrators
• Multiple individuals and conversations within the group could stimulate discussions of topics that may not even have been considered during the evaluation.	• University researchers
Questionnaires and Surveys	
• Likert scales	
• Checklists	
• Open-ended questions	

Nonetheless, there is an important consideration when conducting interviews. As Kvale (2006) emphasizes, there is also potential for dominance and exploitation through these interviews. The personal connections and relationships that are fostered through an individual interview could also reflect differential power because it is not a relationship with dialogue or conversation; rather, the interviewer is gathering sometimes deeply personal narratives from the interviewee (Kvale, 2006). It is important that the practitioner, as an interviewer, review their positionality within the context of the school and community.

[Reflexivity Activity]:

- *What power do I have?*
- *In what ways would this power impact my ability to gather stories?*

A second method of gathering information, including stories, is focus groups. In contrast to individual interviews, focus groups have multiple individuals and conversations within the group that could stimulate discussions of topics that may not have even been considered during the evaluation. Focus groups are useful because they align with how most people typically communicate—in groups and in natural settings (Chilisa, 2020). Stories can be told together, as a group, giving more meaning and nuance than at the individual level. See Appendix 11B for a sample focus group script.

Within focus groups it is important to recognize that individuals may not have equal opportunities to speak, and some individual voices in the groups may be overpowered by others. Thus, it is important that the practitioner validate and respect the various identities among the participants and consider ways to elicit information so that they can share their stories, making it more representative (Rodriguez et al., 2011). There are methods, such as talking circles, to allow for equal opportunities to speak because everyone is respected and encouraged to share their ideas (Chilisa, 2020).

A third method of gathering information is using questionnaires or surveys. The advantage of this approach is that they are an efficient way to gather a lot of data quickly. People who may not have the time or resources to participate in individual interviews or focus groups may be able to complete a question-naire on their own time. Questionnaires could be distributed electronically or in paper format to many people, including parents, educators, students, community members, etc. An already existing questionnaire could be used, or one could be designed specifically for the program.

There are various types of questionnaires, including (1) Likert scales, (2) checklists, and (3) open-ended questions (Spaulding, 2013). In Likert scale questionnaires, respondents are given a statement and asked the degree to which they agree with that statement (e.g., 1, *Strongly Disagree*, to 5, *Strongly Agree*). These types of questionnaires are useful because respondents can complete them relatively quickly, and they allow for obtaining aggregate (e.g., means and standard deviations) information. Questionnaires that use checklists have a se-ries of options, and the respondent checks off those options that are relevant to them, but there may be possible answers of which the evaluation team may not be aware (Spaulding, 2013). Thus, if the evaluation team chooses to create its own questionnaire using checklists, it may be appropriate to conduct interviews with the community first. These questionnaires may not allow for nuance in responses, as there may be variation in perspectives, depending on the topic. Responses based on scores may not fully capture or explain the perceptions of those who completed it.

When creating a questionnaire or using an already existing one, there are a number of considerations. If the team includes an item related to race or eth-nicity, it is important to be aware of the issues related to the use of checklists. If there are a series of options (e.g., "White" or "Black/African American"), it is critical to pay attention to which race or ethnicity was *not* included among the options. For example, Arab ethnicity is often not included on government-level checklists, such as the U.S. Census, and thus questionnaires may similarly ne-glect to include this group among the options. Further, Arab Americans may identify their race as White, Black, or neither. Options should also consider intersectionality of identity, such as gender and sexual identity, or neurodiversity. Further, the team may want to consider whether the questionnaires should be adapted or translated for the community, as well as the literacy level of the ques-tionnaire. Some families, particularly those who may fear deportation, may be confused about the particular purpose of the questionnaire or how results will be used, and the team should consider ways to articulate the goals of the evaluation clearly and include cultural liaisons who have established trust with families.

Interpret Data with a Culturally Responsive Lens

After data have been collected using multiple methods and multiple sources, interpreting those data must be done carefully using culturally responsive approaches. All data, whether they are means and standard deviations, personal narratives, or group discussions, are grounded in culture and context. Although we may believe that a number is entirely "objective," it is not. A number is contextualized in the meaning that we, as evaluators, bring to it. Our training, background, experiences, and biases shape our interpretation of a number. For instance, if a rating scale is given to students to assess for depression, we may obtain a mean and standard deviation (e.g., on average, X number of students experience clinically significant symptoms). That number, however, may be meaningless unless we understand the culture and context of the students' experiences. *Is this number representative of students within the larger community? In what ways does your educational background or training shape your understanding of this number?* Importantly, it is not about being wrong or right; rather, it is about acknowledging that data are always contextualized.

Thus, to contextualize these data, it is imperative that they are interpreted using triangulation of methods and member checking. Triangulation of methods (e.g., questionnaire and focus groups) and sources (e.g., students and parents) can allow for complementary perspectives on a particular question or issue. An analyst triangulation approach can be particularly helpful during the interpretation stage of program evaluation, in which there are multiple perspectives viewing those data, ensuring that the interpretation is robust and comprehensive. As an evaluator, the practitioner would work closely with their team to analyze the data separately first, then to come together to see whether the various interpretations of the data were aligned or not.

Member checking is also a very helpful and important approach to data interpretation. Sometimes called *participant validation*, member checking involves returning to the participants and verifying the interpretation of the data with them (Birt et al., 2016). This approach enhances the rigor of the program evaluation by reducing biases or any misinterpretations that the program evaluators have. There are a number of ways that this could be done, including having people review the interview or focus group transcripts or review the synthesized data (Birt et al., 2016). Thus, in this approach, the team may go back to the individuals with whom they gathered the data to check that the interpretation aligned with the individual's intentions. They may go back to the students who completed a measure or the parents in a focus group, share the interpretation, and obtain their feedback.

Disseminate Results Back to School and Community

Once data have been analyzed and interpreted, an essential next step is to communicate those results to the school and community. Additionally, an important component of program evaluation is collaborating with community members to disseminate the results of the program. Often, information about programs is not disseminated back to the community (Peltier, 2018), which further perpetuates distrust because efforts were not made to ensure they were informed. If the program evaluation team develops and evaluates a program, then the team needs to disseminate that information to the community (e.g., parents, caregivers, spiritual leaders) in an accessible and meaningful way.

If the purpose of the evaluation is for ongoing decision-making (i.e., formative evaluation), the results can be shared through informal means, including phone conversations, brief memos, or written progress reports (Spaulding, 2013). Formative feedback can be helpful in examining any barriers that may not have been foreseen prior to the development or the implementation of the program. For example, if the results of the data suggest that there is a lack of buy-in among educators implementing the program, and thus the fidelity of the intervention is compromised, the progress report could help to initiate conversations between the team and those implementing the program.

If the purpose of the analyses is to determine the effectiveness of the program (i.e., summative evaluation), the results should be shared both in written and oral reports. Written reports are useful for organizing the information so that multiple team members can review the results. Written reports also document the process and outcomes of the program for the future, so that the program could be replicated or modified. Generally, the final written report includes (1) a cover page, (2) an executive summary, (3) an introduction, (4) method, (5) the body of report, and (6) recommendations for next steps (Spaulding, 2013). Throughout the report, it is important that the practitioner minimize the use of any jargon (i.e., terms that only individuals with special training would understand) and make the writing readable to most people. Making a report understandable to most people is actually quite difficult, and using an online readability calculator can be helpful.

The results of the evaluation should not be presented in a standard report given at scientific conferences; rather, the results should be shared in a way that is meaningful and engaging to the audience: for example, at locations where audiences would typically be, such as religious organizations (e.g., mosque), tribal council meetings, or parent–teacher association meetings. Stories and narratives are some of the most helpful and recommended methods for sharing the results of the evaluation, as they can ground the program and evaluation in the roots of that particular culture (LaFrance & Nichols, 2008). Most cultures have cherished traditions around stories, and it is the way that information is shared among family members and communities. Using this tradition, the practitioner can share the results of the evaluation by sharing the meaning behind the evaluation. That is, consider ways to share the story of why the program was developed in the first place, how the program evaluation team collected the information, and then ultimately what the information gathered really means for the students in that school. One approach may be to tell the story of one student (de-identified or fictionalized) and share their lived experience of suicidal ideation and the role of the school in preventing suicide. That story can be used to describe how the student may have navigated a number of barriers in the school and how the school was or was not successful in supporting that student. The results of the evaluation and recommendations can be shared for future actions by highlighting what the school could have done better to help that student and what the school should do next.

Metaphors and images can also be useful in sharing the results of an evaluation and can be integrated within the story or narrative. Often, evaluation reports are designed with a logic model, which is rooted in Western ideas of causal relationships between actions and outcomes (LaFrance & Nichols, 2008). Symbols or images, on the other hand, can be used to represent relationships that have meaning in the context of the program. LaFrance and Nichols (2008) highlighted examples of Indigenous communities that used a metaphor of a Cherokee basket for describing the strength that comes from interconnected relationships within the community or using a cedar tree to represent the roots of their traditions and the strength of the trunk as building trust and relationships. These symbols were created by each community because it was relevant and represented the story (program and outcomes). Importantly, it would be inappropriate and disrespectful for a non-Indigenous member to create the symbol *for* the community; thus, the practitioner must work closely with community members to consider how to present the information in ways that would be meaningful. Community members may choose to create a symbol as a way to tell the story.

ETHICAL ISSUES IN CULTURALLY RESPONSIVE EVALUATION

There are a number of ethical issues that may arise while conducting a culturally responsive program evaluation. Although the process of evaluation differs from research, which often requires proposal submission to an institutional review board, there are nonetheless important steps that the team should take across all stages of the program evaluation process. The codes of ethics across professions (e.g., National Association of Social Workers, National Association of School Psychologists) emphasize the importance of undergoing ethical decision-making in practice. These codes of ethics apply within culturally responsive program evaluation.

Take Steps to Protect Community Members and Participants from Harm

From the beginning of the process, it is imperative that all decisions and processes do not harm anyone. Harm can be defined broadly and can include physical, psychological, or emotional harm. For those practitioners who are White and have more privilege and power, it is especially important to consider how their behavior may impact the community. Harm can be done, even if that was not the intent. The practitioner must be critically reflexive and take actionable steps to listen and learn from those who may have less power but more at stake.

Respect the Dignity of All Members

Throughout the program evaluation, community members and participants should be treated with respect and dignity. As part of the evaluation team, the practitioner should ensure that the dignity of each member of the evaluation, as well as the dignity of educators, administrators, students, parents, and community members, is respected. This means that if community members become uncomfortable with the process or decisions for the program, the practitioner must respect their dignity and have difficult conversations with each stakeholder.

Respect the Rights of Participants Not to Disclose Private Information

Collecting information from educators, parents, students, and community members is an important aspect of the evaluation process. As a result, it is essential that participants fully understand the purpose of the evaluation as well as have a right to choose not to disclose their thoughts, beliefs, or feelings. There is a chance that participants may experience coercion due to the power among those in the evaluation team or the sociopolitical context in which the program evaluation may be occurring. For example, if the members of the evaluation team include community members that hold power within the school or community (e.g., church leaders, parent–teacher association president), participants may feel obligated to complete questionnaires or participate in focus groups even when they are not comfortable doing so. The practitioner's ethical responsibility is to ensure that all participants understand their right to not disclose any information.

Provide Supportive Services to All Community Members and Participants

All community members and participants involved in the evaluation should have an opportunity to access supportive services. During the evaluation process, participants may share their thoughts, feelings, and beliefs about sensitive topics (e.g., suicide, bullying, homelessness). Therefore, if they are participating in the evaluation, the evaluation team should ensure that they have access to supportive services, such as information about accessing counseling services or case management.

SUMMARY

CRE is essential for identifying whether a program works in the specific context of the program and integrates community members, parents, and school personnel throughout the process. CRE uses a strengths-based approach to promote social justice and shifts the conversation from *problems* to *opportunities* for meaningful growth.

There are six steps within the school-based culturally responsive program evaluation model. First, evaluators should critically reflect on their role within the school and community in order to articulate why the evaluation is being conducted and the initial goals of the evaluation. Second, trusting relationships should be developed with various community members, educators, and administrators to establish the evaluation team. This is a critical step that can be accomplished through listening to the stories people tell about themselves, the world, and the community. Third, objectives for the evaluation should be developed collaboratively with community members. AIM outlines steps to use stories as a way to discover what is important to different people. Fourth, data collection should be intentional and use multiple methods and sources, including interviews, structured focus groups, questionnaires, and/or community forums. Fifth, data should be interpreted within a culturally responsive lens—keeping in mind the three major tenets of CRE. Lastly, results of the evaluation should be disseminated back to the community in a meaningful way.

Finally, there are ethical considerations for completing CRE. These steps ensure protection of community members and participants from harm and respect their dignity and privacy, and provision of supportive services to everyone involved.

DISCUSSION QUESTIONS

1. How comfortable/uncomfortable do you feel about sharing the power and acknowledging the wisdom of communities you work with in the process of developing and conducting program evaluation?
2. Traditionally, data collection strategies that aimed to inform program development and support the evaluation process included various types of surveys and interviews. What culturally responsive adaptations could you make to address the needs of the following communities: (a) Indigenous, (b) Black, (c) low SES and rural, (d) refugee, (e) migrant, (f) religious/spiritual followers (e.g., Catholic, Muslim, Jewish)?
3. Based on the vignette, what would be some potential ethical issues that could emerge from implementing culturally responsive evaluation of the suicide prevention program? How would you address these issues?
4. Imagine that you are the lead on developing a suicide prevention program, and a school staff member comes to you and says, "I think that organizing focus groups with the community members and healers is a waste of time." Recognizing the importance of practices described in this chapter, how would you respond to your colleague?

SAMPLE CULTURALLY RESPONSIVE EVALUATION MATRIX

Collaboratively Determined Objectives	Relevant Members	Tools	Timeline	Purpose
1. Identify at-risk individuals.	Counselors, students, parents	Be Well screenings (e.g., BASC-3)	Completed two times each school year	Early identification can lead to more specialized support.
2. Enhance protective factors.	Teachers, students	Be Well training aimed at social skills, communication, problem-solving, and coping	Throughout school year as directed by Be Well curriculum	Build upon existing coping skills and increase efficacy of adaptive coping.
3. Provide education on early warning signs.	Parents, teachers	Psychoeducation	Offer training each quarter for parents who are interested.	Equip parents to look for and seek help for students who may be struggling.
4. Teach students and community about help-seeking.	Community members, students	Clear list of resources and available agencies within the community	Immediately gather information; disseminate routinely at community gatherings and school events.	Help connect the community with resources and accurate information.

NOTE: Adapted from *Program Evaluation in Practice: Core Concepts and Examples for Discussion and Analysis*, by D. T. Spaulding, 2013, John Wiley & Sons, Incorporated.

APPENDIX 11B
SAMPLE FOCUS GROUP SCRIPT

Beginning of Focus Group Script:

Welcome. Thanks again for coming and taking time out of your day to speak with us. We know that you read and responded to the initial email and flyer regarding our interest in better understanding how to support students' well-being here at Mariposa High School. For approximately the next 45 minutes, we will be asking you different questions to learn more about your perspectives about social and emotional learning, and your ideas about how to meet the social and emotional learning needs of students.

Before we begin, let's review the informed consent form. Here is a copy for you to sign acknowledging that you have read and agreed to participate in this focus group. The information that you provide during the focus group will be kept confidential. That is, we will make sure that we do not link your name with any information we share through publications or presentations. It is also important that you do not share what other individuals in the group discuss in the group. *We will also be audiotaping and taking notes to make an accurate record of what is said, including your comments.* There is no right or wrong answer to the questions that will be raised in the group; the important thing is that you share your experiences and opinions.

The notes and the information you provide in the meeting will be kept confidential. Only those of us who are involved in the research team will have access to the information we collect. This information will be kept in password-protected secured cloud storage approved by the SKC Institutional Review Board. No one outside of the research team will see your responses.

Do you have any questions about the informed consent or how we will be spending the next 45 minutes?

Topical Areas for Questions:

- Discussion of individual's beliefs and knowledge about social and emotional learning
- Knowledge of resources available within and outside of the school related to social and emotional learning
- Previous interactions with support professionals in and out of the school who specialize in social and emotional learning
- Experience of how social and emotional learning influences academic performance and preparation
- Role and responsibility of educators to facilitate social and emotional needs of students

Interview Warm-Up:

Have participant(s) flip over demographic information to answer (write down) the following question; Say, "take a couple minutes and describe how you would define social and emotional competence."

Main Guiding Questions:

1. [*Have participants write their definitions of social and emotional learning written on back of demographic form and share.*] How did you come up with that definition?
2. Tell me about how you have learned about social and emotional learning.
3. Tell me about your experiences with social and emotional learning (classroom, conferences)?
4. When you think of social and emotional learning resources, what or who comes to your mind?
5. What are other ways you hope to integrate social and emotional learning?
6. How do you see the relationship between social and emotional learning and students' academic performance?
7. What role or responsibility do you believe educators have in supporting students' social and emotional learning?
8. Is there a connection between social and emotional learning and mental health? If so, tell us about the connection.
9. What role or responsibility do you believe educators have in supporting students' mental health?
10. Are there any points that I missed or things you believe are important in understanding what you know about social and emotional learning in the schools?

Ending the Focus Group:

Thank you again for taking the time to participate in this important research. As said before, you are entitled to $10 cash payment or one OPI Renewed Unit for your time.

Finally, we want to remind you that your name will be kept confidential and separate from any of your answers in the focus group recordings or notes. If at any point you have any questions or are concerned about your comments being used, please contact the primary investigator at the contact numbers provided in the informed consent. Do you have any questions before we end? Thank you.

REFERENCES

INTRODUCTION

Baker, C. N., Peele, H., Daniels, M., Saybe, M., Whalen, K., Overstreet, S., & The New Orleans, T.-I. S. L. C. (2021). The experience of COVID-19 and its impact on teachers' mental health, coping, and teaching. *School Psychology Review, 50*(4), 491–504. https://doi.org/10.1080/2372966X.2020.1855473

Cancio, E. J., Larsen, R., Mathur, S. R., Estes, M. B., Johns, B., & Chang, M. (2018). Special education teacher stress: Coping strategies. *Education and Treatment of Children, 41*(4), 457–481. doi:10.1353/etc.2018.0025.

Crenshaw, K. (1989). Demarginalizing the intersection of race and sex: A Black feminist critique of antidiscrimination doctrine. *University of Chicago Legal Forum, 1989*(1), 139–168.

Department of Health and Human Services. (2021). *U.S. Surgeon General Issues Advisory on Youth Mental Health Crisis Further Exposed by COVID-19 Pandemic.* https://www.hhs.gov/sites/default/files/surgeon-general-youth-mental-health-advisory.pdf

Gay, G. (2018). *Culturally responsive teaching: Theory, research, and practice.* Teachers College Press.

González, N., Moll, L. C., & Amanti, C. (2006). *Funds of knowledge: Theorizing practices in households, communities, and classrooms.* Routledge.

Ladson-Billings, G., & Tate, W. F. (1995). Toward a critical race theory of education. *Teachers College Record, 97*(1), 47–68.

Lazarus, P. J., Doll, B., Song, S. Y., & Radliff, K. (2021). Transforming school mental health services based on a culturally responsible dual-factor model. *School Psychology Review*, 1–16. https://doi.org/10.1080/2372966X.2021.1968282

Masten, A. S., Lucke, C. M., Nelson, K. M., & Stallworthy, I. C. (2021). Resilience in development and psychopathology: Multisystem perspectives. *Annual Review of Clinical Psychology, 17*(1), 521–549. https://doi.org/10.1146/annurev-clinpsy-081219-120307

Roberts, S. O., & Rizzo, M. T. (2020). The psychology of American racism. *American Psychologist.* https://doi.org/http://dx.doi.org/10.1037/amp0000642

Yang, C. (2021). Online teaching self-efficacy, social–emotional learning (SEL) competencies, and compassion fatigue among Educators during the COVID-19 Pandemic. *School Psychology Review, 50*(4), 505–518. https://doi.org/10.1080/2372966X.2021.1903815

CHAPTER 1

American Counseling Association. (2015). *Multicultural and social justice counseling competencies.* https://www.counseling.org/docs/default-source/competencies/multicultural-and-social-justice-counseling-competencies.pdf?sfvrsn=8573422c_22

Applebaum, B. (2009). Is teaching for social justice a "liberal bias"? *Teachers College Record, 111*(2), 376–408.

Bernal, G. (2006). Intervention development and cultural research with diverse families. *Family Process, 45*(2), 143–150.

Bettez, S. C. (2015). Navigating the complexity of qualitative research in postmodern contexts: Assemblage, critical reflexivity, and communion as guides. *International Journal of Qualitative Studies in Education, 28*(8), 932–954. https://doi.org/10.1080/09518398.2014.948096

Bronfenbrenner, U. (2005). Ecological systems theory. In U. Bronfenbrenner (Ed.), *Making human beings human: Bioecological perspectives on human development* (pp. 106–167). Sage Publications.

Castro, F. G., Barrera, M., & Martinez, C. R. (2004). The cultural adaptation of prevention interventions: Resolving tensions between fidelity and fit. *Prevention Science, 5*(1), 41–45.

Christens, B. D. (2012). Toward relational empowerment. *American Journal of Community Psychology, 50*(1–2), 114–128. https://doi.org/10.1007/s10464-011-9483-5

Clarke, B. L., Sheridan, S. M., & Woods, K. E. (2009). Elements of healthy family-school relationships. In S. L. Christenson & A. L. Reschly (Eds.), *Handbook of school-family partnerships* (pp. 61–79). Routledge.

Crenshaw, K. (1989). Demarginalizing the intersection of race and sex: A Black feminist critique of antidiscrimination doctrine. *University of Chicago Legal Forum, 1989*(1), 139–168.

Cunliffe, A. L. (2016). Republication of "On becoming a critically reflexive practitioner." *Journal of Management Education, 40*(6), 747–768. https://doi.org/10.1177/1052562916674465

Dunn, C. W., & Woodard, J. D. (2003). *The conservative tradition in America.* Rowman & Littlefield.

Goforth, A. N. (2016). A cultural humility model of school psychology training and practice. *Trainer's Forum, 34*(1), 3–24.

Hoagwood, K., & Johnson, J. (2003). School psychology: A public health framework: I. From evidence-based practices to evidence-based policies. *Journal of School Psychology, 41*(1), 3–21. https://doi.org/https://doi.org/10.1016/S0022-4405(02)00141-3

Hook, J. N., Davis, D., Owen, J., & DeBlaere, C. (2017). *Cultural humility: Engaging diverse identities in therapy.* American Psychological Association.

Jones, J. (2013). Family, school, and community partnerships. In D. Shriberg, S. Y. Song, A. H. Miranda, & K. M. Radliff (Eds.), *School psychology and social justice: Coneptual foundations and tools for practice* (pp. 270–293). Routledge.

Kratochwill, T. R., & Stoiber, K. C. (2002). Evidence-based interventions in school psychology: Conceptual foundations of the *Procedural and Coding Manual* of Division 16 and the Society for the Study of School Psychology Task Force. *School Psychology Quarterly, 17*(4), 341–389.

Linklater, R. (2014). *Decolonizing trauma work: Indigenous stories and strategies.* Fernwood Publishing.

Linnemeyer, R. M., Nilsson, J. E., Marszalek, J. M., & Khan, M. (2018). Social justice advocacy among doctoral students in professional psychology programs. *Counselling Psychology Quarterly, 31*(1), 98–116. https://doi.org/10.1080/09515 070.2016.1274961

Lord, J., & Hutchison, P. (1993). The process of empowerment: Implications for theory and practice. *Canadian Journal of Community Mental Health, 12,* 5–22.

McCarty, T. L., & Lee, T. S. (2014). Critical culturally sustaining/revitalizing pedagogy and indigenous education sovereignty. *Harvard Educational Review, 84*(1), 101–124.

Ortiz, S. (2014). Best practices in nondiscriminatory assessment. In P. L. Harrison & A. Thomas (Eds.), *Best practices in school psychology: Foundations* (pp. 661–678). National Association of School Psychologists.

Parikh, S. B., Post, P., & Flowers, C. (2011). Relationship between a belief in a just world and social justice advocacy attitudes of school counselors. *Counseling and Values, 56*(1–2), 57–72.

Pham, A. V., Goforth, A. N., Aguilar, L. N., Burt, I., Bastian, R., & Diaków, D. M. (2021). Dismantling systemic inequities in school psychology: Cultural humility as a foundational approach to social justice. *School Psychology Review,* 1–18. https://doi.org/ 10.1080/2372966X.2021.1941245

Prilleltensky, I. (2008). The role of power in wellness, oppression, and liberation: The promise of psychopolitical validity. *Journal of Community Psychology, 36*(2), 116–136. https://doi.org/10.1002/jcop.20225

Shriberg, D., Song, S. L., Miranda, A. H., & Radliff, K. M. (2013). Introduction. In D. Shriberg, S. L. Song, A. H. Miranda, & K. M. Radliff (Eds.), *School psychology and social justice: Conceptual foundations and tools for practice* (pp. 1–11). Routledge.

Stanhope, V., Solomon, P., Pernell-Arnold, A., Sands, R. G., & Bourjolly, J. N. (2005). Evaluating cultural competence among behavioral health professionals. *Psychiatric Rehabilitation Journal, 28*(3), 225–233.

Steele, J. M., Bischof, G. H., & Craig, S. E. (2014). Political ideology and perceptions of social justice advocacy among members of the American Counseling Association. *International Journal for the Advancement of Counselling, 36*(4), 450–467.

Sue, D. W. (2001). Multidimensional facets of cultural competence. *The Counseling Psychologist, 29*(6), 790–821.

Sue, D. W., Bernier, J. E., Duran, A., Feinberg, L., Pedersen, P., Smith, E. J., & Vasquez-Nuttal, E. (1982). Position paper: Cross-cultural counseling competencies. *The Counseling Psychologist, 10*(45), 45–52. https://doi.org/10.1177/0011000082102008

Sue, D. W., & Torino, G. C. (2005). Racial-cultural competence: Awareness, knowledge, and skills. In Robert T. Carter (Ed.), *Handbook of racial-cultural psychology and counseling, Vol 2: Training and practice* (pp. 3–18). John Wiley & Sons, Inc.

Sue, S. (2006). Cultural competency: From philosophy to research and practice. *Journal of Community Psychology, 34*(2), 237–245. http://dx.doi.org/10.1002/jcop.20095

Weidenstedt, L. (2016). Empowerment gone bad: Communicative consequences of power transfers. *Socius, 2,* 1–11. https://doi.org/10.1177/2378023116672869

Wendt, D. C., & Gone, J. P. (2011). Rethinking cultural competence: Insights from indigenous community treatment settings. *Transcultural Psychiatry, 49*(2), 206–222. https://doi.org/10.1177/1363461511425622

Whaley, A. L., & Davis, K. E. (2007). Cultural competence and evidence-based practice in mental health services: A complementary perspective. *American Psychologist*, *62*(6), 563–574. https://doi.org/10.1037/0003-066X.62.6.563

White, J. L., & Kratochwill, T. R. (2005). Practice guidelines in school psychology: Issues and directions for evidence-based interventions in practice and training. *Journal of School Psychology, 43*, 99–115.

CHAPTER 2

Albee, G. W. (2000). Commentary on prevention and counseling psychology. *The Counseling Psychologist, 28*(6), 845–853.

Alfred, T., & Corntassel, J. (2005). Being Indigenous: Resurgences against contemporary colonialism. *Government and Opposition, 40*(4), 597–614.

American Counseling Association. (2014). ACA code of ethics. https://www.counseling.org/resources/aca-code-of-ethics.pdf

American Psychological Association. (2017a). *Ethical principles of psychologists and code of conduct.*

American Psychological Association. (2017b). *Multicultural guidelines: An ecological approach to context, identity, and intersectionality.*

Bear, L., Finer, R., Guo, S., & Lau, A. S. (2014). Building the gateway to success: An appraisal of progress in reaching underserved families and reducing racial disparities in school-based mental health. *Psychological Services, 11*(4), 388–397.

Becker, J. C., Glick, P., Ilic, M., & Bohner, G. (2011). Damned if she does, damned if she doesn't? Social consequences of accepting versus rejecting benevolent sexist offers for the target and perpetrator. *European Journal of Social Psychology, 41*, 761–773.

Bonilla-Silva, E. (2006). *Racism without racists: Color-blind racism and the persistence of racial inequality in the United States.* Rowman & Littlefield Publishers.

Brave Heart, M. Y. H. (1998). The return to the sacred path: Healing the historical trauma and historical unresolved grief response among the Lakota through a psychoeducational group intervention. *Smith College Studies in Social Work, 68*(3), 287–305.

Campbell, C. D., & Evans-Campbell, T. (2011). Historical trauma and Native American child development and mental health: An overview. In M. C. Sarche, P. Spicer, P. Farrell, & H. E. Fitzgerald (Eds.), *American Indian and Alaska Native children and mental health: Development, context, prevention, and treatment* (pp. 1–25). ABC-CLIO.

Christens, B. D. (2012). Toward relational empowerment. *American Journal of Community Psychology, 5*, 114–128.

Coker, T. R., Elliott, M. N., Kanouse, D. E., Grunbaum, J. A., Schwebel, D. C., Gilliland, M. J., . . . & Schuster, M. A. (2009). Perceived racial/ethnic discrimination among fifth-grade students and its association with mental health. *American Journal of Public Health, 99*(5), 878–884.

Cole, E. R. (2009). Intersectionality and research in psychology. *American Psychologist, 64*(3), 170–180.

Crenshaw, K. (1989). Demarginalizing the intersection of race and sex: A Black feminist critique of antidiscrimination doctrine. *University of Chicago Legal Forum, 1989*(1), 139–168.

Crenshaw, K., Gotanda, N., Peller, G., & Thomas, K. (1995). *Critical race theory. The key writings that formed the movement*. The New Press.

Cunliffe, A. L. (2016). Republication of "On becoming a critically reflexive practitioner." *Journal of Management Education, 40*(6), 747–768.

Czopp, A. M., Kay, A. C., & Cheryan, S. (2015). Positive stereotypes are pervasive and powerful. *Perspectives on Psychological Science, 10*(4), 451–463.

Czopp, A. M., Monteith, M. J., & Mark, A. Y. (2006). Standing up for a change: Reducing bias through interpersonal confrontation. *Journal of Personality and Social Psychology, 90*(5), 784–803.

Davis-Delano, L. R., Gone, J. P., & Fryberg, S. A. (2020). The psychosocial effects of Native American mascots: A comprehensive review of empirical research findings. *Race Ethnicity and Education, 23*(5), 613–633.

Delgado, R., & Stefancic, J. (2017). *Critical race theory: An introduction* (Vol. 20). New York University Press.

Devine, P. G., Forscher, P. S., Austin, A. J., & Cox, W. T. (2012). Long-term reduction in implicit race bias: A prejudice habit-breaking intervention. *Journal of Experimental Social Psychology, 48*(6), 1267–1278.

Diemer, M. A., Hsieh, C. A., & Pan, T. (2009). School and parental influences on socio-political development among poor adolescents of color. *The Counseling Psychologist, 37*(2), 317–344.

Dubrow, J. K., & Adams, J. (2012). Hoop inequalities: Race, class and family structure background and the odds of playing in the National Basketball Association. *International Review for the Sociology of Sport, 47*(1), 43–59.

Dunn, C. W., & Woodard, J. D. (2003). *The conservative tradition in America*. Rowman & Littlefield.

Fisher-Borne, M., Cain, J. M., & Martin, S. L. (2015). From mastery to accountability: Cultural humility as an alternative to cultural competence. *Social Work Education, 34*(2), 165–181.

Fraser, N. (2008). *Scales of justice: Reimagining political space in a globalizing world*. Columbia University Press.

French, B. H., Lewis, J. A., Mosley, D. V., Adames, H. Y., Chavez-Dueñas, N. Y., Chen, G. A., & Neville, H. A. (2020). Toward a psychological framework of radical healing in communities of color. *The Counseling Psychologist, 48*(1), 14–46.

Fryberg, S. A., Markus, H. R., Oyserman, D., & Stone, J. M. (2008). Of warrior chiefs and Indian princesses: The psychological consequences of American Indian mascots. *Basic and Applied Social Psychology, 30*(3), 208–218.

Gilliam, W. S., Maupin, A. N., Reyes, C. R., Accavitti, M., & Shic, F. (2016). Do early educators' implicit biases regarding sex and race relate to behavior expectations and recommendations of preschool expulsions and suspensions? *Yale University Child Study Center, 9*(28), 1–16.

Gion, C., McIntosh, K., & Smolkowski, K. (2018). Examinations of American Indian/Alaska Native school discipline disproportionality using the vulnerable decision points approach. *Behavioral Disorders, 44*(1), 40–52.

Girvan, E. J., Gion, C., McIntosh, K., & Smolkowski, K. (2017). The relative contribution of subjective office referrals to racial disproportionality in school discipline. *School Psychology Quarterly, 32*(3), 392–404.

Gladding, S. (2016). *Groups: A counseling specialty* (7th ed.). Pearson.

Goforth, A. N. (2016). A cultural humility model of school psychology training and practice. *Trainer's Forum*, *34*, 3–24.

Grantham, T. C. (2011). New directions for gifted Black males suffering from bystander effects: A call for upstanders. *Roeper Review*, *33*(4), 263–272.

Hays, P. A. (2008). *Addressing cultural complexities in practice: Assessment, diagnosis, and therapy* (2nd ed.). American Psychological Association.

Hook, J. N., Davis, D., Owen, J., & DeBlaere, C. (2017). *Cultural humility: Engaging diverse identities in therapy*. American Psychological Association.

Kosciw, J. G., Clark, C. M., Truong, N. L., & Zongrone, A. D. (2020). The 2019 National School Climate Survey: The experiences of lesbian, gay, bisexual, transgender, and queer youth in our nation's schools. GLSEN.https://www.glsen.org/sites/default/files/2020-10/NSCS-2019-Full-Report_0.pdf

Kumashiro, K. K. (2015). *Against common sense: Teaching and learning toward social justice* (3rd ed.). Routledge.

Leath, S., Mathews, C., Harrison, A., & Chavous, T. (2019). Racial identity, racial discrimination, and classroom engagement outcomes among Black girls and boys in predominantly Black and predominantly White school districts. *American Educational Research Journal*, *56*(4), 1318–1352.

Lenard, P. T., & Balint, P. (2020). What is (the wrong of) cultural appropriation? *Ethnicities*, *20*(2), 331–352.

Leonardo, Z., & Porter, R. K. (2010). Pedagogy of fear: Toward a Fanonian theory of "safety" in race dialogue. *Race, Ethnicity and Education*, *13*(2), 139–157.

Levinson, J. D., Bennett, M. W., & Hioki, K. (2017). Judging implicit bias: A national empirical study of judicial stereotypes. *Florida Law Review*, *69*, 63.

Linnemeyer, R. M., Nilsson, J. E., Marszalek, J. M., & Khan, M. (2018). Social justice advocacy among doctoral students in professional psychology programs. *Counselling Psychology Quarterly*, *31*, 98–116.

Lopez, A. E. (2016). *Culturally responsive and socially just leadership in diverse contexts: From theory to action*. Springer.

McFarland, J., Cui, J., Holmes, J., & Wang, X. (2020). Trends in high school dropout and completion rates in the United States: 2019. Compendium report. NCES 2020-117. National Center for Education Statistics.

McIntosh, P. (1989). White privilege: Unpacking the invisible knapsack. *Peace and Freedom*, 10–12.

Monteith, M. J., Ashburn-Nardo, L., Voils, C. I., & Czopp, A. M. (2002). Putting the brakes on prejudice: On the development and operation of cues for control. *Journal of Personality and Social Psychology*, *83*(5), 1029–1050.

National Association of School Psychologists. (2020). *The professional standards of the National Association of School Psychologists*.

National Center for Education Statistics. (2019). *Status and trends in the education of racial and ethnic groups 2018*. National Center for Education Statistics.

Neblett, E. W., Philip, C. L., Cogburn, C. D., & Sellers, R. M. (2006). African American adolescents' discrimination experiences and academic achievement: Racial socialization as a cultural compensatory and protective factor. *Journal of Black Psychology*, *32*(2), 199–218.

Ostrander, S. (1984). *Women of the upper class*. Temple University Press.

Parikh, S. B., Post, P., & Flowers, C. (2011). Relationship between a belief in a just world and social justice advocacy attitudes of school counselors. *Counseling and Values*, 56(1–2), 57–72.

Peterson, N. A., & Zimmerman, M. A. (2004). Beyond the individual: Toward a nomological network of organizational empowerment. *American Journal of Community Psychology*, 34(1–2), 129–145.

Pon, G. (2009). Cultural competency as new racism: An ontology of forgetting. *Journal of Progressive Human Services*, 20(1), 59–71.

Prilleltensky, I. (2008). The role of power in wellness, oppression, and liberation: The promise of psychopolitical validity. *Journal of Community Psychology*, 36(2), 116–136.

Roberts, S. O., & Rizzo, M. T. (2020). The psychology of American racism. *American Psychologist*. Advance online publication.

Salter, P. S., Adams, G., Perez, M. J. (2018). Racism in the structure of everyday worlds: A cultural-psychological perspective. *Current Directions in Psychological Science*, 27, 150–155.

Sanders-Phillips, K. (2009). Racial discrimination: A continuum of violence exposure for children of color. *Clinical Child and Family Psychology Review*, 12(2), 174–195.

Sellers, R. M., & Kuperminc, G. P. (1997). Goal discrepancy in African American male student-athletes' unrealistic expectations for careers in professional sports. *Journal of Black Psychology*, 23(1), 6–23.

Shriberg, D., Song, S. Y., Miranda, A. H., & Radliff, K. (Eds.). (2013). *School psychology and social justice: Conceptual foundations and tools for practice*. Routledge.

Steele, C. M., & Aronson, J. (1995). Stereotype threat and the intellectual test performance of African Americans. *Journal of Personality and Social Psychology*, 69(5), 797–811.

Steele, J. M., Bischof, G. H., & Craig, S. E. (2014). Political ideology and perceptions of social justice advocacy among members of the American Counseling Association. *International Journal for the Advancement of Counselling*, 36(4), 450–467.

Sue, D. W., Capodilupo, C. M., Torino, G. C., Bucceri, J. M., Holder, A., Nadal, K. L., & Esquilin, M. (2007). Racial microaggressions in everyday life: implications for clinical practice. *American Psychologist*, 62(4), 271–286.

Sue, D. W. (2010). *Microaggressions, marginality, and oppression. Microaggressions and Marginality, Manifestation, Dynamics, and Impact*. Wiley & Sons.

Sue, D. W., Sue, D. (2013). *Counseling the culturally diverse: Theory and practice* (6th ed.). Hoboken, NJ: John Wiley.

Sue, S. (2006). Cultural competency: From philosophy to research and practice. *Journal of Community Psychology*, 34, 237–245.

Sullivan, A. L., & Bal, A. (2013). Disproportionality in special education: Effects of individual and school variables on disability risk. *Exceptional Children*, 79(4), 475–494.

Sutter, M., & Perrin, P. B. (2016). Discrimination, mental health, and suicidal ideation among LGBTQ people of color. *Journal of Counseling Psychology*, 63(1), 98–105.

Tervalon, M., & Murray-Garcia, J. (1998). Cultural humility versus cultural competence: A critical distinction in defining physician training outcomes in multicultural education. *Journal of Health Care for the Poor and Underserved*, 9(2), 117–125.

Tew, J. (2006). Understanding power and powerlessness: Towards a framework for emancipatory practice in social work. *Journal of Social Work*, 6(1), 33–51.

Theoharis, G. (2007). Social justice educational leaders and resistance: Toward a theory of social justice leadership. *Educational Administration Quarterly, 43*(2), 221–258.

Trent, M., Dooley, D. G., Dougé, J., Cavanaugh, R. M., Lacroix, A. E., Fanburg, J., . . . & Wallace, S. B. (2019). The impact of racism on child and adolescent health. *Pediatrics, 144*(2). Article e20191765.

Vera, E. M., & Speight, S. L. (2003). Multicultural competence, social justice, and counseling psychology: Expanding our roles. *The Counseling Psychologist, 31*(3), 253–272.

Watts, R. J., Diemer, M. A., & Voight, A. M. (2011). Critical consciousness: Current status and future directions. *New Directions for Child and Adolescent Development, 2011*(134), 43–57.

Wellman, N., Applegate, J. M., Harlow, J., & Johnston, E. W. (2020). Beyond the pyramid: Alternative formal hierarchical structures and team performance. *Academy of Management Journal, 63*(4), 997–1027.

Wildman, S. M., & Davis, A. D. (1996). Making systems of privilege visible. In *Privilege Revealed* (pp. 7–24). New York University Press.

Wu, E. D. (2015). *The color of success: Asian Americans and the origins of the model minority*. Princeton University Press.

Young, J., Ne'eman, A., & Gelser, S. (2012). Bullying and students with disabilities: A briefing paper from the National Council on Disability. *National Council on Disability*.

CHAPTER 3

Ackerman, S. J., & Hilsenroth, M. J. (2003). A review of therapist characteristics and techniques positively impacting the therapeutic alliance. *Clinical Psychology Review, 23*(1), 1–33. https://doi.org/https://doi.org/10.1016/S0272-7358(02)00146-0

Adams, K. S., & Christenson, S. L. (2000). Trust and the family–school relationship examination of parent–teacher differences in elementary and secondary grades. *Journal of School Psychology, 38*(5), 477–497. https://doi.org/https://doi.org/10.1016/S0022-4405(00)00048-0

Albright, M. I., & Weissberg, R. P. (2010). School-family partnerships to promote social and emotional learning. In S. L. Christenson & A. L. Reschly (Eds.), *Handbook of school-family partnerships* (pp. 246–265). Routledge.

Auerbach, S. (2010). Beyond coffee with the principal: Toward leadership for authentic school-family partnerships. *Journal of School Leadership, 20*.

Brayboy, B. M. J. (2005). Toward a tribal critical race theory in education. *The Urban Review, 37*(5), 425–446. https://doi.org/10.1007/s11256-005-0018-y

Bronfenbrenner, U. (2005). Ecological systems theory. In U. Bronfenbrenner (Ed.), *Making human beings human: Bioecological perspectives on human development* (pp. 106–167). Sage Publications.

Bryan, J., & Henry, L. (2012). A model for building school–family–community partnerships: Principles and process. *Journal of Counseling & Development, 90*(4), 408–420. https://doi.org/https://doi.org/10.1002/j.1556-6676.2012.00052.x

Campbell, C. D., & Evans-Campbell, T. (2011). Historical trauma and Native American child development and mental health: An overview. In M. C. Sarche, P. Spicer, P. Farrell, & H. E. Fitzgerald (Eds.), *American Indian and Alaska Native children and mental health: Development, context, prevention, and treatment* (pp. 1–25). ABC-CLIO.

Christenson, S. L., & Sheridan, S. M. (2001). *School and families: Creating essential connections for learning.* Guilford Press.

Clarke, B. L., Sheridan, S. M., & Woods, K. E. (2009). Elements of health family-school relationships. In S. L. Christenson & A. L. Reschly (Eds.), *Handbook of school-family partnerships* (pp. 61–79). Routledge.

Day, E., & Dotterer, A. M. (2018). Parental involvement and adolescent academic outcomes: Exploring differences in beneficial strategies across racial/ethnic Groups. *Journal of Youth and Adolescence, 47*(6), 1332–1349. https://doi.org/http://dx.doi.org/10.1007/s10964-018-0853-2

Epstein, J. L. (2010). *School, family, and community partnerships: Preparing educators and improving schools.* Taylor & Francis Group. http://ebookcentral.proquest.com/lib/msoumt/detail.action?docID=625094

Fantuzzo, J., Tighe, E., & Childs, S. (2000). Family Involvement Questionnaire: A multivariate assessment of family participation in early childhood education. *Journal of Educational Psychology, 92*(2), 367–376. https://doi.org/http://dx.doi.org/10.1037/0022-0663.92.2.367

Garcia, J. (2019). Critical and culturally sustaining Indigenous family and community engagement in education. In S. B. Sheldon & T. A. Turner-Vorbeck (Eds.), *The Wiley handbook of family, school, and community relationships in education* (pp. 71–90). Wiley. https://doi.org/https://doi.org/10.1002/9781119083054.ch4

Holcomb-McCoy, C., & Bryan, J. (2010). Advocacy and empowerment in parent consultation: Implications for theory and practice. *Journal of Counseling & Development, 88*(3), 259–268. https://doi.org/https://doi.org/10.1002/j.1556-6678.2010.tb00021.x

Izuhara, M. (2010). *Ageing and intergenerational relations: Family reciprocity from a global perspective.* Policy Press.

Jeynes, W. H. (2007). The relationship between parental involvement and urban secondary school student academic achievement: A meta-analysis. *Urban Education, 42*(1), 82–110. https://doi.org/10.1177/0042085906293818

Ji, C. S., & Koblinsky, S. A. (2009). Parent involvement in children's education: An exploratory study of urban, Chinese immigrant families. *Urban Education, 44*(6), 687–709. https://doi.org/10.1177/0042085908322706

Kao, G., & Rutherford, L. T. (2007). Does social capital still matter? Immigrant minority disadvantage in school-specific social capital and its effects on academic achievement. *Sociological Perspectives, 50*(1), 27–52. https://doi.org/10.1525/sop.2007.50.1.27

Lareau, A., & Horvat, E. M. (1999). Moments of social inclusion and exclusion race, class, and cultural capital in family-school relationships. *Sociology of Education, 72*(1), 37–53. https://doi.org/10.2307/2673185

Li, G., & Sun, Z. (2019). Asian immigrant family school relationships and literacy learning: Patterns and explanations. In S. B. Sheldon & T. A. Turner-Vorbeck (Eds.), *The Wiley handbook of family, school, and community relationships in education.*

Ma, X., Shen, J., Krenn, H. Y., Hu, S., & Yuan, J. (2016). A meta-analysis of the relationship between learning outcomes and parental involvement during earlycChildhood education and early elementary education. *Educational Psychology Review, 28*(4), 771–801. https://doi.org/http://dx.doi.org/10.1007/s10648-015-9351-1

Miller, W. R., & Rollnick, S. (2013). *Motivational Interviewing: Helping People Change* (3rd ed.). The Guiford Press.

Milne, E. (2016). "I have the worst fear of teachers": Moments of inclusion and exclusion in family/school relationships among Indigenous families in southern Ontario. *Canadian Review of Sociology/Revue canadienne de sociologie, 53*(3), 270–289. https://doi.org/https://doi.org/10.1111/cars.12109

Olivos, E. M. (2019). Community and school collaborations. In S. B. Sheldon & T. A. Turner-Vorbeck (Eds.), *The Wiley handbook of family, school, and community relationships in education* (pp. 9–27). Wiley. https://doi.org/https://doi.org/10.1002/9781119083054.ch1

Pinquart, M., & Kauser, R. (2018). Do the associations of parenting styles with behavior problems and academic achievement vary by culture? Results from a meta-analysis. *Cultural Diversity and Ethnic Minority Psychology, 24*(1), 75–100. https://doi.org/https://doi.org/10.1037/cdp0000149

Santiago, R. T., Garbacz, S. A., Beattie, T., & Moore, C. L. (2016). Parent-teacher relationships in elementary school: An examination of parent-teacher trust. *Psychology in the Schools, 53*(10), 1003–1017. https://doi.org/https://doi.org/10.1002/pits.21971

Shannon, S. M. (1996). Minority parental involvement: A Mexican mother's experience and a teacher's interpretation. *Education and Urban Society, 29*(1), 71–84.

Sheridan, S. M., & Kratochwill, T. R. (2008). *Conjoint behavioral consultation: Promoting family-school connections and interventions.* Springer.

Shilling, V. (2019). An eagle feather? When representation of a Native Nation gets in the way of graduation. *Indian Country Today.* https://indiancountrytoday.com/news/an-eagle-feather-how-representation-of-a-native-nation-gets-in-the-way-of-graduation

Smith, T. E., Sheridan, S. M., Kim, E. M., Park, S., & Beretvas, S. N. (2020). The effects of family-school partnership interventions on academic and social-emotional functioning: A meta-analysis exploring what works for whom. *Educational Psychology Review, 32*(2), 511–544. https://doi.org/10.1007/s10648-019-09509-w

Stormshak, E., Dishion, T., & Falkenstein, C. (2009). Family-centered, school-based mental health strategies to reduce student behavioral, emotional, and academic risk. In S. L. Christenson & A. L. Reschly (Eds.), *Handbook of School-Family Partnerships* (pp. 228–245). Taylor & Francis Groups.

Tran, Y. (2014). Addressing reciprocity between families and schools: Why these bridges are instrumental for students' academic success. *Improving Schools, 17*(1), 18–29. https://doi.org/10.1177/1365480213515296

Wilson, C. M. (2019). Critical approaches to educational partnerships with African American families: The relevancy of race in ideology and practice. In S. B. Sheldon & T. A. Turner-Vorbeck (Eds.), *The Wiley handbook of family, school, and community relationships in education.* Wiley

Witte, A. L., Schumacher, R. E., & Sheridan, S. M. (2022). The effectiveness of technology-delivered conjoint behavioral consultation: Addressing rural student and family needs. *Journal of Educational and Psychological Consultation*, 1–26. https://www.tandfonline.com/doi/citedby/10.1080/10474412.2022.2083624?scroll=top&needAccess=true

Chapter 4

Aganza, J. S., Godinez, A., Smith, D., Gonzalez, L. G., & Robinson-Zañartu, C. (2015). Using cultural assets to enhance assessment of Latino students. *Contemporary School Psychology, 19*, 30–45. doi: http://dx.doi.org/10.1007/s40688-014-0041-7

American Educational Research Association. (2014). *Standards for educational and psychological testing*. American Educational Research Association.

Beirens, K., & Fontaine, J. R. J. (2010). Somatic and emotional well-being among Turkish immigrants in Belgium: Acculturation or culture? *Journal of Cross-Cultural Psychology, 42*, 56–74. doi: 10.1177/0022022110361773

Brown, M. A., & Di Lallo, S. (2020). Talking circles: A culturally responsive evaluation practice. *American Journal of Evaluation, 41*, 367–383. doi: 10.1177/1098214019899164

Chan, M. E., & Elliott, J. M. (2011). Cross-linguistic differences in digit memory span. *Australian Psychologist, 46*, 25–30. doi: 10.1111/j.1742-9544.2010.00007.x

Chan, P. E., Graham-Day, K. J., Ressa, V. A., Peters, M. T., & Konrad, M. (2014). Beyond involvement: Promoting student ownership of learning in classrooms. *Intervention in School and Clinic, 50*, 105–113.

Chin, M. J., Quinn, D. M., Dhaliwal, T. K., & Lovison, V. S. (2020). Bias in the air: A nationwide exploration of teachers' implicit racial attitudes, aggregate bias, and student outcomes. *Educational Researcher, 49*, 566–578. doi: 10.3102/0013189X20937240

Cook-Cottone, C. P., Kane, L. S., & Anderson, L. M. (2014). *The elements of counseling children and adolescents*. Springer Publishing Company.

Dombrowski, S. C. (2015). Interviewing and gathering data. In S. C. Dombrowski (Ed.), *Psychoeducational Assessment and Report Writing* (pp. 17–42). Springer New York.

Fong, E. H., Catagnus, R. M., Brodhead, M. T., Quigley, S., & Field, S. (2016). Developing the cultural awareness skills of behavior analysts. *Behavior Analysis in Practice, 9*, 84–94. doi: 10.1007/s40617-016-0111-6

Geva, E., & Wiener, J. (2015). *Psychological assessment of culturally and linguistically diverse children and adolescents: A practitioner's guide*. Springer.

Guarnaccia, P. J., Lewis-Fernández, R., & Marano, M. R. (2003). Toward a Puerto Rican popular nosology: Nervios and Ataque de Nervios. *Culture, Medicine and Psychiatry, 27*, 339–366. doi: 10.1023/a:1025303315932

Hydén, M. (2014). The teller-focused interview: Interviewing as a relational practice. *Qualitative Social Work, 13*, 795–812. doi: 10.1177/1473325013506247

Johnston, A., & Claypool, T. (2010). Incorporating a multi-method assessment model in schools that serve First Nations, Inuit, and Métis learners. *Native Studies Review, 19*, 121–138.

Kuwabara, M., & Smith, L. B. (2012). Cross-cultural differences in cognitive development: Attention to relations and objects. *Journal of Experimental Child Psychology, 113*, 20–35. doi: 10.1016/j.jecp.2012.04.009

Kvale, S. (2006). Dominance through interviews and dialogues. *Qualitative Inquiry, 12*, 480–500. doi: 10.1177/1077800406286235

Lau, A. S., Garland, A. F., Yeh, M., McCabe, K. M., Wood, P. A., & Hough, R. L. (2004). Race/ethnicity and inter-informant agreement in assessing adolescent psychopathology. *Journal of Emotional and Behavioral Disorders, 12*, 145–156. doi: 10.1177/10634266040120030201

LeBlanc, L. A., Raetz, P. B., Sellers, T. P., & Carr, J. E. (2016). A proposed model for selecting measurement procedures for the assessment and treatment of problem behavior. *Behavior Analysis in Practice, 9*, 77–83.

Li, C., & Wang, Z. (2014). School-based assessment with Asian children and adolescents. In L. T. Benuto, N. S. Thaler, & B. D. Leany (Eds.), *Guide to psychological assessment with Asians* (pp. 393–405). Springer New York.

Lindsey, K. A., Manis, F. R., & Bailey, C. E. (2003). Prediction of first-grade reading in Spanish-speaking English-language learners. *Journal of Educational Psychology, 95,* 482–494. doi: 10.1037/0022-0663.95.3.482

McGoey, K. E., McCobin, A., & Venesky, L. G. (2016). Early childhood assessment for diverse learners. In S. L. Graves & J. J. Blake (Eds.), *Psychoeducational assessment and intervention for ethnic minority children: Evidence-based approaches* (pp. 115–131, Chapter xiv, 289 Pages). American Psychological Association.

Minsky, S., Petti, T., Gara, M., Vega, W., Lu, W., & Kiely, G. (2006). Ethnicity and clinical psychiatric diagnosis in childhood. *Administration and Policy in Mental Health and Mental Health Services Research, 33,* 558–567. doi: 10.1007/s10488-006-0069-8

Morgan, P. L., Farkas, G., Cook, M., Strassfeld, N. M., Hillemeier, M. M., Pun, W. H., et al. (2018). Are Hispanic, Asian, Native American, or language-minority children overrepresented in special education? *Exceptional Children, 84,* 261–279. doi: 10.1177/0014402917748303

Mzimkulu, K. G., & Simbayi, L. C. (2006). Perspectives and practices of Xhosa-speaking African traditional healers when managing psychosis. *International Journal of Disability, Development and Education, 53,* 417–431. doi: 10.1080/10349120601008563

Okazaki, S., & Sue, S. (1995). Methodological issues in assessment research with ethnic minorities. *Psychological Assessment, 7,* 367–375. doi: 10.1037/1040-3590.7.3.367

Okonofua, J. A., & Eberhardt, J. L. (2015). Two strikes: Race and the disciplining of young students. *Psychological Science, 26,* 617–624. doi: 10.1177/0956797615570365

Ortiz, S. (2002). Multicultural issues in school psychology practice. *Journal of Applied School Psychology, 22,* 151–167.

Pham, A. V., Carlson, J. S., & Kosciulek, J. F. (2010). Ethnic differences in parental beliefs of Attention-Deficit/Hyperactivity Disorder and treatment. *Journal of Attention Disorders, 13*(6), 584–591. https://doi.org/10.1177/1087054709332391

Portman, T. A. A., & Garrett, M. T. (2006). Native American healing traditions. *International Journal of Disability, Development & Education, 53,* 453–469. doi: 10.1080/10349120601008647

Rahill, S. (2014). Theme-based psychological reports: Towards the next generation of report writing. Paper presented at the Trainers' Forum.

Rhodes, R. L., Ochoa, S. H., & Ortiz, S. O. (2005). *Assessing culturally and linguistically diverse students: A practical guide.* Guilford Press.

Sattler, J. M. (2018). *Assessment of Children: Cognitive Foundations and Applications.* Jerome M. Sattler, Publisher, Inc.

Schlosser, A. V., & Ninnemann, K. (2012). Introduction to the special section: The anthropology of psychopharmaceuticals: Cultural and pharmacological efficacies in context. *Culture, Medicine, and Psychiatry, 36,* 2–9. doi: 10.1007/s11013-012-9249-z

Sommers-Flanagan, J., & Sommers-Flanagan, R. (2014). *Clinical Interviewing* (5th ed.). Wiley.

Tenenbaum, H. R., & Ruck, M. D. (2007). Are teachers' expectations different for racial minority than for European American students? *A meta-analysis. Journal of Educational Psychology, 99,* 253–273. doi: 10.1037/0022-0663.99.2.253

Thaler, N. S., Allen, D. N., & Scott, J. G. (2014). Neuropsychological assessment of Asian-American children and adolescents. In L. T. Benuto, N. S. Thaler & B. D. Leany (Eds.), *Guide to Psychological Assessment with Asians* (pp. 407–425). New York, NY: Springer New York.

Tilly, W. D. (2014). The evolution of school psychology to science-based practice: Problem solving and the Three-Tiered Model. In P. Harrison & A. Thomas (Eds.), *Best Practices in School Psychology* (Vol. V). National Association of School Psychologists (pp. 17–36).

van de Vijver, F. J. R., & Poortinga, Y. H. (2020). Dealing with methodological pitfalls in cross-cultural studies of stress. In T. Ringeisen, P. Genkova, & F. T. L. Leong (Eds.), *Handbuch Stress und Kultur: Interkulturelle und kulturvergleichende Perspektiven* (pp. 1–19). Springer Fachmedien Wiesbaden.

Volpe, R. J., & McConaughy, S. H. (2005). Systematic direct observational assessment of student behavior: Its use and interpretation in multiple settings: An introduction to the miniseries. *School Psychology Review, 34,* 451–453.

Zamarripa, M. X., & Lerma, E. (2013). School-based assessment with Latina/o children and adolescents. In L. T. Benuto (Ed.), *Guide to psychological assessment with Hispanics* (pp. 335–349). Springer US.

Zink, D., Lee, B., & Allen, D. (2015). Structured and semistructured clinical interviews available for use among African American clients: Cultural considerations in the diagnostic interview process. In L. T. Benuto & B. D. Leany (Eds.), *Guide to Psychological assessment with African Americans* (pp. 19–42). Springer.

CHAPTER 5

Abedi, J., Hofstetter, C. H., & Lord, C. (2004). Assessment accommodations for English language learners: Implications for policy-based empirical research. *Review of Educational Research, 74*(1), 1–28. https://doi.org/10.3102/00346543074001001

Allinder, R. M., Bolling, R. M., Oats, R. G., & Gagnon, W. A. (2000). Effects of teacher self-monitoring on implementation of curriculum-based measurement and mathematics computation achievement of students with disabilities. *Remedial and Special Education, 21*(4), 219–226. https://doi.org/10.1177/074193250002100403

Alonzo, J., Tindal, G., Ulmer, K., & Glasgow, A. (2006). easyCBM online progress monitoring assessment system [Computer software]. University of Oregon, Behavioral Research and Teaching. http://easycbm.com

Altman, C., Harel, E., Meir, N., Iluz-Cohen, P., Walters, J., & Armon-Lotem, S. (2021). Using a monolingual screening test for assessing bilingual children. *Clinical Linguistics & Phonetics,* 1–21. https://doi.org/10.1080/02699206.2021.2000644

Artiles, A. J., Rueda, R., Salazar, J. J., & Higareda, I. (2005). Within-group diversity in minority disproportionate representation: English language learners in urban school districts. *Exceptional Children, 71*(3), 283–300. https://doi.org/10.1177/0014402 90507100305

Barrueco, S., Lopez, M., Ong, C., & Lozano, P. (2012). *Assessing Spanish-English bilingual preschoolers: A guide to best approaches and measures.* Brookes.

Berry, J. W. (1992). Acculturation and adaptation in a new society. *International Migration, 30,* 69–69.

Brandenburg, J., Klesczewski, J., Schuchardt, K., Fischbach, A., Büttner, G., & Hasselhorn, M. (2017). Phonological processing in children with specific reading disorder versus typical learners: Factor structure and measurement invariance in a transparent orthography. *Journal of Educational Psychology, 109*(5), 709–726. https://doi.org/10.1037/edu0000162

Carley Rizzuto, K. (2017). Teachers' perceptions of ELL students: Do their attitudes shape their instruction? *The Teacher Educator, 52*(3), 182–202. https://doi.org/10.1080/08878730.2017.1296912

Cho, H. (2016). Formal and informal academic language socialization of a bilingual child. *International Journal of Bilingual Education and Bilingualism, 19*(4), 387–407. https://doi.org/10.1080/13670050.2014.993303

Claussenius-Kalman, H., Hernandez, A. E., & Li, P. (2021). Expertise, ecosystem, and emergentism: Dynamic developmental bilingualism. *Brain and Language, 222*, Article 105013. https://doi.org/10.1016/j.bandl.2021.105013

Crutchfield, J., Phillippo, K. L., & Frey, A. (2020). Structural racism in schools: A view through the lens of the national school social work practice model. *Children & Schools, 42*(3), 187–193. https://doi.org/10.1093/cs/cdaa015

Cummins, J. (1979). Cognitive/academic language proficiency, linguistic interdependence, the optimum age question and some other matters. *Working Papers on Bilingualism* (pp. 2–9), *19*.

Darling-Hammond, L., Flook, L., Cook-Harvey, C., Barron, B., & Osher, D. (2020). Implications for educational practice of the science of learning and development. *Applied Developmental Science, 24*(2), 97–140. https://doi.org/10.1080/10888 691.2018.1537791

De Brey, C., Snyder, T. D., Zhang, A., and Dillow, S. A. (2021). Digest of Education Statistics 2019 (NCES 2021–009). National Center for Education Statistics, Institute of Education Sciences, U.S. Department of Education.

Deno, S. L. (2003). Developments in curriculum-based measurement. *The Journal of Special Education, 37*(3), 184–192. https://doi.org/10.1177/00224669030370030801

De Ramírez, R. D., & Shapiro, E. S. (2007). Cross-language relationship between Spanish and English oral reading fluency among Spanish-speaking English language learners in bilingual education classrooms. *Psychology in the Schools, 44*(8), 795–806. https://doi.org/10.1002/pits.20266

Fall, A. M., & Billingsley, B. S. (2011). Disparities in work conditions among early career special educators in high-and low-poverty districts. *Remedial and Special Education, 32*(1), 64–78. https://doi.org/10.1177/0741932510361264

Freeman, Y., & Freeman, D. (2003). Struggling English Language Learners: Keys for Academic Success. *TESOL Journal, 12*(3), 5–10.

Förster, N., & Souvignier, E. (2015). Effects of providing teachers with information about their students' reading progress. *School Psychology Review, 44*(1), 60–75.

García, O., & Wei, L. (2014). Language, bilingualism and education. In O. García & L. Wei (Ed.), *Translanguaging: Language, bilingualism and education* (pp. 46–62). Palgrave Pivot.

García-Sánchez, I. M. (2010). The politics of Arabic language education: Moroccan immigrant children's language socialization into ethnic and religious identities. *Linguistics and Education, 21*(3), 171–196.

Geary, D. C., Hoard, M. K., Nugent, L., & Bailey, D. H. (2012). Mathematical cognition deficits in children with learning disabilities and persistent low achievement: A five-year prospective study. *Journal of Educational Psychology, 104*(1), 206–223. https://doi.org/10.1037/a0025398

Gersten, R., Baker, S. K., Shanahan, T., Linan-Thompson, S., Collins, P., & Scarcella, R. (2007). *Effective literacy and English language instruction for English learners in the elementary grades. IES practice guide.* NCEE 2007–4011. What Works Clearinghouse.

Gleason, P. (2019). *Speaking of diversity: Language and ethnicity in twentieth-century America.* JHU Press.

González, N., Moll, L. C., & Amanti, C. (2005). *Funds of knowledge: Theorizing practices in households, communities, and classrooms.* Lawrence Erlbaum Associates.

Good, R. H., Gruba, J., & Kaminski, R. A. (2002). Best practices in using dynamic indicators of basic early literacy skills (DIBELS) in an outcomes-driven model. In A. Thomas & J. Grimes (Eds.), *Best practices in school psychology IV* (pp. 699–720). National Association of School Psychologists.

Goodrich, J. M., Lonigan, C. J., Phillips, B. M., Farver, J. M., & Wilson, K. D. (2021). Influences of the home language and literacy environment on Spanish and English vocabulary growth among dual language learners. *Early Childhood Research Quarterly, 57,* 27–39. https://doi.org/10.1016/j.ecresq.2021.05.002

Goodrich, J. M., & Namkung, J. M. (2019). Correlates of reading comprehension and word-problem solving skills of Spanish-speaking dual language learners. *Early Childhood Research Quarterly, 48,* 256–266. https://doi.org/10.1016/j.ecr esq.2019.04.006

Gort, M. (2012). Code-switching patterns in the writing-related talk of young emergent bilinguals. *Journal of Literacy Research, 44*(1), 45–75. https://doi.org/10.1177/10862 96X11431626

Gravois, T. A., & Gickling, E. (2008). Best practices in instructional assessment. In A. Thomas & J. Grimes (Eds.), *Best practices in school psychology V* (pp. 503–518). National Association of School Psychologists.

Grosjean, F. (2008). *Studying bilinguals.* Oxford University Press.

Guzman-Orth, D., Lopez, A. A., & Tolentino, F. (2017). A framework for the dual language assessment of young dual language learners in the United States. *ETS Research Report Series, 2017*(1), 1–19.

Han, H. (2012). Being and becoming "a new immigrant" in Canada: How language matters, or not. *Journal of Language, Identity & Education, 11*(2), 136–149. https://doi.org/10.1080/15348458.2012.6673109

Hintze, J. M., Callahan, J. E., III, Matthews, W. J., Williams, S. A., & Tobin, K. G. (2002). Oral reading fluency and prediction of reading comprehension in African American and Caucasian elementary school children. *School Psychology Review, 31*(4), 540–553. https://doi.org/10.1080/02796015.2002.12086173

Hoff, E. (2013). Interpreting the early language trajectories of children from low-SES and language minority homes: Implications for closing achievement gaps. *Developmental Psychology, 49*(1), 4–14. https://doi.org/10.1037/a0027238

Hoff, E., & Core, C. (2015). What clinicians need to know about bilingual development. *Seminars in Speech and Language, 36*(2), 89–99.

Hoover, J. J., & Soltero-González, L. (2018). Educator preparation for developing culturally and linguistically responsive MTSS in rural community elementary schools. *Teacher Education and Special Education, 41*(3), 188–202. https://doi.org/10.1177/0888406417753689

Hopewell, S., & Escamilla, K. (2014). Struggling reader or emerging biliterate student? Reevaluating the criteria for labeling emerging bilingual students as low achieving. *Journal of Literacy Research, 46*(1), 68–89. https://doi.org/10.1177/1086296X13504869

Hussar, B., Zhang, J., Hein, S., Wang, K., Roberts, A., Cui, J., . . . & Dilig, R. (2020). *The Condition of Education 2020*. NCES 2020–144. National Center for Education Statistics.

Individuals with Disabilities Education Improvement Act of 2004. (2004). Public Law 446, U.S. Statutes at Large. *118*, 2647–2808. https://www.congress.gov/bill/108th-congress/house-bill/1350?q=H.R.+1350+%28108%29

Kaminitz- Berkooz, I., & Shapiro, E. (2005). The applicability of curriculum-based measurement to measure reading in Hebrew. *School Psychology International*, *26*(4), 494–519. https://doi.org/10.1177/0143034305059028

Kieffer, M. J., Lesaux, N. K., Rivera, M., & Francis, D. J. (2009). Accommodations for English language learners taking large-scale assessments: A meta-analysis on effectiveness and validity. *Review of Educational Research*, *79*(3), 1168–1201. https://doi.org/10.3102/0034654309332490

Knight, M. G., Roegman, R., & Edstrom, L. (2016). My American dream: The interplay between structure and agency in West African immigrants' educational experiences in the United States. *Education and Urban Society*, *48*(9), 827–851. https://doi.org/10.1177/0013124515589596

Kim, B. S. K. (2009). Acculturation and enculturation of Asian Americans: A primer. In N. Tewari & A. N. Alvarcz (Eds.), *Asian American psychology: Current perspectives* (pp. 97–112). Routledge/Taylor & Francis Group.

Kim, B. S. K., & Abreu, J. M. (2001). Acculturation measurement: Theory, current instruments, and future directions. In J. G. Ponterotto, J. M. Casa, L. Suzuki, & C. M. Alexander (Eds.), *Handbook of multicultural counseling* (2nd ed., pp. 394–424). Sage.

Kim, C. J. H., & Padilla, A. M. (2020). Technology for educational purposes among low-income Latino children living in a mobile park in Silicon Valley: A case study before and during COVID-19. *Hispanic Journal of Behavioral Sciences*, *42*(4), 497–514. https://doi.org/10.1177/0739986320959764

Kim, J. S., Vanderwood, M. L., & Lee, C. Y. (2016). Predictive validity of curriculum-based measures for English learners at varying English proficiency levels. *Educational Assessment*, *21*(1), 1–18. https://doi.org/10.1080/10627197.2015.1127750

Kim, W., & Linan-Thompson, S. (2013). The effects of self-regulation on science vocabulary acquisition of English language learners with learning difficulties. *Remedial and Special Education*, *34*(4), 225–236. https://doi.org/10.1177/0741932513476956

Lenski, S. D., Ehlers-Zavala, F., Daniel, M. C., & Sun-Irminger, X. (2006). Assessing English-language learners in mainstream classrooms. *The Reading Teacher*, *60*(1), 24–34. https://doi.org/10.1598/RT.60.1.3

Lopez, A. A., Pooler, E., & Linquanti, R. (2016). Key issues and opportunities in the initial identification and classification of English learners (Research Report No. RR-16–09). Educational Testing Service. http://dx.doi.org/10.1002/ets2.12090

Martines, D., & Rodriquez-Srednicki, O. (2007) Academic assessment of bilingual and English language learning students. In G. B. Esquivel, E. C. Lopez, & S. G. Nahari (Eds.), *Handbook of multicultural school psychology: An interdisciplinary perspective* (pp. 381–405). Lawrence Erlbaum.

Mechelli, A., Crinion, J. T., Noppeney, U., O'Doherty, J., Ashburner, J., Frackowiak, R. S., & Price, C. J. (2004). Structural plasticity in the bilingual brain. *Nature*, *431*(7010), 757–757. https://doi.org/10.1038/431757a

Moll, L. C. (2019). Elaborating funds of knowledge: Community-oriented practices in international contexts. *Literacy Research: Theory, Method, and Practice, 68*(1), 130–138. https://doi.org/10.1177/2381336919870805

Moll, L. C., Amanti, C., Neff, D., & González, N. (1992). Funds of Knowledge for teaching: Using a qualitative approach to connect homes and classrooms. *Theory Into Practice, 31*(2), 132–141. https://doi.org/10.1080/00405849209543534

Morgan, P. L., Farkas, G., Cook, M., Strassfeld, N. M., Hillemeier, M. M., Pun, W. H., . . . & Schussler, D. L. (2018). Are Hispanic, Asian, Native American, or language-minority children overrepresented in special education? *Exceptional Children, 84*(3), 261–279. https://doi.org/10.1177/0014402917748303

National Center for Education Statistics. (2019). Nation's report card: Reading. National Assessment of Educational Progress. https://www.nationsreportcard.gov/reading/nation/achievement/?grade=4

Notari-Syverson, A., Losardo, A., & Lim, Y. S. (2003). Assessment of young children from culturally diverse backgrounds: A journey in progress. *Intervention, 29*(1), 39–51. https://doi.org/10.1177/073724770302900105

Ortiz, S. O., Flanagan, D. P., & Dynda, A. M. (2008). Best practices in working with culturally diverse children and families. In A. Thomas & J. Grimes (Eds.), *Best practices in school psychology* (Vol. V, pp. 1721–1738). National Association of School Psychologists.

Padilla, A. M., & Gonzalez, R. (2001). Academic performance of immigrant and US-born Mexican heritage students: Effects of schooling in Mexico and bilingual/English language instruction. *American Educational Research Journal, 38*(3), 727–742. https://doi.org/10.3102/00028312038003727

Paige, R., & Witty, E. (2010). *The Black-White achievement gap: Why closing it is the greatest civil rights issues of our time.* Amacom.

Pearson. (2010). *AIMSweb: Assessment and data management for RTI.* Author.

Pham, A. V., Goforth, A. N., Chun, H., Castro-Olivo, S., & Costa, A. (2017). Acculturation and help-seeking behavior in consultation: A sociocultural framework for mental health service. *Journal of Educational and Psychological Consultation*, 1–18. https://doi.org/10.1080/10474412.2017.1287574

Pontier, R., & Gort, M. (2016). Coordinated translanguaging pedagogy as distributed cognition: A case study of two dual language bilingual education preschool coteachers' languaging practices during shared book readings. *International Multilingual Research Journal, 10*(2), 89–106. https://doi.org/10.1080/19313152.2016.1150732

Reardon, S. F., Robinson-Cimpian, J. P., & Weathers, E. S. (2015). Patterns and trends in racial/ethnic and socioeconomic academic achievement gaps. In H. A. Ladd & M. E. Goertz (Eds.), *Handbook of research in education finance and policy* (pp. 491–509). Routledge.

Rojas, R., & Iglesias, A. (2013). The language growth of Spanish-speaking English language learners. *Child Development, 84*(2), 630–646. https://doi.org/10.1111/j.1467-8624.2012.01871.x

Shin, R., Daly, B., & Vera, E. (2007). The relationships of peer norms, ethnic identity, and peer support to school engagement in urban youth. *Professional School Counseling, 10*(4), 379–388. https://doi.org/10.1177/2156759X0701000411

Souto-Manning, M. (2016). Honoring and building on the rich literacy practices of young bilingual and multilingual learners. *The Reading Teacher, 70*(3), 263–271. https://doi.org/10.1002/trtr.1518

Svalberg, A. M. (2016). Language awareness research: Where we are now. *Language Awareness, 25*(1–2), 4–16. https://doi.org/10.1080/09658416.2015.1122027

Trumbull, E., & Nelson-Barber, S. (2019). The ongoing quest for culturally-responsive assessment for Indigenous students in the US. *Frontiers in Education, 4*(40), https://doi.org/10.3389/feduc.2019.00040

Ward, C., & Geeraert, N. (2016). Advancing acculturation theory and research: The acculturation process in its ecological context. *Current Opinion in Psychology, 8*, 98–104. https://doi.org/10.1016/j.copsyc.2015.09.021

WIDA. (2020). ELD standards framework: The 2020 edition. https://wida.wisc.edu/teach/standards/eld/2020

WIDA Consortium. (2007). *WIDA English language proficiency standards and resource guide: prekindergarten–grade 12.* WIDA Consortium.

Chapter 6

Ahram, R., Fergus, E., & Noguera, P. (2011). Addressing racial/ethnic disproportionality in special education: Case studies of suburban school districts. *Teachers College Record, 113*(10), 2233–2266.

Alexander, R. M., & Reynolds, M. R. (2020). Intelligence and adaptive behavior: A meta-analysis. *School Psychology Review, 49*(2), 85–110. https://doi.org/10.1080/2372966X.2020.1717374

Al-Hroub, A., & Whitebread, D. (2019). Dynamic assessment for identification of twice-exceptional learners exhibiting mathematical giftedness and specific learning disabilities. *Roeper Review, 41*(2), 129–142. https://doi.org/10.1080/02783193.2019.1585396

Armour-Thomas, E., & Gopaul-McNicol, S.-A. (1997). Bio-ecological approach to cognitive assessment. *Cultural Diversity and Mental Health, 3*(2), 131–144. https://doi.org/10.1037/1099-9809.3.2.131

Benson, N. F., Maki, K. E., Floyd, R. G., Eckert, T. L., Kranzler, J. H., & Fefer, S. A. (2020). A national survey of school psychologists' practices in identifying specific learning disabilities. *School Psychology, 35*(2), 146–157. https://doi.org/10.1037/spq0000344

Bonner, P. J., Warren, S. R., & Jiang, Y. H. (2018). Voices from urban classrooms: Teachers' perceptions on instructing diverse students and using culturally responsive teaching. *Education and Urban Society, 50*(8), 697–726.

Bronfenbrenner, U. (2005). Ecological systems theory. In U. Bronfenbrenner (Ed.), *Making human beings human: Bioecological perspectives on human development* (pp. 106–167). Sage Publications.

Card, D., & Giuliano, L. (2016). Universal screening increases the representation of low-income and minority students in gifted education. *Proceedings of the National Academy of Sciences, 113*(48), 13678–13683. https://doi.org/10.1073/pnas.1605043113

Christensen, D. L., Schieve, L. A., Devine, O., & Drews-Botsch, C. (2014). Socioeconomic status, child enrichment factors, and cognitive performance among preschool-age children: Results from the Follow-Up of Growth and Development Experiences study. *Research in Developmental Disabilities, 35*(7), 1789–1801.

Climie, E., & Henley, L. (2016). A renewed focus on strengths-based assessment in schools. *British Journal of Special Education, 43*(2), 108–121. https://doi.org/10.1111/1467-8578.12131

Dembitzer, L., & Kettler, R. J. (2018). Testing adaptations: Research to guide practice. In S. N. Elliott, R. J. Kettler, P. A. Beddow & A. Kurz (Eds.), *Handbook of accessible instruction and testing practices* (pp. 213–230). Springer, Cham.

Elliott, C. D. (2007). *Differential ability scales* (2nd ed.). Harcourt Assessment.

Farmer, R. L., Goforth, A. N., Kim, S. Y., Naser, S. C., Lockwood, A. B., & Affrunti, N. W. (2021). Status of school psychology in 2020, Part 2: Professional practices in the NASP membership survey. *Research Reports, 5*, 1–17.

Figueroa, R. A., & Hernandez, S. (2000). *Testing Hispanic students in the United States: Technical and policy issues.* The Commission. Retrieved from: https://files.eric.ed.gov/fulltext/ED441652.pdf

Flanagan, D. P., Ortiz, S. O., & Alfonso, V. C. (2013). *Essentials of cross-battery assessment* (3rd ed.). Wiley.

Fletcher, J. M., & Miciak, J. (2017). Comprehensive cognitive assessments are not necessary for the identification and treatment of learning disabilities. *Archives of Clinical Neuropsychology: The Official Journal of the National Academy of Neuropsychologists, 32*(1), 2–7. https://doi.org/10.1093/arclin/acw103

Ford, D. Y. (2014). Segregation and the underrepresentation of Blacks and Hispanics in gifted education: Social inequality and deficit paradigms. *Roeper Review, 36*(3), 143–154. https://doi.org/10.1080/02783193.2014.919563

Fuchs, D., Compton, D. L., Fuchs, L. S., Bouton, B., & Caffrey, E. (2011). The construct and predictive validity of a dynamic assessment of young children learning to read: Implications for RTI frameworks. *Journal of Learning Disabilities, 44*(4), 339–347. https://doi.org/10.1177/0022219411407864

Gardner, H. (1993). *Multiple intelligences: The theory in practice.* Basic Books.

Gillborn, D. (2016). Softly, softly: Genetics, intelligence and the hidden racism of the new geneism. *Journal of Education Policy, 31*(4), 365–388.

Gilman, R., & Huebner, S. (2003). A review of life satisfaction research with children and adolescents. *School Psychology Quarterly, 18*(2), 192–205. https://doi.org/10.1521/scpq.18.2.192.21858

Girvan, E. J., McIntosh, K., & Santiago-Rosario, M. R. (2021). Associations between community-level racial biases, office discipline referrals, and out-of-school suspensions. *School Psychology Review, 50*(2–3), 288–302.

Graziano, P. A., Reavis, R. D., Keane, S. P., & Calkins, S. D. (2007). The role of emotion regulation in children's early academic success. *Journal of School Psychology, 45*(1), 3–19. https://doi.org/10.1016/j.jsp.2006.09.002

Hackman, D. A., & Farah, M. J. (2009). Socioeconomic status and the developing brain. *Trends in Cognitive Sciences, 13*(2), 65–73. https://doi.org/10.1016/j.tics.2008.11.003

Hattie, J. (2012). *Visible learning for teachers: Maximizing impact on learning.* Routledge.

Helms, J. E., Jernigan, M., & Mascher, J. (2005). The meaning of race in psychology and how to change it: A methodological perspective. *American Psychologist, 60*(1), 27–36. https://doi.org/10.1037/0003-066X.60.1.27

Individuals With Disabilities Education Act, 20 U.S.C. § 1400 (2004).

Jimerson, S. R., Sharkey, J. D., Nyborg, V., & Furlong, M. J. (2004). Strength-based assessment and school psychology: A summary and synthesis. *California School Psychologist, 9*(1), 9–19. https://doi.org/10.1007/BF03340903

Kaufman, A. S., & Kaufman, N. L. (2004). Kaufman assessment battery for children: Second edition (KABC-II). American Guidance Service.

Kettler, R. J. (2012). Testing accommodations: Theory and research to inform practice. *International Journal of Disability, Development and Education, 5*(1), 53–66. https://doi.org/10.1080/1034912X.2012.654952

Knight, D. S. (2019). Are school districts allocating resources equitably? The Every Student Succeeds Act, teacher experience gaps, and equitable resource allocation. *Educational Policy, 33*(4), 615–649.

Kwate, N. O. A. (2001). Intelligence or misorientation? Eurocentrism in the WISC-III. *Journal of Black Psychology, 27*(2), 221–238. https://doi.org/10.1177/009579840102 7002005

Lidz, C. S. (2009). Dynamic assessment in school psychology. *Communique, 38*(2), 16–18.

Lidz, C. S., & Elliott, J. G. (2006). Use of dynamic assessment with gifted students. *Gifted Education International, 21*(2–3), 151–161. https://doi.org/10.1177/02614294060 2100307

Lidz, C. S., & Macrine, S. L. (2001). An alternative approach to the identification of gifted culturally and linguistically diverse learners: The contribution of dynamic assessment. *School Psychology International, 22*(1), 74–96. https://doi.org/10.1177/ 01430343010221006

Lidz, C. S., & Peña, E. D. (1996). Dynamic assessment: The model, its relevance as a nonbiased approach, and its application to Latino American preschool children. *Language, Speech, and Hearing Services in Schools, 27*(4), 367–372. https://doi.org/ 10.1044/0161-1461.2704.367

McGrew, K. S. (2005). The Cattell-Horn-Carroll theory of cognitive abilities: Past, present, and future. In D. P. Flanagan & P. L. Harrison (Eds.), *Contemporary intellectual assessment: Theories, tests, and issues* (pp. 136–181). The Guilford Press.

National Center for Education Statistics. (2019a). Nation's report card. National assessment of educational progress. https://www.nationsreportcard.gov/mathematics/nat ion/achievement/?grade=4

Neisser, U., Boodoo, G., Bouchard, T. J., Jr., Boykin, A. W., Brody, N., Ceci, S. J., Halpern, D. F., Loehlin, J. C., Perloff, R., Sternberg, R. J., & Urbina, S. (1996). Intelligence: Knowns and unknowns. *American Psychologist, 51*(2), 77–101. https:// doi.org/10.1037/0003-066X.51.2.77

Nickerson, A. B., & Fishman, C. E. (2013). Promoting mental health and resilience through strength-based assessment in US schools. *Educational and Child Psychology, 30*(4), 7–17.

Pashler, H., McDaniel, M., Rohrer, D., & Bjork, R. (2008). Learning styles: Concepts and evidence. *Psychological Science in the Public Interest, 9*(3), 105–119. https://doi.org/ 10.1111/j.1539-6053.2009.01038.x

Peters, S. J., Rambo-Hernandez, K., Makel, M. C., Matthews, M. S., & Plucker, J. A. (2019). Effect of local norms on racial and ethnic representation in gifted education. *AERA Open, 5*(2), https://doi.org/10.1177/2332858419848446

Petersen, D. B., Chanthongthip, H., Ukrainetz, T. A., Spencer, T. D., & Steeve, R. W. (2017). Dynamic assessment of narratives: Efficient, accurate identification of language impairment in bilingual students. *Journal of Speech, Language, and Hearing Research*, 60(4), 983–998. https://doi.org/10.1044/2016_JSLHR-L-15-0426

Pham, A. V., Castro-Olivo, S., Chun, H., & Goforth, A. N. (2017). Cognitive abilities in bilinguals in L1 and L2. In A. Ardila, A. B. Cieślicka, R. R. Heredia, M. Rosselli (Eds.), *Psychology of Bilingualism* (pp. 269–291). Springer, Cham.

Pham, A. V., Goforth, A. N., Aguilar, L. N., Burt, I., Bastian, R., & Diaków, D. M. (2021). Dismantling systemic inequities in school psychology: Cultural humility as a foundational approach to social justice. *School Psychology Review*, 1–18. https://doi.org/10.1080/2372966X.2021.1941245

Plomin, R. (2018). *Blueprint: How DNA makes us who we are*. MIT Press.

Plucker, J. A., Peters, S. J., & Schmalensee, S. (2017). Reducing excellence gaps: A research- based model. *Gifted Child Today*, 40(4), 245–250. https://doi.org/10.1177/1076217517723949

Redding, C. (2019). A teacher like me: A review of the effect of student–teacher racial/ethnic matching on teacher perceptions of students and student academic and behavioral outcomes. *Review of Educational Research*, 89(4), 499–535.

Reynolds, C. R., & Suzuki, L. A. (2012). Bias in psychological assessment: An empirical review and recommendations. In Irving Weiner (Ed.), *Handbook of Psychology* (Vol. 10, 2nd ed.), 82–113. https://doi.org/10.1002/9781118133880.hop210004

Rhee, S., Furlong, M. J., Turner, J. A., & Harari, I. (2001). Integrating strength-based perspectives in psychoeducational evaluations. *The California School Psychologist*, 6(1), 5–17. https://doi.org/10.1007/BF03340879

Ricciardi, C., Haag-Wolf, A., & Winsler, A. (2020). Factors associated with gifted identification for ethnically diverse children in poverty. *Gifted Child Quarterly*, 64(4), 243–258. https://doi.org/10.1177/0016986220937685

Rinn, A. N., Mun, R. U., & Hodges, J. (2020). 2018-2019 State of the States in Gifted Education. National Association for Gifted Children and the Council of State Directors of Programs for the Gifted. https://www.nagc.org/2018-2019-state-states-gifted-education

Roth, B., Becker, N., Romeyke, S., Schäfer, S., Domnick, F., & Spinath, F. M. (2015). Intelligence and school grades: A meta-analysis. *Intelligence*, 53, 118–137. https://doi.org/10.1016/j.intell.2015.09.002

Rubie-Davies, C. M. (2010). Teacher expectations and perceptions of student attributes: Is there a relationship? *British Journal of Educational Psychology*, 80(1), 121–135. https://doi.org/10.1348/000709909X466334

Salovey, P., & Mayer, J. D. (2004). Emotional intelligence. In P. Salovey, M. A. Brackett, & J. D. Mayer (Eds.), *Emotional intelligence: Key readings on the Mayer and Salovey model* (pp.1–27). Dude Publishing.

Salvia, J., Ysseldyke, J., & Witmer, S. (2016). *Assessment in special and inclusive education*. Cengage Learning.

Sattler, J. M. (2018). *Assessment of Children: Cognitive Foundations and Applications*. Jerome M. Sattler, Publisher, Inc.

Scheiber, C. (2016). Do the Kaufman tests of cognitive ability and academic achievement display construct bias across a representative sample of Black, Hispanic, and Caucasian school-age children in grades 1 through 12? *Psychological Assessment*, 28(8), 942–952. https://doi.org/10.1037/pas0000236

Serpell, R. (2011). Social responsibility as a dimension of intelligence, and as an educational goal: Insights from programmatic research in an African society. *Child Development Perspectives, 5*(2), 126–133. https://doi.org/10.1111/j.1750-8606.2011.00167.x

Snider, L. A., Talapatra, D., Miller, G., & Zhang, D. (2020). Expanding best practices in assessment for students with intellectual and developmental disabilities. *Contemporary School Psychology, 24*(4), 429–444. https://doi.org/10.1007/s40688-020-00294-w

Sobeck, J. L., Chapleski, E. E., & Fisher, C. (2003). Conducting research with American Indians: A case study of motives, methods, and results. *Journal of Ethnic and Cultural Diversity in Social Work, 12*(1), 69–84. https://doi.org/10.1300/J051v12n01_04

Steele, C. M., & Aronson, J. A. (2004). Stereotype threat does not live by Steele and Aronson (1995) alone. *American Psychologist, 59*(1), 47–48. https://doi.org/10.1037/0003-066X.59.1.47

Sternberg, R. J. (1997). The triarchic theory of intelligence. In D. P. Flanagan, J. L. Genshaft, & P. L. Harrison (Eds.), *Contemporary intellectual assessment: Theories, tests, and issues* (pp. 92–104). The Guilford Press.

Sternberg, R. J. (2004). Culture and intelligence. *American Psychologist, 59*(5), 325–338. https://doi.org/10.1037/0003-066X.59.5.325

Sternberg, R. J. (2007). Who are the bright children? The cultural context of being and acting intelligent. *Educational Researcher, 36*(3), 148–155. https://doi.org/10.3102/0013189X07299881

Sternberg, R. J., & Grigorenko, E. L. (2002a). The theory of successful intelligence as a basis for gifted education. *Gifted Child Quarterly, 46*(4), 265–277. https://doi.org/10.1177/001698620204600403

Sternberg, R. J., & Grigorenko, E. L. (2002b). *Dynamic testing: The nature and measurement of learning potential.* Cambridge University Press.

Styck, K. M., & Watkins, M. W. (2013). Diagnostic utility of the Culture-Language Interpretive Matrix for the Wechsler Intelligence Scales for Children—Fourth Edition among referred students. *School Psychology Review, 42*(4), 367–382. https://doi.org/10.1080/02796015.2013.12087460

Sue, D. W., Arredondo, P., & McDavis, R. J. (1992). Multicultural counseling competencies and standards: A call to the profession. *Journal of Counseling and Development, 70*, 477–486. https://doi.org/10.1002/j.1556-6676.1992.tb01642.x

Sung, H. Y. (2010). The influence of culture on parenting practices of East Asian families and emotional intelligence of older adolescents: A qualitative study. *School Psychology International, 31*(2), 199–214. https://doi.org/10.1177/0143034309352268

Terjesen, M. D., Jacofsky, M., Froh, J., & DiGiuseppe, R. (2004). Integrating positive psychology into schools: Implications for practice. *Psychology in the Schools, 41*(1), 163–172. https://doi.org/10.1002/pits.10148

Torrance, E. P. (1974). *Torrance tests of creative thinking: Norms-technical manual.* Scholastic Testing.

Trundt, K. M., Keith, T. Z., Caemmerer, J. M., & Smith, L. V. (2018). Testing for construct bias in the Differential Ability Scales: A comparison among African American, Asian, Hispanic, and Caucasian children. *Journal of Psychoeducational Assessment, 36*(7), 670–683. https://doi.org/10.1177/0734282917698303

Van De Vijver, F. J. (2008). On the meaning of cross-cultural differences in simple cognitive measures. *Educational Research and Evaluation, 14*(3), 215–234. https://doi.org/10.1080/13803610802048833

von Stumm, S. (2017). Socioeconomic status amplifies the achievement gap throughout compulsory education independent of intelligence. *Intelligence, 60*, 57–62. https://doi.org/10.1016/j.intell.2016.11.006

Warne, R. T., & Burningham, C. (2019). Spearman's g found in 31 non-Western nations: Strong evidence that g is a universal phenomenon. *Psychological Bulletin, 145*(3), 237–272. http://dx.doi.org/10.1037/bul0000184

Waterhouse, L. (2006). Inadequate evidence for multiple intelligences, Mozart effect, and emotional intelligence theories. *Educational Psychologist, 41*(4), 247–255. doi: 10.1207/s15326985ep4104_5

Wechsler, D. (2014). *WISC-V: Technical and interpretive manual.* Pearson.

Weiss, L. G., Saklofske, D. H., Holdnack, J. A., & Prifitera, A. (2015). *WISC-V assessment and interpretation: Scientist-practitioner perspectives.* Academic Press.

Weiss, L. G., & Saklofske, D. H. (2020). Mediators of IQ test score differences across racial and ethnic groups: The case for environmental and social justice. *Personality and Individual Differences, 161*, Article 109962. https://doi.org/10.1016/j.paid.2020.109962

Williams, F. E. (1980). *Creativity assessment packet.* DOK Publishers.

CHAPTER 7

Abdullah, T., & Brown, T. L. (2011). Mental illness stigma and ethnocultural beliefs, values, and norms: An integrative review. *Clinical Psychology Review, 31*(6), 934–948. https://doi.org/https://doi.org/10.1016/j.cpr.2011.05.003

Adams, G., Fryberg, S. A., Garcia, D. M., & Delgado-Torres, E. U. (2006). The psychology of engagement with indigenous identities: A cultural perspective. *Cultural Diversity and Ethnic Minority Psychology, 12*(3), 493–508. https://doi.org/http://dx.doi.org/10.1037/1099-9809.12.3.493

American Psychiatric Association. (2013). *Diagnostic and statistical manual of mental disorders* (5th ed.). American Psychiatric Association.

American Psychological Association. (2010). *Resilience and recovery after war: Refugee children and families in the United States.* American Psychological Association.

American Psychological Association. (2021). *Apology to people of color for APA's role in promoting, perpetuating, and failing to challenge racism, racial discrimination, and human hierarchy in U.S.* American Psychological Association.

Arnetz, J., Rofa, Y., Arnetz, B., Ventimiglia, M., & Jamil, H. (2013). Resilience as a protective factor against the development of psychopathology among refugees. *The Journal of Nervous and Mental Disease, 201*(3), 167–172. https://doi.org/10.1097/NMD.0b013e3182848afe

Arredondo, P., Gallardo-Cooper, M., Delgado-Romero, E. A., & Zapata, A. L. (2014). *Culturally responsive counseling with Latinas/os.* American Counseling Association.

Bal, A., Betters-Bubon, J., & Fish, R. E. (2019). A multilevel analysis of statewide disproportionality in exclusionary discipline and the identification of emotional disturbance. *Education and Urban Society, 51*(2), 247–268. https://doi.org/http://dx.doi.org/10.1177/0013124517716260

Beck, J. S. (2005). *Beck youth inventories: Manual.* San Antonio, TX: Pearson.

Bernhard, A., Martinelli, A., Ackermann, K., Saure, D., & Freitag, C. M. (2018). Association of trauma, posttraumatic stress disorder and conduct disorder: A systematic review and meta-analysis. *Neuroscience & Biobehavioral Reviews, 91*, 153–169. https://doi.org/https://doi.org/10.1016/j.neubiorev.2016.12.019

Betancourt, T. S., Newnham, E. A., Layne, C. M., Kim, S., Steinberg, A. M., Ellis, H., & Birman, D. (2012). Trauma history and psychopathology in war-affected refugee children referred for trauma-related mental health services in the United States. *Journal of Traumatic Stress, 25*(6), 682–690. https://doi.org/http://dx.doi.org/10.1002/jts.21749

Bhugra, D., & Jones, P. (2001). Migration and mental illness. *Advances in Psychiatric Treatment, 7*(3), 216–222. https://doi.org/10.1192/apt.7.3.216

Bitsko, R. H., Holbrook, J. R., Ghandour, R. M., Blumberg, S. J., Visser, S. N., Perou, R., & Walkup, J. T. (2018). Epidemiology and impact of health care provider-diagnosed anxiety and depression among US children. *Journal of Developmental & Behavioral Pediatrics, 39*(5), 395–403. https://doi.org/10.1097/dbp.0000000000000571

Brave Heart, M. Y. H., Chase, J., Elkins, J., & Altschul, D. B. (2011). Historical trauma among indigenous peoples of the Americas: Concepts, research, and clinical considerations. *Journal of Psychoactive Drugs, 43*(4), 282–290. https://doi.org/10.1080/02791072.2011.628913

Briere, J. (1996). Trauma symptom checklist for children. *Odessa, FL: Psychological Assessment Resources*, 00253-8.

Bronfenbrenner, U. (2005). Ecological systems theory. In U. Bronfenbrenner (Ed.), *Making human beings human: Bioecological perspectives on human development* (pp. 106–167). Sage Publications.

Bryant-Davis, T., & Ocampo, C. (2006). A therapeutic approach to the treatment of racist-incident-based trauma. *Journal of Emotional Abuse, 6*(4), 1–22. https://doi.org/10.1300/J135v06n04_01

Campbell, C. D., & Evans-Campbell, T. (2011). Historical trauma and Native American child development and mental health: An overview. In M. C. Sarche, P. Spicer, P. Farrell, & H. E. Fitzgerald (Eds.), *American Indian and Alaska Native children and mental health: Development, context, prevention, and treatment* (pp. 1–25). ABC-CLIO.

Carter, R. T. (2007). Racism and psychological and emotional injury: Recognizing and assessing race-based traumatic stress. *The Counseling Psychologist, 35*(1), 13–105. https://doi.org/10.1177/0011000006292033

Carter, R. T., & Forsyth, J. (2010). Reactions to racial discrimination: Emotional stress and help-seeking behaviors. *Psychological Trauma: Theory, Research, Practice, and Policy, 2*(3), 183–191. https://doi.org/http://dx.doi.org/10.1037/a0020102

Cauce, A. M., Domenech-Rodríguez, M., Paradise, M., Cochran, B. N., Shea, J. M., Srebnik, D., & Baydar, N. (2002). Cultural and contextual influences in mental health help seeking: A focus on ethnic minority youth. *Journal of Consulting and Clinical Psychology, 70*(1), 44–55. https://doi.org/10.1037//0022-006x.70.1.44

Chavez-Dueñas, N. Y., Adames, H. Y., Perez-Chavez, J. G., & Salas, S. P. (2019). Healing ethno-racial trauma in Latinx immigrant communities: Cultivating hope, resistance, and action. *American Psychologist, 74*(1), 49–62. https://doi.org/http://dx.doi.org/10.1037/amp0000289

Christopher, J. C. (1999). Situating psychological well-being: Exploring the cultural roots of its theory and research. *Journal of Counseling & Development, 77*(2), 141–152. https://doi.org/http://dx.doi.org/10.1002/j.1556-6676.1999.tb02434.x

Cohen, J. A., Mannarino, A. P., & Deblinger, E. (2017). *Treating trauma and traumatic grief in children and adolescents* (2nd ed.). Guilford Press.

Cook-Cottone, C. P., Kane, L. S., & Anderson, L. M. (2014). *The elements of counseling children and adolescents*. Springer Publishing Company.

Copeland, W. E., Shanahan, L., Hinesley, J., Chan, R. F., Aberg, K. A., Fairbank, J. A., van den Oord, E. J. C. G., & Costello, E. J. (2018). Association of childhood trauma exposure with adult psychiatric disorders and functional outcomes. *JAMA Network Open, 1*(7), e184493–e184493. https://doi.org/10.1001/jamanetworkopen.2018.4493

Corrigan, P. (2004). How stigma interferes with mental health care. *American Psychologist, 59*(7), 614–625. https://doi.org/http://dx.doi.org/10.1037/0003-066X.59.7.614

Cuffe, S. P., Moore, C. G., & McKeown, R. E. (2005). Prevalence and correlates of ADHD symptoms in the national health interview survey. *Journal of Attention Disorders, 9*(2), 392–401. https://doi.org/10.1177/1087054705280413

de Arellano, M. A., & Danielson, C. K. (2008). Assessment of trauma history and trauma-related problems in ethnic minority child populations: An INFORMED approach. *Cognitive and Behavioral Practice, 15*(1), 53–66. https://doi.org/https://doi.org/10.1016/j.cbpra.2006.09.008

Department of Health and Human Services. (2021). *U.S. Surgeon General issues advisory on youth mental health crisis further exposed by COVID-19 pandemic.* https://www.hhs.gov/sites/default/files/surgeon-general-youth-mental-health-advisory.pdf

Ebigbo, P. O., Lekwas, E. C., & Chukwunenyem, N. F. (2014). Brain fag: New perspectives from case observations. *Transcultural Psychiatry, 52*(3), 311–330. https://doi.org/10.1177/1363461514557064

El-Islam, M. F. (2008). Arab culture and mental health care. *Transcultural Psychiatry, 45*(4), 671–682. https://doi.org/10.1177/1363461508100788

Felitti, V. J., Anda, R. F., Nordenberg, D., Williamson, D. F., Spitz, A. M., Edwards, V., Koss, M. P., & Marks, J. S. (1998). Relationship of childhood abuse and household dysfunction to many of the leading causes of death in adults: The Adverse Childhood Experiences (ACE) Study. *American Journal of Preventive Medicine, 14*(4), 245–258. https://doi.org/https://doi.org/10.1016/S0749-3797(98)00017-8

Garb, H. N. (2021). Race bias and gender bias in the diagnosis of psychological disorders. *Clinical Psychology Review, 90*, 102087. https://doi.org/https://doi.org/10.1016/j.cpr.2021.102087

Garcia Coll, C., Lamberty, G., Jenkins, R., McAdoo, H. P., Crnic, K., Wasik, B. H., & Garcia, H. V. (1996). An integrative model for the study of developmental competencies in minority children. *Child Development, 67*(5), 1891–1914. http://www.jstor.org/stable/1131600

Habib, M., & Labruna, V. (2011). Clinical considerations in assessing trauma and PTSD in adolescents. *Journal of Child & Adolescent Trauma, 4*(3), 198–216. https://doi.org/10.1080/19361521.2011.597684

Hinton, D. E., Hofmann, S. G., Orr, S. P., Pitman, R. K., Pollack, M. H., & Pole, N. (2010). A psychobiocultural model of orthostatic panic among Cambodian refugees: Flashbacks, catastrophic cognitions, and reduced orthostatic blood-pressure response. *Psychological Trauma: Theory, Research, Practice, and Policy, 2*(1), 63–70. https://doi.org/http://dx.doi.org/10.1037/a0018978

Hydén, M. (2014). The teller-focused interview: Interviewing as a relational practice. *Qualitative Social Work, 13*(6), 795–812. https://doi.org/10.1177/1473325013506247

Jones, J. M. (2009). Counseling with multicultural intentionality: The process of counseling and integrating client cultural variables. In J. M. Jones (Ed.), *The psychology of multiculturalism in the schools: A primer for practice, training, and research*. National Association of School Psychologists (pp. 191–213).

Kvale, S. (2006). Dominance through interviews and dialogues. *Journal of Qualitative Inquiry, 12*, 480–500. doi: 10.1177/1077800406286235.

Kisiel, C., Fehrenbach, T., Conradi, L., & Weil, L. (2021). Selecting and integrating trauma-informed assessment tools for children and adolescents. In Cassandra Kisiel, Tracy Fehrenbach, Lisa Conradi, and Lindsey Weil, *Trauma-informed assessment with children and adolescents: Strategies to support clinicians* (pp. 85–106). American Psychological Association, American Psychological Association. https://doi.org/http://dx.doi.org/10.1037/0000233-005

Kung, W. W., & Lu, P. C. (2008). How symptom manifestations affect help seeking for mental health problems among Chinese Americans. *Journal of Nervous and Mental Disease, 196*(1), 46–54. https://doi.org/10.1097/NMD.0b013e31815fa4f9

Lau, A. S., Garland, A. F., Yeh, M., McCabe, K. M., Wood, P. A., & Hough, R. L. (2004). Race/ethnicity and inter-informant agreement in assessing adolescent psychopathology. *Journal of Emotional and Behavioral Disorders, 12*(3), 145–156. https://doi.org/10.1177/10634266040120030201

Lewis-Fernández, R., Aggarwal, N. K., Hinton, L., Hinton, D. E., & Kirmayer, L. J. (2015). *DSM-5° handbook on the cultural formulation interview*. American Psychiatric Publishing.

Liang, J., Matheson, B. E., & Douglas, J. M. (2016). Mental health diagnostic considerations in racial/ethnic minority youth. *Journal of Child and Family Studies, 25*(6), 1926–1940. https://doi.org/10.1007/s10826-015-0351-z

Lopez, M. H., & Minushkin, S. (2008). *2008 national survey of Latinos:Hispanics see their situation in U.S. deteriorating; Oppose key immigration enforcement measures.* https://www.pewresearch.org/hispanic/2008/09/18/2008-national-survey-of-latinos-hispanics-see-their-situation-in-us-deteriorating-oppose-key-immigration-enforcement-measures/

Lyon, A. R., Ludwig, K. A., Stoep, A. V., Gudmundsen, G., & McCauley, E. (2013). Patterns and predictors of mental healthcare utilization in schools and other service sectors among adolescents at risk for depression. *School Mental Health, 5*(3), 155–165. https://doi.org/10.1007/s12310-012-9097-6

March, J. S., Parker, J. D. A., Sullivan, K., Stallings, P., & Conners, C. K. (1997). The Multidimensional Anxiety Scale for Children (MASC): Factor structure, reliability, and validity. *Journal of the American Academy of Child & Adolescent Psychiatry, 36*(4), 554–565. https://doi.org/https://doi.org/10.1097/00004583-199704000-00019

Markus, H. R., & Kitayama, S. (1991). Culture and the self: Implications for cognition, emotion and motivation. *Psychological Review, 988*(2), 224–253.

Minsky, S., Petti, T., Gara, M., Vega, W., Lu, W., & Kiely, G. (2006). Ethnicity and clinical psychiatric diagnosis in childhood. *Administration and Policy in Mental Health and Mental Health Services Research, 33*(5), 558–567. https://doi.org/10.1007/s10488-006-0069-8

Mzimkulu, K. G., & Simbayi, L. C. (2006). Perspectives and practices of Xhosa-speaking African traditional healers when managing psychosis. *International Journal of*

Disability, Development and Education, 53(4), 417–431. https://doi.org/10.1080/10349120601008563

Nader, K. (2007). Culture and the assessment of trauma in youths. In J. P. Wilson & C. S.-k. Tang (Eds.), *Cross-Cultural Assessment of Psychological Trauma and PTSD* (pp. 169–196). Springer US. https://doi.org/10.1007/978-0-387-70990-1_8

Nader, K. (2008). *Understanding and assessing trauma in children and adoescents: Measures, methods, and youth in context.* Routledge.

Neblett, E. W., Jr. (2019). Racism and health: Challenges and future directions in behavioral and psychological research. *Cultural Diversity and Ethnic Minority Psychology, 25*(1), 12–20. https://doi.org/10.1037/cdp0000253

The National Child Traumatic Stress Network. (2021). *About child trauma.* Retrieved September 17, 2021, from https://www.nctsn.org/what-is-child-trauma/about-child-trauma

Pham, A. V., Goforth, A. N., Chun, H., Castro-Olivo, S., & Costa, A. (2017). Acculturation and help-seeking behavior in consultation: A sociocultural framework for mental health service. *Journal of Educational and Psychological Consultation, 27*(3), 271–288. https://doi.org/10.1080/10474412.2017.1287574

Roberts, R. E., Roberts, C. R., & Xing, Y. (2006). Prevalence of youth-reported DSM-IV psychiatric disorders among African, European, and Mexican American adolescents. *Journal of the American Academy of Child & Adolescent Psychiatry, 45*(11), 1329–1337. https://doi.org/10.1097/01.chi.0000235076.25038.81

Rossen, E. (2018, November). Creating trauma-informed individualized education programs: Integration of ACEs into the development of IEPs for students through grade 12. *Children, Youth, and Families News.* Retrieved from: https://www.apa.org/pi/families/resources/newsletter/2018/11/trauma-teaching

Saigh, P. A., Yasik, A. E., Oberfield, R. A., Green, B. L., Halamandaris, P. V., Rubenstein, H., Nester, J., Resko, J., Hetz, B., & McHugh, M. (2000). The children's PTSD inventory: Development and reliability. *Journal of Traumatic Stress, 13*(3), 369–380.

Sanchez, A. L., Comer, J. S., & LaRoche, M. (2021). Enhancing the responsiveness of family-based CBT through culturally informed case conceptualization and treatment planning. *Cognitive and Behavioral Practice, 29*(4), 750–770. https://doi.org/https://doi.org/10.1016/j.cbpra.2021.04.003

Squires, J., Twombly, E., Bricker, D. D., & Potter, L. (2009). *ASQ-3 user's guide.* Paul H. Brookes Publishing Company.

Steinberg, A. M., Brymer, M. J., Decker, K. B., & Pynoos, R. S. (2004). The University of California at Los Angeles post-traumatic stress disorder reaction index. *Current Psychiatry Reports, 6*(2), 96–100.

Sullivan, A. L. (2017). Wading through quicksand: Making sense of minority disproportionality in identification of emotional disturbance. *Behavioral Disorders, 43*(1), 244–252. https://doi.org/http://dx.doi.org/10.1177/0198742917732360

Sullivan, A. L., & Simonson, G. R. (2016). A systematic review of school-based social-emotional interventions for refugee and war-traumatized youth. *Review of Educational Research, 86*(2), 503–530. https://doi.org/10.3102/0034654315609419

Sun, S., Hoyt, W. T., Brockberg, D., Lam, J., & Tiwari, D. (2016). Acculturation and enculturation as predictors of psychological help-seeking attitudes (HSAs) among racial and ethnic minorities: A meta-analytic investigation. *Journal of Counseling Psychology, 63*(6), 617–632. https://doi.org/http://dx.doi.org/10.1037/cou0000172

Tishelman, A. C., Haney, P., O'Brien, J. G., & Blaustein, M. E. (2010). A framework for school-based psychological evaluations: Utilizing a "trauma lens." *Journal of Child and Adolescent Trauma, 3*(4), 279–302. https://doi.org/http://dx.doi.org/10.1080/19361521.2010.523062

Todd-Bazemore, B. (1999). Cultural issues in psychopharmacology: Integrating medication treatment with Lakota Sioux traditions. *Journal of Clinical Psychology in Medical Settings, 6,* 139–150. https://doi.org/10.1023/a:1026211515879

Trimble, J. E. (2010). The virtues of cultural resonance, competence, and relational collaboration with Native American Indian communities: A synthesis of the counseling and psychotherapy literature. *The Counseling Psychologist, 38*(2), 243–256. https://doi.org/10.1177/0011000009344348

van de Vijver, F. J. R., & Poortinga, Y. H. (2020). Dealing with methodological pitfalls in cross-cultural studies of stress. In T. Ringeisen, P. Genkova, & F. T. L. Leong (Eds.), *Handbuch Stress und Kultur: Interkulturelle und kulturvergleichende Perspektiven* (pp. 1–19). Springer Fachmedien Wiesbaden. https://doi.org/10.1007/978-3-658-27825-0_2-1

Varas-Díaz, N., & Serrano-García, I. (2003). The challenge of a positive self-image in a colonial context: A psychology of liberation for the Puerto Rican experience. *American Journal of Community Psychology, 31*(1–2), 103–115. https://doi.org/http://dx.doi.org/10.1023/A:1023078721414

Woolgar, F., Garfield, H., Dalgleish, T., & Meiser-Stedman, R. (2021). Systematic review and meta-analysis: Prevalence of posttraumatic stress disorder in trauma-exposed preschool-aged children. *Journal of the American Academy of Child & Adolescent Psychiatry.* Advance online publication. https://doi.org/http://dx.doi.org/10.1016/j.jaac.2021.05.026

CHAPTER 8

Abreu, R. L., & Kenny, M. C. (2018). Cyberbullying and LGBTQ youth: A systematic literature review and recommendations for prevention and intervention. *Journal of Child & Adolescent Trauma, 11*(1), 81–97. https://doi.org/10.1007/s40653-017-0175-7

Anyon, Y., Zhang, D., & Hazel, C. (2016). Race, exclusionary discipline, and connectedness to adults in secondary schools. *American Journal of Community Psychology, 57*(3–4), 342–352. https://doi.org/https://doi.org/10.1002/ajcp.12061

Askew, K., Beverly, M. G., & Jay, M. L. (2012). Aligning collaborative and culturally responsive evaluation approaches. *Evaluation and Program Planning, 35*(4), 552–557. https://doi.org/https://doi.org/10.1016/j.evalprogplan.2011.12.011

Avalos, B. (2011). Teacher professional development in *Teaching and Teacher Education* over ten years. *Teaching and Teacher Education, 27*(1), 10–20. https://doi.org/https://doi.org/10.1016/j.tate.2010.08.007

Battistich, V., Schaps, E., Watson, M., Solomon, D., & Lewis, C. (2000). Effects of the Child Development Project on students' drug use and other problem behaviors. *Journal of Primary Prevention, 21*(1), 75–99. https://doi.org/10.1023/A:1007057414994

Bear, G. G., Gaskins, C., Blank, J., & Chen, F. F. (2011). Delaware School Climate Survey—Student: Its factor structure, concurrent validity, and reliability. *Journal of School Psychology*, *49*(2), 157–174. https://doi.org/https://doi.org/10.1016/j.jsp.2011.01.001

Berkowitz, R., Moore, H., Astor, R. A., & Benbenishty, R. (2017). A research synthesis of the associations between socioeconomic background, inequality, school climate, and academic achievement. *Review of Educational Research*, *87*(2), 425–469. https://doi.org/10.3102/0034654316669821

Birt, L., Scott, S., Cavers, D., Campbell, C., & Walter, F. (2016). Member checking: A tool to enhance trustworthiness or merely a nod to validation? *Qualitative Health Research*, *26*(13), 1802–1811. https://doi.org/10.1177/1049732316654870

Blitz, L. V., Yull, D., & Clauhs, M. (2016). Bringing sanctuary to school: Assessing school climate as a foundation for culturally responsive trauma-informed approaches for urban schools. *Urban Education*, *55*(1), 95–124. https://doi.org/10.1177/004208591.6651323

Brand, S., Felner, R., Shim, M., Seitsinger, A., & Dumas, T. (2003). Middle school improvement and reform: Development and validation of a school-level assessment of climate, cultural pluralism, and school safety. *Journal of Educational Psychology*, *95*(3), 570–588. https://doi.org/http://dx.doi.org/10.1037/0022-0663.95.3.570

Bronfenbrenner, U. (2005). Ecological systems theory. In U. Bronfenbrenner (Ed.), *Making human beings human: Bioecological perspectives on human development* (pp. 106–167). Sage Publications.

Byrd, C. M. (2015). The associations of intergroup interactions and school racial socialization with academic motivation. *The Journal of Educational Research*, *108*(1), 10–21. https://doi.org/10.1080/00220671.2013.831803

Byrd, C. M., & Chavous, T. (2011). Racial identity, school racial climate, and school intrinsic motivation among African American youth: The importance of person–context congruence. *Journal of Research on Adolescence*, *21*(4), 849–860. https://doi.org/https://doi.org/10.1111/j.1532-7795.2011.00743.x

Centers for Disease Control and Prevention. (2009). *School connectedness: Strategies for increasing protective factors among youth*. U.S. Department of Health and Human Services. https://www.cdc.gov/healthyyouth/protective/pdf/connectedness.pdf

Chilisa, B. (2020). *Indigenous Research Methodologies*. Sage.

Chun, H., Marin, M. R., Schwartz, J. P., Pham, A., & Castro-Olivo, S. M. (2016). Psychosociocultural structural model of college success among Latina/o students in Hispanic-serving institutions. *Journal of Diversity in Higher Education*, *9*(4), 385–400.

Cohen, J., McCabe, L., Michelli, N. M., & Pickeral, T. (2009). School climate: Research, policy, practice, and teacher education. *Teachers College Record*, *111*(1), 180–213.

Daily, S. M., Mann, M. J., Kristjansson, A. L., Smith, M. L., & Zullig, K. J. (2019). School climate and academic achievement in middle and high school students. *Journal of School Health*, *89*(3), 173–180. https://doi.org/https://doi.org/10.1111/josh.12726

Daily, S. M., Mann, M. J., Lilly, C. L., Dyer, A. M., Smith, M. L., & Kristjansson, A. L. (2020). School climate as an intervention to reduce academic failure and educate the whole child: A longitudinal study. *Journal of School Health*, *90*(3), 182–193. https://doi.org/https://doi.org/10.1111/josh.12863

Darling-Hammond, L., & Cook-Harvey, C. M. (2018). *Educating the whole child: Improving school climate to support student success*. Learning Policy Institute. https://learningpolicyinstitute.org/sites/default/files/product-files/Educating_Who le_Child_REPORT.pdf

Demirtas-Zorbaz, S., Akin-Arikan, C., & Terzi, R. (2021). Does school climate that includes students' views deliver academic achievement? A multilevel meta-analysis. *School Effectiveness and School Improvement, 32*(4), 1–21. https://doi.org/10.1080/ 09243453.2021.1920432

Durlak, J. A., Weissberg, R. P., Dymnicki, A. B., Taylor, R. D., & Schellinger, K. B. (2011). The impact of enhancing students' social and emotional learning: A meta-analysis of school-based universal interventions. *Child Development, 82*(1), 405–432. https:// doi.org/10.1111/j.1467-8624.2010.01564.x

Eaton, A. A., & McGlynn, C. (2020). The psychology of nonconsensual porn: Understanding and addressing a growing form of sexual violence. *Policy Insights from the Behavioral and Brain Sciences, 7*(2), 190–197.

Eugene, D. R., Du, X., & Kim, Y. K. (2021). School climate and peer victimization among adolescents: A moderated mediation model of school connectedness and parental involvement. *Children and Youth Services Review, 121*, Article 105854. https://doi. org/https://doi.org/10.1016/j.childyouth.2020.105854

Gay, G. (2018). *Culturally responsive teaching: Theory, research, and practice*. Teachers College Press.

Gregory, A., Cornell, D., Fan, X., Sheras, P., Shih, T.-H., & Huang, F. (2010). Authoritative school discipline: High school practices associated with lower bullying and victimization. *Journal of Educational Psychology, 102*(2), 483–496. https://doi.org/http:// dx.doi.org/10.1037/a0018562

Hamm, M. P., Newton, A. S., Chisholm, A., Shulhan, J., Milne, A., Sundar, P., Ennis, H., Scott, S. D., & Hartling, L. (2015). Prevalence and effect of cyberbullying on children and young people: A scoping review of social media studies. *JAMA Pediatrics, 169*(8), 770–777. https://doi.org/10.1001/jamapediatrics.2015.0944

Hinduja, S., & Patchin, J. W. (2019). Connecting adolescent suicide to the severity of bullying and cyberbullying. *Journal of School Violence, 18*(3), 333–346. https://doi. org/10.1080/15388220.2018.1492417

Huang, S.-T., & Vidourek, R. A. (2019). Bullying victimization among Asian-American youth: A review of the literature. *International Journal of Bullying Prevention, 1*(3), 187–204. https://doi.org/10.1007/s42380-019-00029-3

Iowa City Community School District. (2021). *2021–22 ICCSD School Climate Survey-Students*. https://www.iowacityschools.org/Page/1130

Knoff, H. M. (2000). Organizational development and strategic planning for the millennium: A blueprint toward effective school discipline, safety, and crisis prevention. *Psychology in the Schools, 37*(1), 17–32. https://doi.org/https://doi.org/10.1002/ (SICI)1520-6807(200001)37:1<17::AID-PITS3>3.0.CO;2-K

Koth, C. W., Bradshaw, C. P., & Leaf, P. J. (2008). A multilevel study of predictors of student perceptions of school climate: The effect of classroom-level factors. *Journal of Educational Psychology, 100*(1), 96–104. https://doi.org/http://dx.doi.org/10.1037/ 0022-0663.100.1.96

Kwong, D., & Davis, J. R. (2015). School climate for academic success: A multilevel analysis of school climate and student outcomes. *Journal of Research in Education, 25*(2), 68–81.

La Salle, T. P., McCoach, D. B., & Meyers, J. (2021). Examining measurement invariance and perceptions of school climate across gender and race and ethnicity. *Journal of Psychoeducational Assessment, 39*(7), 800–815. https://doi.org/10.1177/0734282921 1023717

La Salle, T. P., Meyers, J., Varjas, K., & Roach, A. (2015). A cultural-ecological model of school climate. *International Journal of School & Educational Psychology, 3*(3), 157–166. https://doi.org/10.1080/21683603.2015.1047550

Ladson-Billings, G. (2014). Culturally relevant pedagogy 2.0: A.K.A. the Remix. *Harvard Educational Review, 84*(1), 74–84,135.

Ladson-Billings, G., & Tate, W. F. (1995). Toward a critical race theory of education. *Teachers College Record, 97*(1), 47–68.

Lee, T., Cornell, D., Gregory, A., & Fan, X. (2011). High suspension schools and dropout rates for Black and White students. *Education and Treatment of Children, 34*(2), 167–192. http://www.jstor.org/stable/42900581

Mattison, E., & Aber, M. S. (2007). Closing the achievement gap: The association of racial climate with achievement and behavioral outcomes. *American Journal of Community Psychology, 40*(1–2), 1–12. https://doi.org/https://doi.org/10.1007/s10 464-007-9128-x

McCarty, T. L., & Lee, T. S. (2014). Critical culturally sustaining/revitalizing pedagogy and indigenous education sovereignty. *Harvard Educational Review, 84*(1), 101–124.

McNeely, C. A., Nonnemaker, J. M., & Blum, R. W. (2002). Promoting school connectedness: Evidence from the national longitudinal study of adolescent health. *Journal of School Health, 72*(4), 138–146. https://doi.org/10.1111/j.1746-1561.2002.tb06533.x

National Association of School Psychologists. (2021). NASP Condemns Violence Against AAPI Communities, Urges Schools to Reinforce Students' Safety, Well-Being. Retrieved from: https://www.nasponline.org/about-school-psychology/media-room/press-relea ses/nasp-condemns-violence-against-aapi-communities-urges-schools-to-reinforce- students-safety-well-being

National Center on Safe Supportive Learning Environments. (2021). *ED School Climate Surveys (EDSCLS)*. Retrieved December 17, 2021, fromhttps://safesupportivelearn ing.ed.gov/edscls

National School Climate Center. (2021a). *Measuring school climate*. https://schoolclim ate.org/services/measuring-school-climate-csci/csci-report/

National School Climate Center. (2021b). *What is school climate and why is it important?* https://schoolclimate.org/school-climate/

Olweus, D., & Limber, S. P. (2010). Bullying in school: Evaluation and dissemination of the Olweus Bullying Prevention Program. *American Journal of Orthopsychiatry, 80*(1), 124–134. https://doi.org/http://dx.doi.org/10.1111/j.1939-0025.2010.01015.x

Osher, D., Fisher, D., Amos, L., Katz, J., Dwyer, K., Duffey, T., & Colombi, G. D. (2015). *Addressing the root causes of disparities in school discipline: An educator's action planning guide*. National Center on Safe Supportive Learning Environments. https://saf esupportivelearning.ed.gov/sites/default/files/15-1547%20NCSSLE%20Root%20 Causes%20Guide%20FINAL02%20mb.pdf

Parris, L., Neves, J. R., & La Salle, T. (2018). School climate perceptions of ethnically diverse students: Does school diversity matter? *School Psychology International, 39*(6), 625–645. https://doi.org/10.1177/0143034318798419

Pham, A. V. (2014). Navigating social networking and social media in school psychology: Ethical and professional considerations in training programs. *Psychology in the Schools, 51*(7), 767–778. https://doi.org/10.1002/pits.21774

Ross, R. (2013). School climate and equity. In T. Dary & T. Pickeral (Eds.), *School climate practices for implementation and sustainability. A school climate practice brief, Number 1*. National School Climate Center.

Sabol, T. J., & Pianta, R. C. (2012). Recent trends in research on teacher–child relationships. *Attachment & Human Development, 14*(3), 213–231. https://doi.org/10.1080/14616734.2012.672262

Schneider, S. H., & Duran, L. (2010). School climate in middle schools: A cultural perspective. *Journal of Character Education, 8*(2), 25–37.

Segool, N. K., Goforth, A. N., Bowman, N., & Pham, A. (2016). Social networking practices in school psychology: Have moral panic concerns been overstated? *Journal of Applied School Psychology, 32*(1), 66–81. https://doi.org/10.1080/15377903.2015.1121194

Seldin, M., & Yanez, C. (2019). Student reports of bullying: Results from the 2017 School Crime Supplement to the National Crime Victimization Survey. NCES 2019-054. National Center for Education Statistics.

Selkie, E. M., Fales, J. L., & Moreno, M. A. (2016). Cyberbullying prevalence among US middle and high school–aged adolescents: A systematic review and quality assessment. *Journal of Adolescent Health, 58*(2), 125–133. https://doi.org/https://doi.org/10.1016/j.jadohealth.2015.09.026

Skiba, R., Simmons, A. B., Peterson, R., McKelvey, J., Forde, S., & Gallini, S. (2004). Beyond guns, drugs and gangs. *Journal of School Violence, 3*(2–3), 149–171. https://doi.org/10.1300/J202v03n02_09

Smith, L. V., Wang, M.-T., & Hill, D. J. (2020). Black youths' perceptions of school cultural pluralism, school climate and the mediating role of racial identity. *Journal of School Psychology, 83*, 50–65. https://doi.org/https://doi.org/10.1016/j.jsp.2020.09.002

Spaulding, D. T. (2013). *Program evaluation in practice: Core concepts and examples for discussion and analysis*. John Wiley & Sons, Incorporated.

Stone, A. L., & Carlisle, S. K. (2017). Racial bullying and adolescent substance use: An examination of school-attending young adolescents in the United States. *Journal of Ethnicity in Substance Abuse, 16*(1), 23–42. https://doi.org/10.1080/15332640.2015.1095666

Suldo, S. M., McMahan, M. M., Chappel, A. M., & Loker, T. (2012). Relationships between perceived school climate and adolescent mental health across genders. *School Mental Health, 4*(2), 69–80.

Tanrikulu, I. (2018). Cyberbullying prevention and intervention programs in schools: A systematic review. *School Psychology International, 39*(1), 74–91.

Thapa, A., Cohen, J., Guffey, S., & Higgins-D'Alessandro, A. (2013). A review of school climate research. *Review of Educational Research, 83*(3), 357–385. https://doi.org/10.3102/0034654313483907

Uline, C., & Tschannen-Moran, M. (2008). The walls speak: The interplay of quality facilities, school climate, and student achievement. *Journal of Educational Administration, 46*(1), 55–73. https://doi.org/10.1108/09578230810849817

Voight, A., Hanson, T., O'Malley, M., & Adekanye, L. (2015). The racial school climate gap: Within-school disparities in students' experiences of safety, support, and connectedness. *American Journal of Community Psychology, 56*(3), 252–267. https://doi.org/10.1007/s10464-015-9751-x

Wang, M.-T., & Degol, J. L. (2016). School climate: A review of the construct, measurement, and impact on student outcomes. *Educational Psychology Review, 28*(2), 315–352.

Wang, M.-T., Selman, R. L., Dishion, T. J., & Stormshak, E. A. (2010). A tobit regression analysis of the covariation between middle school students' perceived school climate and behavioral problems. *Journal of Research on Adolescence, 20*(2), 274–286. https://doi.org/https://doi.org/10.1111/j.1532-7795.2010.00648.x

CHAPTER 9

Algozzine, B., & Algozzine, K. (2009). Facilitating academic achievement through schoolwide positive behavior support. In Wayne Sailor, Glen Dunlap, George Sugai, and Rob Horner, *Handbook of positive behavior support* (pp. 521–550). Springer.

Bal, A. (2015). *Culturally responsive positive behavioral interventions and supports.* WCER Working Paper. Wisconsin Center for Education Research.

Barrera, M., & Castro, F. G. (2006). A heuristic framework for the cultural adaptation of interventions. *Clinical Psychology: Science and Practice, 13*(4), 311–316. https://doi.org/10.1111/j.1468-2850.2006.00043.x

Bernal, G., Bonilla, J., & Bellido, C. (1995). Ecological validity and cultural sensitivity for outcome research: Issues for the cultural adaptation and development of psychosocial treatments with Hispanics. *Journal of Abnormal Child Psychology, 23*(1), 67–82. https://doi.org/10.1007/BF01447045

Bernal, G., Jiménez-Chafey, M. I., & Domenech Rodríguez, M. M. (2009). Cultural adaptation of treatments: A resource for considering culture in evidence-based practice. *Professional Psychology: Research and Practice, 40*(4), 361–368. https://doi.org/10.1037/a0016401

Blanco-Vega, C. O., Castro-Olivo, S. M., & Merrell, K. W. (2007). Social–emotional needs of Latino immigrant adolescents: A sociocultural model for development and implementation of culturally specific interventions. *Journal of Latinos and Education, 7*(1), 43–61. https://doi.org/10.1080/15348430701693390

Bradshaw, C. P., Mitchell, M. M., O'Brennan, L. M., & Leaf, P. J. (2010). Multilevel exploration of factors contributing to the overrepresentation of black students in office disciplinary referrals. *Journal of Educational Psychology, 102*(2), 508–520. https://doi.org/10.1037/a0018450

Carver-Thomas, D., & Darling-Hammond, L. (2017). *Teacher turnover: Why it matters and what we can do about it.* Learning Policy Institute.

Castro, F. G., Barrera, M., & Martinez, C. R. (2004). The cultural adaptation of prevention interventions: Resolving tensions between fidelity and fit. *Prevention Science, 5*(1), 41–45. https://doi.org/10.1023/B:PREV.0000013980.12412.cd

Castro, F. G., & Yasui, M. (2017). Advances in EBI development for diverse populations: Towards a science of intervention adaptation. *Prevention Science, 18*(6), 623–629. https://doi.org/10.1007/s11121-017-0809-x

Castro-Olivo, S. M., & Merrell, K. W. (2012). Validating cultural adaptations of a school-based social-emotional learning programme for use with Latino immigrant adolescents. *Advances in School Mental Health Promotion, 5*(2), 78–92. https://doi.org/10.1080/1754730X.2012.689193

Fadus, M. C., Valadez, E. A., Bryant, B. E., Garcia, A. M., Neelon, B., Tomko, R. L., & Squeglia, L. M. (2021). Racial disparities in elementary school disciplinary actions: Findings from the ABCD study. *Journal of the American Academy of Child & Adolescent Psychiatry, 60*(8), 998–1009. https://doi.org/10.1016/j.jaac.2020.11.017

Farinde-Wu, A., Glover, C. P., & Williams, N. N. (2017). It's not hard work; it's heart work: Strategies of effective, award-winning culturally responsive teachers. *The Urban Review, 49*(2), 279–299. https://doi.org/10.1007/s11256-017-0401-5

Fryberg, S. A., Troop-Gordon, W., D'Arrisso, A., Flores, H., Ponizovskiy, V., Ranney, J. D., . . . & Burack, J. A. (2013). Cultural mismatch and the education of Aboriginal youths: The interplay of cultural identities and teacher ratings. *Developmental Psychology, 49*(1), 72–79. doi: 10.1037/a0029056

Gay, G. (2002). Preparing for culturally responsive teaching. *Journal of Teacher Education, 53*(2), 106–116. https://doi.org/10.1177/0022487102053002003

Gilliam, W. S., Maupin, A. N., Reyes, C. R., Accavitti, M., & Shic, F. (2016). Do early educators' implicit biases regarding sex and race relate to behavior expectations and recommendations of preschool expulsions and suspensions? *Yale University Child Study Center, 9*(28), 1–16.

Girvan, E. J., McIntosh, K., & Smolkowski, K. (2019). Tail, tusk, and trunk: What different metrics reveal about racial disproportionality in school discipline. *Educational Psychologist, 54*(1), 40–59. https://doi.org/10.1080/00461520.2018.1537125

Hernández Finch, M. E. (2012). Special considerations with response to intervention and instruction for students with diverse backgrounds. *Psychology in the Schools, 49*(3), 285–296. https://doi.org/10.1002/pits.21597

Hollie, S. (2011). *Culturally and linguistically responsive teaching and learning: Classroom practices for student success.* Shell Publications.

Hollie, S. (2019). Branding culturally relevant teaching. *Teacher Education Quarterly, 46*(4), 31–52. https://www.jstor.org/stable/26841575

Hoover, J. J., & Patton, J. R. (2017). *IEPs for ELs: And other diverse learners.* Corwin Press.

Hoover, J. J., & Soltero-González, L. (2018). Educator preparation for developing culturally and linguistically responsive MTSS in rural community elementary schools. *Teacher Education and Special Education, 41*(3), 188–202. https://doi.org/10.1177/0888406417753689

Horner, R. H., Todd, A. W., Lewis-Palmer, T., Irvin, L. K., Sugai, G., & Boland, J. B. (2004). The School-Wide Evaluation Tool (SET): A research instrument for assessing schoolwide positive behavior support. *Journal of Positive Behavior Interventions, 6*(1), 3–12. https://doi.org/10.1177/10983007040060010201

Hwang, W.-C. (2009). The formative method for adapting psychotherapy (FMAP): A community-based developmental approach to culturally adapting therapy. *Professional Psychology: Research and Practice, 40*(4), 369–377. https://doi.org/10.1037/a0016240.

Individuals with Disabilities Education Improvement Act of 2004, Pub. L. No. 108-446, 118 Stat. 2647 (2004).

Irvin, M. J., Byun, S. Y., Meece, J. L., Reed, K. S., & Farmer, T. W. (2016). School characteristics and experiences of African American, Hispanic/Latino, and Native American youth in rural communities: Relation to educational aspirations. *Peabody Journal of Education, 91*(2), 176–202. https://doi.org/10.1080/0161956X.2016.1151739

Kelly, J. A., Heckman, T. G., Stevenson, L. Y., Williams, P. N., et al. (2000). Transfer of research-based HIV prevention interventions to community service providers: Fidelity and adaptation. *AIDS Education and Prevention, 12,* 87–98.

Klinger, J., & Soltero-Gonzalez, L. (2009). Culturally and linguistically responsive instruction for English language learners with learning disabilities. *Multiple Voices for Ethnically Diverse Exceptional Learners, 12,* 5–20.

Kratochwill, T. R. (2007). Preparing psychologists for evidence-based school practice: Lessons learned and challenges ahead. *American Psychologist, 62*(8), 829–843. https://doi.org/10.1037/0003-066X.62.8.829

Kumpfer, K., Magalhães, C., & Xie, J. (2017). Cultural adaptation and implementation of family evidence-based interventions with diverse populations. *Prevention Science, 18*(6), 649–659. https://doi.org/10.1007/s11121-016-0719-3

Lane, K. L., Kalberg, J. R., Bruhn, A. L., Driscoll, S. A., Wehby, J. H., & Elliott, S. N. (2009). Assessing social validity of school-wide positive behavior support plans: Evidence for the reliability and structure of the Primary Intervention Rating Scale. *School Psychology Review, 38*(1), 135–144.

Lau, A. S. (2006). Making the case for selective and directed cultural adaptations of evidence-based treatments: Examples from parent training. *Clinical Psychology: Science and Practice, 13*(4), 295–310. https://doi.org/10.1111/j.1468-2850.2006.00042.x

Leverson, M., Smith, K., McIntosh, K., Rose, J., & Pinkelman, S. (2021). PBIS cultural responsiveness field guide: Resources for trainers and coaches. Center on Positive Behavioral Interventions and Supports, University of Oregon. https://www.pbis.org/resource/pbis-cultural-responsiveness-field-guide-resources-for-trainers-and-coaches

Losen, D., Hodson, C., Keith II, M. A., Morrison, K., & Belway, S. (2015). *Are we closing the school discipline gap?* University of California, Los Angeles.

MacPherson, S. (2010). Teachers' collaborative conversations about culture: Negotiating decision making in intercultural teaching. *Journal of Teacher Education, 61*(3), 271–286.

McIntosh, K., Gion, C., & Bastable, E. (2018). *Do schools implementing SWPBIS have decreased racial and ethnic disproportionality in school discipline?* PBIS evaluation brief. OSEP National Technical Assistance Center on Positive Behavioral Interventions and Supports.

McIntosh, K., Girvan, E. J., Fairbanks Falcon, S., McDaniel, S. C., Smolkowski, K., Bastable, E., Santiago-Rosario, M. R., Izzard, S., Austin, S. C., Nese, R. N. T., & Baldy, T. S. (2021). Equity-focused PBIS approach reduces racial inequities in school discipline: A randomized controlled trial. *School Psychology, 36*(6), 433–444. https://doi.org/10.1037/spq0000466

McIntosh, K., Girvan, E. J., Horner, R. H., & Smolkowski, K. (2014). Education not incarceration: A conceptual model for reducing racial and ethnic disproportionality in school discipline. *Journal of Applied Research on Children, 5*(2), 1–22.

McKleroy, V. S., Galbraith, J. S., Cummings, B., Jones, P., Harshbarger, C., Collins, C., . . . & ADAPT Team. (2006). Adapting evidence-based behavioral interventions for new settings and target populations. *AIDS Education & Prevention, 18*(supp.), 59–73.

Muldrew, A. C., & Miller, F. G. (2021). Examining the effects of the personal matrix activity with diverse students. *Psychology in the Schools, 58*(3), 515–533. https://doi.org/10.1002/pits.22461

Murray, L. K., Dorsey, S., Skavenski, S., Kasoma, M., Imasiku, M., Bolton, P., . . . & Cohen, J. A. (2013). Identification, modification, and implementation of an evidence-based psychotherapy for children in a low-income country: The use of TF-CBT in Zambia. *International Journal of Mental Health Systems, 7*(1), 1–12. https://doi.org/10.1186/1752-4458-7-24

Nese, R. N. T., & McIntosh, K. (2016). Do school-wide positive behavioral interventions and supports, not exclusionary discipline practices. In B. G. Cook, M. Tankersley, & T. J. Landrum (Eds.), *Advances in learning and behavioral disabilities* (pp. 175–196). Emerald Group Publishing.

Nelson, J. R., Benner, G. J., Lane, K., & Smith, B. W. (2004). Academic achievement of K-12 students with emotional and behavioral disorders. *Exceptional Children, 71*(1), 59–73. https://doi.org/10.1177/001440290407100110

Nicolas, G., Arntz, D. L., Hirsch, B., & Schmiedigen, A. (2009). Cultural adaptation of a group treatment for Haitian American adolescents. *Professional Psychology: Research and Practice, 40*(4), 378–384. https://doi.org/10.1037/a0016307

Orosco, M. J., & Klingner, J. (2010). One school's implementation of RTI with English language learners: "Referring into RTI." *Journal of Learning Disabilities, 43*(3), 269–288. https://doi.org/10.1177/0022219409355474

OSEP Technical Assistance Center on Positive Behavioral Interventions and Supports. (2015, October). *Positive behavioral interventions and supports (PBIS) implementation blueprint: Part 1—Foundations and supporting information.* Eugene: University of Oregon. Retrieved from http://www.pbis.org

Pham, A. V., N. Goforth, A. N., Aguilar, L., Burt, I., Bastian, R., & Diaków, D. M. (2021). Dismantling systemic inequities in school psychology: Cultural humility as a foundational approach to social justice. *School Psychology Review*, 1–18. https://doi.org/10.1080/2372966X.2021.1941245

Pina, A. A., Polo, A. J., & Huey, S. J. (2019). Evidence-based psychosocial interventions for ethnic minority youth: The 10-year update. *Journal of Clinical Child & Adolescent Psychology, 48*(2), 179–202. https://doi.org/10.1080/15374416.2019.1567350

Resnicow, K., Soler, R., Braithwaite, R. L., Ahluwalia, J. S., & Butler, J. (2000). Cultural sensitivity in substance use prevention. *Journal of Community Psychology, 28*(3), 271–290. https://doi.org/10.1002/(SICI)1520-6629(200005)28:3<271::AID-JCOP4>3.0.CO;2-I

Rivas-Drake, D., Seaton, E. K., Markstrom, C., Quintana, S., Syed, M., Lee, R. M., . . . & Ethnic and Racial Identity in the 21st Century Study Group. (2014). Ethnic and racial identity in adolescence: Implications for psychosocial, academic, and health outcomes. *Child Development, 85*(1), 40–57. https://doi.org/10.1111/cdev.12200

Sit, H. F., Ling, R., Lam, A. I. F., Chen, W., Latkin, C. A., & Hall, B. J. (2020). The cultural adaptation of Step-by-Step: An intervention to address depression among Chinese young adults. *Frontiers in Psychiatry, 11*, 650. https://doi.org/10.3389/fpsyt.2020.00650

Smith, C. O., Levine, D. W., Smith, E. P., Dumas, J., & Prinz, R. J. (2009). A developmental perspective of the relationship of racial–ethnic identity to self-construct, achievement, and behavior in African American children. *Cultural Diversity and Ethnic Minority Psychology, 15*(2), 145. https://doi.org/10.1037/a0015538

Smolkowski, K., Girvan, E. J., McIntosh, K., Nese, R. N., & Horner, R. H. (2016). Vulnerable decision points for disproportionate office discipline referrals: Comparisons of discipline for African American and White elementary school students. *Behavioral Disorders*, 41(4), 178–195. https://doi.org/10.17988/bedi-41-04-178-195.1

Stephens, N. M., Fryberg, S. A., Markus, H. R., Johnson, C. S., & Covarrubias, R. (2012). Unseen disadvantage: How American universities' focus on independence undermines the academic performance of first-generation college students. *Journal of Personality and Social Psychology*, 102(6), 1178–1197. https://doi.org/10.1037/a0027143

Sugai, G., & Horner, R. H. (2009). Responsiveness-to-intervention and school-wide positive behavior supports: Integration of multi-tiered system approaches. *Exceptionality*, 17(4), 223–237. https://doi.org/10.1080/09362830903235375

Sugai, G., O'Keeffe, B. V., & Fallon, L. M. (2012). A contextual consideration of culture and school-wide positive behavior support. *Journal of Positive Behavior Interventions*, 14(4), 197–208. https://doi.org/10.1177/1098300711426334

Sullivan, A. L., & Bal, A. (2013). Disproportionality in special education: Effects of individual and school variables on disability risk. *Exceptional Children*, 79(4), 475–494. https://doi.org/10.1177/001440291307900406

Vincent, C. G., Randall, C., Cartledge, G., Tobin, T. J., & Swain-Bradway, J. (2011). Toward a conceptual integration of cultural responsiveness and schoolwide positive behavior support. *Journal of Positive Behavior Interventions*, 13(4), 219–229. https://doi.org/10.1177/1098300711399765

Vincent, C. G., Swain-Bradway, J., Tobin, T. J., & May, S. (2011). Disciplinary referrals for culturally and linguistically diverse students with and without disabilities: Patterns resulting from school-wide positive behavior support. *Exceptionality*, 19(3), 175–190.

Zubieta, C., Lichtl, A., Trautman, K., Mentor, S., Cagliero, D., Mensa-Kwao, A., . . . & Kaiser, B. N. (2020). Perceived feasibility, acceptability, and cultural adaptation for a mental health intervention in rural Haiti. *Culture, Medicine, and Psychiatry*, 44(1), 110–134. https://doi.org/10.1007/s11013-019-09640-x

CHAPTER 10

Ahammed, S. (2010). Applying Qur'anic metaphors in counseling. *International Journal for the Advancement of Counselling*, 32(4), 248–255. https://doi.org/http://dx.doi.org/10.1007/s10447-010-9104-2

Alegria, M., Green, J. G., McLaughlin, K. A., & Loder, S. (2015). Dispartities in child and adolescent mental health and mental health services in the U.S. https://wtgrantfoundation.org/library/uploads/2015/09/Disparities-in-Child-and-Adolescent-Mental-Health.pdf

Allison, A. C., & Ferreira, R. J. (2017). Implementing Cognitive Behavioral Intervention for Trauma in Schools (CBITS) with Latino youth. *Child & Adolescent Social Work Journal*, 34(2), 181–189. https://doi.org/http://dx.doi.org/10.1007/s10560-016-0486-9

American Psychological Association. (2017). *Ethical principles of psychologists and code of conduct*.

American Psychological Association Working Group for Addressing Racial and Ethnic Disparities in Youth Mental Health. (2017). *Addressing the mental health needs of racial and ethnic minority youth: A guide for practitioners.* https://www.apa.org/pi/families/resources/mental-health-needs.pdf

Arredondo, P., Gallardo-Cooper, M., Delgado-Romero, E. A., & Zapata, A. L. (2014). *Culturally responsive counseling with Latinas/os.* American Counseling Association.

Beck, A. T., Epstein, N., Brown, G., & Steer, R. (1993). Beck Anxiety Inventory. *Journal of Consulting and Clinical Psychology.*

Beck, A. T., Epstein, N., Brown, G., & Steer, R. (1988). *Beck Anxiety Inventory* [Database record]. APA PsycTests. https://doi.org/10.1037/t02025-000

Berry, J. W. (2005). Acculturation: Living successfully in two cultures. *International Journal of Intercultural Relations, 29,* 697–712. https://doi.org/10.1016/j.ijintrel.2005.07.013

Brennan, C. (2013). Ethics in school counseling. In C. M. Jungers & J. Gregoire (Eds.), *Counseling ethics: Philosophical and professional foundations* (pp. 301–320). Springer.

Bronfenbrenner, U. (2005). Ecological systems theory. In U. Bronfenbrenner (Ed.), *Making human beings human: Bioecological perspectives on human development* (pp. 106–167). Sage Publications.

Chen, E. C., Budianto, L., & Wong, K. (2010). Professional school counselors as social justice advocates for undocumented immigrant students in group work. *The Journal for Specialists in Group Work, 35*(3), 255–261. https://doi.org/10.1080/01933 922.2010.492897 .

Cho, E. (2018). Ethical considerations for psychologists providing treatment to Arab Americans. *Ethics & Behavior, 28*(5), 347–369. https://doi.org/10.1080/10508 422.2018.1435282

Cohen, J. A., Mannarino, A. P., Berliner, L., & Deblinger, E. (2000). Trauma-focused cognitive behavioral therapy for children and adolescents: An empirical update. *Journal of Interpersonal Violence, 15*(11), 1202–1223. https://doi.org/10.1177/08862600001 5011007

Crenshaw, K. (1989). Demarginalizing the intersection of race and sex: A Black feminist critique of antidiscrimination doctrine. *University of Chicago Legal Forum, 1989*(1), 139–168.

Cunliffe, A. L. (2016). Republication of "On becoming a critically reflexive practitioner." *Journal of Management Education, 40*(6), 747–768. https://doi.org/10.1177/10525 62916674465

Danielson, M. L., Bitsko, R. H., Holbrook, J. R., Charania, S. N., Claussen, A. H., McKeown, R. E., Cuffe, S. P., Owens, J. S., Evans, S. W., Kubicek, L., & Flory, K. (2021). Community-based prevalence of externalizing and internalizing disorders among school-aged children and adolescents in four geographically dispersed school districts in the United States. *Child Psychiatry & Human Development, 52*(3), 500–514. https://doi.org/10.1007/s10578-020-01027-z

Day-Vines, N. L., Cluxton-Keller, F., Agorsor, C., Gubara, S., & Otabil, N. A. A. (2020). The multidimensional model of broaching behavior. *Journal of Counseling & Development, 98*(1), 107–118. https://doi.org/https://doi.org/10.1002/jcad.12304

Day-Vines, N. L., Wood, S. M., Grothaus, T., Craigen, L., Holman, A., Dotson-Blake, K., & Douglass, M. J. (2007). Broaching the subjects of race, ethnicity, and culture during the counseling process. *Journal of Counseling & Development, 85*(4), 401–409. https://doi.org/https://doi.org/10.1002/j.1556-6678.2007.tb00608.x

Diamond, G. S., Reis, B. F., Diamond, G. M., Siqueland, L., & Isaacs, L. (2002). Attachment-based family therapy for depressed adolescents: A treatment development study. *Journal of the American Academy of Child and Adolescent Psychiatry, 41*(10), 1190-1196. https://doi.org/10.1097/00004583-200210000-00008

Franco, D. (2018). Trauma without borders: The necessity for school-based interventions in treating unaccompanied refugee minors. *Child & Adolescent Social Work Journal, 35*(6), 551–565. https://doi.org/http://dx.doi.org/10.1007/s10560-018-0552-6

García, M. A. (2014). Society of Indian Psychologists' commentary on the APA Code of Ethics. *American Psychological Association.* Retrieved September 7, 2014, from https://www.apa.org/pi/oema/resources/communique/2014/12/indian-psychologists-ethics

Garcia Coll, C., Lamberty, G., Jenkins, R., McAdoo, H. P., Crnic, K., Wasik, B. H., & Garcia, H. V. (1996). An integrative model for the study of developmental competencies in minority children. *Child Development, 67*(5), 1891–1914. http://www.jstor.org/stable/1131600

Ginsburg, G. S., & Drake, K. L. (2002). School-based treatment for anxious African-American adolescents: A controlled pilot study. *Journal of the American Academy of Child and Adolescent Psychiatry, 41*(7), 768–775.

Goodkind, J. R., LaNoue, M. D., & Milford, J. (2010). Adaptation and implementation of cognitive behavioral intervention for trauma in schools with American Indian youth. *Journal of Clinical Child & Adolescent Psychology, 39*(6), 858–872. https://doi.org/10.1080/15374416.2010.517166

Goodman, R. (2001). Psychometric properties of the strengths and difficulties questionnaire. *Journal of the American Academy of Child & Adolescent Psychiatry, 40*(11), 1337–1345.

Hays, P. A. (2008). Making meaningful connections: Establishing respect and rapport. In P. A. Hays, *Addressing cultural complexities in practice: Assessment, diagnosis, and therapy* (2nd ed., pp. 85–101). American Psychological Association. https://doi.org/http://dx.doi.org/10.1037/11650-005

Hook, J. N., Davis, D., Owen, J., & DeBlaere, C. (2017). *Cultural humility: Engaging diverse identities in therapy.* American Psychological Association.

Huey, S. J., Jr., & Polo, A. J. (2008). Evidence-based psychosocial treatments for ethnic minority youth. *Journal of Clinical Child and Adolescent Psychology, 37*(1), 262–301. https://doi.org/10.1080/15374410701820174

Ibrahim, F. A., & Heuer, J. R. (2016). *Cutural and social justice counseling.* Springer.

Jones, J. (2015). *Culturally responsive interpersonal psychotherapy with children and adolescents.* John Wiley & Sons, Incorporated.

Kamphaus, R. W., & Reynolds, C. R. (2007). *Behavior Assessment System for Children—Second Edition (BASC-2): Behavioral and Emotional Screening System (BESS).* Pearson.

Kataoka, S., Novins, D. K., & DeCarlo Santiago, C. (2010). The practice of evidence-based treatments in ethnic minority youth. *Child and Adolescent Psychiatric Clinics of North America, 19*(4), 775–789. https://doi.org/http://dx.doi.org/10.1016/j.chc.2010.07.008

Killick, S., Curry, V., & Myles, P. (2016). The mighty metaphor: A collection of therapists' favourite metaphors and analogies. *The Cognitive Behaviour Therapist, 9,* Article e37. https://doi.org/10.1017/S1754470X16000210

Liang, J., Matheson, B. E., & Douglas, J. M. (2016). Mental health diagnostic considerations in racial/ethnic minority youth. *Journal of Child and Family Studies*, 25(6), 1926–1940. https://doi.org/10.1007/s10826-015-0351-z

Lim, T.-S. (2017). Verbal communication across cultures. In L. Chen (Ed.), *Intercultural Communication* (pp. 179–198). De Gruyter.

Liu, W. M., & Clay, D. L. (2002). Multicultural counseling competencies: Guidelines in working with children and adolescents. *Journal of Mental Health Counseling*, 24(2), 177.

Lorié, Á., Reinero, D. A., Phillips, M., Zhang, L., & Riess, H. (2017, 2017/03/01/). Culture and nonverbal expressions of empathy in clinical settings: A systematic review. *Patient Education and Counseling*, 100(3), 411–424. https://doi.org/https://doi.org/10.1016/j.pec.2016.09.018

McMahon, H. G., Mason, E. C. M., Daluga-Guenther, N., & Ruiz, A. (2014). An ecological model of professional school counseling. *Journal of Counseling & Development*, 92(4), 459–471. https://doi.org/https://doi.org/10.1002/j.1556-6676.2014.00172.x

Meléndez Guevara, A. M., Lindstrom Johnson, S., Elam, K., Hilley, C., McIntire, C., & Morris, K. (2021). Culturally responsive trauma-informed services: A multilevel perspective from practitioners serving Latinx children and families. *Community Mental Health Journal*, 57(2), 325–339. https://doi.org/10.1007/s10597-020-00651-2

Melhem, I., & Chemali, Z. (2014). Mental health of Arab Americans: Cultural considerations for excellence of care. In P. Ranna (Ed.), *The Massachusetts General Hospital textbook on diversity and cultural sensitivity in mental health* (pp. 3–30). Humana Press. https://doi.org/http://dx.doi.org/10.1007/978-1-4614-8918-4_1

Nagayama Hall, G. C. (2001). Psychotherapy research with ethnic minorities: Empirical, ethical, and conceptual issues. *Journal of Consulting and Clinical Psychology*, 69(3), 502–510.

Nagayama Hall, G. C., Berkman, E. T., Zane, N. W., Leong, F. T. L., Hwang, W.-C., Nezu, A. M., Nezu, C. M., Hong, J. J., Chu, J. P., & Huang, E. R. (2021). Reducing mental health disparities by increasing the personal relevance of interventions. *American Psychologist*, 76(1), 91–103. https://doi.org/http://dx.doi.org/10.1037/amp0000616

National Association of Social Workers. (2021a). Code of ethics. https://www.socialworkers.org/About/Ethics/Code-of-Ethics

National Association of Social Workers. (2021b). National Association of Social Workers code of ethics. https://www.socialworkers.org/About/Ethics/Code-of-Ethics/Code-of-Ethics-English

Norcross, J. C., & Wampold, B. E. (2011). Evidence-based therapy relationships: Research conclusions and clinical practices. In J. C. Norcross (Ed.), *Psychotherapy relationships that work: Evidence-based responsiveness* (2nd ed., pp. 423–430). Oxford University Press. https://doi.org/10.1093/acprof:oso/9780199737208.003.0021

Overington, L., & Ionita, G. (2012). Progress monitoring measures: A brief guide. *Canadian Psychology*, 53(2), 82–92. https://doi.org/https://doi.org/10.1037/a0028017

Paone, T. R., & Malott, K. M. (2008). Using interpreters in mental health counseling: A literature review and recommendations. *Journal of Multicultural Counseling and Development*, 36(3), 130–142. https://doi.org/https://doi.org/10.1002/j.2161-1912.2008.tb00077.x

Park, N., & Peterson, C. (2008). Positive psychology and character strengths: Application to strengths-based school counseling. *Professional School Counseling*, 12(2), 85–92. http://www.jstor.org.weblib.lib.umt.edu:8080/stable/23801059

Pedersen, P. (2009). Inclusive cultural empathy: A relationship-centred alternative to individualism. *South African Journal of Psychology, 39*(2), 143–156. https://doi.org/10.1177/008124630903900201

Rosselló, J., Bernal, G., & Rivera-Medina, C. (2008). Individual and group CBT and IPT for Puerto Rican adolescents with depressive symptoms. *Cultural Diversity & Ethnic Minority Psychology, 14*(3), 234–245. https://doi.org/http://dx.doi.org/10.1037/1099-9809.14.3.234

Silverman, W. K., Kurtines, W. M., Ginsburg, G. S., Weems, C. F., Lumpkin, P. W., & Carmichael, D. H. (1999). Treating anxiety disorders in children with group cognitive-behaviorial therapy: A randomized clinical trial. *Journal of Consulting and Clinical Psychology, 67*(6), 995–1003.

Sori, C. F., & Hecker, L. L. (2015). Ethical and legal considerations when counselling children and families. *Australian and New Zealand Journal of Family Therapy, 36*(4), 450–464. https://doi.org/https://doi.org/10.1002/anzf.1126

Squires, J., Bricker, D., & Twombly, E. (2002). *Ages & stages questionnaires: Social-emotional* (Vol. 2). Paul H. Brookes Publishing Company.

Sue, D. W., & Sue, D. (2013). *Counseling the culturally diverse: Theory and practice.* John Wiley & Sons.

Wendt, D. C., & Gone, J. P. (2011). Rethinking cultural competence: Insights from indigenous community treatment settings. *Transcultural Psychiatry, 49*(2), 206–222. https://doi.org/10.1177/1363461511425622

Woods-Jaeger, B., Briggs, E. C., Gaylord-Harden, N., Cho, B., & Lemon, E. (2021). Translating cultural assets research into action to mitigate adverse childhood experience–related health disparities among African American youth. *American Psychologist, 76*(2), 326–336. https://doi.org/http://dx.doi.org/10.1037/amp0000779

CHAPTER 11

Askew, K., Beverly, M. G., & Jay, M. L. (2012). Aligning collaborative and culturally responsive evaluation approaches. *Evaluation and Program Planning, 35*(4), 552–557. https://doi.org/https://doi.org/10.1016/j.evalprogplan.2011.12.011

Birt, L., Scott, S., Cavers, D., Campbell, C., & Walter, F. (2016). Member checking: A tool to enhance trustworthiness or merely a nod to validation? *Qualitative Health Research, 26*(13), 1802–1811. https://doi.org/10.1177/1049732316654870

Boyd, N. M., & Bright, D. S. (2007). Appreciative inquiry as a mode of action research for community psychology. *Journal of Community Psychology, 35*(8), 1019–1036. https://doi.org/https://doi.org/10.1002/jcop.20208

Chilisa, B. (2020). *Indigenous Research Methodologies.* Sage.

Cunliffe, A. L. (2016). Republication of "On becoming a critically reflexive practitioner." *Journal of Management Education, 40*(6), 747–768. https://doi.org/10.1177/1052562916674465

Holden, D. J., & Zimmerman, M. A. (2009). In *A practical guide to program evaluation planning: Theory and case examples* (pp. 7–32). Sage.

Hood, S., Hopson, R. K., & Kirkhart, K. E. (2015). Culturally responsive evaluation: Theory, practice, and future implications. In K. E. Newcomer, H. P. Hatry, & J. S. Wholey (Eds.), *Handbook of Practical Program Evaluation* (pp. 281–318). Wiley.

Kirkhart, K. E. (2005). Through a cultural lens: Reflections on validity and theory in evaluation. In S. Hood, H. Frierson, & R. Hopson (Eds.), *The Role of Culture and Cultural Context in Evaluation: A Mandate for Inclusion, the Discovery of Truth and Understanding* (pp. 21–39). Information Age Publishing.

Kvale, S. (2006). Dominance through interviews and dialogues. *Qualitative Inquiry*, *12*(3), 480–500. https://doi.org/10.1177/1077800406286235

LaFrance, J., & Nichols, R. (2008). Reframing evaluation: Defining an indigenous evaluation framework. *Canadian Journal of Program Evaluation*, *23*(2), 13–31.

LaFrance, J., Nichols, R., & Kirkhart, K. E. (2012). Culture writes the script: On the centrality of context in indigenous evaluation. *New Directions for Evaluation*, *2012*(135), 59–74. https://doi.org/10.1002/ev.20027

Peltier, C. (2018). An application of Two-Eyed Seeing: Indigenous research methods with participatory action research. *International Journal of Qualitative Methods*, *17*(1), 1609406918812346. https://doi.org/10.1177/1609406918812346

Rodriguez, K. L., Schwartz, J. L., Lahman, M. K. E., & Geist, M. R. (2011). Culturally responsive focus groups: Reframing the research experience to focus on participants. *International Journal of Qualitative Methods*, *10*(4), 400–417. https://doi.org/10.1177/160940691101000407

Schwandt, T. A. (2005). The centrality of practice to evaluation. *American Journal of Evaluation*, *26*(1), 95–105. https://doi.org/10.1177/1098214004273184

Spaulding, D. T. (2013). *Program evaluation in practice: Core concepts and examples for discussion and analysis*. John Wiley & Sons, Incorporated.

Thomas, V. G., Madison, A., Rockcliffe, F., DeLaine, K., & Lowe, S. M. (2018). Racism, social programming, and evaluation: Where do we go from here? *American Journal of Evaluation*, *39*(4), 514–526. https://doi.org/10.1177/1098214018772910

Thomas, V. G., & Parsons, B. A. (2017). Culturally responsive evaluation meets systems-oriented evaluation. *American Journal of Evaluation*, *38*(1), 7–28. https://doi.org/10.1177/1098214016644069

For the benefit of digital users, indexed terms that span two pages (e.g., 52–53) may, on occasion, appear on only one of those pages.

Tables, figures, and boxes are indicated by *t*, *f*, and *b* following the page number